PRAISE FOR *A CRISIS OF BRILLIANCE*

'Haycock manages the drama in this tale with such skill that his story unfolds like a well-plotted novel ... Never before have the private vicissitudes of these artists' lives been made so real, or their exuberance so vivid'
Frances Spalding, *Daily Mail*

'A vintage decade of early twentieth-century British art, told in vivid and entertaining detail through the adventures of five highly gifted young painters. I greatly enjoyed it'
Michael Holroyd

'What gives David Boyd Haycock's book its freshness is that, through skilful use of letters and memoirs left by his five subjects, he injects it with the anxiety, ambition, self-doubt and jealousy that possessors of youth and talent are fated to feel'
John Carey, *Sunday Times*

'Haycock's narrative of this entangled, war-defined group is so strong that it often has the force of a novel, hard to put down ... We should call for a joint exhibition of their work, to complement the moving portrayal of their lives in this engrossing and enjoyable book'
Jenny Uglow, *Guardian*

'An extraordinary book. I read it avidly ... The familiar cast is handled in a quite new and original way. They have been made fresh and vulnerable once more, and their work re-evaluated – made new to us'
Ronald Blythe

'Truly fascinating from every angle – almost a work of art in itself'

Books Quarterly

'Haycock wears his learning lightly and has an enviably fluent and assured style of writing: you pick this book up and simply start reading. Rarely has art history seemed so agreeable'

The Art Newspaper

'A sad tale, wonderfully told … Haycock fades the many different narratives in and out with ease'

Country Life

ALSO BY DAVID BOYD HAYCOCK

A Crisis of Brilliance: Five Young British Artists and the Great War
Paul Nash

'To defend Madrid is to defend Catalonia' by Martí Bas (V&A)

I AM SPAIN

The Spanish Civil War and the
men and women who went to fight Fascism

DAVID BOYD HAYCOCK

First published in 2012 by Old Street Publishing Ltd
Trebinshun House, Brecon LD3 7PX
www.oldstreetpublishing.co.uk

ISBN 978-1-908699-10-7

10 9 8 7 6 5 4 3 2 1

A CIP catalogue record for this title is available from the British Library.

Printed and bound by CPI Group (UK) Ltd, Croydon, CR0 4YY

For Genevieve and Nathaniel

CONTENTS

CHRONOLOGY

1936

17 July: Military rebellion against the Republican Government starts in Spanish North Africa.

18 July: Military rebellion spreads to mainland Spain.

20 July: General Franco sends emissaries to Mussolini and Hitler, requesting military assistance. General José Sanjurjo, nominal leader of the revolt, killed in an air crash.

20 July: Republican siege of the Alcázar in Toledo begins.

26 July: Comintern agrees to raise funds and send international volunteers to support the Republic.

27 July: German and Italian airlift of the Army of Africa from Morocco to mainland Spain begins.

27 September: Rebels retake Toledo and lift the siege of the Alcázar.

14 August: The Army of Africa storms Badajoz.

16 August: Catalan Republican forces attack Majorca.

3 September: Republican assault on Majorca abandoned.

24 August: Accompanied by numerous 'advisors', the Russian Ambassador to Spain arrives.

28 August: First bombing of Madrid by rebel planes.

4 September: Socialist leader Largo Caballero becomes Prime Minister.

9 September: In London, the Non-Intervention Committee holds its first meeting.

18 September: The International Brigades established by the Comintern.

1 October: General Franco proclaimed rebel Commander-in-Chief and Head of State.

6 November: Republican government quits Madrid for Valencia.

7 November: start of the battle for Madrid.

18 November: Franco's regime is officially recognized by Germany and Italy.

14 December: The battle of Boadilla begins.

24 December: First Company of the English-Speaking Battalion mobilized.

1937

17 January: Rebels forces capture Malaga.

6 February: Rebels attempt again to capture Madrid, and the battle of Jarama begins.

8 March: Battle of Guadalajara begins as rebels attempt to take Madrid from the north.

26 April: German and Italian planes bomb Guernica.

3 May: Street fighting breaks out in Barcelona as anarchists and the POUM fight with communists.

15 May: Largo Caballero resigns as Prime Minister and is soon succeeded by Juan Negrín.

6 July: Battle of Brunete begins with a major Republican offensive.

25 August: Rebels capture Santander on the north coast of Spain.

31 November: Republican government moves from Valencia to Barcelona.

15 December: The Battle of Teruel begins.

1938

12 March: The *Anschluss*: Austria is annexed by Germany.

16 March: Italian bombers begin three days of intensive air raids on Barcelona.

1 May: Juan Negrín's attempts to negotiate peace with Franco are rejected.

24 July: The Battle of the Ebro begins with a major Republican offensive.

21 September: Juan Negrín announces in Geneva that the International Brigades will be withdrawn from action.

15 November: the International Brigades hold leaving parade in Barcelona.

29 September: British Prime Minister Neville Chamberlain flies to Munich to meet Hitler in attempt to end the Czechoslovakian crisis.

9 November: *Kristallnacht*: Nazi pogrom against Jews in Austria and Germany.

23 December: Rebels launch offensive to capture Catalonia.

1939

26 January: Rebel forces capture Barcelona.

27 February: The British and French governments recognize Franco's regime.

27 March: Rebel forces march into Madrid.

1 April: General Franco announces that the Spanish Civil War is over. US Government recognizes his regime.

1 September: Germany invades Poland.

3 September: Britain and France declare war on Germany.

GLOSSARY

Carlism: A political movement originating in the early 19th century with the aim of establishing a separate Bourbon monarchy in Spain.

CEDA: The Spanish Confederation of Right-Wing Groups, established in 1933.

CNT: The National Confederation of Labour: an anarcho-syndicalist labour union founded in Barcelona in 1910.

Comintern: The Communist International, established by Lenin in 1919 as a world-wide union of communist parties.

Commune de Paris Battalion: A unit of the International Brigades, chiefly made up of French and Belgian anti-Fascists.

CPGB: The Communist Party of Great Britain

CPUSA: The Communist Party of the United States of America.

Falange: The Spanish fascist party, founded by José Antonio Primo de Rivera in 1933.

FAI: The Iberian Anarchist Federation, founded in Valencia in 1927.

Garibaldi Battalion: A unit of the International Brigades, chiefly made up of Italian anti-fascists.

League of Nations: An international organization founded in 1919 with the aim of keeping world peace through disarmament and arbitration. Its effectiveness was undermined by the failure of the US to join.

PCE: The Spanish Communist Party.

POUM: The Workers' Party of Marxist Unification: a chiefly Catalan anti-Stalinist communist organization founded by Andrés Nin in 1935.

PSOE: The Spanish Socialist Workers' Party, founded in 1879.

Thälmann Battalion: A unit of the International Brigades, chiefly made up of German and Austrian anti-fascists.

UGT: The Amalgamated Union of Workers: A Spanish socialist trade union founded in 1888.

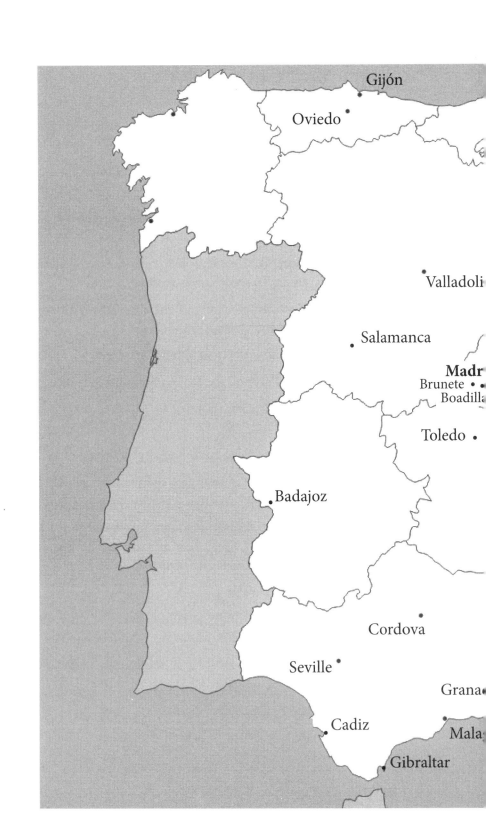

Introduction

'The Politics of Desperation'

> What's your proposal? To build the just city? I will.
> I agree. Or is it the suicide pact, the romantic
> Death? Very well, I accept, for
> I am your choice, your decision. Yes, I am Spain.
> W.H. Auden, *Spain* (May 1937)

The Civil War that raged through Spain between 1936 and 1939 was a ruthless conflict: a local catastrophe that, in a world seemingly poised on the brink of another global war, quickly acquired international significance. As Ernest Hemingway's Spanish friend José Luis Castillo-Puche reflected long afterwards, the war was

> a direct confrontation between two radically different, fanatical, totally irreconcilable antagonists who had sworn to destroy each other. The issues were black and white; what was at stake was a whole style of life, a worldview, the acceptance or the rejection of all human history. This was not a war fought in the front line according to tactical plans drawn up by general staffs; it was a battle fought in the streets and the countryside according to the instincts of the people, a total destruction of the enemy improvised from moment to moment. Not only were there grimacing corpses on the battlefields; civilians, too, died dramatic deaths. Above and beyond the horror of soldiers whose dead bodies were riddled with machine-gun bullets, there was the brutal,

inhuman slaughter of non-combatants, a collective sadism, senseless cruelty.

Yet this war was not simply a Spanish affair. The overt involvement of the fascist forces of Adolf Hitler and Benito Mussolini, and the communists of Joseph Stalin's Soviet Union – as well as thousands of international volunteers from over forty countries, fighting on both sides of the political divide – created what many contemporaries called 'a world war in miniature', a microcosm of greater forces at work, greater conflicts. For as the English poet Stephen Spender observed, within a few weeks of the outbreak of the Civil War, Spain had become 'the symbol of hope' for anti-fascists everywhere. And as he added, 'since the area of struggle in Spain was confined, and the methods of warfare comparatively restrained, the voices of human individuals were not overwhelmed, as in 1939, by vast military machines and by propaganda. The Spanish war remained to some extent a debate, both within and outside Spain, in which the three great political ideas of our time – Fascism, Communism, and Liberal-Socialism – were discussed and heard.'

This book tells the story of the war through the interwoven voices of just a handful of those many individuals who came from outside Spain either to fight or to observe and record the war. The principal British participants whose letters, diaries, newspaper reports and recollections I draw upon are Felicia Browne, Claud Cockburn, John Cornford, George Orwell, Esmond Romilly and Tom Wintringham; the Americans are Alvah Bessie, Ernest Hemingway, John Dos Passos and William Herrick (who later changed his name to William Horvitz). But the Spanish war touched the lives of many other foreign anti-fascists, and the names that appear in this book include Britons, Americans, Irishmen, Spaniards, Frenchmen, Germans and a Hungarian: names such as W.H. Auden, Kitty Bowler, Robert Capa, Cyril Connolly, Martha Gellhorn, Laurie Lee, Herbert Matthews, Dorothy Parker, Gustav Regler, Frank Ryan, Stephen Spender, George Steer, Gerda Taro and Philip Toynbee.

That most of these foreign participants were writers and artists is not intended to diminish the role played by the tens of thousands of other men and women who travelled to Spain to aid the Republican cause, nor that of the millions of Spaniards who fought or endured the war. Furthermore, this is a story of only one side of the conflict: the Republican side, a loose affiliation of leftists, liberals and anarchists who for almost three years stood up to a repressive tyranny of militarism, repression, dictatorship and fascism. For this was a war that almost compelled people to take sides. As Ernest Hemingway (who already knew Spain well) told a young American writer in February 1937:

> The Spanish war is a bad war, Harry, and nobody is right. All I care about is human beings and alleviating their suffering, which is why I back ambulances and hospitals. The Rebels have plenty of good Italian ambulances. But it's not very Catholic or Christian to kill the wounded in the hospital in Toledo with hand-grenades or to bomb the working quarter of Madrid for no military reason except to kill poor people, whose politics are only the politics of desperation. I know they have shot priests and bishops but why was the church in politics on the side of the oppressors instead of for the people – or instead of not being in politics at all?
>
> It's none of my business and I'm not making it mine but my sympathies are always for exploited working people against absentee landlords even if I drink around with the landlords and shoot pigeons with them. I would as soon shoot them as the pigeons.

Inevitably, this is a book with both a position and an opinion, but these, I hope, emerge through the voices of those who were there and who saw it happen. 'In case I have not said this somewhere earlier in the book,' George Orwell counselled in his classic 1938 account of his war-time experiences in Catalonia, 'I will say it now: beware of my partisanship, my mistakes of fact, and the distortion inevitably caused by my having seen only one corner of events. And beware of exactly the same things when you read any other book on this period of the Spanish war.'

Chapter 1

The Sun Also Rises

|

S pain in 1936 was a land not well known to many foreigners. W.H. Auden memorably described it as 'that arid square, that fragment nipped off from hot Africa, soldered so crudely to inventive Europe'. To George Orwell, writing of how he pictured Spain before he first travelled there, it was a land of white sierras and Moorish palaces, of goatherds and olive trees and lemon groves; of gypsies and girls in black mantillas, bullfights, cardinals and the half-forgotten terrors of the Inquisition. Of all Europe, he would write in 1937, Spain was the one country that had the most hold upon his imagination.

But Spain was not simply a land of the imagination. In the years immediately around the Great War a number of British and American writer and artists travelled – even settled – there. Their books and paintings added layers of modernity to Orwell's almost oriental vision. Yet they, too, sometimes mirrored his exotic impression. For Spain was a land not quite like anywhere else in Western Europe.

The American novelist John Dos Passos first visited Spain in 1916, a few months after graduating from Harvard. He had travelled already in France, Italy and Greece, yet wrote that nowhere else in Europe had he so felt 'the *strata* of civilization – Celt-Iberians, Romans, Moors and French have each passed through Spain and left something there – alive … It's the most wonderful jumble – the peaceful Roman world; the sadness of the Semitic nations, their mysticism; the grace – a little provincialized, a little barbarized – of a Greek colony; the sensuous dream of Moorish Spain; and little yellow trains and American automobiles and German locomotives – all in a tangle together!' When the author Lytton Strachey visited Granada in the spring of 1920 he too was captivated: 'Never have I seen a country on so vast a scale,' he wrote home, 'wild, violent, spectacular – enormous mountains, desperate chasms, endless distances – colours everywhere of deep orange and brilliant green – a wonderful place, but easier to get to with a finger on the map than in reality!'

Strachey's travelling companion, the artist Dora Carrington, would be equally moved, capturing the landscape and its people in scintillating oil colours. She would be one of the first in a long line of post-war British artists to visit Spain: Ben and William Nicholson, Augustus John, David Bomberg, Mark Gertler, Henry Moore, Edward Burra, to name only the most well-known. And there were English-speaking writers, too, making of Spain a place to wander: Ralph Bates, Waldo Frank, Robert Graves, Ernest Hemingway, Laurie Lee, Malcolm Lowry, V.S. Pritchett, as well as Dos Passos. According to one contemporary literary critic, what had initially attracted Dos Passos (and no doubt some of the others, too) was the discovery in Spain of 'an attitude toward life and a way of living which are in pleasant contrast to the mad turmoil of industrial Europe and America'. Nonetheless, in his 1917 essay 'Young Spain', Dos Passos observed a country – with its corrupt, inefficient politicians and its ill-educated, underpaid workforce – ripe for revolution. It was only, Dos Passos considered, a sort of despairing inaction that prevented it.

Insight into the country's deeper complexities often came only with time. Strachey and Carrington's host in Spain, the writer and Great War veteran Gerald Brenan, admitted that when he had chosen to settle there the previous year he had known next to nothing about the country. In due course, and over many decades, he wrote a series of books that would bring Spain – its language, its culture, its politics – to life for many English-speaking readers. Ernest Hemingway would call Brenan's 1943 study, *The Spanish Labyrinth*, a 'splendid book', 'the best book I know on Spain politically'.

Hemingway was the writer who really captured for a broader audience the foreigner's experience of Spain in the decade following the Great War. Born in Chicago in 1899, the son of a prosperous doctor, Hemingway passed a seemingly idyllic childhood, enjoying sports and writing at school and long summers hunting and fishing with family and friends. Having launched on a career as a journalist with *The Kansas City Star*, early in 1918 he decided to head for Europe and the Great War, volunteering with the Red Cross. He served (like John Dos Passos) as an ambulance driver in Italy, where he was seriously wounded by a mortar burst and machine-gun fire. This – and the doomed romance with an American nurse that followed – would prove life-defining experiences.

It was on his way home to a hero's welcome that Hemingway made his first, short stop in Spain. Having married and settled in Paris as a journalist for the Toronto *Star Weekly*, in 1923 he made two longer trips. Seeking the truth and courage and conviction in human experience that Hemingway believed existed only in the face of imminent death, he was almost immediately transfixed by the *corrida de toros*. Before his first visit, he thought bullfights 'would be simple and barbarous and cruel and that I would not like them'; but he also hoped that he would witness in them the 'certain definite action which would give me the feeling of life and death' that he was looking to describe in his fiction.

In July at Pamplona Hemingway and his wife Hadley attended the San Fermín fiesta: 'five days of bull fighting dancing all day and all night,' he told a friend, 'wonderful music – drums, reed pipes, fifes … all the men in blue shirts and red handkerchiefs circling lifting floating dance. We the only foreigners at the damn fair.'

'It isn't just brutal,' he wrote of the *corrida*. 'It's a great tragedy – and the most beautiful thing I've ever seen and takes more guts and skill and guts again than anything possibly could. It's just like having a ringside seat at the war with nothing going to happen to you. I've seen 20 of them.' To use the Spanish word for a devotee of bullfighting, Hemingway was already an *aficionado*.

The couple returned the following year with a group of friends, including Dos Passos. After the fiesta they explored the Basque country and the foothills of the Pyrenees, where they hiked and fished. Hemingway had travelled extensively in Europe, and like Dos Passos felt that Spain was 'the only country left that hasn't been shot to pieces … Spain is the real old stuff.'

Ernest Hemingway, Duff Twysden, Hadley Hemingway and friends, Pamplona, July 1925
(JFK Library)

It was a visit to Pamplona in 1925 that provided Hemingway with the material for his breakthrough book, *The Sun Also Rises*.[1] Published when he was still only in his mid-twenties, the novel told the story of a handful of British and American tourists who (according to one reviewer) 'belong to the curious and sad little world of disillusioned and aimless expatriates who make what home they can in the cafés of Paris.' Closely based on Hemingway's unrequited love for a beautiful Englishwoman, Duff (Lady) Twysden, its finest passages related with brusque relish the Pamplona bullfights. As Dorothy Parker observed in *The New Yorker*, almost as soon as *The Sun Also Rises* was published its author 'was praised, adored, analyzed, best-sold, argued about, and banned in Boston … and some, they of the cool, tall foreheads, called it the greatest American novel … I was never so sick of a book in my life.' Hemingway's sparse prose and gritty, realistic dialogue would quickly spawn dozens of less gifted imitators.

However, *The Sun Also Rises* said more about Hemingway, bullfighting, fishing, drinking, loving and the post-war malaise than it did about Spain. Its epigraph was a truncated version of a remark Gertrude Stein had

---

1 The book appeared in Britain as *Fiesta*, Hemingway's original choice of title.

once made to Hemingway: 'That's what you all are,' she had told him. 'All of you young people who served in the war. You are a lost generation.' The effects and after-effects of the Great War permeated the book: one approving American reviewer – the critic Edmund Wilson – considered 'the barbarity of the world since the War' to be its very theme: a theme that was then still consuming Western culture. 'What gives the book its profound unity and its disquieting effectiveness,' Wilson suggested, 'is the intimate relation established between the Spanish fiesta with its processions, its revelry and its bull-fighting and the atrocious behavior of the group of Americans and English who have come down from Paris to enjoy it.'

Hemingway's novel – like his letters and short stories – had almost nothing to say about Spanish politics. Yet in September 1923, only a couple of months after Hemingway's first extended visit to Spain, General Miguel Primo de Rivera had led a *coup d'état* that established him as dictator. Perhaps this was unremarkable to Hemingway because coups, revolutions and revolts had become relatively common events in recent Spanish history. Since the extraordinary heights of imperial power and wealth it had enjoyed in the seventeenth century, the country's standing had steadily declined. After the forces of Napoleon Bonaparte occupied the peninsula in 1808 they left behind a country economically ruined and politically divided.

By 1898 Spain had lost those New World colonies that had once brought its ruling classes great wealth. With the Philippines, Mexico and Cuba gone, the acquisition of northern Morocco as a colony in 1904 was nothing but an expensive, troublesome burden. Compared to the rest of Western Europe, early twentieth-century Spain was a poor and (with the exception of Catalonia) under-industrialized backwater. Two-thirds of its twenty million or so population lived and worked in the countryside, with large tracts of land owned by a tiny minority of the population. Productivity was low, mass education minimal, and in many regions of the rural south poverty was endemic. The Church appeared to take little interest in the plight of the poor, perpetuating a *status quo* that had lasted centuries, an attitude which resulted in widespread resentment of the clergy. This was a land of stark contrasts. 'You can't be in Spain more than half an hour,' wrote one English visitor in 1936, 'without becoming painfully aware of the extremes of feudalism that still linger on side by side with the growth of modern capitalism.'

The political situation was no happier. The 1830s had seen a seven-year civil war, and the Republic declared in 1873 was short-lived. Foreign monarchs were invited to intervene, and attempts at introducing land reform, and loosening the grip of the Church and Army, made little progress. Despite the introduction of universal male suffrage in 1890, government was characterized by factionalism, corruption and rigged elections. In Barcelona in 1899 only ten per cent of the electorate bothered to vote. 'Wretched Castile,' wrote the poet Antonio Machado, a member of a turn-of-the century group of intellectuals and liberals who sought a way to redeem Spain, 'once supreme, now forlorn, wrapping herself in rags, closes her mind in scorn.'

More powerful than the new Republican movement – more powerful, perhaps, than the upsurge in regional nationalism – was anarchism. Drawing on the ideas of the Russian revolutionary and philosopher Mikhail Bakunin, Spanish anarchists rejected all forms of government: instead, free individuals would manage their own affairs through consensus and co-operation. Anarchists promised their followers freedom, social justice, land reform and the total destruction of the capitalist system, ideals that caught the imagination of Andalusia's largely illiterate, landless peasantry and Catalonia's exploited factory workers. Tens of thousands of Spaniards joined this visionary, idealistic movement, and as the Spanish anarchist Juan García Oliver would tell the English author Cyril Connolly in 1937: 'If I had to sum up Anarchism in a phrase I would say it was the ideal of eliminating the beast in man.' In response to the charge of anarchist violence, Oliver replied: 'Anarchism has been violent in Spain because oppression has been violent.'

And violent it certainly was, for anarchists believed in direct action. A bomb dropped into the audience of Barcelona's Liceu Opera House in 1893 killed twenty-two people, and by 1921 Spanish anarchists had assassinated three prime ministers. Repression followed, and violence exploded periodically into chaos and devastation. The Church – which owned much of the land and along with the Army shouldered the State's authority – was a frequent target of public anger. During Barcelona's 'Tragic Week' of July 1909 an orgy of anticlericalism saw 42 churches and convents attacked. Soldiers crushed the uprising with considerable bloodshed.

Barcelona, the so-called 'city of bombs,' was the epicentre of Spanish anarchism. A large proportion of the million inhabitants of the 'Manchester of the Mediterranean' worked in the textile factories that, through the city's busy port and railway network, supplied Spain, Cuba and South America with cloth. In 1926 an American tourist described the outskirts of Barcelona as 'a rampart of warehouses, machine shops, flour, cotton and textile mills, dyeworks, chemical factories'. By contrast, its broad, tree-lined boulevards and wide, residential streets reminded many a visitor of Paris. When the Bolshevik revolutionary Leon Trotsky passed through Barcelona in 1916 he noted in his diary: 'Big Spanish-French kind of city. Like Nice in a hell of factories. Smoke and flames on the one hand, flowers and fruit on the other.'

Barcelona considered itself different from the rest of Spain; it was more industrialized and modernized, the people spoke Catalan, they were wealthier, and thought themselves more cosmopolitan, more European. There was a flourishing artistic scene: Pablo Picasso, Antoni Gaudí, Joan Miró and Salvador Dalí were all either natives or residents of Catalonia. Distant Castile, and its government in Madrid, was regarded with caution, and sometimes fear. As in the Basque region of northern Spain, there was a burgeoning independence movement.

When the horror of the Great War rolled across Europe in 1914 Spain remained neutral. For a while, the country's economy thrived on supplying the Allies with minerals and industrial goods. But there was also rampant inflation, and affiliation to workers' organizations soared. Membership of the anarchist trade union, the CNT, ballooned fifty-fold.

Inspired by the Bolshevik revolutionaries who had helped overthrow the Russian Tsar in 1917, anarchists and socialists in Spain attempted to foment an armed rebellion. Even liberal elements in Catalonia began demanding home rule, the first step on what traditionalists feared would be the road to independence and the break-up of their country.

It was in Barcelona in 1923 that General de Rivera staged his 'proclamation'. King Alfonso XIII appointed him head of a military directorate, charged with restoring order, stability and unity. The General curbed press freedom, outlawed strikes and restricted political activity, but he also encouraged capital investment, and there was a period of economic growth.

There was plenty of drama for a novel in these political upheavals. But it was not a story Hemingway chose to tell. His next book on Spain, *Death in the Afternoon*, was an idiosyncratic guide to bullfighting. Published in 1932, after he had witnessed the deaths of over a thousand bulls in the *corrida*, its one reference to Primo de Rivera was to remark that under the dictator a more humane measure had been introduced into the ring. Padding would now protect the picadors' horses from goring by the bulls' horns. Though Hemingway admitted that the frequent death of the horses was one of its most sickening aspects, he considered the move 'the first step toward the suppression of the bullfight'.

II

Even dictators fall. By 1930 General Primo de Rivera had become unpopular with both the Army and the people; facing a rising tide of republicanism he retired to Paris, where he soon died. Municipal elections held in 1931 sent a clear message to King Alfonso: he too was no longer wanted. Declaring that he was 'determined to have nothing to do with setting one of my countrymen against another in a fratricidal civil war,' he too went into exile. To widespread celebration – but also some trepidation – the Second Republic was declared.

For much of the population, expectations were enormous. A general election saw a landslide victory for the parties of the Republican-Socialist coalition. Immediate improvements followed: women received the vote, divorce was legalized, land and labour laws were reformed, with attempts made to redistribute land from the large estate owners to the peasants who actually tilled the soil; home rule was granted to Catalonia, which established its own parliament in Barcelona – the *Generalitat* – and measures were passed to relax the Army's grip on the state, with many senior officers forced into retirement. Action was also taken against the Church: schooling was taken from clerical control, religious symbols were removed from classrooms and public buildings, and freedom of belief was declared. Even this, though, was not enough for some: in Madrid, Seville and several other cities churches were torched, and there were rural insurrections and even an anarchist uprising near Cadiz.

Unfortunately, the birth of the Second Spanish Republic coincided with the Great Depression. If the Great War had been the first global disaster of the twentieth century, the Wall Street Crash of 1929 was the second. After the Crash, the Depression descended upon the world (to use George Orwell's apt phrase) 'like a new ice age,' spawning the conditions for the rapid rise to power of fascists in Germany, and the emergence of potent right-wing forces in Britain, France, the US and Japan. It was no exaggeration to say that many liberal thinkers in the 1930s saw Western civilization as on the brink of collapse: with world trade declining, exports fell sharply, unemployment rose and state finances collapsed. The Spanish Government, saddled with a huge deficit following the profligate years of de Rivera's dictatorship, lacked funds to carry forward its programme of reform. The Right, still fearing Bolshevism and the break-up of Spain into independent states, united with the Church to obstruct further change.

Elsewhere in the world there were many who believed that only strong leadership and a mass ideology could solve national problems of mass unemployment, labour unrest, debt and rampant inflation. The few countries appearing to have bucked these trends were the Soviet Union and Germany, and they offered two contrasting visions – or delusions

– of hope. As the English philosopher Bertrand Russell wrote after visiting Russia in 1920, 'the war has left throughout Europe a mood of disillusionment and despair which calls aloud for a new religion, as the only force capable of giving men the energy to live vigorously. Bolshevism has supplied the new religion.' Then, in a 1931 book simply titled *Hitler*, the Anglo-American artist and writer Percy Wyndham Lewis aired a cautious judgment in favour of Nazism, suggesting that since the 'political and economic structure of Western Europe and of America are in a state of violent disequilibrium,' something 'has to be done of a most radical sort, very rapidly indeed, it seems. And I suggest that sort of solution indicated in Hitlerism is not entirely to be despised …' Yet both these new ideologies were based on oppression, and they were dangerous – if also tempting – choices. 'Cruelty lurks in our instincts,' Russell had warned, 'and fanaticism is a camouflage for cruelty. Fanatics are seldom genuinely humane, and those who sincerely dread cruelty will be slow to adopt a fanatical creed.' Nazism, of course, was just as fanatical as Bolshevism. Following their rise to power in 1933 the Nazis had set about ruthlessly crushing Germany's communist and socialist opposition, as well as its Jewish population and other marginalized minorities, exiling, oppressing, imprisoning, executing. 'In the political panorama of Europe I can see only the formation of Marxist and anti-Marxist groups,' the right-wing Spanish politician José María Gil Robles declared at a rally in Madrid. 'This is what is happening in Germany and in Spain also. This is the great battle which we must fight.'

That fight was close at hand. When John Dos Passos revisited Spain shortly after the foundation of the Second Republic he was deeply troubled by what he saw. The Prime Minister, Manuel Azaña, told him that his country had escaped 'the uncivilizing influences' of the Great War, and that Spain had nothing to fear from fascism. But after witnessing a left-wing rally in Santander, Dos Passos was sceptical. He saw 'the hatred in the faces of the well-dressed people seated at the café tables … as they stared at the sweaty Socialists straggling back from the bullring with their children and their picnic baskets and their bunting. If eyes had been machine guns not one of them would have survived that day.' He jotted in his notebook: 'Socialists innocent as a flock of sheep in the wolf country.'

In 1933 two powerful new elements entered Spanish politics. A nationwide confederation of Catholic parties, the CEDA, was formed, taking much assistance from the organizational networks of the Church; so too was the Falange Española, the 'Spanish Phalanx'. Founded by General Primo de Rivera's son, José Antonio, the Falange was Spain's fascist party, and it spawned a cult of violence with its blue-shirted militias, its mass rallies and war cry of *¡Arriba España!* ('Arise, Spain!'). With the Left divided between anarchists and socialists, a centre-right coalition won that year's general election, and the so-called 'two black years' followed. The liberal programme of social improvement was halted; Catalonia's statute of autonomy was suspended, agricultural wages were cut, land reform was abandoned, and unemployment soared. The Left did not sit still: 'It is better to die on your feet,' declared Dolores Ibárruri, figurehead of the small Spanish Communist Party, 'than to live on your knees.' An attempt to launch a revolutionary general strike in October 1934 failed, but in the coal-mining region of Asturias in northern Spain some 40,000 workers formed an armed 'Workers' Alliance'. The government sent in the Spanish Foreign Legion and colonial African troops from Morocco, led by an ambitious and brutal young general called Francisco Franco. A miniature civil war ensued. After two weeks of fierce fighting the miners were defeated, leaving over a thousand dead. In the ensuing clampdown, some 30,000 political opponents were jailed throughout Spain.

As the Right had united into a National Front, so too did the Left, forming a Popular Front that fought the elections of 1936 as a coalition of socialists, communists and moderate republicans. By a fraction of the vote, and to the horror of the Right, they won a majority of seats in the *Cortes*.

Immediately the working class took revenge. Political prisoners were released; the estates of wealthy landowners were raided and lands seized; churches were burnt; workers went on strike. Having failed at the ballot box, both Gil Robles and the Falange abandoned the democratic process in favour of bullets. They deliberately fomented disorder and unrest, pushing forward the moment when an authoritarian regime could impose itself by force; anarchists likewise attempted to undermine the state system they despised with their own acts of brutal resistance, whilst socialists intensified their violent attempts to bring revolutionary change. Activists of the Left and Right clashed on the streets; political opponents and bystanders were shot down in public. Falangists in motorcars opened fire with machineguns on demonstrators and picket lines, killing women and children as well as workers. Anarchists murdered their opponents; politicians carried revolvers into Parliament, where they spoke to their opponents in increasingly inflammatory terms; the Government, clearly weak, did not know how to respond.

May Day in Madrid saw workers bearing red banners and huge portraits of Stalin and Lenin. Graffiti around the country declared 'Death to Gil Robles,' '*Viva Rusia*,' 'Down with Fascism,' while the illiterate drew hammers and sickles on walls. Workers and peasants raised clenched fists in the salute of international socialism; supporters of the Right responded with the raised arm and outstretched palm of fascism.

The young English artist Edward Burra was holidaying in Spain at this time. He later recalled sitting in a restaurant in Madrid as smoke blew past the window. He asked where it came from. 'Oh, it's nothing,' someone answered, with a gesture of impatience. 'It's only a church being burnt.'

The response sickened him. 'It was terrifying: constant strikes, churches on fire, and pent-up hatred everywhere. Everybody knew that something appalling was about to happen.'

III

Things were not quite so bad in Barcelona; some in Madrid were even calling the city 'an oasis of peace' (though this was a comparative judgment). With regional autonomy re-established, this semi-independence (together with a Catalan sense of superiority) gave a different perspective on events. Politically motivated murders were still commonplace (at the start of July union gangsters murdered a Scottish businessman, whilst right-wing troublemakers sent threatening notes to union officials; the dockers were out on strike, with the railwaymen threatening to join them). But the church burnings and provocative acts of random violence were less widespread, and for a while at least, sport offered an alternative to fighting.

In 1931 Barcelona had been the chief contender with Berlin to host the 1936 Olympic Games; it was of course the German bid that won the approval of the International Olympic Committee. Little more than a year later, however, in January 1933, Adolf Hitler was appointed Chancellor of Germany, and the political situation was transformed. The repressive nature of the Nazi regime was apparent, made obvious to the sporting community by the treatment of Germany's Jewish athletes, most of whom were banned from competing. Hitler was soon turning the Berlin Games into a propaganda stunt, a symbol of Germanic 'efficiency' and Aryan 'superiority'.

Late in 1935 a US member of the International Olympic Committee warned the organization's Belgian Chairman that if he permitted the Games to go ahead in Berlin, 'the Olympic idea will cease to be the conception of physical strength and fair play in unison, and there will be nothing left to distinguish it from the Nazi ideal of physical power.' His warning was ignored. Though *The Times* of London admitted that there existed 'a very ugly background to the glittering pageant' in Berlin, boycott campaigns on both sides of the Atlantic failed. But there was an alternative. In 1936 the new Spanish government declared that its athletes *would* boycott the Games. Instead, Barcelona would host a rival 'People's Olympiad'.

The first such 'Workers' Olympics' had been staged in Prague in 1921; the one held in Vienna in 1931 was said to have compared favourably with the 'official' Games in Los Angeles the following year. But the Spanish had only a few months to organise their event. It was not until 22 June – only four weeks before the planned opening – that a letter of invitation reached the American Amateur Athletic Union. The Spaniards apologised for the short notice: 'we hope that you will do your utmost to attend the Games,' they urged. 'In the struggle against fascism, the broad masses of all countries must stand shoulder to shoulder, and Popular Sport is a valuable medium through which they may demonstrate their international solidarity.'

Jesse Owens, the brilliant African-American sprinter, had already told a reporter: 'if there is discrimination against minorities in Germany then we must withdraw from the Olympics.' His coach had immediately warned him to lay off politics: he was going to Berlin. Nevertheless, in mid-July eight American athletes arrived in London en route for Barcelona. 'This team,' their manager told a reporter from the communist newspaper *The Daily Worker*, 'compose real fair play lovers, ready to strike a blow for the Olympic Spirit and ideal.'

Despite last-minute attempts by the Amateur Athletic Association to prevent any of its members attending, 41 British athletes also went to

Spain. They would step into Barcelona's Montjuïc stadium, *The Daily Worker* declared, as 'standard bearers of clean sport, fair play and racial equality.' The paper added: 'Every lover of peace and progressive culture, every opponent to fascism or reaction in any form, is intimately bound to the People's Olympiad … The People's Olympiad is the true Olympic Games.'

The British team was a mixed bag of amateurs and enthusiasts (including a sixteen-year-old schoolgirl); they would be competing in athletics, wrestling, cycling, swimming, table tennis and chess tournaments. On the morning of Friday 17 July they gathered for a rowdy send-off from London's Victoria Station, accompanied by the four Scots bagpipers who would be participating in the folklore events that would form an integral part of the Games. Despite the short time that had been available to prepare, the Spanish organizing committee claimed that over 10,000 athletes from some twenty countries would be participating. Most came from Spain and France, but there were competitors from the USSR, Canada, Poland, Scandinavia, Holland, Britain and the USA, as well as a Jewish team from Palestine. Lluís Companys, the President of Catalonia, would officially open the Games that Sunday.

IV

The British team arrived in Barcelona late in the afternoon of 18 July. The city was decked with brilliantly coloured posters advertising the forthcoming events, and the mood that weekend should have been light-hearted. Instead, the visitors felt an ominous atmosphere.

They checked into a hotel just off Las Ramblas, Barcelona's handsome main thoroughfare, but trouble was already threatening. As the athletes strolled in the warm evening streets they were disconcerted to see armed civilians in the boulevards, and policemen stopping cars: suspected right-wing agitators and Falangists were being arrested. Almost everyone seemed to know what was coming. As several Catalans warned them, making hand gestures imitating guns firing, 'Plenty revolution soon.'

Only a few days before in Madrid a young police officer had been machine-gunned from a passing car. At first it seemed just another incident in weeks of random attacks. This murder, however, was not random. The dead man was a popular left-wing officer of the Assault Guards, the Republic's armed police. Seeking retaliation, his colleagues had searched that night in vain for Gil Robles; instead, they arrested and shot dead another leading right-wing politician, dumping his corpse outside the city cemetery. It was the spark that would ignite the Spanish tinderbox.

Yet in fact the plan for an armed rebellion had already been hatched and launched. On the day the British Olympiad team left London, an English plane flown by an English pilot transported General Franco from the Canary Islands to mainland North Africa. Franco had agreed only at the last minute to join the more senior generals in a conspiracy that had been long in the making; but he was a crucial recruit. That night, the Army in Spanish Morocco rose in rebellion, and Franco issued a proclamation claiming that he was obliged 'to restore the empire of ORDER within the Republic,' and re-establish 'the principle of AUTHORITY, forgotten in these past years,' through the use of serious and rapid 'exemplary … punishments'. Martial law was declared. Army officers in Morocco who remained loyal to the Republic were summarily executed; likewise any officials, workers or citizens who attempted to resist. From there, the military revolt spread to Spain.

In Madrid, the Popular Front government continued to hesitate. For weeks, rumours – and intercepted plans – of a military rising had been reaching the President, Manuel Azaña. Yet despite a tradition of coups dating back to the previous century, he had refused to believe what was before his eyes, and could not believe that the Army's senior officers were not loyal to the Republic. As Pamplona, Saragossa, Oviedo, Salamanca and Cadiz fell into rebel hands, socialists, communists and anarchists demanded that the workers be armed. The government, fearing the far Left almost as much as it feared the far Right, did nothing.

In Barcelona the President of Catalonia refused to issue weapons to the people. So the workers prepared to defend their city any way they could. Through the night dockers fashioned hand grenades from dynamite; a prison was raided and weapons were seized from the warders; gun shops were stripped bare, even air rifles being taken. Vehicles were commandeered and fashioned into makeshift armoured cars. At dawn on Sunday 19 July the rebel officers led their men from their barracks, and people woke to the noise of shooting. As the morning progressed, the sounds of machineguns, heavier guns and government aeroplanes joined the fray. The foreign athletes remained in their hotels, watching from windows as armed men poured into the streets.

One of the first international reporters on the scene was the British journalist Claud Cockburn. He had come out to Spain to cover the Olympiad for *The Daily Worker*, and (at least from a left-wing perspective) was one of the best people the paper could have had to cover such a story. Though Cockburn possessed a lax attitude to facts, his old school friend, the novelist Graham Greene, would call him one of the greatest journalists of the twentieth century. The British Secret Service was perhaps more accurate in its assessment: one report described him as a 'professional mischief maker' whose 'intelligence', 'capability' and 'unscrupulous nature' made him 'a formidable factor with which to reckon.'

A graduate of Oxford University, Cockburn had worked in the late 1920s for that bulwark of the British establishment, *The Times*, first in Berlin, then in America. Arriving in New York City in 1929, he had soon realized that what was happening on Wall Street was what mattered most. 'You could talk about prohibition, or Hemingway, or air conditioning, or music, or horses,' he later wrote, 'but in the end you had to talk about the stock market, and that was where the conversation became serious.'

Cockburn had read Karl Marx in Germany, and he was a convinced communist, certain that 'the Party' was the one organization with the power to resist the rising tide of fascism. In 1932 he had quit *The Times* to launch his own political paper, *The Week*. Relying on a network of sometimes brave, sometimes corrupt fellow-journalists, as well as inside informers, disaffected civil servants, tip-off merchants and whistle-blowers, Cockburn published on three pages of foolscap accounts of international rumour, supposed plots, libellous gossip, plausible intrigues and assertive opinions (largely his own). For it was Cockburn's opinion 'that rumours were just as important, just as significant, just as – in the last analysis – "valid" as "facts" ... unless one imagines one is God, how on earth can one tell truth from rumour in less than perhaps fifty years?

And fifty years is too long to wait if one is in the business of issuing a weekly newspaper.' He later boasted that readers of his scurrilous periodical included the foreign ministers of eleven nations, the staff of all the embassies in London, a dozen US Senators, fifty MPs, the King of England and the Nazi Minister of Propaganda, Joseph Goebbels.

Cockburn had travelled down the Catalan coast for a few days of sunshine and bathing before the Olympiad opened. But as soon as he heard news of the revolt he caught a train back to Barcelona. At each stop on the line people surged round the carriages, reporting the news of the fighting as it came through the railway telephone service. 'At first the people in the train stood silent,' Cockburn wrote, 'or murmuring to one another as the news of the attack sank in and became real.' Then a young bank clerk, standing beside Cockburn in his Sunday suit, leaned out from the window and shouted: *Long Live the Republic!'*

As his cry rang out across the station, railway workers, peasant women, fisherfolk, clerks, businessmen and hotel porters surged towards the train, everyone taking up his call. Suddenly people were shaking hands with strangers and calling one another 'Comrade'. As the train pulled on towards Barcelona, 'Long Live Democracy! Long Live the Republic!' thundered down the crowded corridors.

Another foreign journalist with a grandstand view of the day's events was an American, F. Theo Rogers. Having served with the US Army in Cuba and the Philippines, he was holidaying in Barcelona when the rebellion erupted. His hotel room overlooked the wide expanse of the Plaça de Catalunya, the broad open square at the head of Las Ramblas. Woken by gunfire, Rogers watched as hundreds of rebel soldiers and cavalry, supported by civilian Falangist gunmen, stormed into the square. 'And with them,' he later wrote, 'from all side streets, came the armed Anarchists, running, nondescript, mad and wild.' He watched from his balcony as 'carnage reigned supreme for the next fourteen hours.'

The Plaça de Catalunya was the heart of Barcelona, the strategic key to the city. It included the Telefónica building, where both the central telephone exchange and one of the city's two radio stations were located;

Armed civilians manning a barricade in Barcelona, July 1936 (Imperial War Museum)

the Presidential Palace itself was only a few hundred yards away, down the narrow streets of the old city. A machinegun placed at the centre of the square could command every important thoroughfare. It was here that the principal battle for Barcelona would be fought.

At first only a few thousand badly-armed civilians opposed the rebels. They pulled up cobblestones to erect barricades to block the streets, trams were driven at the soldiers to break up their columns, while those with guns fired down from windows and rooftops. Neither President Companys nor his Chief of Police knew whether the Civil or Assault Guards would remain loyal; traditionally, these armed police units had favoured the Right, and in many parts of Spain they had come out on the side of the rebels. In Barcelona, however, they threw their weight behind the Republic, to the amazement and delight of the people in the streets.

A police captain led the charge against the machinegun nest placed by the rebels in a flowerbed at the centre of the Plaça de Catalunya: it was a suicidal dash of fifty or sixty yards across open ground. According to one account, the policeman was hit eight times before he reached the gun. 'He must have been dead while he was still running,' it was reported, 'as a shot rabbit is dead but still goes on kicking and leaping. He fell over the machine-gun, and the weight of his body knocked it off its tripod. The men who had followed him picked it up and turned it against the rebel soldiers.' The Generals had never anticipated such fanatical resistance to their coup, and for some time the fighting in the Plaça de Catalunya hung in the balance.

Forced off the streets, rebel snipers occupied rooftops and built strong points inside churches; the Telefónica building was taken, then lost and retaken by anarchists. From his vantage point, Theo Rogers watched it all. When it appeared that the rebels were gaining the upper hand, he was surprised by a sudden lull in the fighting.

A worker shouted: 'Soldiers, brothers, why are you fighting us?'

'We don't know,' one replied.

A flag of truce appeared, followed by calls for talk. Their officers had told the soldiers they were quelling an anti-Republican uprising. Now they realized they were on the wrong side. Abruptly, they changed allegiance and disarmed their superiors. By late afternoon the only resistance in the Plaça de Catalunya came from a group of rebels keeping up desultory gunfire from one of the larger hotels. Assault Guards turned a captured field gun on them, and they surrendered.

The Army General who had flown in from the Balearic Isles to command the revolt in Barcelona soon found himself a prisoner. Fortunate not to be killed on the spot, he was persuaded to make a radio broadcast admitting defeat. Streets that had been almost deserted now filled with jubilant crowds, mopping up the last resistance. Then the arsenal at the artillery barracks was broken open. Within a few hours 10,000 rifles and machine guns were 'liberated'. 'That was the moment,' a Catalan textile worker later recalled, 'when the people of Barcelona were armed; that was the moment, in consequence, when power fell into the masses' hands.'

The workers and their leaders had not set out to make a revolution; but when the opportunity came, they had seized it.

Having witnessed the street fighting and the immediate aftermath of the rebellion in Barcelona, Claud Cockburn rushed off to file an uncensored story across the French border. Passing through Gerona on his way north, he reported in *The Daily Worker*, it had been 'a magnificent sight to see the workers drawn up to receive their rifles beneath the ancient panelled roof and golden candelabra' of the government building.

That evening the US Consul General in Barcelona informed Washington that 'the life of the city appeared to be assuming a more normal aspect.' He added, however, that 'it remains to be seen whether or not the radical labor elements now in possession of guns and ammunition will confine their use to legitimate purposes or return them to the constituted authorities, or vest vengeance on their enemies such as church elements and adherents to the subdued Fascists.'

They did the latter. There had been numerous reports of armed priests joining the rebellion, and of religious buildings being used as rebel armouries and strong points. Within hours, an Englishman peering inside one of Barcelona's burning churches saw the body of an elderly priest hanging from the pulpit 'by his sickeningly elongated neck'. Near the British consulate a crowd gathered outside a convent: 'coffins were being excavated from the convent burial ground, and a peseta was being charged for the hire of a long stick with which to strike or insult with unprintable obscenities these sightless, shrunken relics. A charnel house stench and my own sick horror drove me back into the street.'

The British athletes helped to extinguish a fire in the church beside their hotel. Inside they discovered the body of a priest. 'So badly was it burned,' recalled the team's triple-jumper, 'that it was completely beyond recognition. Only a limb or two and some ribs could be distinguished.'

With the authority of the sate shattered in the aftermath of the rebellion, the following weeks witnessed a frenzy of vengeance throughout Spain. In Barcelona the bishop was ejected from his palace and the Diocesan Seminary was converted into a Workers' University.

More churches were sacked or burnt, and across the country thousands of bishops, priests, monks and nuns were murdered. A member of the British consulate in Barcelona claimed to have seen 'Red militiamen' with 'huge road hammers' smashing in the heads of monks. 'We witness here in 1936 scenes reminiscent of the French Revolution,' the Mexican Consul General reported home, 'the only difference being that Madame Guillotine has been replaced by the modern Mauser. Every day people accused of being fascists, industrialists, landlords, etc. are taken from their homes and shot.'

Anarchists formed judicial committees: Theo Rogers called them 'police, jury, judge and executioner combined'. By night, people were visited at home or picked off the streets and 'taken for a ride'. Known supporters of the Right – Falangists, conservative politicians, landowners, businessmen – were the principal victims, whilst captured rebel officers were courtmartialled and executed. This period of lawlessness also offered an opportunity to settle grudges: some of those murdered were actually supporters of the Republic.

The revolution extended to the workplace. Waiters and chefs took over cafés and restaurants abandoned by their owners; hats and ties were discarded in favour of neckerchiefs and overalls; factories and businesses were appropriated by the workers and collectivized. Ford Motor Company and General Motors were confiscated by the Central Committee of the Marxist Militia of Catalonia and turned over to the production of armoured cars. By October around 400 factories employing some 85,000 workers were manufacturing weapons, explosives, gas masks, plane engines. Over the coming months the various political parties and trade unions would enact a wide range of policies to improve working conditions, from increases in wages and reduction of working hours to the provision of free medical cover, pensions and maternity benefits. In certain sectors of the economy, anarchists outlawed money altogether, introducing a barter system instead. In a heady, revolutionary rush hundreds of new schools would be opened.

On 1 August a report in *The Times* was headlined 'Red Rule in

Barcelona'. The newspaper's special correspondent on the Spanish frontier claimed that whilst the city presented 'an appearance of outward calm' it was in fact 'under a reign of terror'. The 'extremists' were 'out of hand' and 'purification squads' had 'assassinated many of the supporters of the Right.' One of the so-called 'revolutionary chiefs' told the British journalist that this was the way of revolutions: 'These excesses are a retaliation to be expected of persons who have been the victims of the terrible and merciless repressions by the Government of the Right.'

What had started as an Army coup had turned – in Catalonia, at least – into a full-scale workers' revolution. The rebel Generals had expected to be in control of Spain within a matter of days. Instead, most of the country's chief cities, including Madrid – where the fighting and subsequent retribution had been equally vicious – were still in Republican hands. But Morocco, a considerable swathe of southern Spain and large parts of the north were now in rebel hands. Their supporters included much of the landed class, the fascists of the Falange, Carlists who wanted a return of a monarchy, and those many devout working-class Catholics who resented the Republic's attacks on the Church. And they too were committing mass murder in an orgy of revenge. 'It is necessary to spread an atmosphere of terror,' one rebel General declared. 'We have to create an impression of mastery.' Union members, Popular Front politicians, intellectuals, bohemians, freemasons, pro-Republican officers and any suspected supporters of the Left were rounded up; many were simply shot out of hand, executed either by the Army or by their fellow citizens. Meanwhile, the Church welcomed the rebels as the liberators of Spain who would purify it of extremism.

A letter from the US Ambassador in Spain to the Secretary of State in Washington set out the exact elements supporting the rebellion. It was a catalogue of conservatism:

> The monarchists, who wanted the King back with the old regime.
> The great landowners, who wished to preserve the feudalistic system by ending agrarian reforms.

The industrialists and financiers, who wished to put, and keep, the workers 'in their place'.

The hierarchy of the Church, hostile to the separation of Church and State.

The military clique that had in mind a military dictatorship.

The fascist element, which was bent on the creation of a totalitarian state.

At his home in Key West, Ernest Hemingway – who loved Spain and the Spanish people dearly – wanted to be where the action was. But he was finishing a book. Developed from a short story he had started writing in Madrid in 1933, *To Have and Have Not* told the interlocking stories of life in Depression-era Florida and Cuba. This was his first novel since *A Farewell to Arms* – the story based on his experiences in Italy during the Great War, the story of a wounded young American who falls in love with a beautiful British nurse and loses her, the story that had *really* made him famous. It had been published to great acclaim almost seven years before.

'I hate to have missed this Spanish thing worse than anything in the world,' he would tell his literary editor in September. But for the time being he waited. He left the heat and interruptions of Key West in the summertime and headed for the solitude of Wyoming. There he worked on his book. It seemed that the fighting in Spain might well be over before he could return to Madrid.

Chapter 2

After the Storm

|

The rebellion that had started on 18 July 1936 would not be over quickly. Within a few days, a Royal Navy cruiser had arrived off Barcelona to evacuate Britons and Americans caught up in the fighting, for as the British Consul in the city told a bespectacled young Englishwoman that a 'period of unbridled licence' had begun. Do not to go out of doors, he advised her. 'But if you are in the street,' he counselled, 'and you meet any of *those fellows* with guns, just do this' – he clenched his fist delicately in the air – 'and smile nicely.'

In fact, visiting the Consul was about the first time Felicia Browne had been *in*doors since the fighting began. She had driven over from England with a friend to attend an anti-fascist conference in Paris and then watch the People's Olympiad, but a real revolution breaking out around her was more excitement than she had anticipated. For the time being, at least, she had little intention either of staying indoors, or of being evacuated.

The daughter of a West End actress and her playboy husband, Felicia Browne was no ordinary woman. Her parents had separated when she was only three, and she had then spent years under the eye of a governess, 'drowning' in what she called 'the well-upholstered family household'. Following the end of the Great War (in which her elder brother died flying with the RAF) she studied at the Slade School of Art in London. When her father died in 1924 she received a legacy that permitted her to travel. For some years she lived in Berlin, where she studied sculpture and metalwork whilst living alongside unemployed German artists. She joined in the vicious street fighting between communists and Nazis, an experience that turned her to politics.

Back in London in the early 1930s Browne had joined the Communist Party, one of the few international organizations taking a firm stand against fascism, inequality and poverty. This was no straightforward undertaking, however: the Party vetted applicants, and it demanded their total devotion. Rajani Palme Dutt, the brilliant young Oxford graduate

Felicia Browne with unknown companion (Tate Gallery archive)

who proved a leading figure in the Communist Party of Great Britain (the CPGB) through the 1920s and '30s, made this clear as early as 1921. As he explained, the Party required 'absolutely everything' from its members in its pursuit of a Marxist utopia in which class differences would be eradicated and property shared by all in an epoch of freedom and plenty. This compelling vision of the future required utter dedication. For, as Dutt continued, the Party 'can tolerate neither conscience, cowardice, nor compassion. You must be prepared for the ruthless sacrifice of self, then of others, and if required, of so called moral scruples also … But if you attempt to enter the arena of the struggle armed with your particular ideas, you will be mercilessly crushed between the millstones of Revolution and Reaction.'

Browne accepted the Party's staggering ideological commitment, giving much of her time to the cause. She sold copies of *The Daily Worker* on street corners, improved her street-fighting skills by learning ju-jitsu, and dispersed her inheritance helping friends escape Nazi Germany. At the same time she visited Russia, Hungary and Czechoslovakia, making drawings of peasants and workers. During a period of illness in a London hospital she so incited the nurses with revolutionary talk that MI5 began intercepting her letters. And this plain, rather dumpy young woman was also a lesbian, besotted with her travelling companion in Spain, the Hungarian communist photographer Edith ('Ed') Bone.

During the first confused days of the Spanish revolution, Browne and Bone ran into Claud Cockburn. Cockburn needed a photographer to take pictures to accompany his *Daily Worker* articles, and Bone and Browne's appearance was fortuitous: immediately they were 'ferociously occupied'. As Browne explained to a friend: 'Sunday and Monday were terrific days, spent in searching Barcelona for Ed and later for her photographic apparatus which she needed badly (extra films, etc.) dodging guns and firing all over the place. I landed (unexpectedly, not knowing my way about) on the edge of the battlefield Plaza Cataluna at 11 a.m. on Sunday, terrific firing going on.'

By Wednesday the fighting was over, and Catalonia was held for the Republic. In neighbouring Aragon, however, the rebels had been far more successful. Its chief towns, Huesca and Saragossa, had both been taken, along with many villages in the surrounding countryside; in Barcelona, bands of armed civilians were forming themselves into militia units to retake them. A column of volunteers setting out on the hundred-mile journey to Saragossa was accompanied down Las Ramblas by the British Olympiad team and its Scottish bagpipers. It was 'only with the greatest difficulty,' *The Daily Worker* reported, that some of the British athletes were prevented from joining them. However, around 200 competitors of other nationalities – including most of the Jewish team from Palestine – immediately joined the fight.

Bone and Cockburn followed this so-called 'Army of Freedom' westward by car. The charismatic anarchist leader Buenaventura Durruti led the most celebrated and ruthless militia unit. A veteran of the Catalan workers' movement, he had helped lead the fight against the rebel uprising in Barcelona, and the Durruti Column (as Cockburn recorded) advanced impetuously on Saragossa in an amazing assortment of vehicles, 'from Barcelona motor-buses and taxi-cabs to Rolls-Royce

Limousines', mattresses strapped to their roofs as protection from bullets and flying the black and red flag of the anarchists. A rebel army officer would call the Catalan militias 'so completely uncoordinated and so divorced from the norms of military technique that their movements resembled the arbitrary efforts of disintegrated hordes.' But in places where there was little organized resistance, they were deadly. Villages liberated by the Durruti Column would have their church torched, with clergymen and suspected fascists rounded up and shot.

Anarchist militiamen from Barcelona head for the Aragon front, July/August 1936 (IWM)

Felicia Browne was left behind in Barcelona. She had tried to join the militia – women were being accepted into the ranks, and there was even talk of forming a female battalion – but there were too many volunteers and insufficient weapons, and she was turned away.[1] She attempted to join the Red Cross instead; but for every person they needed, there were six volunteers. Uncertain what to do next, and since the endless waiting in Barcelona 'provoked savage melancholy,' Browne decided to go in search of Cockburn and Bone.

She caught a train as far as Lérida (Lleida), but found it impossible to reach Saragossa.

Gerda Taro, *Republican militiawomen training near Barcelona, August 1936* (Magnum Photos)

---

1 According to some observers, one of the most striking things was not that these militia women carried guns, but that they wore trousers, a thing almost unthinkable only a few days before.

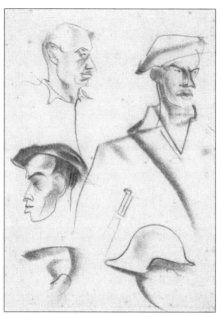

Felicia Browne, *sketch of Spanish Republican militiamen, July 1936* (Tate)

Setting out on foot, she was soon picked up by a car full of militiamen and arrested. For a few hours she was questioned in the Casa del Pueblo in Lérida. When it was finally accepted that she was not a rebel spy, she was allowed to sketch the militiamen and women, and the civilian workers. It was a thrilling opportunity, and her drawings were vivid and animated (though she thought them 'mostly very bad'). In recent months she had felt blocked in her work, had in fact virtually stopped painting or sculpting altogether. This was perhaps unsurprising, as prior to coming to Spain she had been working ten and eleven-hour shifts in a tearoom (where she had encouraged her fellow workers to form a union). As she had explained to a friend, 'the first and true reason' for her not painting was 'actual conditions in the world today which stop one from painting when there are other things to be done.' The thing 'more valid and more urgent' to her was 'the earthquake which is happening in the revolution.' This she had expressed through her work with the trade unions, and for the Artists International Association, which since its conception in 1933 had become a significant force in British left-wing cultural politics.

Here in Spain, however, she was excited to find that numerous artists had joined the militia, and also that it was 'definitely a country for painting'. The saw-toothed mountain of Montserrat, she told her friend, 'would be a good place if it were at all possible to get there. Country beyond that is superb, from Lérida to Bujarelos mainly desert, spotted hills … and earth coloured towns only distinguishable from the hills by shadows, very thin colour, delicate; hard country.' For the time being she could only observe this fantastic landscape, and make ink drawings with the hope that they might be useful to illustrate Cockburn's articles. She tried to reach the Aragon front to find him, but instead encountered a 'very berserk' Edith Bone, who 'with heavy curses' told her to 'get the hell out of here.' It transpired that the militia column Bone and Cockburn had been following had been bombed by rebel planes; they had escaped unharmed, but others were killed nearby, and Bone was clearly anxious.

So Browne returned to Barcelona. 'There have been terrible losses, here in this city and everywhere,' she wrote home. (Cockburn reported in *The Daily Worker* that at least two hundred 'anti-Fascists' had been killed defending the Republic in Barcelona, and around a thousand wounded.) Although the state had effectively been taken over by the workers, and official policing had largely been abandoned, she was impressed by the sense of order, organization and control. The trams – now vividly painted in black and red diagonals – were running again, food was reaching the city, and the large hotels on the Plaça de Catalunya (including the Ritz) had been turned into political command centres, their dining rooms now crowded restaurants for the people.

After the days of mayhem, Browne found it strange to see the shops open again, 'and cars going around without guns sticking out of them and streets without barricades.'

II

At the same time that Felicia Browne was trying and failing to join the militia, another young English Communist was on his way to Spain. John Cornford had just graduated with a starred first in History from Trinity College, Cambridge, where he had been a leading light among the University's left-wing student body. The great-grandson of Charles Darwin, and son of the University's Professor of Ancient Philosophy, Cornford was a handsome, precocious, unconventional twenty-year-old. His younger brother would speak glowingly of John's 'burning energy …

Trying to know him was like standing on a railway embankment and trying to grab an express train.'

Cornford's intention was simply to take a quick look around Spain before the action subsided, and perhaps to write a few newspaper articles: he had some contacts at *The Daily Worker*, Claud Cockburn among them. Then he would join his new girlfriend Margot Heinemann on holiday in the south of France, before returning to Cambridge to take up the Research Scholarship in History he had just been awarded at his old college.

Immediately he was impressed by what he saw in the Catalan capital. Writing in a letter to Margot, Cornford explained that Barcelona's streets were filled with

> armed workers and militiamen, and sitting in the cafés which used to belong to the bourgeoisie. The huge Hotel Colon overlooking the main square is occupied by the United Socialist Party of Catalonia. Further down, in a huge block opposite the Bank of Spain, is the Anarchist headquarters. The palace of a marquis in the Rambla is a Communist Party headquarters. But one does not feel the tension. The mass of the people … simply are enjoying their freedom. The streets are crowded all day, and there are big crowds round the radio palaces. But there is nothing at all like tension or hysteria. It's as if in London the armed workers were dominating the streets … It is genuinely a dictatorship of the majority, supported by the overwhelming majority.

It was a picture that contrasted sharply with reports appearing in the British and American press. When the British Olympiad team disembarked from HMS *London* in Marseilles, they were shocked to read the exaggerated newspaper reports of what was supposedly happening in Spain. One French paper claimed that Barcelona was 'in the hands of a riotous mob,' whilst another reported that it was estimated anarchists in

Madrid had murdered 40,000 men, women and children: 'They assemble people in courtyards, in the prisons, in the squares, and shoot into the crowds. Sharpshooters pick off whole lines of people as they pass.' Back in England a *Daily Mail* poster screamed 'REDS CRUCIFY NUNS.' Arriving home, the British athletes told a reporter from *The Manchester Guardian* that they did not believe sensational stories 'about the heads of priests being carried through the streets'.

Though *The Times* was itself guilty of some misrepresentation, on 19 August it printed a letter from prominent British intellectuals, criticising the press coverage. The signatories included John Cornford's father, together with the writers E.M. Forster, H.G. Wells, Cecil Day Lewis and Leonard and Virginia Woolf, as well as the composer Ralph Vaughan Williams. 'At any other time during the last 150 years of our history,' they complained,

> the sympathies of practically all classes in this country and of our Government would have been with the Spanish people and its Government in such a struggle of democracy against military despotism, and of freedom against Fascism. It is, therefore, a matter of grave concern to find that in many quarters, particularly in the popular Press, a persistent attempt is being made to misrepresent the nature of this struggle, and to enlist the sympathies of Britain for the military rebels, on the ground that the Government is Bolshevist or Communist. The Spanish Government is, we repeat, a democratic Government, elected by the people … it is fighting against military despotism and Fascism for liberty and for what in our country we have for more than a century considered to be the bare minimum of political civilization.

Yet clearly what was happening in Catalonia *was* revolutionary, if not quite as bloodthirsty as the press was claiming. When the Austrian Marxist writer Franz Borkenau arrived in Barcelona at around the same time as John Cornford he was amazed when, on turning into Las Ramblas, he saw 'in a flash' the revolution right before his eyes. 'It was overwhelming,' he wrote. 'It was as if we had been landed on a continent different from anything I had seen before.' There were the workers with rifles over their shoulder, the almost complete absence of police, and the 'innumerable fashionable cars,' appropriated and daubed with the acronyms of the parties and unions of the Spanish Left: CNT (the anarchist Confederation of Workers), FAI (the Federation of Iberian Anarchists), POUM (the breakaway Marxist/Trotskyist party), UGT (the General Workers' Union), PSUC (the Catalan Socialist Party). 'The fact that all these armed men walked about, marched, and drove in their ordinary clothes made the thing only more impressive as a display of the power of the factory workers. The anarchists, recognizable by badges and insignia in red and black, were obviously in overwhelming number. And no "bourgeoisie" whatever!'

Equally striking to Borkenau was the large number of foreigners, all eager to take up arms against the rebels. Among the POUM, he noted, 'there are Germans, Italians, Swiss, Austrians, Dutch, English, a few Americans, and a considerable number of young women of all these nations … All languages are spoken, and there is an indescribable atmosphere of political enthusiasm, of enjoying the adventure of war … of absolute confidence in speedy success. And everybody is friends with everybody in a minute.'

III

In early August, as the Olympic Games opened in Berlin to fanfares and fascist salutes, Felicia Browne wrote home from Barcelona. Since there seemed 'no prospect of exploring, painting, or getting anywhere beyond this monstrous city,' she was trying again to join the militia. Entering the Communist militia office, she demanded to be enlisted.

'I am a member of the London Communists,' she declared, 'and can fight as well as any man.'

This time she was accepted. On the way from the militia office to the garrison she encountered a British journalist from *The Daily Express*. 'I am not at all afraid,' she told him. 'I am fighting for a different country, but the same cause.'

The militia barracks, which had been appropriated from the Army, were filthy; there were no proper uniforms to be had, and 'everybody looks like pirates,' she wrote. She was not the only British volunteer. 'Three Yiddish tailors from Stepney bicycled here from England in order to join up,' she informed her friend in a letter written between stints of guard duty. Nat Cohen, Sam Masters and Allick Sheller were all CPGB members, and had been cycling to Barcelona for the Olympiad when the rebellion broke out. Cohen, the eldest, had learnt Spanish in South America, where he had held down various rough jobs, and had been imprisoned for his communist beliefs. Though he had no military experience, Cohen wanted to join a machinegun unit, and Browne joined with him. However, they immediately encountered a problem: there were no machineguns, nor even any rifles.

Nevertheless, by mid-August Browne was in Tardienta, a small Aragon town some fifteen miles from the rebel forces holed up in Huesca. According to a reporter from *The Manchester Guardian*, as well as being the headquarters of a Republican militia column, Tardienta was home to 'what one might call an anti-Fascist Foreign Legion'. These international volunteers had gathered from all over Europe; they included a large number of Germans and Italians, mostly left-wing exiles from the fascist regimes in their home countries. There were also French and Belgians, and 'one lone Englishman from Stepney'. The town had the feel of 'a big holiday camp,' the journalist reported, before adding ominously that 'this civil war is being fought virtually with the weapons of the Boer War.'

The supply of modern arms, armament and ammunition would prove the Republic's greatest obstacle in defeating the rebels. Spain had no domestic arms industry to speak of, and much of the weaponry needed to fight a large-scale war had to be imported. In France, the recently elected Popular Front government led by the socialist Léon Blum was keen to aid its neighbour. (In Paris on Bastille Day, Felicia Browne had been hugely impressed by the 'hundreds of women, representing anti-fascist, anti-war women's groups all over France. People here are sincerely alive,' she wrote to a friend, and wondered 'why the devil have we not got the same sort of thing in England, which seems to be in a sort of dream.') It was not only a sense of political loyalty to the Left that made some key figures in the French administration natural allies with Spain's Government: *realpolitik* also played its part. Already bordered by Italy and Germany, a third fascist neighbour would exacerbate France's perilous sense of encirclement. Yet at the same time, France's right-wing press – as well as some members of Blum's cabinet – feared abetting a civil war in their own politically-divided country if they helped arm the Spanish Republic.

Blum visited London in late July. There the Foreign Secretary, Anthony Eden, advised him that providing military aid to Spain might not be 'prudent'. As the Conservative MP Winston Churchill suggested in an unofficial letter to the French Ambassador, 'the great bulk of the Conservative Party are very much inclined to cheer the so-called Spanish rebels,' who appeared to represent the forces of order, stability, privilege, commerce and tradition. Besides, the British Government had no wish to see the straits of Gibraltar controlled by a revolutionary state, and British banks and businesses also had considerable sums invested in Spain.

More pressingly, however, the British Government feared that French aid for Spain risked bringing a resurgent Germany into the conflict, and sparking a second world war. For many, such a war already seemed almost inevitable: Hemingway had first heard this gloomy prognosis in Paris as early as 1933, and had soon reached a similar conclusion. Only a few months before the outbreak of the Spanish Civil War, the British Prime Minister, Stanley Baldwin, told a meeting of fellow Conservatives that whilst he was not one of the many who saw a future world war 'inevitable,' he certainly saw it as 'a ghastly possibility'. He considered it 'our duty' to prevent it from happening 'in every we way we can'.

The British people, still reeling from the appalling losses of the Great

War, largely supported this ambition. They could not believe that any other European leader – even Hitler – wished to provoke another such mass bloodletting. One chapter of Wyndham Lewis's 1931 analysis of the Nazi leader was titled, 'Adolf Hitler a Man of Peace'. Though Lewis admitted that it was an often-asked question 'whether Germany contemplates a War of Revenge' for its defeat and humiliation in 1918–19, he advised his readers that it was 'essential to understand that Adolf Hitler is not a sabre-rattler at all.' Meanwhile Lloyd George, the Prime Minister who had led Britain to victory in the Great War but who had suggested that the Treaty of Versailles in 1919 would lead to another world war within twenty years, called Hitler 'the greatest German of the age'.

Deluded as to Hitler's true ambitions, the British public for the most part did not see the cause of Spanish democracy as worth the risk of another global war. For them, as for other foreigners, the Spanish Civil War had been quickly simplified into easy polarities: Communism versus Fascism, Atheism versus Catholicism, Revolution versus Tradition. Only a minority believed that by fighting fascism now they might prevent a greater clash in the future; besides, many people saw Bolshevism as the equal or greater threat to world peace. The official British Government position was soon formulated. As a representative informed the League of Nations in December 1936, offers had been made to help end the fighting by mediation, but 'the unhappy conflict in Spain is, in its inception, an internal affair of the Spanish people,' and therefore 'the political issues involved should not become the concerns of other nations.'

Most Americans were similarly unwilling to spark a global conflict by becoming embroiled in Spain; Congress had already passed Neutrality Acts in an effort either to prevent such a future cataclysm or – if one did occur – to keep the US out. Increasingly through the 1920s it was felt that American involvement in the Great War had been a mistake. And when France defaulted on its massive US war debt in 1933, many Americans became even warier of ever involving themselves in European affairs again.

Furthermore, US investments in Spain were substantial, and the Catholic Church and big business both backed the rebels. (The Texas Oil Company would go so far as delivering $6 million worth of oil to Franco on credit over the course of the war.) A large part of the American press reinforced the image of the Republicans as dangerous revolutionaries: 'Red Madrid Ruled by Trotsky,' barked one of William Randolph Hearst's papers in August. That same month President F.D. Roosevelt's Secretary of State announced that the US would 'scrupulously refrain from any interference whatsoever in the unfortunate Spanish situation.'

Thus within a week of the uprising the French Prime Minister was isolated; he was obliged by circumstance to change tack. Though the Spanish government had every right in international law to buy arms on the open market, Blum decided that, with the support of the League of Nations, a Non-Intervention Agreement was the best he could do to support the Republican Government. If *neither* side had the means to procure weapons or munitions, the war would inevitably end sooner rather than later, perhaps with an internationally mediated peace agreement.

Non-Intervention, however, would never prove anything more than a charade. Although by late August Germany, Italy, France, Britain, the USSR and twenty-two other European nations had signed up to non-intervention, the fascist states were *already* intervening in Spain. The rebels' two best military units were the colonial Army of Africa, which was composed of native Moroccans (known as Moors), and led by Spanish officers; and the Foreign Legion, which was modelled on the French Foreign Legion, but was composed largely of Spaniards. Under the command of General Franco, at the start of the war both these armies had been stationed – and effectively isolated – in Morocco. The rebels' attempt to take the Spanish Navy had failed, and most vessels remained loyal to the Government. (The fact that the crews of a number of Spanish ships had machinegunned their rebellious officers did not endear them to the Royal Navy staff at Gibraltar.) If the rebels were to win the war, they needed to move men and equipment rapidly from North Africa to Spain. After the defeat of their forces in Barcelona, Madrid and other major cities, the rising seemed doomed to failure without the rapid intervention of General Franco's élite forces in Morocco.

Franco therefore approached Benito Mussolini to request transport planes. At first the Italian dictator was wary: he did not wish to provoke a conflict with France or Britain. But he had seen the French government pull back from offering assistance, and suspecting that the British establishment was pro-Franco, he saw another chance to boost his own reputation and Italian prestige after his recent success in subjugating Abyssinia.[1] Within days, a squadron of twelve Italian bombers was heading for Spanish Morocco. Adolf Hitler, meanwhile, was attending the annual Wagner festival in Bayreuth when he received Franco's request for help. Though his initial response was cautious ('That's no way to start a war,' he observed), he was quickly convinced that assisting the rebels was in the Third Reich's political interests: a rebel victory in Spain would bring the country into the fold of European fascism, whereas a Spain ruled by the Left would prove a buttress for France and Russia. Dubbing German involvement 'Operation Magic Fire', he despatched thirty Junker transport planes to Morocco.

By mid-August these foreign aircraft had helped ferry 15,000 rebel soldiers across the Straits of Gibraltar into Spain. Thousands more German and Italian airmen, soldiers and technicians – as well as state-of-the-art planes, machineguns, tanks, artillery, ammunition and other equipment – would arrive over the following months. It was their involvement that made this an overtly fascist war; for whilst the Falange *was* a fascist movement, neither Franco nor the rest of the rebel generals could be considered such. They were soldiers, not politicians.[2] Nonetheless,

---

1 Italian forces had invaded Abyssinia (Ethiopia) in October 1935; the response of the League of Nations and the Western democracies (who feared pushing the Italians into an alliance with Germany) had been grossly ineffectual.

2 As Franz Borkenau observed in 1937, 'The Franco rising is usually described as a fascist revolt; this habit partly derives from the fact that Franco himself identifies with international fascism. And, in a scientific sense, the term might pass, provided every dictatorship is called "fascist" and fascism is simply used in the sense of "a non-democratic régime".' This, no doubt, is how many of those foreigners who went to Spain saw the situation.

their ambitions were totalitarian, and plainly anti-communist. For, as with Hitler and Musolini's support the Army of Africa marched northwards, Franco told the *Chicago Tribune* journalist Jay Allan, 'I will save Spain from Marxism whatever the cost,' even if that meant shooting half of its population. That he was prepared to use an army partly made up of Islamic North Africans against his own people signalled the strength of his commitment to 'cleanse' the country and destroy what he considered 'Red Spain'. But this use of African troops shocked many foreigners. As the British war correspondent Henry Nevinson suggested in *The Daily Herald,* it was comparable to British fascists importing 'an armed force of Zulus to overthrow our Constitution and established Government'.

The rebels' final target was Madrid, and in their wake they left a trail of horror. 'Liberated' towns and villages became scenes of butchery. Badajoz, defended by some 7,000 poorly armed civilians, was the most notorious incident. The Army of Africa stormed the town on 14 August and Jay Allen, fresh from his interview with Franco, reported the aftermath. Those who had survived the hand-to-hand fighting were ushered in batches into the bullring, sometimes roped together: 'There machine guns await them. After the first night the blood was supposed to be palm deep … I don't doubt it. Eighteen hundred men – there were women, too – mowed down there in some twelve hours. There is more blood than you would think in 1,800 bodies.' Altogether, Allen reckoned that some 4,000 people were murdered at Badajoz.[1] Bodies were burnt, and publicly displayed in the street. It was the same wherever the rebels took territory: murder and intimidation followed. Among the most renowned victims was the poet Federico García Lorca, killed in Granada apparently on account of his homosexuality. Spain, the rebels decreed, was to be purged of liberal modernity in all its forms.

Nonetheless the Nationalist press service denied the atrocity at Badajoz, well aware that any negative propaganda would work against

---

1 Allen's horrifying report would help make the Spanish Civil War front page news around the world; but his conservative paper would eventually fire him, feeling that his stories provoked too much sympathy for the Republic.

their cause. But the General commanding the rebel column told Allen, 'Of course we shot them.' And another American journalist reported from Talavera that not a single night went by without his being awakened at dawn 'by the volleys of the firing squads. There seemed no end to the killing.' He reckoned that an average of thirty people were shot every night for some two months. 'They were simple peasants and workers. It was sufficient to have carried a trade-union card, to have been a free-mason, to have voted for the Republic.' The Foreign Legion lived up to their sinister motto 'Long Live Death,' while the Moors fulfilled their fearsome reputation: their Spanish officers encouraged rape, murder, mutilation and despoliation as a deliberate policy of subjugation. As the rebel General Mola stated: 'we have to terrorise, we have to show we are in control by rapidly and ruthlessly eliminating all those who do not think as we do.' Whilst the violence in the centres held by the Republic had been spontaneous and brutal, the authorities did their best to quell it; in rebel-controlled territory, however, it became a matter of policy, and it lasted the course of the war.

Frank Thomas, a young Welshman who had volunteered to fight with the Spanish Foreign Legion three months after the start of the Civil War, thought that his 'rough-humoured *compañeros*' had been 'brutalized by years of warfare' against the 'barbaric' Moors who were now their brothers-in-arms. Though he considered the shooting of prisoners (much like the burning of churches) to be 'an old Spanish custom' common to both sides, he noted that the Legionnaires shot their victims in the stomach, ensuring a slow, agonising death. He also recorded a number of Republican atrocities. A Legionnaire motorcycle despatch rider who rode by accident into a village still held by militiamen was 'beaten to death with rifle butts and sticks,' and his 'mutilated and jelly-like body' left in the street. Another captured Legionnaire was discovered 'with his eyes, tongue, and worse, removed'. These incidents were cruel retribution for the murders committed by Foreign Legionnaires. Though both sides would deny many of these incidents, neither had clean hands.

After his experience of the Barcelona uprising, the journalist Theo

Rogers backed the rebels. But when he returned to the States he was surprised to find that 'the support of Hitler seemed to turn many a fair-minded American from Franco.' He blamed the press, suggesting that some reports of the war published in Britain and the States were 'so far from the truth' that he suspected they were consciously pro-Republican. Many, however, argued exactly the opposite: most notably, the President. When Claude Bowers, the US Ambassador to Spain, told him that nine-tenths of the press reports coming from the country were false, Roosevelt responded: 'You are right about the distortion of the news … Over here the Hearst papers and most of the conservative editors are playing up all kinds of atrocities on the part of what they call the Communist government in Madrid – nothing about atrocities on the part of the rebels.'[1]

The picture was similar in Britain. One journalist who had witnessed the first days of the war expostulated: 'Today most English people have been convinced that the government supporters are not only "reds" but ghouls; that the reason why they have not defeated the fascists is that they spend their time raping nuns and watching them dance naked.' In fact, rebel atrocities now far outstripped those committed by 'Reds'. But any attempts to unravel and report on the true story in Spain became increasingly embroiled in prejudice, propaganda, fear and rumour.

Though it was already apparent that the fascist powers were actively arming the rebels, the German and Italian members of the Non-Intervention Committee assembled in London denied any involvement by their governments in Spain. Despite the overwhelming evidence to the contrary, the Committee's ineffective Chairman, the Tory Lord Plymouth, was not the man to call their bluff, nor was the British Government keen to cause an international scene. (The Soviet Ambassador in London later described Lord Plymouth as possessing an 'imposing and well-groomed body' that hosted 'a small, slow-moving and timid mind. Nature and education had made [him] a practically ideal personification of English

---

1 Roosevelt was despondent about 'press freedom' in the US, feeling that it was largely the freedom to make things up.

political mediocrity. As Chairman of the Committee [he] presented an entirely helpless and often comic figure.') So whilst no action was taken against Germany or Italy, the British Government continued to block any foreign attempts to arm the Republic. The only country prepared openly to offer military assistance was Mexico: 20,000 Mausers and twenty million cartridges were soon on their way across the Atlantic. Until the Soviet Union also offered its clandestine support, the Republic was forced to buy arms on the black market: these weapons, unfortunately, would frequently prove to be outdated, unreliable and over-priced.

IV

The fluid, ever-changing nature of the front during the early stages of the war, and the lack of sufficient troops to secure a clear dividing line between the two sides, was made clear to Claud Cockburn when he visited the headquarters of Colonel Julio Mangada. Described by Cockburn as looking 'like some sort of cross between Gandhi and Gandhi's goat,' Mangada was one of the few senior Army officers to have remained loyal to the Government. Cockburn was accompanied by a man who claimed to be Mexican, but was in fact one of the first Russian 'technical advisers' to have arrived in Spain. (The first wave of Russians travelled incognito since, as Cockburn observed, they 'were rather naturally anxious to avoid doing anything that would give the Western Governments an excuse to turn the Germans loose on them in a war which would be described as having been "provoked" by "Red intervention" in Spain.' They were therefore 'leaning over backwards being discreet'.)

Mangada invited Cockburn and his 'Mexican' colleague to view the front line. 'We walked for a mile or so across lovely, deserted country – partly a sort of parkland, partly mountain foothills, with outcrops of rock baking in the sun.' They passed a few detachments of Republican troops sitting in the shade, and then after another mile or so, 'saw, perhaps six or seven hundred yards away, a line of riflemen in open order, moving about on the low ground ahead of us.'

'Those, I suppose,' said the 'Mexican, 'are your advance patrols?'

'Not at all,' said Mangada, obviously surprised. 'Those must be the advance patrols of the enemy.'

For Cockburn and the Russian advisor it was 'an ugly little moment. There we stood in no-man's-land, and there seemed a high possibility that within about ten minutes Spain's only Loyal General was going to be captured by the enemy, I was going to be shot as a Red Agent, and the "Mexican" … was going to be Exhibit Number One in a nasty international incident.

'Awfully slowly, as it seemed to me, the General – who had the air of a man walking around his estate in Somerset on a Sunday afternoon – turned from his dreamy contemplation of the enemy patrols and we strolled back to his headquarters.'

Such large swathes of no-man's-land and the discomforting ease with which the front could be crossed made commando-style operations relatively easy. It was just such an operation that gave Felicia Browne her chance of action. After only three days at the Aragon front – and refusing to be put off by warnings of how dangerous the undertaking would be – she volunteered to join a mission to destroy an ammunition train carrying supplies along the railway linking the rebel strongholds of Huesca and Saragossa.

Ten volunteers left Tardienta by car early one afternoon in late August. The last ten miles to their target was on foot; on arrival, Browne and two others acted as look-outs, while the others set the explosives. Having carried out their mission, on the way back they stumbled upon a crashed Republican airplane, the dead pilot still trapped in the wreckage. Hastily they buried him; but then they encountered a patrol of thirty or forty rebels. As the group fell back under fire, an Italian anti-Fascist volunteer was wounded. A colleague dragged him into the cover offered by a slight rise in the ground, whilst Browne rushed forward to administer first aid.

She was shot several times as she ran. Spinning around she was hit again in the back, then fell dead to the ground. The wounded Italian was also killed as the militiamen retreated. There was no chance of retrieving their bodies.

At the age of just thirty-two, Felicia Browne was the first British casualty of the war. Her friend Nan Youngman read of her death in a newspaper whilst on holiday in Cornwall. 'I did not want to believe it,' she later recalled. 'I was horrified, and from that moment I began to be aware of living in history ... I was 30, but I was a child.' A number of British papers had run the story. They had few facts to go on. Claud Cockburn reported that Browne had been 'shot through the head as she worked a machinegun at Tardienta,' while *The Manchester Guardian* stated that this 'pilgrim of art' was 'slain in the rebel attack on Barcelona.' No one knew the exact date of her death. As one journalist commented, the young artist had 'fought for what she thought was right, and – whatever her politics – she remains a sad monument to the futility and barbarism of war.'

V

As Felicia Browne was falling for the cause of Republican Spain, John Cornford was being drawn further into its almost irresistible embrace.

Like Browne, Cornford was a committed bourgeois communist. Unlike her, his conversion to the Left had started early, gradually replacing his adolescent interests of cricket and poetry. As a teenager at public school, resentful of its rules, petty restrictions and irritating discipline, he had discussed with his younger brother 'half-jokingly but in great detail, plans for a revolution'. He was not suited to the public-school system, which he detested: he was too individualistic, too imaginative, too ready to question the *status quo*.

At Cambridge, where he cut a strange figure tramping across Trinity College's vast Great Court 'wrapped in portentous gloom and an antique raincoat,' Cornford had dedicated himself to two causes: communism and pacifism. The former was quickly becoming one of the defining ideologies among Cornford's young, radical contemporaries at Trinity, who included the future spies Guy Burgess, Kim Philby and Anthony Blunt. As Claud Cockburn later observed, in the 'desert of misery' that was life for many of Britain's working-class in the years of the Great Depression,

> Cambridge was an ostentatious oasis of civilized comfort. It is not at all surprising that Blunt and others should have, with some deep feelings of guilt, questioned the justification for such a state of affairs. On the contrary, it would have been surprising had any sensitive and informed young man coolly accepted his position as though by divine right. The Communists did not require secret recruiting sergeants; the economics of the time were doing the job quite well enough.

Despite being dismissed by John Maynard Keynes as 'complicated hocus-pocus', Marxism – as one of Cornford's student friend's observed – was 'the new orthodoxy that had fastened itself upon the minds of the undergraduates'.

For a while, however, pacifism proved equally popular among more radical students. On 11 November 1933, during his first term at Cambridge, Cornford helped to organise an anti-war demonstration: a procession of left-wing, pacifist and Christian students planned to lay a wreath at the Cambridge war memorial. It was to carry the inscription *'To the victims of the Great War, from those who are determined to prevent similar crimes of imperialism.'* It was a provocative gesture for Armistice Day, and the police insisted that the inscription be removed since it was 'likely to lead to a breach of the peace'. Even without the inscription, the peace was breached. The demonstration – which many viewed as dishonouring the dead of the Great War – was met by a mob of students and 'townies' throwing eggs, tomatoes, flour and white feathers. The banner-pole of the Socialist Club was broken, and police used their batons to break up the fights that resulted. The clash made the national press, provoking similar public outrage to that caused by the debate at the Oxford Union nine months earlier, when students had supported the motion 'This House will in no circumstances fight for King and Country.'

With the recent rise to power of the Nazis in Germany, the emergence of a domestic fascist party under the leadership of Sir Oswald Mosley, and the ongoing effects of the Great Depression, the political atmosphere in Britain was tense. Numerous students had visited the continent, where the situation was even more alarming. (Having recently returned from a vacation in Vienna, one freshman turned up at Cambridge with a revolver in his luggage, 'under the belief that firearms were carried to political meetings as a matter of course'.) To many left-wing students at the University, Cornford became a kind of symbol. As one friend described him, he was 'the most brilliant, the most sectarian, the most conspiratorial, the most devoted and full of animal energy, the most in need, at times, of a haircut and a shave. Just because he was not merely

John Cornford and his former girlfriend Rachel Peters in a studio portrait by Ramsey & Muspratt, 1934 (National Portrait Gallery)

an isolated heroic figure, but one of many trying to build up a disciplined movement, his actions were significant.'

One unrequited lover described Cornford as 'a hard boiled intellectual ... I believe he'll make the Revolution,' she told the young man's mother, 'destroy and kill – but I shall always be too sensitive and care too much about people being made unhappy and suffering ... To make a Revolution you have to hate and have class consciousness.' A romance with a working-class activist, Rachel Peters, had led to the birth of a son. But Cornford had soon left them both for Margot Heinemann, a fellow student at Cambridge and the daughter of German-Jewish émigrés who would go on to have her own remarkable career as a writer and teacher.

Heinemann was also a member of the Communist Party, and together with the University's left-wing students Cornford and Heinemann helped to organise study groups of Marxist texts, distribute leaflets, sell copies of *The Daily Worker*, and advise the town's workers on political issues, even joining them in picket lines; and they attended public meetings of the British Union of Fascists in order to heckle. In 1934 the students organised a reception for the Hunger Marchers who passed through Cambridge on their way to a mass rally in London, raising money for food and clothing. An Anti-War Exhibition presented a 'huge collection of horror-pictures of corpses and mutilated men'; it was said to have made some visitors physically sick.

Cornford's hatred of fascism, one fellow student wrote, 'amounted to physical loathing, and to break up a fascist meeting was perhaps his highest enjoyment.' When the same friend asked whether he would not have preferred to live a century *after* the Revolution, 'in an era of peaceful construction,' Cornford said, decidedly, 'No,' adding that he 'did in fact *enjoy* finding himself in an epoch of storm and stress, oppression and revolt, tyranny and heroism.' Only the Revolution would overthrow what he saw as the oppressive, empty-headed bourgeoisie who obliged others to live wretchedly in order to maintain a lifestyle that did not even make them happy. For Cornford, the Revolution was as unquestionable a certainty as the Resurrection was to a Christian. It was simply a matter of time.

But Cornford eventually came to the realisation, as he had already acknowledged in a letter to his mother while still a schoolboy, 'that it's impossible to be a pacifist and a Communist … I really don't see how any pacifist organisation would be strong enough to fight the Armament Firms, the Banks, and the Newspapers.' If there was to be a revolution – and how else was capitalism to be overthrown? – it would be an armed event; if there was to be a world without fascism, it was clear that it could not be achieved by intellectual arguments and demonstrations alone. Perhaps only a global revolution in 1918, he told his mother, 'might have ended war forever. "The war to end wars" has simply made the technique of beastliness in war a great deal more efficient … That's why I'm not a pacifist – however good the ideal, the absolute impossibility of attaining it without a fight.'

Events in Spain made this obvious. Having arrived in Barcelona, Cornford quickly realized both that the situation was more serious than he had first imagined, and that his lack of Spanish meant he could do no meaningful work as a journalist. However, on his second day in the city, he met Franz Borkenau. This was a fortuitous encounter: the Austrian writer was an experienced observer of European politics; moreover he spoke Castilian. Exiled from his homeland on account of his left-wing beliefs, Borkenau had nevertheless possessed the self-confidence to resign from the Communist Party when Stalin began eliminating his former Bolshevik colleagues. He would prove a useful guide to the young Englishman.

Accompanied by a French journalist from *Paris Flèche*, Cornford and Borkenau set off for Aragon in a car provided by the Militia Central Committee. They were repeatedly stopped at barricaded and heavily guarded villages, where each time their papers were checked before they could pass on. They were both impressed and shocked by what they saw. 'Assisted by the militia,' Cornford later wrote, 'there is a peasant war raging in the countryside.' The landowners, bourgeoisie and priests had fled or been killed, and the peasants had elected 'Committees of the People' to administer the abandoned estates and agricultural machinery. Rents were wiped out, the Committee redistributed the land, and machines were used in common. In a small town some fifteen miles from Huesca he saw young anarchists make a huge bonfire of title deeds in the market square. 'It was by no means just a matter-of-fact destruction of some unwanted documents,' wrote Borkenau, 'but an act carrying for its participants a deep significance as a symbol of the destruction of the old economic order.'

At Leciñena they encountered a column of militia from the breakaway Marxist/Trotskyist party, the POUM. These anti-Stalinist Catalan workers were an 'incoherent mass,' Cornford wrote, 'a curious mixture of amateur and professional,' their operations 'more picturesque than military'. Their principal weapons were the Mauser rifles liberated from the Barcelona arsenal in July, but they had little of the heavier equipment necessary for fighting a modern war, and only half wore the blue or brown overalls and blue shirts that had become the militias' improvised uniform. There was no saluting, junior officers were elected, and decisions were made only after group discussion. In the evening the men ate, danced and sang,

Robert Capa, POUM *militiamen dancing in Leciñena. Aragon, 1936* (Magnum)

frenetic scenes captured on film by another young foreign anti-fascist when he passed through Leciñena at around this time: the Hungarian photographer Robert Capa. He had come out to Spain from Paris at the start of the war with his German girlfriend, Gerda Taro, an equally brave and even more talented photographer.

It was all so exhilarating that, when Borkenau returned to Barcelona the next day, Cornford decided to stay behind. Presenting his CPGB card as evidence of his anti-fascist credentials, he volunteered to join the POUM militia. It was a spur-of-the-moment decision; unable to speak Spanish, and with nothing to do or to read, he felt lonely, 'a bit useless' and rather isolated. It was a strange change in circumstance for the one-time pacifist who as a schoolboy had refused to 'play at being a soldier' in the Officers' Training Corps. 'But I am settling down,' he explained in a long letter to Margot Heinemann, 'picking up scraps of the language and beginning to feel happy. I think I'll make a good fighter, and I'm glad to be here.'

There was no going back. As he told Margot, who was expecting to join him soon on holiday in the south of France:

> I came out with the intention of staying a few days, firing a few shots, and then coming home. Sounded fine, but you just can't do things like that. You can't play at civil war, or fight with a reservation that you don't mean to get killed. It didn't take long to realise that either I was here in earnest or else I'd better clear out. Then I felt so lonely and bad I tried to get a pass back to Barcelona. But the question was decided for me. Having joined, I am in whether I like it or not. And I like it. Yesterday we went out to attack, and the prospect of action was terribly exhilarating.

Having told Margot that he intended to 'fight like a Communist if not like a soldier,' in the event Cornford and his fellow militiamen had returned to their base without doing anything.

He reckoned he would be with the POUM militia until Saragossa was taken – a couple of months, at least – but that he would learn 'a hell of a lot'. He told Margot not to worry. There was of course a chance that he might be killed, but statistically it was 'not very great … There is a 70 per cent chance of getting back uninjured and 90 per cent of getting back alive; which is, on the whole, worth while …'

Chapter 3

The Soul of Spain

|

In the closing days of August, as John Cornford and his comrades in the POUM were turning their attention to capturing Huesca, Tom Wintringham arrived in Barcelona. A tall, prematurely bald man in his late thirties, he came from an upper-middle-class Lincolnshire family: his father was a prosperous lawyer, whilst an aunt and uncle had been Liberal MPs. After the Great War, during which he had served for two years as a motorcycle despatch rider, Wintringham had gone up to Oxford to read History. Friends made there had included Ralph Fox, an aspiring writer with left-wing sensibilities, and Andrew Rothstein, son of a Lithuanian-born Jew who since 1912 had been London correspondent for the Bolshevik newspaper *Pravda*, and from 1917 Lenin's chief agent in London. These friendships helped move him to the Left, and in 1920 Wintringham visited the Soviet Union. It was only three years after the Revolution, and in the young Socialist state everything good still appeared possible.

By 1936, and despite his bourgeois background, Wintringham had become a leading figure in the Communist Party of Great Britain. In 1925 he had gained notoriety when he and some colleagues were imprisoned on charges of sedition and incitement to mutiny on account of articles they published in a communist newspaper, warning soldiers that a General Strike was coming, and advising them 'if you must shoot, don't shoot the workers.' This episode had put paid to Wintringham's nascent legal career. Instead, he focused even more on writing, helping to found both *The Daily Worker* and *The Left Review*, as well as publishing a number of books (including, in 1935, his stark warning, *The Coming World War*).

Although he was *The Daily Worker*'s military correspondent, Wintringham had been running a 'peace camp' for youngsters in Dorset when Harry Pollitt, the CPGB's Secretary-General, sent a telegram telling him to pack his bags and head immediately for Spain. Claud Cockburn was already there, of course, covering events for *The Daily Worker*, but at only thirty-two he was too young to have served in the Great War, and he had never seen combat before. Wintringham would bring his military experience, as well as the ability to report expertly on Europe's first full-blown military confrontation since the end of the Russian Civil War in 1921. Furthermore (and more importantly) Wintringham would act as the CPGB's advance guard in Spain, representing the organisation politically, and preparing a route out for other British communists to follow.

Kitted out with an army-surplus knapsack and trench coat, Wintringham spent a few days in Paris making contact with fellow communists. Then he caught a train south to Perpignan, and from there, via the railway tunnel beneath the foothills of the Pyrenees, he crossed the border to Portbou and Barcelona. One of his first tasks on arriving in Spain was to sort out Felicia Browne's remaining effects. These included what he called 'a first-rate sketch book full of studies of the militia'; he sent it to Harry Pollitt with the suggestion that the Artists' International Association might sell it to raise funds for the Spanish Republic. His idea was welcomed, and an exhibition was quickly organised in London by Browne's friends.[1] And Wintringham already had another idea of how to aid Spain: raising a legion of British volunteers to fight alongside the workers' militias. Initially this suggestion did not go down so well in London, however: the Labour Party would not support it, he was told.

---

1 When it opened in October, *The Manchester Guardian*'s reviewer observed: 'These heavy unshaven men with the jutting chins and the thin, disdainful little men looking at nothing are terribly authentic. Death seems to brood over that part of the show, but how much is evoked through her art and how much through the waste of this young, talented life and of what we feel about the horrors to-day in Spain one cannot say.'

'But why?' he had asked.

'It isn't respectable,' he was told (presumably by Pollitt), 'and they will think of the Catholic vote and the pacifists. And such a legion would be sure to be labelled Red or Communist. We must avoid having those labels stuck on the war in Spain, which is a defence of democracy, of a democratic republic, against Fascism.'

With the right-wing press continuing to present the Spanish situation as a dangerous threat to Western capitalism – another (if smaller) Soviet Union in the making – moderates in Europe and America had to be kept on side if their support for the Republic was to be counted on. If, indeed, they were going to be interested at all: Winston Churchill's son, Randolph expressed his opinion that in Britain, at least, it was only 'a few excitable Catholics and ardent Socialists' who thought the war mattered: 'for the general public it's just a lot of bloody dagoes killing each other.' A remark attributed to the Prime Minister, Stanley Baldwin, was only a little more considered: 'We English hate Fascism,' he allegedly observed, 'but we loathe Bolshevism as much. So, if there is somewhere where Fascists and Bolsheviks can kill each other off, so much the better.' So for the time being, Wintringham kept quiet about his idea of forming a British legion.

On the journey to Spain Wintringham had shared a carriage with another group of British volunteers. Their passage and equipment paid for by voluntary contributions from concerned British civilians, they were the first contingent of the British Medical Unit. At the head of this group of some twenty doctors and nurses was a twenty-three-year-old medical student, Kenneth Sinclair-Loutit. He had been at Trinity College with John Cornford and had participated with him in the Cambridge Armistice Day peace demonstration three years earlier. Though not fired with Cornford's passion for the Communist Party, he was still firmly anti-fascist. He had recently made a cycling tour through Germany, where he had witnessed first-hand the sinister threat posed by fascism.

The arrival in Barcelona of Sinclair-Loutit's 'band of innocents' (they had no inkling of the complex political situation into which they were plunging) was even more feted than their departure from London had been. The BMU constituted what Sinclair-Loutit called 'the first visible sign of collective international support' for the Republic. Within a few hours of reaching Spain Sinclair-Loutit was invited to meet Lluís Companys, President of Catalonia, in the Renaissance palace of Barcelona's *Generalitat*, with its cloistered rose garden and peacocks.

In a brief audience, the President impressed upon Sinclair-Loutit the importance of their having come to the Spain's aid: 'he wanted me to know that he had given instructions that we should be given every facility.' Sinclair-Loutit was exhilarated, and at that moment defeat for the Republic and its revolutionary militias seemed unthinkable.

II

Accompanying Kenneth Sinclair-Loutit and the BMU was Hugh O'Donnell, a young CPGB apparatchik unpromisingly described by one of his group as 'stupid, conceited and erratic'. Together with Wintringham they set about establishing what exactly the British Medical Unit should do: it was stressful, confusing and time-consuming work. But all the time new faces were appearing to help. The communist writer and poet Sylvia Townsend Warner and her lover, Valentine Ackland, had offered their assistance even before Wintrigham had left England. He telegraphed them, asking them to come out to Barcelona to assist O'Donnell with the administrative work. 'The position of the medical service on this front is tragic,' Wintringham had recently written to Harry Pollitt at CPGB headquarters in London: 'wounded bleed slowly to death while being carried on springless lorries over hill roads for hours. There is not enough organization to run a cafe.'

There was plenty to do, but the two women were unimpressed by what they found: they were soon protesting to Pollitt that 'the atmosphere among the English in Barcelona is the atmosphere of the English in India.' They had even heard it reported (with approval) that Sinclair-Loutit had remarked, 'The best way to speak to the Spaniards is with a whip.' They found their colleagues isolated from their Spanish comrades, who complained that the British lacked discipline and drank too much. Warner and Ackland added that 'much time was wasted in aimless discussion in cafés,' and there was endless gossip. 'The general effect was of a clique absorbed in their own affairs and managing them badly.' Hugh O'Donnell, in particular, was a disaster: his apparently deteriorating mental and physical health made it 'imperative that he should be replaced. His state of nervous tension grows worse every day and his lack of self control must grievously endanger Party prestige and safety … while he gives an appearance of great activity no work gets done.' Feeling they were wasting both their time and the scarce resources of the city, Warner and Ackland returned home within a month.

Others who joined Sinclair-Loutit's medical team included an old Cambridge colleague, Stanley Richardson, and Peter Spencer, the Viscount Churchill (a cousin of Winston Churchill). They arrived with the convoy of ambulances and trucks belonging to the Medical Unit that had driven down through France, cheered all the way to the border by the French, and on down Las Ramblas to a welcome from thousands of delighted Spaniards: it appeared that Britain was, perhaps, on their side after all.

These new arrivals were a curious pair. Richardson, who had studied Spanish at Cambridge, was a talented interpreter – as well as a promising young poet – but Sinclair-Loutit described him as 'wildly gay and oddly innocent'. And Viscount Churchill was a dilettantish aristocrat: after a stint as a very young staff officer during the Great War he had acted on Broadway, written a successful play, and dabbled in journalism before turning to left-wing politics early in the 1930s. Both were homosexual, and notwithstanding their respective talents Sinclair-Loutit wondered if either was suited to the prevailing atmosphere in Barcelona. One evening shortly after their arrival they went in search of a café frequented by the city's left-wing gays and non-conformists. Sinclair-Loutit's worries proved unfounded, however: Richardson was a surprising success with Spanish 'macho types, especially big, ferocious, pistol-toting anarchists,' whilst the Viscount with his seemingly limitless expense account 'certainly pleased the communists'.

Arriving in the same convoy was Archie Cochrane, a Scottish medical student. Another brilliant Cambridge graduate, Cochrane had read Natural Sciences before studying psychoanalysis in Vienna and Berlin as the Nazis rose to power. He had driven down to Spain in his Triumph Gloria, an open-topped sports car more suited to the gentle lanes of England than the dusty roads of Catalonia. As Cochrane surveyed his new colleagues, and contemplated Barcelona's unsettled political situation, he felt disheartened. Though fearful that if Spain fell to Franco and joined forces with Hitler and Mussolini, then France and Britain were 'doomed', Cochrane was not a member of any political party, and from this non-partisan position, the twenty-eight men and women that the Spanish Medical Aid Committee had selected for the Unit struck him as 'unsatisfactory and possibly dangerous'. According to his early assessment, there were at least two homosexuals, one alcoholic, a schizophrenic, eight open and about ten secret members of the Communist Party. Sinclair-Loutit, meanwhile, was 'likeable' but with 'a weak streak,' and neither the medical personnel nor their drivers appeared to have much (if any) surgical or military experience.

Indeed, within a fortnight, two of the doctors had been sent home: Wintringham had discovered that one 'had been in a mental home for alcoholic poisoning for some time, and the other drank with him.' Both, he told Harry Pollitt, 'were thoroughly bad lots for this sort of mixture of war, democratic and proletarian revolution.' An American doctor, Randolph Sollenberger, of whom Cochrane took an equally dim view, remained.

Cochrane was not happy. He feared that he had unwittingly volunteered to help run a communist-dominated hospital partaking in an anarchist uprising, with no one having a real clue of what they were doing, or where they ought to be doing it.

III

Through the late summer and autumn of 1936 endless parades wound their way through Barcelona's Plaça de Catalunya and down Las Ramblas, usually led by great banners: the red and gold of Catalonia, the red, gold and purple of the Republic, or (more frequently) the red and black of the anarchists. Some were demonstrations, others were funerals; many more were farewell marches for the militia columns heading off to the front lines in Aragon, Andalusia, Extremadura and Madrid.

Then one night a column marched slowly up from the harbour, the men and women 'ragged and stained,' their clothes revealing as clearly as their manner that they had suffered and survived a demoralizing encounter. 'They had a dogged, rather unhappy air,' Wintringham later recalled; 'they seemed not defeated men but men foiled by an implacable fate.' They were part of a Catalan expeditionary force that had attempted to retake the island of Majorca from the rebels. Among them was Nat Cohen, one of the three 'yids on bikes' that Felicia Browne had encountered in August.

Cohen had begun by leading a *grupo* of ten men in the first stage of the failed operation; he had soon been promoted captain, in charge of a *centuria* of 100 volunteers. His unit had done well, and he had been elected 'delegate' of his Column, becoming one of a handful of men responsible for several hundred or even a thousand soldiers. Accompanying him down Las Ramblas over the following days, Wintringham watched as Spaniards threw themselves upon this 'lean, hard-bitten Jew,' shouting greetings, and waving their guns as they slapped him on the back. Suddenly Wintringham's idea for a British column seemed a possibility, and on 5 September Wintringham wrote to Harry Pollitt that under Cohen's leadership there were now enough willing British volunteers to form an efficient militia unit. But he needed help: 'If you know any good fellow who is taking a holiday soon in this lovely town – very cheap too – send me a selection.' This would let Wintringham take up arms, something he was eager to do.

Five days later Wintringham wrote that Cohen was 'busy raising a

TOM MANN centuria[1], which will include now 10 or 12 English & can accommodate as many likely lads as you can send out.' Seven of the first recruits posed for a photograph with their rifles and banner: they included Wintringham and Cohen with his Spanish fiancée, Ramona (in her blue worker's overalls), together with three other British volunteers and a handsome young Italian Communist, George Tioli, who had recently been living in England. Wintringham also requested that Pollitt send them books, as Cohen 'wants to study war properly'. He requested copies of Liddell Hart's *A History of the World War*, Major-General Altham's *Principles of War* and Stalin's *Leninism*, as well as copies of Wintringham's own recently published volume, *The Coming World War*.

A few days later John Cornford appeared back in Barcelona, having spent only four weeks with the POUM militia in Aragon. He was sick with diarrhoea, feverish and physically exhausted. Wintringham already knew all about Cornford: they had first met when Cornford was still at Cambridge, and he had marked the young undergraduate down as someone worth watching. 'He gave an impression of force, will, certainty, that was remarkable in so young a man.'

The Tom Mann Centuria, Barcelona, August 1936, including Nat Cohen (standing, left) and Tom Wintringham (centre left, kneeling) (Marx Mem. Lib.)

'Who's the lad who talks like a machine-gun?' a friend had whispered to Wintringham at a London conference a few months before the war in Spain broke out. The description seemed to fit, though Wintringham (who

---

1 Tom Mann (1856–1941) was one of Britain's leading trades unionists and an early member of the CPGB. He wrote and travelled extensively, promoting socialism, and on the outbreak of the Spanish Civil War became a member of the Spanish Medical Aid Committee in London.

knew what he was talking about when it came to machineguns) reckoned Cornford 'was quicker and more level than a machine-gun: he spoke with a cold, almost scornful, impetus.' Now he was so utterly exhausted that he could scarcely speak at all.

Cornford's time with the POUM had not impressed him. Their militia, he wrote a few weeks later, were 'the worst organised on the Aragon front … They have little left beyond their sectarian political leaders; a well-produced newspaper, *La Batalla*, and two to three thousand of the worst-organised militia; brave enough, but incapable of a real sustained offensive through sheer inefficiency.' Worst of all, they wanted to emulate the Bolsheviks of 1917, even down to forming cavalry units: 'So the handsome young men of POUM ride round the Barcelona bull-ring with flashing sabres and officiate splendidly as "red Generals": but are not so useful at the front.' His first action – a dawn attack on a rebel-held village near Saragossa – had been a disorganised, ill-prepared and ill-disciplined 'fiasco' that left five comrades dead.

Tom Wintringham had an equally low opinion of the POUM, a relatively marginal political party that had been founded only the previous year, and which numbered around 40,000 members. He dubbed them 'political surrealists,' observing that their taste in transport 'ran to flashy and high-powered private cars' rather than the trucks and lorries favoured by other units. Cornford and Wintringham's judgment was prejudiced, however: the POUM were one of the few Marxist organisations openly critical of the Soviet Union. No doubt Cornford was embarrassed when he discovered that his comrades-in-arms called communists 'dirty Stalinists,' and that they spoke of Stalin's Russian 'dictatorship'.

Whatever his reservations about the POUM, Cornford's service with their militia had helped rekindle his love of poetry, a love that had (along with cricket) been subsumed by the discovery of politics. His mother was a poet, and in her youth had been friends with Rupert Brooke (after whom she had named her eldest son, though he had dropped Rupert in favour of John). As a schoolboy, his English master had sent one of Cornford's poems to W.H. Auden. 'I think your power of writing, of using words is very good indeed,' Auden had replied. 'Considered as a craftsman you have nothing to fear.'

One of Cornford's untitled poems – written in Aragon and addressed to Margot Heinemann – would become his most famous. 'Heart of the heartless world,' it opened, 'Dear heart, the thought of you / Is the pain at my side, / The shadow that chills my view.' By contrast, 'The funeral in the rubbish dump' was more prosaic. Bluntly it related a recently witnessed incident:

> We buried Ruiz in a new pine coffin,
> But the shroud was too small and his washed feet stuck out.
> The stink of his corpse came through the clean pine boards
> And some of the bearers wrapped handkerchiefs round their
>   faces.
> Death was not dignified.
> We hacked a ragged grave in the unfriendly earth
> And fired a ragged volley over the grave.

Another poem recounted the message a Catalan anarchist had asked Cornford to take home with him:

> 'Tell the workers of England
> This was not a war of our own making,
> We did not seek it.
> But if ever the Fascists again rule Barcelona
> It will be as a heap of ruins with us workers beneath it.'

Wintringham agreed that Cornford should indeed return home. There he could convalesce; and, at the same time, the young man could convey an uncensored report to Harry Pollitt, telling him that 'the need that all the English comrades here feel is most urgent.' On the evening of 12 September Wintringham, Nat Cohen and Hugh O'Donnell, the BMU's inexperienced political commissar, sat down to discuss the situation, laying out a series of points for Pollitt's attention. Firstly, they needed someone to come and help raise the profile of the Tom Mann Centuria. 'This is a bloody political town,' Wintringham explained, 'you join the militia through your political party and the parties are almost running everything.' He was pushing forcefully now to assemble a British unit of volunteers. Handfuls of men were arriving from Britain to fight alongside their Spanish comrades, and with or without the CPGB's approval, Wintringham's idea of a British 'column' was gaining traction.

But the Tom Mann Centuria still needed to assemble 'a respectable number of English comrades' – members of the Communist or Labour Parties, and trade unionists – 'to make the centuria largely English in fact as well as in name.' They should bring khaki shirts and shorts, he instructed, as well as warmer kit for the winter: 'then they'll be dressed alike,' he explained to Pollitt, 'and will be the only centuria in Spain, except for the Germans, to look disciplined … send ten per cent trained men if you can to act as corporals, and the rest kids and enthusiasts. Most of them will come back with very valuable experience.' He also set out for Pollitt the broader needs of the Republic: 'planes and pilots, *light* machine guns, rifles, ammunition, and a general staff. Of these the first and last are probably the most important.' The militias did not lack courage, but this on its own would not be enough to beat the rebels. It was clear that without military equipment and a qualified chain of command that could enforce training and discipline, they did not have a hope of defeating the experienced and increasingly well-supplied army that opposed them.

Finally, he asked Pollitt to do all he could to encourage Cornford's return to Spain as soon as he was recovered: within two or three weeks at most. 'He has had a very bad time with the worst-organised gang on an unorganised front, but he can help us all the more by knowing the necessary comparisons.'

At best, Wintringham thought he might recruit fifty British volunteers. 'I was pessimistic about getting them,' he later recalled, and was frustrated that his friends back home had evidently not seen 'the need for a legion of foreign volunteers'. But he knew he had to do something. 'I feel certain that this tragedy will be spreading to swallow us if this war is not ended quickly,' he wrote home to his mother. And as he waited for a reply from his superiors in London he buried himself in work.

IV

A few days after their arrival in Barcelona, as Wintringham, Sinclair-Loutit and colleagues from the British Medical Unit sat at a café in Las Ramblas, a rather forlorn and shy-looking American approached their table. From the men's fresh faces and their forest of bare knees (the weather was still warm, and they all wore shorts), Kitty Bowler was convinced they must be British.

All conversation stopped as the young woman approached. 'Blankly and coldly they looked at me,' she later recalled, 'as only the English can.' Then Wintringham touched her arm, remarking in his soft voice, 'You must join us.'

As Sinclair-Loutit described her, this wealthy, attractive twenty-eight-year-old with large brown eyes and a tousled bob was 'a neat, active, progressive, American,' a 'college-girl archetype' whose 'quick-fire, clear, zesty, American speech came out of a neatly lip-sticked mouth.' Wintringham would jokingly describe her as 'like a wide-eyed child of

Kitty Bowler (KCL Library)

eighteen' (she later admitted that prior to her recent arrival in Spain her knowledge of the country had been 'almost nil', and she had never even heard of Catalonia).

Kitty Bowler had reached Barcelona via Paris and the USSR, and – like her new companions – was keenly anti-Fascist. A descendant of Edward Everett, who had been President of Harvard College and (briefly) Abraham Lincoln's Secretary of State and a Massachusetts senator, Bowler hailed from a distinguished and wealthy line of New

England liberals. (It was a relative with an office on Wall Street who gave her the money to help her travels through Europe.) At Bryn Mawr, the prestigious Pennsylvania women's college, she had majored in Economics and Politics before volunteering with the League Against War and Fascism and the International Labour Defence. While in the Soviet Union she had met *The New York Times*' Pulitzer-prize winning Moscow correspondent, Walter Duranty; in Paris they had embarked on a whirlwind romance. 'My whole generation is being drawn into politics whether they will or no,' she had told him. 'I prefer to be conscious about it.'

'I don't like Fascism,' she had added, but liberalism was 'as seductive and untrustworthy as a mistress … In these tumultuous days I prefer a good trustworthy companion, who'll stick by me thick and thin. I want something that works. So it will have to be one of the brands of Socialism … the one that works best and gives the greatest good to the greatest number.' She was not a member of the Communist Party, however, a fact that would, in due course, bring her serious trouble.

Since Wintringham had also visited Russia the two had plenty to talk about, and Bowler relaxed: 'I realised I was talking to a gifted conversationalist, cultured, intelligent, witty. I liked this man's mind and the amusing twist he would give a phrase. But I was puzzled. This quiet literary individual wasn't my idea of a military man. "That's Tom Wintringham," I was told, "the author of a book on Marxist military strategy. He's a big shot in the English Communist Party, but he's an old sweetie."'

Bowler was impressed by Wintringham, and by Spain: 'this is the most exciting and interesting thing that has ever happened to me in my life,' she wrote home to her mother in Manhattan. 'A new world is in the making here … you are never bored.' She added, 'Don't believe all the crazy things that you read in the papers because I assure you that I am not in the slightest danger.'

She had intended only a brief visit to Spain; having left most of her luggage behind in Paris, she was soon wearing the blue overalls of the militia. By late September, however, Bowler was writing home of her intention 'to stay on more or less indefinitely and see this show through. If you get as deep into it as I have it is hard to break away. Also it is a sort of American pride, every nationality is represented here except Americans, I seem to be practically the only one and it makes me rather ashamed.'

In fact, there *were* already more Americans in Barcelona. They included Lois Orr, a nineteen-year-old socialist from Kentucky, and her husband, Charles. They had been in Germany on honeymoon when the news broke of the Civil War in Spain. Hitch-hiking down through France they had arrived in Barcelona in mid-September; Charles, an economics graduate, hoped to find work with the Catalan government, but they soon found employment instead with the POUM, alongside a few Dutch and German volunteers. In return for free board and lodging at the Hotel Falcón, which the POUM had appropriated as their new headquarters, their job involved translating articles from the POUM's newspaper, *La Batalla*. These were read out over short-wave radio, and used to produce an English edition of the paper.

Ten years younger than her well-travelled husband, Lois Orr was as excited as Kitty Bowler by her new experiences abroad. 'I'm having the time of my life here,' she wrote to her parents in Louisville. She was 'right in the middle of making history,' and 'the people, of course, are the cream of the intellectual crop of Germany, and the French and English comrades are all intensely interesting.' Those with the POUM included a young Scotsman, Bob Smillie, who had studied chemistry at Glasgow University, and who 'is going to work, we think, in a new gun factory to be directed by a Belgian comrade,' a man named Georges Kopp. And there was an Englishwoman, Mary Low, and her Cuban husband, Juan Breá. Lois was excited to report that this young couple 'are surrealists of the most advanced type, having lived in Paris for years.'

Many young foreigners were similarly excited by what was happening in Spain: the uprising appeared less of a threat to democracy than an opportunity, finally, to act, not simply against fascism, but against the mundanity and deprivations of everyday life. Mary Low told how, as she and Juan travelled by train from Paris to Barcelona, a young Frenchman wearing golfing trousers and carrying a knapsack climbed aboard their carriage and looked round eagerly.

'Isn't it wonderful?' he declared. 'Isn't it wonderful something like this happening while we're still alive – I mean, happening in the very middle of the kind of life we live. I work in an office. Now I'm off to see something real … Isn't it wonderful that something like this should really happen and give one a chance in life?'

Lois Orr was also seized by this sense of exhilaration, optimism and opportunity. Despite her youth, she soon had a sharp insight into the Spanish situation, albeit from an anti-Stalinist, POUM perspective. As she explained to her family, while the Spanish Government and the Communist and Socialist Parties were 'trying to make out that this is a war to save democracy,' the men and women 'who are going to the front to get their arms legs heads etc shot off don't have any illusions. They are fighting for a social revolution and not to save some bourgeois republican government which would give right back to the capitalists the factories, railroads, buildings that they have claimed as their own.' In her opinion, it was the anarchists 'who are the key as to whether the revolution will succeed here or not.'

As well as being attuned to the complex political situation, Lois also had an eye for the humorous details of the revolution. Another letter home described how Barcelona's anarchists

> have adopted Popeye as their own pet mascot. In the little stands on the Ramblas everywhere they sell pins, scarves and statues of Popeye waving an anarchist flag of black and red. Betty Boop is also much in favor among the Anarchists, but Mickey Mouse, who is the idol of the people, is so popular that it is necessary that he be non-partisan. The anarchists all wear tiny silk triangles instead of neckties, painted red and black with various designs – a victory wreath, pictures of dead comrades, a clenched fist, and, most popular of all, a nude woman.

'Please for goodness sake don't worry about us,' she told her parents. 'This is a gloriously exciting place to be – the morale and spirit are high and of course it is the most interesting spot in the world at this particular moment. And quite safe.'

V

But Barcelona was not as safe as it appeared, as Keith Sinclair-Loutit was discovering.

His priority was to establish a base for the British Medical Unit, and a Spaniard named Pujol was appointed to advise him. Pujol had lived in the USA, where he had gained what Sinclair-Loutit considered his only asset: excellent English. Pujol and some of his superiors thought that the British should attach themselves to a hospital in Barcelona; but the more Pujol told them that it was 'crazy to go to the ill-defined front,' the more determined the British were to get there. They had not come to Spain to stay away from the action.

The first problem was getting out of Barcelona. There were roadblocks everywhere; some manned by anarchist militia, some by POUM, others by the PSUC. The first two groups were inclined to liberate property from individual hands for their own communal use; however, once they got to know the British and recognized their vehicle they would greet them, waving them through their barricades.

In their chauffeur-driven car Sinclair-Loutit and Pujol reconnoitered the western exits of the city. They were exploring short cuts to the inland highway when they found themselves in the western suburbs on a semi-rural street. A man lay dead by the road.

'Let's get the Hell out of here!' Pujol immediately shouted.

Instead, Sinclair-Loutit signalled for the driver to stop. There was a hole in the centre of the dead man's forehead, and more wounds in his body, blood oozing into the dust.

'Get the fucking-hell out of here, you'll have us all shot!' screamed Pujol, now hysterical.

Sinclair-Loutit had never seen a violent death before, still less one from bullets. Their driver coolly remarked that it was almost certainly anarchists who had carried out this summary execution.

'Why?' asked Sinclair-Loutit.

'*¿Quien sabe?*' replied the driver. '*Matar es muy fácil.*'[1]

These extra-judicial killings continued through the autumn. While Lois Orr assured her father 'that there is no red terror here,' late in September the American Consul in Barcelona received an estimate that in Catalonia alone there had been 'some 10,000 persons executed since the beginning of the present troubles.' It was not just fascists and clergy who were being killed: rivalries between various left-wing groups were also being settled with blood.

Under the headline '*Enough!! Enough!!*', one of Barcelona's daily newspapers, *La Humanitat*, called for an immediate end to what it called these 'personal vengeances, all the private hatred, all the insane fury of the sick and the degenerate, all the venting of the basest passions' which were 'being tragically settled in nightly incursions that dishonour the revolution.' The men undertaking such abhorrent acts, the article declared, were too cowardly to go out and fight fascists at the front; instead they killed unarmed men, alone and at night. It had to stop, and – for a while at least – it did.

Terrified by what he had seen, Pujol did not appear the next day. Sinclair-Loutit was told to make do without him, and advised that if he wanted to leave the city the best time to go was before dawn, when the principal checkpoints could be warned of his approach.

Early the following morning, armed only with a Michelin 1:200,000 scale map and driving Archie Cochrane's Triumph Gloria, Sinclair-Loutit and Peter Spencer headed off on the hundred-mile journey west to the Aragon front. Spencer had learned to read a map with impeccable judgment during the Great War, and it was already clear to him where they should make their medical base: Grañén was a market town centred on a fan-work of roads and tracks; it was near the front, and it was the railhead for Barcelona

---

1 'Who knows? To kill is very easy.'

and Lérida. It looked ideal. Once there, they found a large abandoned farmhouse, and when the Unit arrived they spent days converting its buildings into a field hospital, with wards and two operating theatres.

Spencer then made his first reconnaissance of the front. As he neared the Republican trenches, in the sunlight beneath the olive trees, he passed close to a road where women carrying up rations the previous night had been shot down by a rebel machinegun. 'It is one thing to see dead soldiers,' Spencer later recalled, 'but these young girls, who had been bringing food to their men, were lying there in their clean bright clothes with their shining well-brushed hair spread out in the dust amongst the spilled soup and scattered blood-stained rice and the newly baked loaves. It was not a sight easily forgotten.'

The columns of militia marching up to the front made a more cheering impression on him. 'It was a whole people at war – you could see that. There were grandfathers and young boys, strong-handed peasants, clerks and teachers in horn-rimmed glasses, burly farmers and thin-faced shopkeepers – every type you could imagine.' The combined imprint of a people co-operating in a common cause was unlike anything Spencer had seen before. 'Strangers helped each other and petty jealousies seemed to have been forgotten … The cheerfulness with which backbreaking work was done and suffering endured was amazing … It seemed too good to be true.'

The fact that Cochrane's car was soon 'liberated' by anarchists was perhaps an indication that it was. As Sinclair-Loutit would wistfully recall, 'The doctrine of Anarchy may have its noble abstract beauty, but it is not easy to live with.' A less charitable English observer wrote that whilst the anarchists' doctrines were certainly appealing, anyone who 'is not either a hopelessly impractical dreamer, or else a certifiable half-wit, realizes that the programme that it wishes to introduce is utterly impossible unless you can first eliminate one or two trifling little disadvantages, such as human nature and the basic laws of economics.' Such debates made little difference to Archie Cochrane, who grieved the loss of his car, and plunged further into depression.

The people's optimism could not be question, but these Spanish peasants, factory workers and petty bourgeoisie were far from being soldiers capable of defeating the trained professionals of the rebel army. Wintringham saw this clearly when he made his first visit to the front. He was apprehensive at the prospect: despite being a specialist on the subject, he hated war, knowing it all too well from his service in 1916–18. And he had also fallen in love, with the American ingénue, Kitty Bowler.

So far as his comrades in the Communist Party were concerned, women were Wintringham's greatest weakness. Back in London he had a wife who had been expelled from her Oxford college for joining his Russian trip in 1920, as well as a mistress. Both women were keenly involved in politics (his wife had been a founder member of the CPGB), and between them had borne him four children. This was not something to deter Wintringham, however. Before setting off on the ten-hour drive from Barcelona to Grañén he 'proposed' to Bowler, 'curtly and nervously,' and notwithstanding the fact that he was still married. They had known one another for only a few weeks, but she was as equally keen on the bald Englishman with his bad teeth.

Wintringham left early the following morning, driving through rain and over bad roads broken up by heavy lorries. At Grañén he met Sinclair-Loutit, and together they travelled the last few miles to the front. In the distance they could glimpse Huesca, with the Pyrenees beyond, 'abrupt and fantastic,' as Wintringham described them, 'as if painted on the back-cloth of a theatre-scene'. Their objective was the Thälmann Centuria, a company largely made up of German volunteers: communists, Jews, anti-fascists, exiled over the previous three years by the Nazi takeover of their homeland. Many had survived spells in prison or concentration camps; some had been in Barcelona for the People's Olympiad; others had arrived quickly from Paris. They were named after Ernst Thälmann, one-time leader of the Red Front Fighters' League and the imprisoned head of the Communist Party of Germany.

Their number included two notable anti-fascist veterans of the Great War. Hans Beimler had been Communist deputy to the Reichstag until Hitler took power; thrown into prison, he had managed to escape, recording his exploit in the short book *Four Weeks in the Hands of Hitler's Hell-Hounds: The Nazi Murder Camp of Dachau*. Published in 1933, it was one of the earliest first-hand accounts of how the new German government was treating political opponents. Ludwig Renn, meanwhile, was the author of the influential anti-war novel, *Krieg*. John Cornford had been immensely impressed by the handful of Germans he had encountered in Spain: 'They are the finest people in some ways I've ever met,' he had told his girlfriend. 'In a way they have lost everything, have been through enough to break most people, and [yet] remain strong and cheerful and humorous. If anything is revolutionary it is these comrades.'

Wintringham parked by a bombed-out cottage close to the Thälmann's

David Seymour, *German volunteers of the Thälmann Centuria, 1936* (Magnum)

field kitchen. Spread-eagled in the wreckage of the roof was a woman's body; she had been dead some time. They paused for a moment. It was another first for Sinclair-Loutit: the nasty smell of human decomposition. For Wintringham, though, it was a step back almost two decades to the Great War and its signature odour of putrefaction.

All the way up to the front Wintringham had been surveying the landscape, wondering what it would be like to fight in this kind of terrain. Difficult, was his

74

conclusion. The rocks would give shelter to machineguns and riflemen, whilst it was too broken by cliff-banked rivers and rocks to be easily traversed by tanks. But he soon discovered that the Thälmann Centuria and their Spanish neighbours in the line had made little provision for defence. The cover leading to the forward positions was rudimentary. Wintringham and Sinclair-Loutit made their way up under regular bursts of machinegun and sniper fire, through a crude array of shallow trenches, ditches, tiny parapet shelters and wide-open spaces, which they waited in turns to cross, as the rebels waited for them to move, their bullets twanging and buzzing overhead like angry wasps.

'Was I afraid?' Wintringham asked himself a few months later. 'Of course I was afraid. It is a soldier's job to be afraid at the right time … My pulse made a little pattern of taps at the back of my throat. It was my turn to go and I was not moving.'

He forced himself forward. Sinclair-Loutit followed. In the squalid fashion of the front line, the next trench they landed in also doubled up as a latrine. Six shots hit the tree above them with a great tearing and whacking.

'Bad shots, these Fascists,' said a militiaman, doing up his trousers. 'Too high, much too high, very much too high.'

When Wintringham and Sinclair-Loutit finally reached the forward position scared but unscathed, they found only some fifteen Germans among the Spaniards, along with an Englishman: Nat Cohen's East End companion, Sam Masters.

Meeting the Germans and hearing their stories immediately rekindled Wintringham's awareness of the pressing need for trained, experienced units who could teach the Spanish the techniques of modern warfare. Rather than showing the Spanish militiamen how to fight – how to dig decent trenches, how to organise themselves, how to survive – the Germans of the Thälmann Centuria had simply adopted local customs. Like the anarchists and the POUM, they elected their officers, and they changed their group leader fortnightly so that (for fairness's sake) everyone had a turn in command. Wintringham hardly needed his experience in the art of war to see that this system did not work: it could not function for a debating club, never mind an army.

Even worse, the Thälmann Centuria had willingly accepted the role of 'shock troops,' and the Germans were proud to have participated in what Wintringham called 'the almost suicidal unsupported Republican offensives and counter-attacks'. They had been used 'mainly in very gallant, almost futile, repeated attacks on an impossible position.' They were allowed – and allowed themselves – to be used in assault after assault upon impenetrable positions as if they were waging the Great War all over again. The casualty rate amongst these fervent Germans had been appalling, and an incredible waste.

On his return to Barcelona Wintringham argued endlessly against these brave but foolhardy frontal attacks: it 'was the worst, most hopeless, way of fighting a war,' he told anyone who would listen, a method invented 'by the incredible stupidity' of the generals of 1914–18.

Yet he had no idea whether those to whom he raged had any power to alter what was happening. 'Barcelona seemed leaderless, and talked of glory, not of war.'

Chapter 4

Armies of Free Men

|

On the night of 14 September 1936 John Cornford, carrying Tom Wintringham's report to Harry Pollitt, crossed the border back into France. At dawn in Toulouse railway station he penned a letter home: 'I haven't yet been discharged from the militia,' he explained to his father, 'but have been sent back for a period of three weeks on a special propaganda mission.' He added that he had had 'a fairly quiet month on the Saragossa and Huesca fronts,' and 'actively only did a little skirmishing ... I hope you haven't been too much worried about me.'

Once back in London Cornford met his brother, Christopher, who was an art student in Chelsea. Dressed in old flannel trousers and the rope-soled shoes of the Spanish worker, John's face was yellow with the effects of his illness and his recent journey. 'He was at a high pitch of nervous excitement,' Christopher later recalled. 'Unable to speak fast enough to keep pace with his ideas, he recounted his experiences, analysed the situation in Catalonia, speculated on the future of the struggle ("I have no doubt whatever who's going to win this war"). We walked together, as so often before, down the King's Road, he talking and I listening. People in the street watched us curiously. Then we parted, John still too excited to sleep; and that was the last time I ever saw him.'

Cornford's 'special mission' took him to the CPGB's headquarters in central London and a meeting with Harry Pollitt. There he relayed the urgency of the military situation in Spain, and repeated Wintringham's plea for a disciplined unit of British volunteers.

Pollitt was no fan of war – at least, not of capitalist, imperialist wars. Born into a working-class family in Lancashire in 1890, as a boilermaker and union leader he had been a vocal opponent of the Great War. 'Your class caused this war,' he had told a government representative in 1915. 'Mine wants to stop it.' But the conflict in Spain was different. As Claud Cockburn reported in *The Daily Worker*, the front line now protecting Madrid from the rebels was 'the front-line defence of *your* democracy, *your* freedom, *your* peace'.

The war in Spain (at least in so far as it was being portrayed in the international press) was not simply a domestic issue: its ramifications were global. 'Let us organise a mighty united movement of solidarity,' Pollitt had told a pro-Spain rally at Trafalgar Square in July. He was a powerful orator who made good use of the men and women eager to help the Communist Party, especially writers and intellectuals such as Wintringham, Cornford and Cockburn. Like the others, Cockburn had not been satisfied with standing on the sidelines and watching as others fought. Having left Barcelona to report on the war in Madrid, he had enlisted in what he called 'a company of barely trained peasants': a section of the Fifth Regiment, a communist corps of volunteers that would eventually prove one of the best units in the Republican army. Cockburn soon saw frantic action on the front line, resisting the rebel advance on Madrid, and witnessing first hand the true face of 'Non-Intervention' as German bombs fell from German aeroplanes. He was soon promoted to corporal after two sergeants deserted to join the rebels, and was lucky not be killed. Eventually persuaded that he could do a better job as a propagandist than a soldier, Cockburn had returned briefly to England. There Pollitt told him to write a book about his experiences, and gave him a week in which to do it. Published under Cockburn's *nom de plume* 'Frank Pitcairn', *Reporter in Spain* was an early example of what for a while became a bestselling new genre. Accounts of the Civil War would soon be churning off the presses, revealing a readership avid for information.

But Pollitt could only go so far in supporting fighting volunteers in Spain. As he was also responsible for pursuing the Communist policy of a Popular Front that would unite all parties of the Left into an anti-fascist alliance, he did not want to alienate the Labour Party, which (as fearful as the Government of provoking a war with the Fascist Powers) was supporting Non-Intervention. So whilst he now gave his approval to the recruitment of British volunteers to serve in Spain, any such movement would have to be clandestine.

So for Cornford, the three weeks following his meeting with Pollitt were a whirlwind of visits to family and friends as he prepared to return to Spain with a detachment of volunteers. Margot Heinemann came down from Birmingham to see him, but her work teaching young factory girls prevented her from joining him on a visit to an old Cambridge friend. Michael Straight was the son of a wealthy American investment banker who had died in the Great War; his mother had gone on to marry a British educationalist and they had settled in Devon, founding a progressive school in the run-down medieval buildings of Dartington Hall.

Straight had first met Cornford when the latter visited his digs in Cambridge to recruit the young American into the University Socialist Society. When Cornford had insisted that the class struggle was the central reality of life in Britain, Straight had responded that he had lived for eight years in Britain, 'and it was not the central reality for me'. Despite this disagreement they had soon become good friends. Though Straight was never a card-carrying communist (and he had no wish to go to Spain himself), he had been persuaded by members of the Socialist Society to give as much money as he could to Harry Pollitt and the CPGB.[1]

At Dartington, Straight found Cornford 'greatly changed' after his recent adventures. 'He was quiet, sombre. He was, in his own mind, still in Spain.' For a lot of the time Cornford – who told Straight that 'he felt like a deserter' – worked in a guest bedroom, writing a long article 'On

---

1 This flirtation with the far Left brought Straight into the orbit of a number of other Cambridge communists, including Anthony Blunt and Guy Burgess. Burgess attempted to recruit Straight into the infamous Cambridge spy ring, and it would be Straight's testimony that decades later led to Anthony Blunt being unmasked as a Soviet spy.

Michael Straight, *John Cornford at Dartington*

the Catalonian Front'. Straight typed it up, and it would be published in *The New Republic* in December, giving the American magazine's readers a first-hand insight to the Spanish Civil War, and the effects of so-called 'Non-Intervention' in particular (what Cornford called 'the pseudo-neutrality of the British Government'). As Cornford explained, 'I do not think the Fascists will ever succeed in subduing Spain: to do so they would have to wipe out a third of the population – which the Badajoz massacre shows they are ready to do; but the policy of "neutrality" will prolong for months and even years a war that could speedily be ended.' What the Spanish Republic needed most – besides immediate medical supplies, guns and money – was for its supporters 'to redouble the campaign against neutrality … Give the Spanish Republic the arms it has a right to, and it can win in a few months.'

Before they left Dartington, Straight took Cornford's photograph. 'I crouched beneath him with my Leica,' he later recalled. 'It took me a minute or two to adjust the focus and the exposure. I thought to myself: *He wouldn't stand still for this long if he believed that he was coming back.*'

They returned to London together, four hours by train, talking endlessly, though not about Spain. At one point Straight remarked how the intensity of his desire to excel in everything he did disturbed him. Cornford grinned, 'and said that it was the same with him, only a thousand times more so'.

Once back in Cambridge Cornford visited another friend, Bernard Knox, who had just graduated from St John's College with a degree in Classics. Like many young men of his generation, the Great War fascinated Knox. His two earliest memories, he later wrote, were of 1917, when he was barely three years old: the first was of the London street where he lived illuminated by moonlight and the moving beams of searchlights searching for German zeppelins, and hurrying with his mother for an air-raid shelter; the second was of his father home on leave from Passchendaele, kitbag and rifle propped up against the sitting-room wall. Knox's father survived the war, but would never talk about his experiences. Instead, Knox learnt about the conflict from books: Robert Graves' *Goodbye to All That*, Henri Barbusse's *Le Feu*, and the poets: Wilfred Owen, Siegfried Sassoon, Isaac Rosenberg. 'All that we read induced in us a horror at what seemed a senseless waste of human lives and a fear that, in spite of the League of Nations, war might recur.' Knox had also joined Cornford in the 1933 Armistice demonstration at Cambridge's war memorial, and was also a member of the University Socialist Society. Only Marx and Engels struck him as having an answer to the economic crisis enveloping Western capitalism, whilst the prospect of a renewed European war struck him as 'a grim reality'.

Knox immediately agreed to go with Cornford to Spain, even though he later admitted that he 'knew no more about Spanish politics and history than most of my fellow-countrymen, that is to say, not much.' His familiarity with things Spanish stretched little further than having read (in translation) *Don Quixote* and having seen (in reproduction) the works of Velázquez and Goya. Unlike Cornford, however, Knox had participated in the Officer Training Corps at school, and had fired rifles and light machineguns on exercise with the Territorial Army. His knowledge of French would also prove indispensable.

It was in Cambridge that Cornford solved the problem of getting hold of a gun. His father had served as a musketry instructor during the Great War, and gave him his old service revolver as a parting gift. Professor Cornford was, understandably, distressed to see his young son go voluntarily to war. But he knew there was nothing he could do to stop him.

On his last day at home before leaving for Spain Cornford wrote to his tutor at Trinity College, resigning his scholarship: 'by the time this reaches you,' he explained, 'I shall already be on the way to rejoin the unit of the Anti-Fascist Militia with which I have been fighting this summer. I am sorry I did not have time to discuss it personally.

'I should like to take this opportunity of thanking you, and through you other Fellows of the College I have not had time to write to, for the tremendous personal kindness and interest you have always shown me, even though you must have looked with disfavour on many of my activities.'

II

In London on the evening of 5 October 1936 five other recruits joined John Cornford and Bernard Knox on the boat-train to Paris. All were fellow members of the Communist Party: John Sommerfield was another Cambridge graduate, and an aspiring writer; Jan Kurzke was a German refugee artist living in London who had served in the *Reichswehr*; George Sowersby and Robert Clarke were Scottish veterans of the British Army; and Chris Thorneycroft was an Oxford University engineering student. They wore large new boots and carried khaki overalls in their rucksacks. On Cornford's advice they had brought plenty of books, as well as a pocket chess set: 'The worst thing about this war,' he had told them, 'is not discomfort, nor even danger, but boredom.' Cornford's reading matter consisted of Volume I of Marx's classic text, *Das Kapital*, and a collected edition of Shakespeare's *Tragedies*. Since his passport showed that Cornford had recently been in Spain – which would draw the attention of French Customs officers at Dieppe – Knox concealed the revolver in his own luggage.

They arrived in Paris without incident and then bought guns: small automatics, as John Sommerfield later recalled, that fitted neatly in their pockets. Then it was on to a hotel in the working-class suburb of Belleville; they whiled away impatient days awaiting instructions from a communist committee that had taken over the organization of volunteers arriving in France from around Europe. It was here that they discovered that Cornford's scheme for a small British unit to serve with the Tom Mann Centuria on the Aragon front would never materialize. Instead, they found themselves 'a tiny English drop in a sea of large national groups'. In Belleville hundreds of volunteers were gathering – from Poland, Belgium, Germany, Italy, France – all of them bound for Spain. For Wintringham had not been alone in seeing the need for a disciplined corps of experienced foreign volunteers. Many people, separately and spontaneously, had also seen an opportunity to fight fascism face on. And the Communist International had recognised the need to raise an army that could match the forces being thrown into Spain by Hitler and Mussolini.

At first Stalin had been reluctant to commit the USSR to such an undertaking. He, too, felt threatened by the burgeoning power of Hitler's Germany, for the Nazi leader had made quite clear both his anti-Bolshevism and his interest in expanding German territory eastwards. Stalin was thus seeking a joint alliance with the capitalist powers of France and Britain, and openly supporting the Spanish Republic would not serve that cause. And paradoxically, to foment a communist, revolutionary war was even less in his interest: the circulating stories of 'Red Terror' in Spain were anathema to the Soviet leader. As Wintringham's superiors in the CPGB had told him, moderates would never back such extremism. Since 1935 a 'Popular Front' that united all the forces of the Left – not just the hardcore extremists – had become the official line of the Communist International.[1] As the recent elections in Spain and France had shown, the united forces of the Left *could* win power.

Yet, clearly, Stalin could not be seen to sit on his hands and do nothing as fellow communists fought for the workers and peasants of Spain. It was a conundrum. Hence, in public, Stalin (like Hitler and Mussolini) supported Non-Intervention. But behind the scenes, in late July the Comintern and the Red International of Labour Unions (the Profintern) had met in Prague

---

1 Established in 1919, the Communist International ('the Comintern') had the declared aim of creating an international Soviet republic.

and secretly set aside 1,000 million francs to form and arm a brigade of 5,000 men to fight in Spain. The funds would come from donations made by sympathisers worldwide, whilst volunteers would be encouraged from the global Party membership. Paris would be the assembly point, from where the Communist Party of France would transport the men to Spain. Unwittingly – but to their great joy – Cornford and his comrades suddenly found that they had landed amongst a global brigade of fellow militants. They were warned, however, not to call themselves communists: they were simply 'anti-fascists'. Any overt political symbols were banned, and as far as possible, the force's true origins were to be kept secret; in fact roughly one in five of the volunteers with the 'International Column' were not communists at all.

Francisco Largo Caballero, Spain's socialist Prime Minister, did not embrace this offer of covert assistance with much enthusiasm. He did not trust the communists, and when the Comintern's Italian representative, Luigi Longo, came to make arrangements for the International Column's imminent arrival, he found himself shunted from office to office. Nor were the anarchists keen on these foreigners who preached a domineering political system that contradicted their own ambitions of individual liberty. Besides, 'arms were needed,' they complained, 'not men.' Caballero perhaps shared this opinion, for despite his indifferent reception of Longo, the previous month the Prime Minister and his Minister of Finance, Juan Negrín, had persuaded the Cabinet to approve the removal of Spain's gold reserves to a place of greater safety: the People's Commissariat of Finances in Moscow. On 25 October, 10,000 cases of gold that was then worth over half a billion US dollars arrived at the Soviet port of Odessa under NKVD escort.[1] In return (and after deducting a considerable fee for transporting and safekeeping the gold), the Russians would supply Spain with arms and food.

In Madrid, Longo found the Spanish government apathetic and unsupportive in the face of the steady advance northwards of Franco's

---

1 The Russian secret police, the NKVD (the People's Commissariat for Internal Affairs) was the precursor of the KGB.

forces. Eventually, it was the small Communist Party of Spain that came to his assistance: their Fifth Regiment had a base at Albacete, 130 miles south-east of the capital in the plains of La Mancha. They offered it to Longo. He arrived on 12 October, exactly a week after Cornford and his friends had left London. Two days later the first foreign volunteers followed him by train; over the next few months hundreds more disembarked there each day.

With a destination now confirmed, Cornford and the rest of the impatient mass of volunteers that had been gathering in Paris received instructions to move out. Packed into a night-train bound for Marseilles, the small British group was a curiosity among this mass of continental revolutionaries.

'So there are communists in England?' one French volunteer muttered. '*C'est formidable!*'

The following evening Cornford and his companions joined eight hundred men boarding a Spanish ship manned by anarchists. To evade the Italian submarines that were already stalking Republican vessels at sea they departed at midnight, and once clear of the harbour sailed without lights. At dawn they passed Barcelona ('a smear of buildings and factory smoke low down on the horizon') and Valencia, then steamed past Royal Navy destroyers stationed off the Costa Blanca and into Alicante, with its bright stucco houses and palm trees, shuttered cafés and yellow trams, and the long white road that wound up the hillside to the Castillo de Santa Bárbara.

As the men marched into town they sang the *Internationale*, the revolutionary anthem of the Left:

> *Enslaved masses, stand up, stand up,*
> *The world is about to change foundation!*
> *We who are nothing, let us be everything.*
>
> *This is the final fight,*
> *Let us unite, and tomorrow*

The International
Will be the human race!

After a joyful reception there was another train journey, this time inland through a strange, moonlit landscape. John Sommerfield was amazed when at every station they were offered wine and baskets of grapes by crowds of well-wishers. Women held children up to them to kiss whilst old ladies 'with magnificent ancient wrinkled faces, stamped with the history of fifty years of toil, shrieked curses at the Fascists and urged us to disembowel them.'

Everyone thought they were Russians. '*Viva Rusia,*' they cried. '*¡Viva el Partido Comunista!*'

III

The man the Comintern placed in command of the International Column was André Marty. With his beret and large walrus moustache he was unmistakably French. Now approaching his fiftieth birthday, Marty was a celebrated veteran of the French Communist Party. During the Great War he had served as a machinist in the French Navy, and in 1919 had participated in a mutiny in which the crews of two destroyers of the Black Sea Fleet refused to aid White Russians fighting the revolutionary Red Army. Marty had been sentenced to twenty years hard labour for his role, though in fact he had soon been released.

Like Longo and Wintringham, Marty was unimpressed by what he saw of the Spanish Government's response to the Civil War. He was particularly critical of the situation in Barcelona, where 'Anarchists from every corner of the world are thronging': 'they turn out armoured cars,' he reported to the Comintern, 'but they are so heavy that they can move only on flat terrain and very quickly break down.' And at the factories for war production 'all sorts of rogues and frauds have flocked to the workers' committees with the most fantastic proposals. The engineers do not dare to object, because they are afraid that they will be shot as saboteurs. The result is that the Catalan industry is almost paralyzed by the anarchists. The little that they still manufacture remains in Catalonia itself; the Anarchists give nothing to Madrid.'

According to Marty, in Madrid it was the communists who had mobilized the public to prepare for the forthcoming assault by the Army of Africa. Their own Prime Minister, he observed, had stated approvingly that the Spanish were 'too proud to dig in the ground'. In response, the Communist Party had organised the construction of a fortified line around the city, assigning a French military engineer to supervise the task. 'At every step, our party has run into opposition from Caballero,' Marty complained. 'He is completely absorbed in the thought of his political career. It has never occurred to him that if the Fascists win, then all his career will turn to dust.'

The communists also worked hard to improve the public image of the Republic. In an effort to reassure Catholics horrified by the murder of priests and bishops they arranged for a prominent Catholic, Don Ángel Ossorio y Gallardo, to speak on the radio. As Claud Cockburn reported, this ex-Cabinet Minister and former Governor of Barcelona stated:

A Christian cannot be a Fascist because Catholicism means liberty of spirit and respect for human thought, whereas Fascism means the rule of force to protect the privileged class. A Catholic cannot follow those teachings which demand the extermination of the Communists and the Jews because the Catholic doctrine demands that one should love one's enemies.

Gallardo concluded with the declaration that, though he was a Catholic, he supported the Republic 'for genuine spiritual values, for self-determination of the people and the liberty of man.'[1]

---

1 Another leading Spanish figure, Miguel de Unamuno, rector of the University of Salamanca, would echo these words. Having started out as a supporter of the rebellion, he changed his mind when he saw its vicious nature and bravely told an audience of rebel supporters in October:

Marty told the Comintern that he was 'convinced that we can be victorious,' but only through a concerted effort that was more than simply achieving military success: 'Franco has published his programme. We must make our programme, the programme of the Popular Front, known to all the people.' This would include the introduction of social security measures ('protection for old age, for accidents at work, aid for pregnant women, and so on'); independence for Morocco; freedom of religion, and an end to the apparent persecution of the Church: 'Believers ought to know that we will arrest priests not because they serve God but because they serve fascism – that is, they are shooting at the people and spreading fascist propaganda.' Finally, the anarchists had to be 'drawn into the state machinery … We need to defeat them not with the threat of being shot … but through the excellence of our work among the masses.' It would be disastrous to try to fight the anarchists at this moment, Marty warned, when fascism had to be defeated first: 'after victory we will get even with them, all the more so since at that point we will have a strong army.'

Marty's second-in-command at Albacete was a man who in Spain went by the name of Emilio Kléber. Born Moishe Stern in 1896 to a Jewish family in what is now Ukraine, he had been conscripted into the Austro-Hungarian army at the start of the Great War. Captured by the Russians and freed during the 1917 revolution, he joined the Bolsheviks and became a staff officer in the Red Army. Since then he had worked as a spy in America, and as an advisor to the Chinese Army. When he was first introduced to the volunteers crowded in Albacete – stepping forward and giving the clenched fist salute – he was met with a roar of applause.

IV

Many of the commanding officers in the International Brigades were veterans of the Red Army, but their first quartermaster was its first

---

'You will win, because you have more than enough brute force. But you will not convince. For to convince, you need to persuade. And in order to persuade you would need what you lack: reason and right in the struggle.'

American volunteer: the journalist Louis Fischer. He had the onerous job of feeding and clothing the men arriving daily in Albacete, of arming and accommodating them. 'Each one of these tasks was a nightmare,' he wrote, 'because of the disorganization, the shortage of supplies, and the crowding.' The peacetime population of Albacete was about 10,000. It had swelled to twice this number with refugees, and there was little room for the Brigaders. The first to arrive slept in the bull-ring. Eventually an assortment of billets were found, including the office of the Bank of Spain, an old nunnery, and the former Civil Guard barracks (where the washrooms were still caked in blood, and sheds on the roof held civilians suspected of rebel sympathies).

The volunteers spent their days queuing for meals; by the time they received breakfast, it was often time to start queuing again for lunch. Many found the Spanish food disagreeable; diarrhoea was soon rampant, and the lavatories overflowing. There were virtually no weapons and, at first, very little to do.

Gradually the men were grouped into battalions by nationality. For a while no one knew what to do with Cornford and the tiny and seemingly anomalous band of English-speakers that congregated around him. Their number had slowly grown to nineteen: they included another University friend of Cornford's, Griffith Maclaurin, a New Zealander with some military training who until a few weeks before had been running a left-wing bookshop in Cambridge. The most experienced of the group was 'Jock' Cunningham, a British Army veteran from Glasgow. Since they included a number of experienced machine-gunners, and since Bernard Knox spoke fluent French, these English-speakers were assigned eventually to the *compagnie mitrailleuse* of the Commune de Paris Battalion. Their new French comrades were not impressed: they regarded these 'Anglo-Saxons' as a nuisance, since every order had to be translated for their benefit. The English-speakers were equally exasperated at having to follow commands in a language most did not understand. An ex-Guardsman, Fred Jones, was made section leader as he too spoke good French. But, as Knox later wrote, it was Cornford who assumed responsibility 'for maintaining discipline and harmony in the group'. Such was Cornford's 'political experience and integrity' that before long even 'hardened old soldiers had come to respect his judgment and seek his advice.'

The Commune de Paris Battalion was sent to a more distant village for training. For many weeks there were scarcely any rifles, and only one battered, worn-out machinegun. Since it had no ammunition, they practised taking it to pieces and reassembling it. Their only item of uniform was a large black beret. Cornford told his friends not to take it all too seriously: 'The only thing to do is to laugh at it,' he advised. 'If you look at it long enough it seems funny.'

Although Cornford and Sommerfield could laugh together for hours, Bernard Knox found it a hard lesson. 'But I was to learn; and I think that there were times when the way we learned to see the funny side of a hopeless situation was the only thing that kept us alive and sane.'

'The days went by,' wrote John Sommerfield, 'and the war went on while we ran about the fields and drank in cafés.'

V

In fact, John Cornford's was not the only native English-speaking group in Albacete, but in the mass of volunteers their paths had not crossed with the others. One of the most unusual men amongst this other group of volunteers was a young acquaintance of Cornford's, Esmond Romilly, the eighteen-year-old nephew of Winston Churchill.

Even whilst he was still a schoolboy, Romilly and his elder brother Giles had attracted the attention of the press. Though the sons of an Army Colonel attending the prestigious private school Wellington College (which had been founded in honour of the great British General of the Peninsular War and Waterloo), both had refused to join the school's OTC. While Giles openly declared that he was a communist, on Armistice Day 1933 Esmond had inserted pacifist leaflets into the hymnbooks. The brothers followed this escapade by launching an anti-public school, anti-war magazine, *Out of Bounds*. They invited contributions from other disaffected public schoolboys, and it was through this that Esmond and John Cornford first met. Their activities seemed more than high spirits, however, and Scotland Yard had their eye on the boys: the *Daily Mail* even ran an article about the brothers (who were soon dubbed 'Winston's Red Nephews') headlined 'Red Menace in Public Schools'. Threatened with expulsion, Esmond ran away to London; following a drunken night out with his friend Philip Toynbee (son of the distinguished historian, Arnold), he was sentenced to a spell in a remand home. He followed this by publishing a precocious joint autobiography with his brother, *Out of Bounds: the Education of Giles and Esmond Romilly*.

Winston Churchill's 'Red Nephews': Esmond and Giles Romilly in a studio portrait by Howard Coster, 1934 (NPG)

Finally leaving school at sixteen, Esmond Romilly found intermittent work as a door-to-door salesman and then as an advertising copywriter. It was not long after the outbreak of the Civil War that he decided to go to Spain. That this one-time pacifist felt the need to go to war was a curious volte-face. But as Philip Toynbee later reflected, as schoolboys they had devoured the poems of Siegfried Sassoon and Wilfred Owen, as well as Erich Maria Remarque's novelistic memoir, *All Quiet on the Western Front*. And they had been awed by Paul Nash's desolate oil paintings of no-man's-land. Rather than convincing them that war was 'dull and dispiriting,' these influences

> had made a powerful, complex and stimulating impression on us, so that we felt less pity than envy of a generation which had experienced so much. Even in our Anti-War

campaigns of the early thirties we were half in love with
the horrors which we cried out against, and, as a boy, I can
remember murmuring the name 'Passchendaele' in an ecstasy
of excitement and regret.

Romilly's response to the 'people's war' in Spain was thus both earnest
and eager. It was a mixture of what Toynbee called a 'secret, unadmitted
longing' and a 'shame-faced romanticism'.

Though a remarkable young man, his lack of any military training
and his unfortunate capacity for losing things meant Romilly was ill-
suited to the demands that lay ahead. Telling no one of his plans, he
sold the furniture in his London flat to raise money, then caught a ferry
to Dieppe. There he bought a bicycle, with the intention of cycling
to Spain. But with his jacket slung carelessly over the handlebars, in
the south of France he dropped his wallet: it contained his money, his
passport and his Labour Party membership card. This loss, however,
did not unduly deter him: whatever he lacked in organizational ability,
he made up for with extraordinary energy and self-confidence. He
detoured to Marseilles, where after a week of living as a down-and-out
he found a Spanish ship bound for Valencia. On board were another
six hundred volunteers, all of them en route for Albacete and the
International Brigades.

The teenager was not overawed by this mass of strangers: working-
class men mostly, French, Germans, Italians, Yugoslavians, Belgians,
Poles, Russians. Their reception in Spain was fantastic: as they steamed
into Valencia there was a huge, cheering crowd, and marching through
the streets he was struck by the slogans and colourful posters and military
flags and badges everywhere. Their send-off at the station surpassed their
reception at the port. 'In the first hour the train stopped at every little
station on the way – and at each one there was the same crowd, the same
friendly words, the same forest of clenched fists as we moved on.' Nor
was he daunted by the idea of war. During an air-raid warning shortly
their arrival in Albacete their barracks fell silent: 'I did not think of the

wickedness and frightfulness and horror of air bombardments,' he later recalled, 'I was wildly excited.'

Over the following days Romilly ran into a handful of English-speakers. There was an American, 'Jerry' Fontana, who had lost two fingers in an explosion in a munitions factory, and had been working on the docks in Marseilles; there was an Australian tramp; and a young Cambridge graduate, Lorimer Birch, a committed Communist who had arrived in Barcelona in September, where – alongside Tom Wintringham – he had joined the Tom Mann Centuria. There Birch had met Arnold Jeans who, with his missing front teeth and six passports, would prove to be the group's enigma, its leader, and its hero: though he had travelled out from Manchester, he had a slight foreign accent, and spoke numerous languages, including German. No one knew for certain whether he was Russian, Latvian or Polish, though it was known he had been through the Russian revolution as a boy, and had been imprisoned in (and deported from) several countries.

After the break-up of the Tom Mann Centuria following the establishment of the International Brigades, Wintringham had remained in Barcelona with Kitty Bowler as the CPGB's representative in the city. Nat Cohen and Sam Masters had returned to militia units on the Aragon Front, while the rest of the nascent British unit had gone to Albacete. They included Bill Scott, an ex-IRA man from County Kerry; Raymond Cox, a young clerk from Southampton; David Marshall, 'a boy of 23' who had brought copies of Keats, Swinburne and Shelley with him; and Sidney Avener, 'called Long Sid on account of his unwieldy bulk,' a Jewish student from London University.

The only English-speaking group remaining on the Aragon front was the British Medical Unit. But the whole focus of the war, as well as most of the fighting, was now in central and southern Spain. Kenneth Sinclair-Loutit, Archie Cochrane and their colleagues soon found themselves isolated, and largely idle.

Esmond Romilly felt 'very lucky' in his new companions at Albacete. 'I had expected them all to be tougher, more frighteningly efficient.' In fact, the ten others were mostly young – 'all about twenty-two' – and almost all were communists. One exception was the twenty-four-year-old London University graduate, Keith Scott Watson. Described by the journalist Sefton Delmer as 'a tall myopic Bloomsbury Bohemian, with a gift for sardonic irony,' and 'a mop of blond hair which kept flopping into his spectacles,' Scott Watson had been a journalist before hitch-hiking around Europe. His travels had taken him to both Germany and the USSR. At the start of the Civil War he had joined an anarchist column in Barcelona, before transferring to the International Brigades. He refused to take the rules and regulations at Albacete seriously.

Romilly first met him over lunch.

'Are you one of the faithful?' Scott Watson asked.

'Faithful? How do you mean?'

'Member of the Communist Party, I mean, you know, seen the holy light.'

Romilly replied that he belonged to the Labour Party.

'It's religion, you know,' Scott Watson went on, meaning Communism. 'You'll have enough of it in the next few weeks.'

Romilly's group was given the option either of joining the French Battalion or the much-expanded corps of Germans, who were now transforming the remnants of the Thälmann Centuria that Wintringham had visited on the Aragon Front into a full-scale Battalion. Lorimer Birch summoned a Group Meeting to decide. They voted, almost unanimously, to join the Germans. Like Cornford's group in the Commune de Paris Battalion, they would be attached to a machinegun squad.

The Thälmann Battalion was divided into three companies, and the companies into *Zug*s of thirty men. Along with a dozen Flemings and a few Germans, the English-speakers formed the 3rd *Zug* of the 1st Company. They met the Battalion's political commissar, whose job it was to maintain discipline and morale, and to provide political education and information.[1] He asked them their name and age, their parents' occupations, their party political membership, and, lastly: 'Why have you come to Spain?' This was an easy one to answer, as a poster on the barracks wall proclaimed: '*To smash fascism.*' Then all they had to do was practice drill, wait for their weapons to arrive, and listen to rumours. There were many: Russia was about to declare war on Germany; a thousand rebels had surrendered on the Madrid front; Madrid had fallen. They did not pay much attention to them. Yet newspaper placards back in England were already proclaiming that the rebels were about to take Madrid.

While Romilly and his new friends waited, they were frequently told that there were more 'Englishmen' in town; this became a bit of a joke, as they rarely turned out to be English. When he was told after a week that there were Englishmen at the Café de Albacete, Romilly expected 'more Latvians'. In fact, there were nine British men, drinking coffee. Older and tougher, they were very different from Romilly's group. They included Harry Addley (nicknamed 'Tich' on account of his size) and his friend Arthur 'Babs' Ovenden, both of whom had served with the British Army during the Great War. They had been running a restaurant in Dover when the Civil War broke out, and decided that their military experience would be of use to the people of Spain. And there was 'Joe' Gough, an unemployed metal finisher from Luton (an 'extraordinary-looking fellow with red face and glasses'), who had travelled in Russia and Germany. He had brought with him a brand-new suit in which he intended to march down Luton High Street on his glorious return home. (Even better, he

---

1 The position of commissar had its origins in the Republican armies of the French Revolution, and subsequently the Soviet Red Army. According to *The Book of the 15th International Brigade* (1938), their purpose was 'to inspire their unit with the highest spirit of discipline and loyalty to the Republican cause and establish a feeling of mutual confidence and good comradeship between Commanders and men … In an Imperialist Army soldiers are kept forward in the attack by another file of soldiers who will shoot them if they retreat; the Commissar aims at keeping the soldiers forward in the attack by their own passionate devotion to the cause for which they fight.' They were not always popular: the American volunteers dubbed them 'comic stars', and one of their number later defined them as 'thought control agents, intellectual policemen'.

thought, if he could replace the suit with a Spanish general's uniform and a row of medals.)

The ex-soldiers were fed up. 'What we've been doing here is waiting about and eating and then waiting about for the next bit of grub,' Ovenden complained. 'Then they've started some jolly game of hauling ourselves out at six in the morning to go on parade and listen to some fat bastard gassing his head off in some language we don't understand. When someone tried to get us up this morning, we just stayed fixed where we were.' The men considered themselves volunteers: they should be allowed to do what they wanted, and damn any 'regulations'.

The following day André Marty made a long speech, explaining why the Republican militias had not yet defeated the rebels:

> Is it because they have lacked enthusiasm? A thousand times no. Is it because they have lacked courage? I say ten thousand times no … There are three things that they have lacked, three things that are essential for victory, three things which we must have – which we *will* have. The first is political unity; the second is military leaders; the third is discipline.

He then reminded the men that they were no longer communists or socialists or Republicans or radicals: they were anti-fascists. Then Kléber stepped forward:

> There are those who are impatient, who wish to rush off to the front at once, untrained, without proper arms. I say those people who spread those ideas – though they mean well – they are criminals. We are preparing for war, not massacre. When the first International Brigade goes into action, they will be properly trained men, with good rifles, a well-equipped corps.

But they were still waiting for those weapons. Through October they waited, days spent practising close-order drill, or field manoeuvres, or marching along the dusty roads of Murcia.

Finally, early in November, they received rudimentary uniforms. Romilly's unit was issued with thick khaki coats, brown corduroy trousers, belts, bayonets, boots, socks, plates, knives, spoons, mugs 'and every sort of underwear'. The trousers were all one size, and that size was large. Cornford's group was equally unlucky. 'Everybody got *something* and no one everything,' and John Sommerfield thought they looked like 'a lot of scarecrows'. But at last they had rifles.

These were unloaded from huge wooden crates at the railway yards. The cases were covered with all kinds of stamps and bills of lading: whilst some were in Arabic, one was branded 'IRA'. Inside, packed in grease, there were old American Springfields and Remingtons: the weapons the US Infantry had carried to France back in 1918. Sommerfield recorded his 'pang of delight' at first getting his hands on one. 'Everyone was quiet, almost sulky, like dogs with bones. They wanted to get back to the barracks and be alone with their guns and take them to pieces and play with them.' Some were less battered than others. Sommerfield peered down the barrel of his: 'it was a silver-shining tunnel … I'd got a good gun; it was the best thing that had happened since I left London.'

On 4 November André Marty sent Stalin a top-secret telegram. There were now 3,000 men at Albacete, he declared, with 2,000 more expected to arrive over the next ten days: 'The morale of the brigades is strong. Lacking are automatic weapons and artillery; one-third have insufficient military training. The command staff is extremely small and insufficiently qualified.' Some of these problems Marty expected to rectify over the coming weeks. Those men who had received arms were now receiving instruction. Before long, they would be ready for action.

That action, however, came much sooner than Marty expected. A request suddenly came instructing Marty to send men to aid the defence of Madrid from imminent rebel assault. The recently formed XI International Brigade would be the first to be sent in to action.[1] Under

---

1 The International Brigades began their numbering from eleven upwards.

the command of Emilio Kléber, it numbered 1,900 men and was made up of four battalions: the principally Polish Dombrowski Battalion, the Austro-German Edgar André Battalion, the Italian Garibaldi Battalion, and the French and Belgian Commune de Paris Battalion with its handful of British machine-gunners. John Cornford and his friends were about to see action.

The International Brigades' courage 'was tremendous,' one of their German commissars later wrote in recollection of this historic moment, 'its weapons poor, its notions of discipline wild, its staff weak. Chaos reigned amid all their heroic resistance – a chaos of tongues, a chaos of organization, a chaos of illusions.'

Chapter 5

The Spanish Cockpit

|

Since being airlifted across the Straits of Gibraltar in late July General Franco's Army of Africa had been fighting its way steadily northwards. They had easily pushed the untrained, inexperienced militiamen of the Republic back before them. At the same time, rebel soldiers from the north were marching on Madrid. Altogether, four columns were converging on the capital; and as the rebel General Emilio Mola boasted in a radio broadcast, a 'fifth column' of armed supporters trapped in the capital would augment their attack.

'The Fascists will stop at nothing,' Claud Cockburn warned in *The Daily Worker*. 'One can be sure that Madrid will fight to the death, but world public opinion in all countries must make itself heard by raising its voice against the new and monstrous crime of mass slaughter which the Fascist war instigators are preparing.' The rebel assault on the city was preceded by artillery bombardments and aerial attacks, and on 2 November Cockburn reported on a recent raid by German and Italian planes that – it was claimed – had left between 140 and 160 dead:

> The reason for the doubt in the figures is simple and ghastly. It is that in many cases groups of people – particularly women standing close together in queues, sometimes with babies in their arms – were torn so violently to pieces by the bombs that it was impossible to be sure how many bodies

were represented by the horrible, mangled and scattered remains of flesh and bones.

At one spot 'there were bits of flesh and brains plastered against walls many yards from the actual scene of the explosion.' To add insult, these bombs 'fell within a few hours of the British delegate to the Non-Intervention Committee solemnly recording his vote on behalf of the assertion that German and Italian planes are not here.'

On 6 November, despite the strong opposition of its anarchist cabinet ministers, the government abandoned Spain's capital and re-established itself in Valencia. They left the last-ditch defence of Madrid to two loyal army officers, General José Miaja and his chief of staff, Colonel Vicente Rojo; Miaja was said to have turned pale when given this awesome – and seemingly impossible – task. For although the confident slogan of the people was that Madrid would be 'the tomb of Fascism,' Franco expected to take the city within days. Both the Prime Minister of the Republic and the international press thought likewise. On 7 November it was reported in *The New York Times* that the 'fall of Madrid' was 'apparently only a matter of hours' away.

But had Franco left the assault on Madrid too late? Hemingway considered the mountain city a 'natural fortress,' and the longer Franco delayed his attack, the stiffer resistance would prove. And Franco *had* delayed. In late September, with the capital seemingly ripe for the picking, he had diverted the advancing Army of Africa to capture Toledo, forty-five miles south of Madrid. There, since the first day of the rebellion in July, around a thousand Civil Guards and Falangists had been under siege in the Alcázar, a sixteenth-century fortified palace. The relief of the Alcázar would an important propaganda coup for Franco: before, he had simply been one of the movement's chief officers. Now, with the charismatic leader of the Falange soon to be executed in a Republican jail, and with General José Sanjurjo (who had helped mastermind the rebellion) dead in an air-crash, Franco could establish himself as the rebels' figurehead, their *Generalissimo* and *Caudillo*.

While Franco delayed the attack on Madrid, General Miaja and fellow loyalists strengthened its defences: *The New York Times* reported how columns of raw recruits were marching to the firing lines on the edge of the city, whilst well-armed men manned barricades of paving stones as Government artillery 'blazed continuously at the Insurgent troops'. Madrid Radio encouraged the population to join the resistance, loudspeakers in the street rang to the powerful words of the communist orator, Dolores Ibárruri, and banners bore the slogan she made famous '*¡No pasarán!*': 'They shall not pass!' More importantly, weapons had started arriving from Russia: modern tanks and aeroplanes were suddenly available, as well as guns and ammunition. And the first International Brigade had now mobilized.

It was a freezing, desperately uncomfortable 36-hour journey by train and lorry for those first 1,900 volunteers to go into action. Only John Cornford and Fred Jones had brought overcoats with them from England; the others, knowing no better, had too easily believed the tourist propaganda about 'sunny Spain'. Cornford's greatcoat reached almost to his feet, and with an ammunition belt strapped around him and his rifle and blanket over his shoulders he looked – thought Sommerfield – like a bad picture of one Napoleon's soldiers on the retreat from Moscow. But he was warm: Madrid's winter nights could be bitterly cold.

'Do you think we're really going to the wars?' Sommerfield asked Cornford. 'The Front, I mean.'

'Dunno,' he replied,

'We've got no machine-guns.'

'True. It's not like the books, is it?'

'I'll say it isn't.'

Now, at the final hour, at their assembly point on the outskirts of Madrid, they got their machineguns, packed in wooden cases as heavy and narrow as coffins. They were doubly excited, for the date was significant: it was 7 November, the nineteenth anniversary of the Russian Revolution. Their commanding officer made a short speech in the thin drizzle, and they sang the *Internationale*. But the machineguns did not live up to expectations. They were 'a sad disappointment,' Knox complained, 'antique models that sported a bicycle seat for the gunner high up in the air, real suicide traps.' Though the packing-cases bore French stamps, not even their French Army veterans knew what the guns were until one old soldier identified them as St Étiennes, a heavy weapon that had proved so 'insanely complicated' and unreliable in the Great War that it had been taken out of service. Nobody in the whole machinegun company knew how to operate them.

So they spent the night in the attic of a farmhouse, practising by candlelight over and over again how to take the gun to pieces, how to remount it, how to work it. They grumbled incessantly about the British Government, for they knew Non-Intervention was to blame for the inadequacy of their arms. Kléber appeared, looking every inch a general, and speaking English with an American accent. They told him that their section included some experienced handlers of the British Army's efficient light machinegun, the Lewis gun. Kléber promised them they could have some – if he could find any.

Before dawn the next day XI International Brigade made the short train journey into Madrid. Weighed down by guns and tripods, Sommerfield did not feel they cut a dashing sight marching up the Gran Via. 'Ours was no triumphant entry,' he would write the following year: 'we were a last, desperate hope, and as, tired-out, ill-equipped, and hungry, we marched through the windswept streets, past the shuttered shops and the food queues, I thought that the hurrying people on the pavements looked at us as if we were too late and had come only in time to die.' Once again, many observers assumed they were Russians.

The Commune de Paris Battalion was sent to the unfinished University City complex on the western edge of Madrid. The attractive modern buildings overlooked the extensive wooded parkland of the Casa del Campo, a former royal hunting ground. Cornford thought it 'rather Sussexy to look at: but behind to the right a range of the Guadarama, a real good range with snow against a very blue sky.' His group made themselves comfortable in the Faculty of Philosophy and Letters, delighting in the glistening, pristine washrooms and the brand new lavatories. Then Kléber came good with his promise: eight Lewis guns with thousands of rounds of ammunition were unloaded from trucks.

Their 'baptism of fire,' wrote Knox, 'was sharp and unexpected.' Moving out of their overnight accommodation, they dug in the next day with their Lewis guns scattered along a ridge. An incoming shell screamed overhead, landing forty yards behind them and throwing up a fountain of earth. The next shell fell closer; and within a few minutes, everybody was leaping over the ridge, pell-mell into the little valley in front of them. They were lucky. They all survived.

The real fighting began when the rebel infantry advanced into the Casa del Campo. Franco had committed his best troops to the attack: the Moors of the Army of Africa. Over the next ten days the volunteers of the International Brigade and their Spanish comrades were shelled, bombed and machinegunned by planes: one barrage killed seven Frenchmen in only a few minutes. 'Jerking limb-stumps with the blood gushing from them bright and sparkling in the sunshine,' Sommerfield wrote of the dead and wounded they saw over the following days, 'entrails palpitating amongst rags of torn underwear ... a man staring at his arm on the ground ... we learned a whole dance of shudderings and writhings and convulsions, an opera of moans and howls and whimpers.'

They buried and burnt the corpses of both sides, and were soon familiar with every manner of death. 'We knew them slain suddenly,' wrote Sommerfield, or

> frozen in the gestures of fear and surprise, their legs drawn up, arms lifted to protect dead faces; we knew them stretched gently on the ground as if they slept, we knew them killed running, killed eating, killed excreting; we became familiar with all the vile ridiculousness of spoiled flesh; we knew the huddled bloody messes of frost-covered rags strewn upon frozen earth like overturned scarecrows, the rents in whose clothes disclosing surprisingly not straw but dead, mottled

flesh. We knew them in the cold dawns, frozen stiff as statues, we knew them in the last stages of being dead, when they were picked up to be shovelled into the earth and the skin slid down the arm like a loose glove, when the limbs themselves broke off like rotten wood and that which was left bore no relation to humanity.

They slept out in the open, numb with cold – damp, filthy, hungry – and fought day and night. Sometimes they simply fired their Lewis guns into the darkness at an invisible enemy, with the sound reverberating in the wooded hills, like (as Sommerfield recorded) 'a rushing, dying sigh, a disembodied sobbing, an infinitely melancholy complaint of pierced and wounded air.'

Finally there was a lull in the battle. In an oak-filled valley Cornford found time to write a letter home. 'This is a real war,' he admitted to Margot Heinemann, 'not a military holiday like the Catalan affair … But our International Brigade has done well. Continuous fighting, heavy losses, many of them simply due to inexperience, but we've been on the whole successful.'

The worst news concerned four machine-gunners from their section who had been sent forward to defend a key building near the University complex: Moors, who were experts in stealth and the use of dead ground, had stormed their positions during the night. One British Army veteran was in hospital 'with two bullets in the guts,' another was missing, 'believed 90 per cent certain dead … worst of all, Maclaurin, picked up dead on his gun after covering a retreat.'

Having coming out to Spain from his Cambridge bookshop Maclaurin had done 'really well,' Cornford told his girlfriend. 'Continuously cheerful, however uncomfortable, and here that matters a hell of a lot. Well, it's useless to say how sorry we are; nothing can bring him back now. But if you meet any of his pals, tell them (and I wouldn't say it if it weren't true) he did well here, and died bloody well.'

Equally sickening, their section leader, Fred Jones, had been killed in a freak accident. During a night march a Republican lorry struck a cable that was being used to block a road. The wire snapped, catching Jones round the neck. 'We didn't see what happened,' Cornford told Margot, 'and to give some idea of the way we felt about him, after his death none dared to tell the English section for several hours. Well, we shall get along somehow. But that's a hell of a way to have your best man killed.'

Sommerfield was devastated: he thought Jones had the air of a man who would never be killed. Joe Hinks, a British Army veteran, initially took over command. Since he did not speak French, however, he soon resigned. Cornford, whose French had rapidly improved, was elected in his place.

Cornford also told Margot that Bernard Knox, though exhausted, was 'doing fine'. Two nights running he had fainted from the cold, 'but [he] hasn't made any complaints'. As the letter progressed, Cornford's façade of confidence slipped. He admitted that everyone was

> a bit shaken and upset by our losses, depressed. And it's affected me a bit, though I'm getting a thick skin … For five weeks I scarcely missed you, everything was so new and different, and I couldn't write but formal letters. Now I'm beginning to wake up a bit, and I'm as glad as I could be that the last few days I had with you were as good as they could be …
>
> I don't know what's going to happen, but I do know we're in for a tough time. And I am glad that you are behind me, glad and proud. The losses are heavy, but there's still a big chance of getting back alive, a big majority chance. And if I didn't, we can't help that. Be happy, darling. Things here aren't easy, but I never expected them to be. And we'll get through them somehow, and I'll see you again, bless you, darling.
>
> JOHN.

Esmond Romilly and the other English-speaking machine-gunners with the Thälmann Battalion experienced an equally punishing 'baptism of fire'. The 1,500 men of the three hastily-assembled battalions of XII International Brigade were placed under the command of a Hungarian Red Army officer, who in Spain went by the name Pavol Lukács. They received orders to move out from Albacete and join XI Brigade in the defence of Madrid; they were packed into lorries and driven, cold and uncomfortable, through the countryside. Romilly was gripped by diarrhoea, whilst the smell of food being eaten in the back of the lorry (tinned fish, bread and pomegranates) made him vomit.

At midnight they were unloaded in the market town of Chinchón, still some thirty miles from Madrid. In the morning they received ammunition, and two days later, on 12 November, they were back in their lorries. Their next stop was a quiet country village five miles southwest of the capital. It was a beautiful, sunny day, and the gentle hills reminded Romilly – as they had Cornford – of the Sussex Downs.

In an effort to prevent the rebels from encircling Madrid, they were to attack a fortified hilltop position. Their inexperience and lack of training was quickly apparent (at least one of their number was under the impression that they were still on exercise). Crossing a field they came under fire, the *swish – swish – swish* of the bullets was like a cool breeze whistling through grass. Romilly's initial feeling was excitement – until the smack of a round in the earth nearby unsettled this confidence.

Their progress was slow, and as darkness fell they set up their machinegun. Romilly let off five rounds with his rifle; astonishingly, it was the first time in his life he had ever fired a gun. Rebel bullets splashed around him. 'I had little time to reflect on the occasion,' he later recalled; 'it seemed very unfair that the enemy now seemed to be able to see me but I could not see them.'

Then a German in their Battalion was hit. Romilly volunteered to help him back. They were soon lost in the darkness. Eventually they found a

French unit that had had six of its men killed by an unseen machinegun: 'it's terrible,' they despaired, 'we don't know anything – there's no organisation, there's nothing.'

The Frenchmen took the wounded German with them, and Romilly tried to retrace his steps. He roamed uncertainly for hours in search of his colleagues before running into Bill Scott, the IRA man. Stumbling into empty enemy trenches, and hearing the distant, intermittent report of heavy guns, Romilly was reminded of stories he had read of the Great War, of no-man's-land. He asked Scott how this compared to the fighting in Ireland.

'This is a proper war all right,' Scott replied.

By morning they had found Arnold Jeans and the remainder of their unit and – at long last – food. As their group reassembled, it was found that only one of them – David Marshall a 'veteran' of the Tom Mann Centuria – had been injured. It also transpired that Keith Scott Watson had deserted.

Birch and another of the more earnest British communists urged that Scott Watson should be found, brought back, and shot. Romilly and the others looked at each other aghast, not so much at the ruthlessness of the proposal, but at its absurdity. Then they burst out laughing.

'With the best will in the world,' Romilly later told a friend, 'we couldn't have arranged him against a tree and taken aim at him. It would have been too pompous for us.' And others in the Battalion were also voicing a wish to quit. Faced with the reality of war, and the apparent incompetence of their command, the morale of the international volunteers had plummeted.

Though the tactics used in the attack had astonished Tich, his quiet, reassuring manner gave Romilly the confidence that at least something of the British Army was present. 'Knowing nothing of war, nothing surprised me much in the way it was fought.'

The following day they were bombed by German planes, but the next night's action was more successful, when they overtook a patrol of Moorish cavalry. 'I would have sworn my cartridge had got one of them,'

Romilly wrote, 'but then, everyone afterwards claimed dozens of victims.' One of their own *Zugs*, flushed with success, then opened fire on them; luckily no one was hit, but friendly fire would prove a frequent danger throughout the war, especially among the International Brigades, where the babble of languages caused frequent confusion.

The younger men celebrated their first action by getting drunk, to the disapproval of the ex-soldiers. Then came the order to move into Madrid. Inauspiciously, they arrived during an air-raid. The city, thought Romilly, 'didn't look very exciting – mostly tramlines and barricades,' like London in road-works. 'It was an anticlimax.'

They were sent to a reserve position on the edge of University City, and waited.

III

At a crucial stage in the November fighting around University City, 4,000 Catalan anarchists from the Durruti Column arrived in Madrid. When Durruti was given orders to attack, one of his colleagues called the plan 'an imbecility'. The anarchists suspected that the communists were deliberately trying to see them defeated in order to discredit them, suspecting that 'the communists cannot permit Durruti to be the saviour of the capital.'

Overawed by the withering fire of the Moroccan machine-guns, Durruti's independently-minded irregulars refused to follow orders. One source would claim that the ill-disciplined, disorganized and inexperienced anarchists 'ran like rabbits' in the face of the enemy's well-placed guns. In the ensuing confusion, the rebels successfully stormed the university buildings.

A few days later, in the environs of University City, Durruti was killed: perhaps by a stray bullet, or (it was claimed in some quarters) by one of his own disgruntled men. More probably, he was killed by an accidental discharge from his or a colleague's gun, a not uncommon occurrence among soldiers unfamiliar with firearms. His body was taken back to

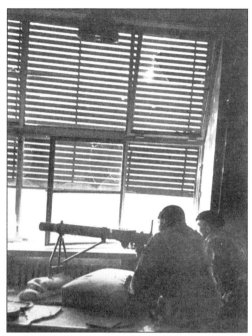

Robert Capa, *Lewis gun section of Commune de Paris Battalion, XI International Brigade, University City, Madrid. November/December 1936* (Magnum)

Barcelona, where the crowd at his funeral numbered some 200,000 mourners.[1]

The XI International Brigade was sent back to try to retake University City. Extraordinary scenes of house-to-house fighting followed in the tall red and white buildings (some six or even eight stories high). Sometimes the International Brigaders held the top floors and fired from the roofs whilst Moors held the lower floors; sometimes it was the other way round. One volunteer became expert in slinging homemade bombs out of the window on a length of string, so that they plunged in through windows three floors below. Some Spanish soldiers dumped grenades and high explosives into a lift, attached a long time-fuse, then sent it up to the rebels in the upper stories.

Cornford's group found themselves back in the Faculty of Philosophy and Letters. It was now no longer a plush residence, but rather a 'great gutted building,' as Cornford described it, 'with broken glass all over'. Encamped there, Knox would recall, they were 'as happy as I think men can possibly be in the front line of a modern war'. Though they had to

<hr>

1 Lois Orr, the nineteen-year-old from Kentucky working for the POUM, attended Durruti's funeral, and in the immense crowd proceeding to Montjuïc cemetery lost herself in what she described as 'a tremendous sense of identification with these swarthy, silent, wonderful people. I felt for them, I loved them, I wanted to be one of them ... From this day on I was emotionally and intellectually committed to the antifascist revolution as a wonderful human experiment and the last doubts and reservations were swept away.'

smash the windows to remove the threat of flying glass, they still had some protection from the terrible cold outside.

With thick volumes of Indian metaphysics and German philosophy from the Faculty Library they blockaded the windows against snipers; there were sofas to sleep on, and in the long periods between the fighting they had time and relative comfort to talk and smoke, to read, to play chess. For Knox, the greatest pleasure was being able to take his boots off at night, free from the fear that they might suddenly be called into action. 'Here we discussed art and literature, life and death and Marxism during the long day, and as the evening drew on, we sang. Nothing delighted John Cornford more than the sort of crude community singing that is common to undergraduate parties and public bars alike.'

Positioning a large armchair behind a loophole, John Sommerfield spent hours sniping at the enemy. (One of the reasons Cornford had selected him to come to Spain was because he was a good shot.) It was 'impersonal,' Sommerfield wrote, like clay pigeon shooting:

> you did not think that you were making widows and orphans, robbing mothers of their children. You fired at something dark and moving and if you hit it, you felt 'good shot.' At other times you fired and killed because they were coming at you, and it was you or them, but it was still impersonal, and if you advanced later and saw the corpses they were dead men and anything might have killed them.

But increasingly there were few targets to shoot at. The enemy – surprised at the resistance they had encountered, and suffering heavy casualties – had learnt their lesson. The rebel soldiers were learning to respect their enemy, and they were keeping their heads down.

IV

Esmond Romilly and his comrades in the Thälmann Battalion soon joined the fighting. John Sommerfield watched them in their khaki uniforms, marching 'magnificently' into Madrid, singing songs from their street demonstrations in Germany before the Nazis had driven them into exile. Their voices were 'low and deep and beautifully together, the words of the song and the beat of the marching feet all together making one single noise.' The men of the Commune de Paris saluted them with clenched fists. 'And we felt the song and the marching feet right down inside us,' Sommerfield wrote, 'seeing the red banners and the rifles all sloped together and the determined faces, and knowing that our dreams of justice and liberty … could at last be defended with the weapons that had always been used before to shatter them.'

At dawn, as Romilly and the other English speakers of the Thälmann Battalion waited near the Casa del Campo for the order to attack, Arnold Jeans relayed the sensational news that, on the pretext that Franco was now in control of Madrid, Germany and Italy had formally recognised the rebels as Spain's legitimate government. And Portugal had followed suit. It was, of course, a lie: Franco was far from controlling Madrid. As Jeans told his men, their forthcoming fight 'would have a decisive effect on the future of international relations.'

Romilly found the suspense of waiting to go into action 'maddening'. Again he recalled books about the Great War, 'and for the first time the expression "going over the top" had some meaning. I felt an urgent desire to relieve myself, but decided there would not be time.'

Jeans shouted, 'Fix bayonets, everyone ready!'

Their objective was a complex of farm buildings and the White House where Maclaurin, the Lewis gunner with Cornford's section, had been killed. An artillery barrage had preceded their attack, and a unit of Italian anti-fascists covered their advance with rifles and machine-guns.

'It was a mad scramble,' Romilly recalled afterwards. 'A few of the Germans dropped on the way – it was just like seeing people killed running in an American film.'

Within the farmhouse and its surrounding barns, sheds and stables there were at least a hundred dead Moors. 'Most were not killed by bullets – their bodies had been torn apart by shells, limbs blown off by hand grenades … In the middle of the mud I watched a little blaze crackling away – two dead men were burning steadily.'

Then they saw Moors running down the road towards the university buildings. Mad with excitement, Romilly fired wildly, 'never stopping to take aim, I was desperate to discharge as many shots as I could now – for the first time in the war – I had a clear target.'

Later their officer asked for volunteers to dig forward positions. Romilly, Tich, Ovenden and a number of others dashed forward from the cover of the White House, crossing the road one at a time.

A German volunteer was hit in the forehead. 'Someone got his body,' Romilly remembered afterwards. 'It left a red smear on the road. I felt a little sick. The enemy had some first-class marksmen, and a lot of men who moved a few feet out of safety got a bullet through their heads that afternoon.'

Then Romilly shot a rebel carrying ammunition, albeit in his reckoning more by accident than aim. Back under cover they cleaned their weapons. Corpses still lay everywhere: 'in the room, in the passage, and heaped up on the stairs.' The First Company was now barely sixty strong; remarkably, none of Romilly's section had yet been injured.

By nightfall, and despite the rain, all the buildings were ablaze. Romilly found that the 'overpowering stench' inside the house and the 'peculiar combination' of dead men, crackling flames and drizzle almost defied description. Under cover of darkness the Thälmann Battalion retreated, carrying their dead with them.

Over the next five days they remained in the front line. Shivering from cold, they were bombed, shelled and machinegunned from the air. Despite Tom Wintringham's hope that a British force would show the Spanish how to fight a modern war, Romilly and his companions displayed no greater enthusiasm for digging trenches.

As the lines moved forwards and backwards, as buildings were won and lost, chaos reigned. A German patrol returning with five Italians was disappointed to discover that their prisoners were anti-fascists from the

Garibaldi Battalion. On another occasion, Germans with XII International Brigade watched from a rooftop as a Moor, lost in the warren of the university buildings, ran back and forth 'like a hunted animal'. They argued whether or not it was right to shoot him. 'The majority were against it,' one later recalled, 'because one does not shoot a man in the back, and because after all he was only a man, a victim of colonialism.' But then, he admitted, 'the desire to destroy the enemy triumphed over principle.' They shot the African, and 'did not shoot any less well because they had hesitated, and they were fortified in the last resort by the hideous memory of Hitler, or simply by the ruthlessness of war.'

One highpoint for the British volunteers in the Thälmann Battalion was a visit by the *Daily Express* reporter, Sefton Delmer. He told them that they were 'occupying the most vital sector of the Madrid defence,' an observation that was received 'with mixed feelings'.

'We've got nothing to complain of here,' Joe Gough joked to the embarrassment of the others, 'except the Russian grub and the Fritzies now and again.' He told Delmer how he would soon be marching down Luton High Street, a row of medals pinned on his chest.

Delmer promised to get them newspapers, chocolate and cigarettes, then gave them the surprising news that their old colleague, Keith Scott Watson, was now working for him. Scott Watson had decided that returning to his old job as a journalist was much safer than soldiering, telling Delmer that 'he had come out to Spain to "fight for freedom" but had changed his mind when he found it meant charging up hills against machineguns.'

Though *The Daily Express* was broadly pro-Franco ('a fascist paper,' in Lorimer Birch's opinion), Delmer's subsequent article painted a heroic picture of the Thälmann Battalion's tiny British section. 'I don't think I have ever seen a finer body of men,' he wrote under the headline 'British Storm Troop Defend Madrid,' 'all of them with the real fighting enthusiasm unquenched by the continual bombing, shelling, machine-gun and tank attacks.' This picture contrasted markedly with his private opinion, however. The British volunteers quite obviously 'stood out from the … barrel-chested Germans,' he later wrote: 'they looked smaller and younger and less self-assured.' And as Romilly himself later admitted:

> I somehow could never really believe the enemy were occupying themselves with *us*; we were only playing at soldiers, we were only amateurs. It seemed impossible that over there, beyond the outline of the fort, someone was scheming how *we* were to be destroyed, eliminated, or – the simplest and most expressive word of all – killed. Delmer had said we were holding the most vital position; it was ridiculous that we should be doing this – we who were surely concerned all the time only with seeing that we had the same food rations as the Flems and quarrelling among ourselves and holding Group Meetings. It was all wrong.

Whilst the situation might have seemed shambolic and unprofessional on the Republican side, things appeared little better to the rebels' foreign allies. As the German Embassy in Seville reported to the German Foreign Ministry on 24 November, 'the military situation is not very satisfactory … The difficulty of taking Madrid is obviously underestimated. The Red government's announcement that Madrid would fall into White hands only as a field of ruin and carnage threatens to become a reality.'

It appeared to official Nazi observers that Franco might actually be in danger of losing the war. With the support and advice of the communists and the Russians, the Spanish Government appeared to be winning the propaganda war as well. The German Embassy emphasized the need to mobilize the Spanish population in support of the rebellion: 'This is of primary importance because the necessity of crushing Bolshevism here, come what may, would force us to make up the deficit with German blood.' For as the Embassy acknowledged, 'Even in leading government circles the opinion is already fairly prevalent that the war is not being fought in the interest of Spain, but is a showdown between Fascism and Bolshevism on Spanish soil.'

In comparison to Romilly's situation, life for John Cornford and his friends in the University's Faculty of Philosophy and Letters was comfortable. One day they were delighted to discover a cache of English books in the departmental library, and staggered upstairs with armfuls of Everyman Classics. Sommerfield settled down to read Thomas De Quincey's *Recollections of the Lake Poets* – burying himself in stories of Coleridge, Wordsworth and Southey – whilst Cornford relaxed with a Victorian historical novel.

After half an hour's silent reading there was a sudden explosion which, Knox wrote, 'seemed to rip my head open and I was thrown to the floor. When I looked up, the room was full of filthy black smoke and John was stumbling past me, his face bloody.' When the dust cleared, they found that one wall had a three-foot hole blown in it, whilst the one opposite was riddled with shrapnel.

Fortunately Cornford's injury was not too serious. Sent off to hospital, he returned to University City the following day, weak from loss of blood and his head swathed in bandages. Knox had discovered that the shell that had hit them had come from a Republican anti-aircraft gun, and Cornford roared with laughter when he heard that he had nearly been killed by friendly fire. But as he admitted to Margot Heinemann, 'We were lucky as hell not to be wiped out completely.'

Still not fully recovered, he returned to hospital a few days later. There in a long letter to Margot he outlined his recent exploits:

> I think I killed a Fascist. Fifteen or sixteen of them were running from a bombardment. I and two Frenchmen were firing from our barricades with sights at 900 [yards]: We got one, and both said it was I that hit him, though I couldn't be sure. If it is true, it's a fluke, and I'm not likely to do as good a shot as that again.
>
> Well, that's how far we've got. No wars are nice, and even

a revolutionary war is ugly enough. But I'm becoming a good soldier, longish endurance and a capacity for living in the present and enjoying all that can be enjoyed. There's a tough time ahead but I've plenty of strength left for it.

Well, one day the war will end – I'd give it till June or July, and then if I'm alive I'm coming back to you. I think about you often, but there's nothing I can do but say again, be happy, darling. And I'll see you one day.

Bless you, JOHN.

VI

Still stationed in open ground on the edge of University City, Esmond Romilly was reading a book 'about snobbery in the United Sates of America' when the Thälmann Battalion was suddenly almost overrun. Without warning, the Italians in front of them started falling back, and when two dropped dead it was abruptly apparent that they were under attack. 'We shoved in clip after clip of cartridges,' Romilly recorded,

> until the breaches and barrels of our guns were red hot. I never took aim. I never looked up to see what I was firing at, I never heard the order to open fire. I never saw the enemy – never knew for certain where they were … It was a mad scramble – pressing my elbows into the earth, bruising them on the stones, to get my rifle to my shoulder, pressing the trigger, rasping back the bolt, then shoving it home, then onto my elbows again.

When their company officer shouted 'Forward,' he stumbled down the bank in front of them, waving a muddy bayonet in his hand. Dead Moors lay everywhere. The attack had been repulsed.

In response, Hans Beimler organised a raiding party. After so many days in action Romilly felt 'heavy and sticky and dirty – it was an exaggeration of the sensation you have after driving a car a very long way.' Lorimer Birch was keen to join Beimler's operation, and was desperately disappointed when he was overlooked. Beimler was the communist former Deputy of the Reichstag who in 1933 had escaped from Dachau, and who had been with the Thälmann Centuria when Tom Wintringham had visited the Aragon Front. He was a talismanic figure among the Germans, and seemed almost invincible. Gustav Regler, a thirty-eight-year-old veteran of the Great War who had recently joined XII International Brigade as their political commissar, was amazed at his countryman's 'almost superhuman intensity'. Regler had hated his experience in the trenches of the Western Front, and found 'something gluttonous' in Beimler's 'ardour' for war, 'as though he was afraid of not getting his fill'. Manning a machinegun with deadly effect, yet without any signs of hatred in his face, Beimler made Regler feel 'that after all this war could be won, for the example he set was worth battalions.'

Beimler equally impressed Claud Cockburn, who had interviewed the German communist in the Casa del Campo a few weeks before. A bullet had narrowly missed head. Beimler had shrugged it off: he had been closer to death than that, he told Cockburn, before relating the story of how he had escaped from Dachau.

One night, Beimler's SS guards had told him to hang himself (as one of his comrades had already done). If he did not, they promised to return to his cell in the morning and kill him themselves. 'He very nearly did commit suicide there and then,' Cockburn wrote, 'making an end to all the horrible physical pain and agony, not to mention the mental pain and agony that went with it. Then he pulled himself together and calculated that after all a dead man is a dead man, and utterly harmless and useless, and that he might anyway make one more effort.' A guard had made the error of entering Beimler's cell alone: Beimler strangled him, took his uniform, and escaped. Beimler's anti-fascist fervour was obvious. As if any further proof were necessary, in the Casa del Campo Cockburn saw him shoot a Republican militia officer who was deserting his post.

The Spanish war had given Beimler an opportunity to fight his enemies face to face. Cockburn thought that he had 'never seen a man who seemed so confident and happy. He was without illusions. He had seen the front. He had seen the casualties. He knew what the difficulties and dangers were.' Yet Beimler was happy because he was 'entirely … engaged in something which he knew to be a decisive action for the liberation of the world from the threat of Fascism and war which hangs over us.'

Arnold Jeans joined Beimler's raiding party. Regler warned them of the snipers, but Beimler simply laughed. 'I'm bullet-proof,' he joked. Ten minutes later he was brought back on a stretcher, shot through the heart. Though he knew it was pointless, Regler touched Beimler's body to see if he was really dead.

When Cockburn heard the news, he wrote a powerful obituary in *The Daily Worker*: 'We have often said that from the blood of our murdered comrades new men, new champions would spring … The new champions are really there. They are there in that roaring semi-circle of shellfire, bursting bombs, gas, machine-gun bullets and mud, around the city of Madrid, the men of the International Brigades.' After lying in state in Madrid, Beimler's body was sent to Moscow, to be buried with full honours in Red Square.

In its first three weeks in action, half of XII International Brigade had been killed or wounded. Romilly's company had left Albacete with 120 men; it now numbered 37. Miraculously, since arriving in University City Romilly's little English-speaking contingent had not suffered a single casualty. They felt guilty to have had such good fortune.

Then one night the Thälmann Battalion was relieved. Falling back to the lorries that would take them from the front they passed the wooden crosses marking their comrades' last resting place. The survivors stood to attention, fists clenched. For the Germans of XII International Brigade, this had not been a clash with Franco; it had been a direct engagement with National Socialism. 'We are fighting Hitler's Germany,' one of their officers explained. 'The real Germany of the German people will remember those who fought and died here.'

As Romilly observed, for these exiles, their homeland under the imprint of the swastika, its Führer leading their people towards another genocidal world war, 'there could be no surrender, no return … I felt deeply for the first time a sense of the tragedy inherent in the very fact of these German volunteers – a tragedy almost as great as that of the Spanish war itself.'

Through Europe and America, however, the popular press was more interested in the British constitutional crisis. 'Spain, Germany, Russia – all are elbowed out,' Virginia Woolf wrote in her diary on 7 December. 'The marriage stretches from one end of the paper to another.' The king, Edward VIII, was about to abdicate and wed his American lover, Mrs Wallis Simpson. His stammering younger brother would succeed him as George VI. This – not the defence of Madrid – was the big news story. 'The massacre of a hundred Spanish children is less interesting than a sigh from Mrs Simpson,' one French correspondent complained from Madrid.

Chapter 6

Boadilla

|

Through December 1936 the Republican government continued its efforts to create a Popular Army that would turn peasants and factory workers into soldiers. As it did so, the rebel land and air assault on Madrid continued. Often led by the German planes and pilots of the Condor Legion, the raids were intended to break the morale of the population, in which ambition they largely failed. Nevertheless, as Claud Cockburn had witnessed, they could be both terrifying and deadly. Romilly and Birch were on leave from the front when they were caught by an air-raid in an underground station: 'We tried to get out on to the street, but a panic-stricken crowd made it impossible to move. The fear of suffocation was stronger than that of bombs – women screamed and on the steps men were fighting to get inside the shelter … there were twelve bursts – twelve explosions, each the signal for screaming hysteria – then silence.'

In Madrid, half-encircled by the rebels and flooded with refugees, food and drink were becoming increasingly scarce. So Romilly and Birch sought out the hospitality of the British news pack. They tracked Sefton Delmer down to the Gran Via Hotel, and he provided them with brandy 'and a gorgeous hot bath'. But Birch was not in good humour. As he told Romilly, their 'British group' depressed him.

'They all want to go home,' he complained, 'or most of them, as far as I can see.'

Robert Capa, *Republican defences around University City, Madrid, 1936/7* (Magnum)

With Christmas approaching, it was perhaps not surprising that the thoughts of some foreign volunteers were turning towards home. And indeed, the very next day the group's one American, Jerry, told them he was quitting the International Brigades, and he disappeared into Madrid. Romilly realized that Birch was possibly right, and that many in the Thälmann Battalion had been broken by their recent experiences in University City. Romilly himself had discovered that he 'didn't like war,' and thought that even their British Army veterans 'looked less tough now.' Only Jeans and Birch seemed to be standing up to it, albeit in a slightly unsettling, almost inhuman way.

It was not simply the intensity of the fighting that was undermining their morale. Another concern was the language barrier, which isolated the English-speakers from their German comrades. This problem transcended their small unit. Very often, when liaison was needed between the Thälmann and French battalions, the messages had to be translated from German into English by Jeans, and then from English into French by Romilly. However, there was a chance of breaking away: they now knew for certain that the rumours they had heard of 'another group of about a dozen Englishmen' serving with the Commune de Paris were correct, and Jeans had inquired about the possibility of transferring to join them. Whilst in Madrid, Romilly had run into David Mackenzie, a nineteen-year-old Scottish volunteer in Cornford's group. Mackenzie had told him that *they* had asked for a transfer to join Romilly's group. 'They thought the Germans were easier to get on with than the French. I thought the reverse, but I didn't say so.' For the time being, however, the two English-speaking units were told to remain with their original battalions.

On returning to their unit after their night's leave in Madrid, Arnold Jeans confronted Romilly with news from home. A journalist from *The Star* had informed Romilly's mother that her teenage son was fighting on the front line in Madrid. 'We have been living in agony wondering what has become of him,' she had told the reporter. 'Please, please help me to get a message to him.'

'With great emotion,' *The Star* reported, 'her voice broken by sobs, she dictated a message, conveying her love and that of her husband to their son.' The fact that Romilly was Winston Churchill's nephew – previously unknown to his comrades – was also out of the bag.

Jeans told him that, if he wanted, he could go home. Glad though he was to have survived the fighting in University City unscathed, Romilly replied that he 'hadn't the slightest wish to return to England.'

Instead, he wrote to a friend in confident mood: 'This is a note to tell you I've found a whole lot of blood and violent destruction all around … Before I left England, I read that Madrid would fall in a day or two. It is certain now that it can never fall.'

Nevertheless, the British volunteers could not see how the Civil War would ever end, since the two opposing sides appeared so evenly balanced.

'I can't see it, honestly I can't, how this is going to finish,' Joe Gough mused. Although the Republicans still held Spain's industrials heartlands as well as it financial reserves, and although they had more men (and women) in arms, their soldiers were less experienced, and (despite some Russian aid) they were much less well equipped. 'Look at all the stuff the fascists have got, all them German aeroplanes and tanks and guns. It's a blooming stalemate, that's all it is.'

||

With Madrid seemingly secured, Claud Cockburn took a break from the capital to visit Albacete. Two or three hundred English-speaking volunteers had now assembled there, and – in the expectation of further arrivals – they were forming themselves into a Battalion.

Cockburn met Ralph Fox (one of the most important up-and-coming left-wing writers in Britain). He was to become the Brigade's Assistant-Commissar; and he also met Fox's old Oxford University friend, Tom Wintringham.

Keener to fight than to write, Wintringham had eventually quit his job in Barcelona for the excitement of the International Brigades. Unsure quite what to do with this enthusiastic English communist, Andre Marty had eventually appointed him the Brigades' chief machinegun. Though during the Great War Wintringham had been a despatch rider with the Royal Air Force, not an infantryman, Claud Cockburn did his best to build his colleague up in the pages of *The Daily Worker*, describing Wintringham as 'one of the best machine-gun experts' in Albacete, and explaining that he had been going through 'a stiff course' of training 'in order to familiarise himself perfectly with the different types of machine-guns which are to be used by the defending troops.'

Given only a few days to master five different types of weapon, Wintringham was spending ten days with each of the national camps, passing on what he had learnt. Just ten days to learn, he observed, what usually took a professional soldier a year or more. Nevertheless, he was loving the challenge. 'Think of me with my devil-guns,' he wrote to Kitty Bowler, who was still in Barcelona. 'There's a certain exact, free of frills sensible beauty about a good piece of engineering. I can get in a daze and thrill writing, sometimes, that is more exciting but much less satisfying than discovering the timing of an ejector or the way a barrel is released.'

And he was excited by everything else that was happening in Albacete. Almost all the men with posts of responsibility – the heads of departments and brigades, the political commissars, the controllers of transport, food, clothing – wore shaggy sheepskins to keep themselves warm. As they hurried down the narrow, muddy winter streets they seemed to Wintringham like wolves in sheep's clothing: 'And like wolves they raided, got things' – everything to make an army possible, from guns and boots to food. Though signs had begun to appear in the few shops of the little town and surrounding villages announcing that much of their stock had sold out, the locals accepted the foreign soldiers 'with good temper and Spanish courtesy and delay'.

And Wintringham was impressed by the officers and commissars of the International Brigades sitting around in Albacete's Gran Hotel, waiting to be fed, with their array of imposing boots and pistols, semi-military hats and caps, 'talking all the languages of Europe' whilst drinking coffee or vermouth or foul-tasting cognac:

> The Germans card-indexed each other and every one else, sitting at these café tables, and the French darted from table to table like agile fishes with new assignments of work, with exclamations of 'Formidable!' and 'Bougre!' and with plans, scandals, news from the front. And when the doors of the dining-room opened a tidal wave of leather-faced men jammed through them, racing for seats.

His enthusiasm extended to the British battalion – the first, he later wrote, 'put together by English speaking people – the first since Cromwell's day – to be part of a people's army. It's as important as the New Model Army.' But the British volunteers were, he realized, 'a mixed mob – ex-servicemen, hunger-marchers, political enthusiasts, and honest toughs and queer queer 'uns.' The youngest was only sixteen, the eldest fifty-six. Only one in three had any military experience, whilst about ten per cent were – as Wintringham told Harry Pollitt – 'drunks and flunkers'. All that they had needed to get out to Spain was a weekend passport for Paris, and the money for the journey. The CPGB had been willing to help most of them with both, and only a few of the more obviously unsuitable volunteers had been turned away in London.

'I can't understand why you've sent out such useless material,' Wintringham complained to Pollitt. 'We call them "Harry's anarchists".' And few would ever learn to speak the language. 'If you ask one of our boys how much Spanish he knows,' he told Kitty Bowler, 'he'll answer, "I know all anyone needs: Mañana, mañana, mañana. No hay, no sé, salud!"'

Far worse than the men were the weapons he was supposed to be showing them how to use. These, as he later admitted, were 'mostly a job lot of junk … hastily scraped together, from unreliable and extortionate sources all over Europe and America, by improvised purchasing committees that … did not always have the initiative (or the ready cash at hand) to close bargains quickly.' Still, he could not have been happier. 'I believe I can write war like no-one else,' he told Kitty; 'now I think I can fight it too, this time like anyone else. I'm blooming with uppishness at having vicious little guns to learn to handle.'

Also recently arrived in Albacete was Kenneth Sinclair-Loutit and the British Medical Unit. Fed up with inactivity, they had almost been tearing themselves apart with in-fighting and boredom on the Aragon front. Now Marty had accepted them into the International Brigades. But instead of placing their expertise and vehicles at the disposal of the nascent British Battalion, Marty attached them to the French soldiers of XIV Brigade. The British volunteers would soon be complaining that 'every bastard in Spain has our ambulances, bar us.'

As with the British Medical Unit, Wintringham's move to Albacete had been timely. He had not been a great success as CPGB co-ordinator in Barcelona, and was glad to have escaped its intrigues and responsibilities. Sylvia Townsend Warner and Valentine Ackland had complained to

Harry Pollitt that Wintringham had shown 'too little stability,' that he had been more interested in his journalism, and his new mistress, than the demands of the Party. Another CPGB member in Barcelona, the writer Ralph Bates, had likewise been critical of Wintringham's performance. Bates reported to Pollitt that it was 'not unjust to say that everyone here was very disappointed with Comrade Wintringham.' He was particularly critical that Wintringham had taken Kitty Bowler to the Aragon Front, where she had worked for a while as a nurse with the BMU.

By then, the CPGB had already had first-hand experience of Bowler. She had gone to England in November, in an attempt to find work writing for *The Manchester Guardian* and *The News Chronicle*. (As she told her mother, 'my line is "little girl wide-eyed in Spain".') Wintringham had sent with her a verbal message for Pollitt, emphasising once again that what they needed in the International Brigades was not more safely orthodox communists, but more ex-soldiers with military experience. However, as Kenneth Sinclair-Loutit realized, sending Bowler had been 'a tactical error'. In trying to look her best, the young American had made completely the wrong impression: 'Poor Kitty must have exemplified the very licentiousness of the class-enemy, the bourgeoisie,' he wrote afterwards. 'Tom had certainly chosen Kitty as courier because he knew that she would get there, through Hell or high-water, without fail. What he failed to see was that her appearance, and her frank drive, would serve to weaken the force of his dispatches.'

Wintringham's new mistress shocked his strait-laced comrades in London (one later claimed that the well-dressed American 'smelt like a whorehouse'). It was their impression that Tom 'had sent back a bourgeois tart,' a 'great talker,' and one possibly with dangerous Trotskyist leanings. 'The Party has punished members for far less serious examples of levity than this,' as Ralph Bates observed.

As Barcelona was a key staging post for the British volunteers coming out to Spain, it was Bates who now kept Pollitt informed of developments within the International Brigades. An NCO in the Great War, Bates had joined the trickle of British veterans who after 1918 had sought a new life abroad. Eventually he had settled in the Pyrenees with his wife, Winifred, burying himself in the working-class life of Spain: he harvested olives, studied the techniques of winemaking and cork gathering, even worked on the docks in Barcelona. He also wrote a number of books, including *The Olive Field*, which had been published to great success earlier in 1936. That December, Bates reiterated Wintringham's key point to Pollitt, that what they needed most was volunteers with military experience, 'and only a very small proportion of those without should be allowed.' These, he told Pollitt, need 'to be good, loyal and tried comrades, not odds and sods from Bloomsbury, of whom we have had a few, or the poor kind of student (not the best kind like Knox and Cornford). This is a matter of lives, with our short training too many inexperienced men may prove fatal.'

Bates added that the make-up of the so-called 'British' Battalion would be multinational: there were already Irish, Cypriots, Canadians, Australians and even Dutch. Someone at CPGB headquarters therefore suggested they name themselves after Shapurji Saklatvala, the Indian politician who in 1922 had become one of Britain's first Communist MPs, and who had died earlier in the year. It was also thought, perhaps, that his name might attract Indian volunteers, whilst at the same indicating that it was not some kind of imperial, colonial army. As Bates explained, 'we are men of all English-speaking nationalities fighting for the freedom and equality of all peoples.' Though officially known thereafter as the Saklatvala Battalion, the headed paper used for official correspondence carried the rather unwieldy title, 'The English-Speaking Battalion'. Mostly, however, it was known simply as the British Battalion, or – to the Spanish – *el Batallón Inglés*.

Following his visit to Albacete, Cockburn returned to Madrid. There, in the candlelight of their 'vast rest barracks,' he interviewed the twelve British veterans of the Commune de Paris Battalion. Alfred Brugère, their young French commander, told Cockburn that John Cornford, Bernard Knox, John Sommerfield and the other British volunteers had 'given nothing but the most absolute satisfaction. Alike on the front and in the rest camp their calm conduct is the best of the entire battalion. They have been praised for special valour by all the commanders of the company. How happy I should be if I could have a whole company made up of such men.'

'As we lay wrapped in blankets on the stone floor of their barracks,' Cockburn reported in *The Daily Worker*, 'they told me part of their story.' They related how they been rushed to Madrid, of the unfamiliar machineguns they had first received, and how – hungry and tired – they had spent the night stripping them down and reassembling them. Of how one of their number, Edward Burke, who till recently had been working at *The Daily Worker*, was now 'found to possess an extraordinary flair for machinery,' and how David Mackenzie, the medical student from Edinburgh, had quickly become a proficient Lewis gunner.

Cockburn asked Sommerfield and Cornford (whose head was still wrapped in bandages) about their experiences.

'Well, I don't know why they keep thinking we have done such great things,' the young men replied. 'Looking back, it does not seem as though we have done anything very special.'

Their French commandant interrupted. 'No,' he said, 'we have not done anything special – except help our Spanish comrades save Madrid.'

Brugère was right: saving Madrid had been a joint effort. Nevertheless, the myth quickly emerged that it was the International Brigades, almost alone, who had prevented the rebels from taking Madrid. Others, though, would claim that it was the Russians who had saved the capital. As Theo Rogers, the retired US Army officer who had witnessed the start of the war for America from his Barcelona hotel room, wrote the following year, some of his Spanish friends 'have assured me that on the Madrid front there are entire Regiments of Russians, officered by Russians, fighting for the Madrid government. This I am inclined to believe is absolutely true.'

The men of the International Brigades knew that none of these things were correct. 'Don't let us exaggerate,' Tom Wintringham told his British comrades that winter, 'our Brigade did not save Madrid. Madrid would have saved itself without us. But without us Franco would have got farther into Madrid … There street-fighting would have stopped him; but he would have had a foothold in the city. That he has not got; thanks to the fighting quality, the skill in action, the digging powers of our first International Brigade.'

The successful defence of Madrid was a dazzling signal of Spanish determination to resist Franco. It was also a sign of the determination and organizational skills of the communists, and they quickly saw an enormous growth in their prestige. Membership of the Party surged over the following months, and with the support of the Soviets they quickly became one of the most powerful political forces in Republican Spain. One of their first aims would be to replace the disorganized (and often revolutionary) militias with a well-trained, disciplined and professionally-led Popular Army.

III

In mid-December, Esmond Romilly and his British and German comrades in the Thälmann Battalion were sent to a country house appropriated from the Duke of Alba. Some twenty miles north of Madrid, they had the opportunity to recover from the recent fighting, and to receive further training.

One particular day would remain etched in Romilly's memory, when he took a long walk with Joe Gough through the grounds of the estate. Gough had now become Romilly's closest friend in Spain; 'Babs' Ovenden described him as like 'a favourite uncle' to the teenager. They followed little lanes down into the peaceful town of Aravaca, with the snow-capped peaks of the Guadarrama mountains towering beyond. For a moment they forget the war. This moment of peace did not last long.

With his forces checked in the western sector, Franco launched a new offensive to try and cut the main road linking Madrid with the north-west of Spain. Immediately the Thälmann and Commune de Paris Battalions had their leave cancelled. They were rushed to the isolated village of Boadilla del Monte, a dozen miles west of Madrid and the spearhead of the new Rebel attack.

The French Battalion arrived first. John Cornford's unit spent the night in the ruins of the village church. They now had a Lewis gun and a water-cooled Maxim, mounted on a heavy steel carriage and with a metal shield to cover the gunner. Cornford manned one gun, and Jock Cunningham the other. In thin rain the following morning they set up their weapons in defensive positions in front of Boadilla, and spent the day watching as Republican militiamen counter-attacked up the hills, only to be driven back down again in the afternoon.

The following morning Cornford's isolated little section was still defending the road into Boadilla. Over the course of the day, as the Republican units in front of them retreated, they fired at close range as their attackers attempted to outflank them. Two of their men were killed, and then the Maxim gun badly jammed. Nevertheless, it was obviously their job, as Bernard Knox realized,

> to cover the retreat and not a man murmured when John announced that we were to hold on. Meanwhile the aeroplanes came over and added to the confusion. We were getting at last to the stage where we could cease worrying and laugh. We sighted four Fascist tanks coming up the road towards us, and just at that moment big shells began to fall on the village just behind us. The sight of this concentrated destruction being hurled on twelve men and one Lewis-gun was too much for me. I turned to John and we burst out laughing.

By this time the Thälmann and Edgar André Battalions had arrived in support. Romilly and Birch were sent forward into Boadilla, dodging as best they could the attacking aircraft and exploding shells. A red flag flew from the church, its door and windows shielding more Republican machine-gunners behind hastily erected barricades. A Spanish captain told them about the rear-guard action they had fought the previous night, and that their losses had been terrible. Everything appeared to be in a state of complete confusion. Eventually they found the commander of the Commune de Paris Battalion. He told them where the Thälmann should dig in.

It was clear the position defended by Cornford's unit had become untenable. Knox dashed back to Boadilla for permission to retreat. He found his French comrades preparing to evacuate.

'*Bordel de Dieu!*' their officer exclaimed. 'Are you still out there? Tell Cornford to retire on the village.'

They were dragging their Maxim back to Boadilla when Knox was hit. He fell to the ground, blood spurting like a fountain from a gun-shot wound in his neck.

David Mackenzie examined him. A bullet had passed right through Knox's neck and shoulder, grazing his carotid artery.

Mackenzie had spent barely a year as a medical student at Oxford University. 'I can't do anything about that,' he told Cornford.

John bent down over his friend. 'Good luck, and God bless you, Bernard,' he said.

There was nothing they could do: they had to cover the withdrawal of the other gun crew. They left Knox to bleed to death where he had fallen.

With the Republican line breaking, the Thälmann Battalion was ordered to counter-attack. As company runner, Romilly had to carry messages between the units. Scouting out the enemy positions, he was surprised when everything suddenly turned 'curiously peaceful … I might have been going for a walk in the woods in England,' he later recalled. 'I had time to realise how lovely the country was – and ten minutes before I had had to lie behind a tree with someone pouring lead in my direction … Like so many actions in this war, this one was evidently taking place on a very small front – probably the only objective of the rebels' attack was Boadilla.'

By then, Cornford's machinegun section had fallen back on a defensive position at the edge of a small wood. They were astonished when Bernard Knox rejoined them.

Knox had no idea how long he had lain unconscious in the road outside Boadilla. When he had come round, blood was no longer spouting from his neck. Too weak to dodge the bullets, he had somehow staggered back to his lines without being seen. All the way he had passed other wounded soldiers, unable to walk, 'hoping that one of the company's four stretcher teams would find them, and ready to shoot themselves if the Fascists came first.'

Over the coming years, Knox would read many accounts written by people who, like him, slipping into unconsciousness,

> were sure they were dying but survived. Many of them speak of a feeling of heavenly peace, others of visions of angels welcoming them to Heaven. I had no such feelings or visions; I was consumed with rage – furious, violent rage. Why me? I was just twenty-one and had barely begun living my life. Why should I have to die? It was unjust. And, as I felt my whole being sliding into nothingness, I cursed. I cursed God and the world and everyone in it as the darkness fell.

Towards evening a munitions lorry took Knox to a dressing-station; then he was driven by car to a hospital in Madrid. For Knox and the remaining men of the Commune de Paris Battalion, this battle was over.

IV

Though Boadilla had been lost, a defensive line formed just beyond the village. There, among the ilex trees, and for the first and last time in Spain, Romilly and Cornford met. For Romilly, meeting his old colleague from the war against English public schools was 'the most important incident' in the battle. He was deeply impressed by Cornford, and his whole-hearted commitment to communism.

Whilst Cornford and the hammered remnants of the Commune de Paris were withdrawn from action, the Thälmann Battalion was ordered to dig in. With the Edgar André Battalion and a column of anarchist militia units, they waited for the next rebel attack.

For three days a fog hung over Boadilla, preventing any action. Romilly and his companions, thinly spread out amongst the trees, spent the time digging a series of shallow defences. Hidden beyond a ridge, the enemy was only half a mile away. There was food, wine and cognac, and as they waited, Tich talked about the restaurant he and Ovenden had been running in Dover. They agreed that when they got back from Spain they would start another business, this time in London, with Birch and Raymond Cox as their partners. But Romilly was apprehensive about what lay ahead. It seemed a miracle that none of them had been killed, and their luck could surely not continue. 'Being here is ridiculous,' he told Ovenden. 'Sooner or later we're all going to be killed.'

On the morning of the third day, 20 December, their medical officer appeared: it was Randolph Sollenberger, the American doctor who had been with the British Medical Unit, but who had transferred to the Thälmann Battalion. Romilly was suffering from neuralgia, and Sollenberger gave him aspirin for the pain in his head. He swigged down the pills with brandy.

Then they started to come under irregular fire. Panicking anarchist militiamen fell back into the Thälmann's dugouts. The International Brigaders received orders to move forward, and a patrol disappeared over the ridge into the ilex trees below, never to be seen again. The anarchists began to fall further back. What was supposed to be an advance started looking to Romilly more like 'a disorganised retreat'. Disorder unfolded: following orders, Romilly's section moved forward, but the rest of their company (apparently having received new orders) remained in their trenches.

Romilly had no idea where they were supposed to be going, or what was happening. In a little group of their own, the British were dangerously exposed on the lightly wooded slope. Rebel bullets started raining in from the ridge in front of them that the anarchists had recently abandoned.

Arnold Jeans was hit in the head. Caught in a cross-fire, they ducked as a 'hurricane of lead' flew over them.

Flattened on the ground, Romilly turned to say something to Joe

Gough. His friend was kneeling on the grass, his gun pointing downwards, his head sunk forward on his chest. He was close enough for Romilly to touch: 'I felt I was in the presence of something horrifying,' Romilly later wrote. 'I didn't think about where we were, or the bullets – I didn't think about Joe being dead – I just thought it was all wrong Joe's head being like that.'

Nearby Tich and Birch were arguing about Jeans.

'He's finished,' one of them said.

Despite what was happening, Romilly felt oddly calm. 'All right, Joe's killed,' he kept telling himself, 'that's finished, absolutely settled, that's all right, Joe's killed, that's the end of that.' He kept repeating the words till they screamed in his head. Everything up to that moment would remain clear in his memory. After that, all was disorder.

'Get back, all of you,' Tich was shouting, 'quick as you can.' Then Raymond Cox, firing his rifle from in front of a tree, collapsed.

Rebel tanks had joined the attack. A group of forty British, Germans and Spaniards retreated through the woods. It was a shambles: there were no officers, no one in command. They would get up and run fifty or sixty yards, before dropping back behind another ridge.

A German from the Edgar André Battalion appeared. He cursed everyone for running away. They saw a group of anarchists, led by two young women, also retreating. Ovenden knew that if they weren't all to be killed, they had to make a stand. He shouted at the Spaniards to stop, striking one of the women down when she refused.

'When the enemy comes fire a magazine and retreat,' Ovenden ordered.

Even Randolph Sollenberger, the medical officer, found a rifle and joined the fight. Romilly was almost crying; this, he thought, was surely the end. 'We were firing all the time,' he later recalled. 'I copied the others and fired in the same direction till the barrel was red-hot. And always, starting every few minutes, there was the deadly crossfire.'

Their commanding officer, General Walter, arrived on a Republican tank. Ovenden told him there was no one in command.

'You're in command,' he responded.

The fighting retreat lasted hours. By nightfall another defensive position was established. This new line held, and the mad rush was over. But many of their number, including Tich and Lorimer Birch, were missing.

Just before midnight their German company commander took a roll call. After calling each name from his list he paused for a response, waiting for an answer until the suspense was unbearable: Harry Addley, Sidney Avener, Lorimer Birch, Raymond Cox, Joe Gough, Arnold Jeans, Martin Messer. None of them replied.

'We knew they were killed, but yet we did not believe it,' Romilly wrote. 'It was as if this was their last chance to plead before the final death sentence of the word written against their names.' By each name their officer wrote '*gefallen*'. Of the ten men who had been with the British section that morning, only three remained. By some miracle Romilly – the youngest, the most inexperienced – was among them.

For a further three days the fighting around Boadilla continued. By the time the rebels were pushed back, the woods and grassy slopes were littered with corpses, abandoned rifles and ammunition. Again their attack had failed, and Madrid was still safe.

After Boadilla, the French Battalion returned to Albacete. 'In the battles of the future,' their commanding officer told them, 'if we know that there are Englishmen on our left flank, or Englishmen on our right, then we shall know that we need give no thought nor worry to those positions.'

Romilly and Ovenden – as well as John Sommerfield and David Mackenzie – now called it a day. They would not be joining John Cornford and the handful of surviving English-speaking volunteers from the Commune de Paris and Thälmann Battalions who were now transferring to the British Battalion. Instead, they chose to go home. Within a few days Romilly and Ovenden would be happily posing together for a photograph in the London offices of *The Daily Worker*.

Shortly after returning to London Romilly met his old friend Philip Toynbee. Toynbee was also just back from Spain (which he had visited as part of an international delegation of communist students), and he had found the revolutionary atmosphere there 'intoxicating'. He later recorded that, although Romilly 'was serious, quiet and reasonable,' he was 'not in the least embittered' by his recent experiences. Certainly Romilly told him of the 'awful disorganisation in the International Column, of disgruntlement, harsh mutual criticism, disgraceful retreats, cold, uncongenial company and the rapid fading of romance.' And he told him 'of the terror of being machine-gunned from the air, and how the shells and bombs sickened one with long-accumulated fear.' But he also told him 'of his admiration for the communists who alone, he said, had been responsible for saving Madrid,' and he 'never suggested that the war should not be fought simply because there was drab and ugly side to fighting it.'

When Toynbee asked Romilly whether he now considered himself a communist, Romilly replied 'that he was afraid he would have to say yes. It was an unwilling admission because he also believed that the authoritarian commonsense of the communists would destroy the beauty and natural anarchism of the Spanish character.'

Romilly's intention was to return to Spain as soon as possible, as there was still 'work to be done,' though not, this time, with a rifle. He planned to go back as a journalist, covering the war in the Basque country of northern Spain. These plans were temporarily stymied, however, when he suddenly fell ill. After ten days in a London hospital, cared for by his doting mother, he went to recover at a cousin's country retreat.

There he met another relative: his nineteen-year-old second cousin, Jessica Mitford. Decca, as she was known, was one of the six Mitford sisters, whose eccentric, upper-class upbringing would be fictionalized in Nancy Mitford's 1949 novel, *Love in a Cold Climate*. Unlike Decca, who read *The Daily Worker* and called herself a communist, her sisters Diana and Unity were fascists. Only the previous December, in the Berlin drawing room of the Nazi propaganda minister, Joseph Goebbels, Diana Mitford had married Sir Oswald Ernald Mosley, leader of the British Union of Fascists. Hitler's wedding present to the couple had been a signed photograph in a silver frame.

Now Decca asked Romilly if she could go back to Spain with him. He said yes; and within weeks, the teenagers had eloped. Bizarrely, Romilly would soon find himself the brother-in-law of the public face of fascism in Britain. On the eve of their departure for Paris, Keith Scott Watson – back home from Spain and now working on a memoir of his recent experiences – treated them to champagne and foie gras at a London restaurant.

'Esmond has got a very good job as a journalist so I expect we will be in Spain and will have a mass of dough,' Decca had written to her mother. 'Do remember that I *won't* be in any danger and it will be terrific fun. You will honestly *adore* Esmond when you know him so please don't be put off by all the secrecy, the only reason for it was because I wanted to go to Spain with him and thought you might try and stop me.'

Romilly's attempt to cover the war in northern Spain would prove short-lived, however. *The Daily Express* was soon carrying the headline 'Peer's Daughter Elopes to Spain.' The British Consulate in Bilbao received a telegram from no less a person than the Foreign Secretary, Anthony Eden. 'FIND JESSICA MITFORD AND PERSUADE HER TO RETURN,' he instructed. Romilly telegrammed back: 'HAVE FOUND JESSICA MITFORD. IMPOSSIBLE TO PERSUADE HER TO RETURN.'

Eventually, when Romilly realized that he was in danger of embarrassing the Basque government, the couple agreed to return to France on board a Royal Navy destroyer. They then set up temporary home in Bayonne, where – already expecting a baby – they married. Rather than 'a mass of dough' they had the £50 advance that Romilly had received for his account of his war service, plus whatever money he could make from the occasional article he wrote for the British press on events in Spain. Decca would later recall watching her young husband 'as he worked furiously' on his book, 'brown head bent over the typewriter, papers scattered all over the floor, wondering how much he minded being separated from the struggle in Spain.'

In the final paragraph of his memoir, Romilly reflected on the seven friends who had died fighting alongside him in the International Brigades, and to whom *Boadilla* was dedicated:

> There is something frightening, something shocking about the way the world does not stop because those men are dead. Over all this war there is that feeling … I am not a pacifist, though I wish it were possible to lead one's life without the intrusion of this ugly monster of force and killing – war – and its preparation. And it is not with the happiness of the convinced communist, but reluctantly that I realise that there will never be peace or any of the things I like and want, until that mixture of profit-seeking, self-interest, cheap emotion and organised brutality which is called fascism has been fought and destroyed for ever.

VI

As Romilly was resuming his pre-war life in England, Bernard Knox was still recovering in a hospital in Madrid. When the doctor came on his rounds, he pointed out to his students the two wounds in Knox's neck, saying: 'Tell me all the things the bullet missed that would have killed this man.'

It hardly required a professional to tell Knox that he was lucky to be alive. Following the exhilaration of having survived, however, he fell into what he later called a 'frightful state of depression'. When John Cornford visited, he found Knox nearly crying at the thought of not being able to shoulder a gun again. 'Never mind, Bernard,' Cornford joked, 'we'll make you an officer, and you can carry a little revolver on condition you never fire it.' The company's machinegun officer also visited, telling Knox that, 'in the desperate defence that followed the evacuation of Boadilla del Monte, John's crew had set an example of discipline, tenacity and courage that went far towards saving the day.'

Having transferred with Jock Cunningham to the British Battalion, and with Christmas now fast approaching, Cornford found himself some twenty miles from Albacete, in what one volunteer described as 'a wretched little village called Madrigueras.' The Battalion's new headquarters shocked even those men used to the deprived state of Depression-era Britain: there were no pavements, and just a dirt track down the middle of the street. The locals were desperately poor, and there was little to buy other than the cheap wine sold in the village bar. It was bitterly cold, and though it did not snow, in the mornings puddles would be frozen over. The men burnt whatever they could find to keep themselves warm.

Though clearly exhausted, Cornford had no wish to rest, or to be held back from further active service in order to help train the new arrivals. Tom Wintringham found him 'looking bored and lonely. The life of the front was real to him, but waiting and training seemed unreal.' He invited the young man to dinner at Brigade headquarters in Albacete, but Cornford politely declined, preferring to share the privations of his comrades in Madrigueras.

He soon had his chance to get back to the fighting. Within a few days of his arrival at Madrigueras, some of the more experienced volunteers in the International Brigades were called back into action, this time to join a Republican attack on the rebels' southern flank, in the hope of retaking Cordova and relieving the pressure on Madrid. One hundred and fifty English-speaking volunteers were asked to form a company in a new French battalion that would form part of the hastily assembled XIV International Brigade.[1] They included around fifty of the eighty or so Irishmen who had recently arrived in Spain under the leadership of Frank

---

1 It would later be observed that one of XIV Brigade's Battalions 'was gathered, staffed, and armed in one day,' with sub-units 'that contained dozens of nationalities'.

Senior figures of the English-speaking Battalion, Madrid, winter 1936/7. From left to right: Wilfred Macartney, Dave Springhall, Peter Kerrigan, Tom Wintringham and Frank Ryan (IWM)

Ryan, a young officer in the Irish Republican Army. Responding to some of his men who did not like the idea of joining a 'British' Battalion, Ryan had told them that 'Irish, English, Scots and Welsh comrades will fight side by side against the common enemy – fascism.' In the International Brigades, he explained, 'there are no national differences. We are all comrades ... [we are] soldiers of liberty.' And since Ryan and most of his men were Roman Catholics, there was a strong incentive for them to show a united front: the rebels claimed that they were leading a 'Crusade' against atheist 'Reds' in Spain, and the Pope had given them his backing. One of Ryan's former colleagues in the IRA, Eoin O'Duffy, had even recruited a battalion of volunteers to fight for Franco. If there was a reason to stress their Irishness, Frank Ryan told his men, it was 'to show the world that the majority of the Irish people repudiate fascist O'Duffy and his mercenaries.'

Though still only twenty years old, Cornford was now a seasoned veteran, and he chose to join this British and Irish company in the new offensive. Another volunteer was Ralph Fox, and Tom Wintringham described his old university friend departing for action 'like a schoolboy released for vacation'. The man leading them was an ex-British Army officer named George Nathan. Although 'rather gaunt' and 'long-nosed,' Wintringham saw that Nathan carried himself well and he 'looked a soldier; but his mixture of military and civilian clothes, his sweater and cheap shoes, made him also look like a hard-luck story from a queue of unemployed … His accent was sometimes too gentlemanly to be real. He swanked – yes, there was a pile of peculiarities about George Nathan.'

A working-class Jew from the East End of London, Nathan was hardly a stereotypical British Army officer. In 1916 he had volunteered for the élite Brigade of Guards, and having dropped his Shoreditch accent he rose through the ranks to become an NCO and then – remaining with the Brigade after the Great War – a Colour Sergeant Major. It was the General Strike of 1926, however, that made him realize where his true loyalties lay. When the Guards were sent to support strike-breakers in the London Docks, Nathan's men were issued with rounds of live ammunition. When Nathan questioned the appropriateness of armed British soldiers confronting their fellow-citizens, a senior officer told him: 'Well, none of us will have any compunction in putting this dock-land scum in its place. If we have to fire, we cannot have any shilly-shallying in front of the men.'

As Kenneth Sinclair-Loutit would record, 'in a flash' Nathan realized 'that for years he had been deceiving himself; not only was he no longer a member of that family of "brother officers", but most probably, and this was a bitter realisation, he had never been "one of us" … The next day he was put on an infantry training course at some place in the country; as soon as he arrived there he resigned his commission.'

Over the ensuing decade Nathan had worked in a string of jobs, from a butcher to department-store doorman. It was even rumoured that he served with the notorious Black and Tans in Ireland. By the time he arrived in Spain in 1936 he was clearly down-at-heel, but soon transformed himself back into a British Army officer, carrying a swagger stick whose brass tip shone so brightly it was said to be made of gold.

In time he would acquire an equally well-presented – and handsome – batman (another rumour, probably correct, was that Nathan was homosexual). As Sinclair-Loutit observed, Nathan 'found his place in the International Brigade. Everything that he had ever learnt in his old life took on a new meaningfulness so, as an officer, he shone with a rare brilliance.'

Nathan, Cornford, Fox and the rest of the volunteers in XIV International Brigade left Albacete on Christmas Eve. The French Battalion commander, Major Delasalle, was a veteran of the Great War, but he seemed to have little clue of the challenges facing his men. It seemed that he was never to be found where the fighting was, and when enemy planes attacked his headquarters he fell back even further. Repeatedly he ordered the British Company to take the village of Lopera. Over the course of three days George Nathan did his best, but the support Delasalle repeatedly promised never materialised. British casualties were heavy: around fifty per cent, Tom Wintringham reckoned. The whole offensive was a failure.

Within a few days of this debacle, the International Brigades' commandant, André Marty, ordered Major Delasalle's arrest. He was courtmartialled for cowardice, with the additional charge that he was a rebel spy. 'It was a very fair court martial,' according to Wintringham, 'deliberate and meticulous. It gave LaSalle a hearing.'

The Frenchman was found guilty. Though he protested his innocence, sentence was passed immediately. A comrade stepped up and shot him in the head.

This episode disgusted some of the British volunteers; one would later call Marty 'a bloody madman'. It would later be claimed that over the course of the war the Brigades' commandant was responsible for the execution of some five hundred volunteers. But Delasalle's inadequacies had cost the British some of their best men, including Ralph Fox – and also John Cornford.

Such was the confusion at Lopera that it was never established exactly how – or even when – Cornford died. He was killed on either 27

December 1936 – his twenty-first birthday – or the day after. The first news that eventually reached his friend Michael Straight in Cambridge was that Cornford's own sentries had shot him whilst he was returning from a night patrol. Other accounts stated that he had been killed trying to retrieve Ralph Fox's body (who had himself been killed during a forward reconnaissance). Others reported that a rebel sniper had shot him, Cornford's bandaged head making him a clear target on the ridge above Lopera. When Bernard Knox overheard from some wounded volunteers that a machinegun had killed his friend, 'I didn't want to hear any more. John had always been so gloriously alive, so smiling and confident, that I for one, had come to look on him as immortal.'

Tom Wintringham would later write that Cornford's 'burning anger against Fascism' was part of the 'armour' that his comrades carried with them after his death. Back home in Edinburgh, young David Mackenzie would tell the press that Cornford was 'the finest of all the fine characters I met in Spain … He felt the losses and the horror of the war more deeply than any of us, yet he was the most cheering influence in the group.' Though Mackenzie acknowledged that there would be some who would say 'that the loss of such talent is a waste,' Cornford's 'influence in the International Column was such that its results would achieve more for the working-class of the world than any single man could in a lifetime. His death has made that inspiration unforgettable.'

A fund was soon established in Cambridge in memory of Cornford and Griffith Maclaurin, the New Zealander who had been killed during the fighting in Madrid. The money raised would support dependants of dead and injured British volunteers of the International Brigade, as well as the British Medical Units. 'Cornford and Maclaurin were willing to pay a heavy price to secure the defeat of Franco and his allies,' a pamphlet announcing the Fund explained, 'because they knew that in fighting against fascism they were fighting for the future of peace, democracy, and a better life for all the peoples of the world.'

'We are the future,' Cornford had concluded in one of his last poems. Yet many of his Cambridge friends saw his sacrifice as having been, ultimately, futile. In a memorial volume published the following year one recalled listening to Cornford 'talking one night of the futility of conventional existence, and saying, "*I* am learning to live by *living*." What he learned was to die.'

When the young poet Stephen Spender came to review that same memorial volume, however, he was more optimistic. He visited Spain in 1937, and on the invitation of Harry Pollitt had briefly joined the Communist Party. 'This book inspires me,' he would write in 1938,

> and fills me with shame … Cornford's life speaks for itself in a way that burns the imagination … If civilization is to be saved from barbarism it will be by people who have transformed it into a way of life which they are willing to defend with their lives. The alternative is for it to be surrendered to the barbarians by commercial cynics who do not think it worth saving.

The fact that Cornford lived and that others like him still live, is an important lesson to the leaders of democracies. It shows that people will live and die and fight for democracy if it gives them the justice and freedom which are worth fighting for.

Chapter 7

Looking for Trouble

|

Ａmerican volunteers had been arriving in Spain in small numbers since the start of the war. Ernest Hemingway had bankrolled at least two of them. As he told his literary editor, Maxwell Perkins, on 15 December 1936:

> I've *got* to get to Spain. But there's no great hurry. They'll be fighting for a long time and it's cold as hell around Madrid now! I've paid two guys over there to fight (transportation and cash to Spanish Border) already. If I could send seven more could probably be a corporal … Franco is a good general but a son of a bitch of the first magnitude and he lost his chance to take Madrid for nothing by being over cautious.

With Madrid still in the hands of the Republic, Hemingway rightly saw a longer war ahead. He continued work on his new novel. Only when a complete draft of *To Have and to Have Not* was finished would he consider going to Spain.

Most of the Americans who were already in Spain had been in Europe when the Civil War broke out. With much further to travel, those in the States who wanted to get involved in the action would inevitably take longer to arrive. The American Communist Party (CPUSA) did not start its recruitment drive for volunteers to join the International Brigades until early November, and with Manhattan as the assembly point, most of the first recruits came from New York, Boston and Philadelphia. Eventually more would arrive from as far afield as California and Texas, often making the long journey by railroad or Greyhound bus. None would reach Spain until early in January 1937.

But Spain was within easy reach of London, and on almost the same day that John Cornford died, another left-wing English writer arrived in Barcelona. Like John Cornford, his initial intention was to gather material for some newspaper articles, though he also had what he called 'some vague idea of fighting if it seemed worthwhile'.

Eric Blair, as he would be known to everyone he met in Spain, was thirty-three years old. Born in India to an English civil servant and his Anglo-French wife, he was already the author of a number of books, all of them published under his *nom de plume*, George Orwell. He would become the most famous British participant in the Civil War, Hemingway's English equivalent. Though superficially quite different characters – the brash and reckless American versus the levelheaded Englishman – the two writers had a surprising amount in common: both resented authority, and both had spent a stint of their twenties living in Paris; both fancied themselves with firearms, females and fishing rods (and both sported unfashionable moustaches). Like Hemingway, Orwell based his novels on personal experience, blending fact with fiction to create stories that dwelled on the individual; like Hemingway, he was (in a quieter, subtler way) a lustful, ambitious, egotistical, highly intelligent self-fashioner, a teller of plausible-sounding stories who had forsaken the opportunity of a university education for an adventurous life overseas. (Stephen Spender would call Orwell a 'phoney,' likening him to 'a character in a Charlie Chaplin movie, if not like Charlie Chaplin himself. He was a person who was always playing a role, but with great pathos and great sincerity.')

Again like Hemingway, Orwell used his novelist's skills to write idiosyncratic works of non-fiction. His first book, *Down and Out in Paris and London*, described the indigent life he had lived on returning to Europe after six years' service with the Indian Imperial Police, an experience that also inspired his first novel, *Burmese Days* (which was published first in the US for fear the individuals upon whom it was based might sue for libel). Two more novels followed in 1935 and 1936: *A Clergyman's Daughter* and *Keep the Aspidistra Flying* were both founded on personal experiences, and in style and subject matter were a world away from what Orwell considered the violent, 'would-be tough American school' of writing that he saw Ernest Hemingway as epitomizing.

Unlike Hemingway, and despite their promising critical reception, none of Orwell's early books had been especially successful. Unable to support himself by writing alone, after leaving the Imperial Police and his months of poverty in Paris, he had worked first as a prep school teacher, then as an assistant in a second-hand bookshop. Most recently, he had married and taken over with his wife, Eileen, a run-down grocery store in a small Hertfordshire village.

Orwell's departure for Spain had also been delayed by the need to complete his latest book. Chosen by the publisher Victor Gollancz's Left Book Club for a print run of over forty thousand copies, *The Road to Wigan Pier* would prove far more successful and controversial than anything Orwell had previously written. The first part of the book was an account of working-class life in England's depressed industrial north, the slums and slag heaps, the mill-girls and miners; the second part charted Orwell's personal journey to socialism. It concluded with the suggestion that Britain faced two alternative futures: either socialism, or fascism (albeit, he wrote, 'probably a slimy Anglicized form of Fascism, with cultured policemen instead of Nazi gorillas and the lion and the unicorn instead of the swastika'). Given Orwell's increasing concern with politics, as well as his life-long desire to visit Spain, Barcelona was a logical progression from Lancashire. Already, what he called the growing 'international prestige of Fascism' was haunting him 'like a nightmare'.

'Since 1930 the Fascists had won all the victories,' he later wrote; 'it was time they got a beating, it hardly mattered from whom. If we could drive Franco and his foreign mercenaries into the sea it might make an immense improvement in the world situation.' It would also give him the chance to prove himself. Though only four years younger than Hemingway, he had not been old enough to serve in the Great War of 1914–18. 'You felt yourself a little less than a man,' he noted, 'because you had missed it.'

Yet Orwell's decision to go to Spain surprised his friend Richard Rees, editor of the literary quarterly *The Adelphi*. Till then, Rees had never thought that this seemingly ordinary, everyday and rather 'old-fashioned' writer was 'the sort of person who would do anything so dramatic'. He was impressed, and for the first time realized what an extraordinary individual George Orwell actually was.

In London just before Christmas 1936, Orwell sought Harry Pollitt's advice on how to join the International Brigades. Orwell had moved on the fringes of the Communist Party ever since his time in Paris, and local Lancashire communists had assisted him while he was researching his recent book in Wigan, associations that had been sufficient to attract the attention of MI5. As a confidential Special Branch report written that March had noted that in Paris Orwell had taken 'an interest in the activities of the French Communist Party … Information is not available to shew whether he was an active supporter of the revolutionary movement in France, but it is known that whilst there, he offered his services to the "Workers' Life", the forerunner of the "Daily Worker", as Paris correspondent.'

The CPGB's director, however, was as suspicious of Orwell as the secret service: prior to his six years as a policeman in British-occupied Burma, Orwell had been at Eton, the bastion and symbol of English class privilege; and though his family was hardly rich, his ancestry was wealthy and aristocratic: his great-grandfather had owned a slave plantation in Jamaica, whilst his great-great-grandfather had been the Earl of Westmorland. It was hardly the thing to endear him to a working-class communist like Pollitt. Furthermore, in *The Road to Wigan Pier* Orwell wrote disparagingly of English socialism's 'stupid cult of Russia,' in which Stalin could do no wrong.

Pollitt was not impressed by Orwell's penchant for 'roughing it' with down-and-outs and the working class and then writing about his experiences afterwards. Following the publication of *Wigan Pier*, he would describe Orwell in *The Daily Worker* as 'a late imperialist policeman ... a disillusioned little middle-class boy,' a snob obsessed with the idea that the working class 'smell,' publishing books on a 'subject that he does not understand'. To Orwell, this was narrow-minded nonsense. 'The young Communist who died heroically in the International Brigade was public school to the core,' Orwell would write of John Cornford. 'He had changed his allegiance but not his emotions.' It was quite possible for 'one kind of loyalty to transmute itself into another,' for an Old Etonian to recognise the need for an English revolution that might see London's gutters running with blood, whilst continuing at the same time to love the country that had made him; or for an imperial policeman to realize that he was a tool of oppression.

But Pollitt saw things differently. He refused to help, and even tried to frighten Orwell out of going to Spain altogether 'by talking a lot about Anarchist terrorism'. Not to be thwarted, Orwell obtained a letter of introduction to John McNair, the Independent Labour Party's representative in Barcelona. Founded in 1893, the ILP had been a precursor of the Labour Party; by 1936, however, it was in decline, with only four MPs and a membership of about 4,000. Like its Spanish sister organization the POUM, it was pro-revolutionary and anti-Stalinist. This fact would be key to Orwell's future.

Having pawned the family silver to raise the cash for his journey, Orwell set off for Spain on 23 December, leaving behind his new wife and their dilapidated shop. In Paris, before catching the train to Spain, he called on Henry Miller. He had admired Miller's controversial (and sexually explicit) 1934 novel *Tropic of Cancer* – 'It is as though you could hear a voice speaking to you, a friendly American voice, with no humbug in it, no moral purpose'. Banned in Britain and America, the book would later be seen as one of the defining literary works of the age, and the two writers had corresponded. But Miller told Orwell that going to Spain out of some sense of obligation or guilt was 'sheer stupidity,' and that the Englishman's ideas 'about combating Fascism, defending democracy, etc., etc., were all baloney.'

It must have been disappointing for Orwell to hear this from a man who had written in *Tropic of Cancer*, 'Only the killers seem to be extracting from life some satisfactory measure of what they are putting into it. The age demands violence, but we are getting only abortive explosions. Revolutions are nipped in the bud, or else succeed too quickly.' He felt that the American's apparent acceptance of the status quo might be fair enough in 'an epoch of expansion and liberty,' but not in one of 'fear tyranny, and regimentation. To say "I accept" in an age like our own is to say that you accept concentration camps, rubber truncheons, Hitler, Stalin, bombs, aeroplanes, tinned food, machine guns, putsches, purges, slogans, Bedaux belts, gas masks, submarines, spies, provocateurs, press censorship, secret prisons, aspirins, Hollywood films, and political murders.' One could not sit by and watch, he told Miller: the age demanded action. Miller responded by giving the impoverished Englishman a jacket to take with him to Spain.

Convinced he was doing the right thing, Orwell headed south. The train was 'packed with Czechs, Germans, Frenchmen, all bound on the same mission,' and his third-class carriage was 'full of very young, fair-haired, underfed Germans in suits of incredible shoddiness … who rushed out at every stopping-place to buy bottles of cheap wine and later fell asleep in a sort of pyramid on the floor of the carriage.' Half way through its journey most other passengers had disembarked, and 'the train was practically a troop train,' Orwell wrote, 'and the countryside knew it. In the morning, as we crawled across southern France, every peasant working in the fields turned round, stood solemnly upright and gave the anti-Fascist salute. They were like a guard of honour, greeting the train mile after mile.'

As the train approached Spain a Frenchman advised him to remove his collar and tie, bourgeois symbols that would be unwelcome in Catalonia. Arriving in Barcelona on Boxing Day he went in search of John McNair at the Executive Building of the POUM, the small revolutionary Marxist organization with which the Independent Labour Party was affiliated, and with whose militia Cornford had briefly served. The first English-speaking person Orwell met was Charles Orr, the young American economist who had arrived in Barcelona with his teenage wife, Lois, back in September. McNair was Orr's boss, and since McNair was away from the office the morning Orwell arrived, it was Orr who met the 'tall, lanky and tired' new arrival. As he would later recall, at first Orr had not taken Orwell very seriously. 'Just one more foreigner come to help,' he thought to himself, 'but not a party man, apparently a political innocent, blundering into a milieu which placed a premium on political acumen and partisan pedigree. Lucky, I thought, that we could lay hold on him before he fell into communist hands.' As both men had lived in Paris, they found they had plenty to talk about.

When McNair met Orwell a few hours later, he too was initially suspicious. A Tynesider who had left school aged twelve, McNair was initially put off by what he called Orwell's 'distinctly bourgeois accent'. But when he realized that he had read and 'greatly admired' two of Orwell's books, he was more helpful.

'I have come to Spain to join the militia to fight against Fascism,' Orwell told him, adding that he wanted 'to write about the situation and endeavour to stir working-class opinion in Britain and France.'

At first McNair suggested that Orwell base himself in his office, and advised him to visit Madrid, Valencia and the Aragon front, 'and then get down to writing a book'. But – like John Cornford before him – Orwell had already been swept up in the revolutionary atmosphere of Barcelona: the large buildings draped with coloured flags; the churches slowly being demolished by teams of workers; the loudspeakers in Las Ramblas 'bellowing revolutionary songs all day and far into the night'; the waiters and shop assistants who 'looked you in the face and treated you as an equal'; the revolutionary posters 'flaming from the walls in clean reds and blues that made the few remaining advertisements look like daubs of mud'; the people in the streets dressed in 'rough working-class clothes, or blue overalls, or some variant of the militia uniform'.

Despite the long queues for food, the half-empty shops, and the gaunt, untidy look to the city, Orwell had recognized almost immediately that this was 'a state of affairs worth fighting for'. And one glimpse of the Spanish troops was enough to tell him that his military experience – limited though it was to Eton College's Officers' Training Corps – was more than most.

So McNair took Orwell to the Lenin Barracks, a splendid former cavalry quarters that had been converted into the POUM's garrison. There, around a thousand militiamen and women were slowly being taught drill and issued with rudimentary uniforms.

The POUM militia (including George Orwell, left, towards the rear) on parade at the Lenin Barracks, Barcelona, December 1936 (UCL)

Though he could speak no Spanish and suffered from recurrent bronchial problems, Orwell enlisted. Giving his profession as 'grocer,' his stated intention was 'to fight against Fascism' in the name of what he called 'common decency'. As he later admitted, he had naively accepted the left-wing press's simplistic interpretation of the Civil War 'as the defence of civilization against a maniacal outbreak by an army of Colonel Blimps in the pay of Hitler.' It would take him some months to realize that things were far more complicated. 'The revolutionary atmosphere of Barcelona had attracted me deeply, but I had made no attempt to understand it.'

A chance photograph caught the six-foot-two-inch Englishman at the back of a column of volunteers, his face peering above the others. But he was dismayed to discover that there were virtually no weapons in the Lenin Barracks. He would later describe the POUM as 'the most extreme of the revolutionary parties' in Spain, and for this reason, together with their links to Trotsky, they had been ostracized by the communists, who were wielding ever increasing influence in Spain. A month prior to Orwell's arrival in Barcelona, the recently established Soviet Ambassador had sent a letter to all the newspapers in the Republic. As Lois Orr reported it to her family, 'It was a violent attack on the POUM, saying that we were agents of Hitler, paid to stop the revolution here, that we were counter-revolutionaries etc.' This had been followed on 17 December by the ejection of the POUM from the Catalan government, the *Generalitat*. It was not, therefore, surprising that the POUM had not received any of the new armaments arriving from Russia.

Even if the POUM's militiamen had received better armaments, it was not at all clear that they would have known what to do with them. Orwell soon discovered that in his whole section, he was the only one who knew how to load a rifle, let alone aim and fire it. Some recruits were as young as sixteen, and though 'full of revolutionary ardour' they were 'completely ignorant of the meaning of war'. By contrast, Orwell admitted that he had been

> toting a rifle ever since I was ten, in preparation not only
> for war but for a particular kind of war, a war in which the
> guns rise to a frantic orgasm of sound, and at the appointed
> moment you clamber out of the trench … and stumble

across mud and wire into the machine-gun barrage. I am convinced that part of the reason for the fascination that the Spanish civil war had for people of about my age was that it was so like the Great War.

After a week of rudimentary drill instruction, Orwell was posted to the Aragon front. His departure was preceded by what he called the usual 'conquering-hero stuff – shouting and enthusiasm, red flags and red and black flags everywhere, friendly crowds thronging the pavement to look at us, women waving from the windows.' He was now heading for the cold and tedium of the sieges of Saragossa and Huesca: exactly what the POUM militia had been doing when Cornford was serving with them four months earlier.

Nearing the front line the militiamen finally received rifles: forty-year-old German Mausers, rusty old things with corroded barrels. Secretly, Orwell was frightened. The less romantic stories of the Great War now filled his imagination: 'roaring projectiles and skipping shards of steel,' not to mention the 'mud, lice, hunger, and cold.'

Marching up to the trenches to join the POUM's Lenin Division he was filled with a kind of horror at the 'rabble' he was now a part of. 'We straggled along with far less cohesion than a flock of sheep … It seemed dreadful that the defenders of the Republic should be this mob of ragged children carrying worn-out rifles which they did not know how to use.' He wondered what would happen if an enemy plane saw them, if the pilot would bother attacking them. 'Surely even from the air he could see that we were not real soldiers.'

Such was the defensive limitations of their positions when he reached the front, and the youth and inexperience of his comrades, Orwell felt there were nights 'when it seemed to me that our positions could be stormed by twenty Boy Scouts armed with airguns.'

His company commander was Georges Kopp, the Russian-born Belgian engineer whom Lois Orr had met in Barcelona back in September. 'This is not a war,' Kopp joked with the new arrival. 'It is a comic opera with an occasional death.' Sharing a similar dry sense of humour, the two men soon became friends.

Though Orwell found the cold almost unbearable, he found that the food was not bad, there was wine with their meals, and for a while a regular supply of cigarettes. And the scenery in Aragon, he wrote, was 'stupendous': their trenches zig-zagged through the hills, whilst in the distance loomed the 'monstrous peaks' of the Pyrenees. And the POUM were pleased to have him. Their English-language paper (edited by Charles Orr) soon heralded the arrival of 'the well-known British author, whose work is so much appreciated in all English-speaking left circles of thought ... he is now fighting with the Spanish comrades of the POUM on the Aragon front.'

But there was little actual fighting to be done. This, for the next four months or so, would be Orwell's home; his days would be a monotonous repetition of guard duty, with occasional night patrols to break the monotony. He filled his spare time reading books, and writing his diary, recording his impressions for the book he intended to write when the war was over.

II

At the time George Orwell was arriving in Barcelona Bernard Knox was still recovering in a Madrid hospital. His doctors were soon advising him to return to England to seek further treatment for the gunshot wound in his neck. Uncertain whether or not to go home, Knox travelled to Albacete. It was the news he heard there of John Cornford's death that decided the issue. With his friend gone, there seemed no point remaining in Spain.

Knox was not completely disheartened, however. On the rail journey from Madrid to Albacete he had seen 'an encouraging sight. We stopped at one point to let an oncoming train go by. As it rattled past, I saw men waving and giving us the salute with the clenched fist; evidently, these were reinforcements for Madrid. As the coach passed, I saw that it displayed a long white banner that read THE YANKS ARE COMING. It was a contingent of the Lincoln Brigade on its way to the front.'

This first organized group of American volunteers had left New York on Boxing Day 1936. They had been recruited by the CPUSA, and according to one of their number were 'a young, poorly dressed bunch of proles' who half recognized each other 'from demonstrations, picket lines, mass meetings'. Francoist propaganda claimed, more colourfully, that they included 'Negroes from Broadway, Chinese from the ports of New York and Los Angeles, gangsters from Chicago, and militants from the Communist cells of Philadelphia.'

These claims might have been half true; that they had each received 'a large sum of money' for enlisting was not. Though the International Brigades' volunteers would frequently be disparaged as mercenaries, none were in it for money (of which there was little: the volunteers of the International Brigades all received the same pay as regular Spanish Republican recruits). Most of the Americans were communists, many were students, and only a few had any previous military experience; as many as a third, even half, were Jewish (a proportion reflecting the large number of Jews in the CPUSA). A typical example was William Horvitz, who was amongst the first volunteers to appear at the makeshift training depot in the Ukrainian Hall on East 3rd Street.

Born in New Jersey in 1915, Horvitz's working-class parents were Jewish immigrants from what is now Belarus. Images of Lenin, Trotsky and Stalin hung in the family home, and by the time Horvitz graduated from high school in 1932 he was 'a fundamentalist' in his belief that the Soviet Union and the Communist Party

were the answer to every single problem faced by the human race ... Greed, envy, brutality, power; all would vanish from the earth ... We believed beyond reason, and pretended that what we believed was founded on pure reason. We believed what we believed so profoundly that our beliefs became the very foundation of our existence. Our minds were closed to all else … I was a Communist, that was my creed, my religion, my blood.

For a while, Horvitz had belonged to an anarchist Jewish co-operative farm in Michigan. He also spent time on the road, fought on picket lines and worked to save money for college; his ambition was to become a doctor. But always the Party drew him back: going south to work in a Miami Beach restaurant he became involved in Party activism with black sharecroppers in South Georgia, urging them to unite, to hire a lawyer, and to improve their wages, meanwhile aiming to bring them into the CPUSA. He was afraid of tar and feathering, of lynching, of the Ku Klux Klan; men with dogs and guns broke up one clandestine meeting. Back home in New York he fell for a taxi dancer in Harlem, and realized that he was 'madly in love with the Negro people'.

White supremacists such as the racist Mississippi Congressman Theodore Bilbo, 'vomiting pure right shit right here in the good old US of A,' appalled Horvitz. And there were the anti-Semitic rantings of Father Charles Coughlin (allegedly bankrolled by Henry Ford), who, like the fascists in Germany and Spain, used the radio to reach an audience of millions. Policemen armed with truncheons and guns broke up picket lines outside factories. With these provocations, it seemed that revolution was possible even in America.

When Earl Browder, the CPUSA's energetic leader, followed the Comintern's orders and started supporting Roosevelt's New Deal, he made this 'Popular Front' approach remarkably successful. In 1930 membership of the Party had stood at around 7,000; by the early 1940s it had soared to 100,000. Though it was still, comparatively speaking, a tiny player in American politics, as Horvitz later recalled,

> Actors, painters, writers, lawyers, doctors, priests, rabbis, the
> rich and the poor, active trade unionists, even an occasional
> Negro, joined up. Workers, too. Madison Square Garden
> wasn't large enough to hold the crowds coming to hear Earl

Browder, the Kansas Twang, aver our patriotism and our love for America … We were for collective security against Hitler. We were the Popular Front. And we won a great victory: FDR recognized the USSR.

III

At the Ukrainian Hall in New York City the American volunteers for Spain were drilled and received rudimentary military instruction. 'There was no hacking around,' William Horvitz later recalled, 'very little laughter.' Were they, he wondered, 'all as scared as I was? You didn't mention your fear, you were too scared even to think it.' There would be many moments in the coming months when Horvitz would ask himself, 'what am I doing here?'

The men were given money to buy Great War 'doughboy' uniforms, as well as boots and equipment (but not weapons) from the Army and Navy stores. Of the first hundred volunteers, four backed out at the last minute. The send-off for the other ninety-six – Horvitz among them – was low-key. They assembled at the Yiddish Theater on Second Avenue, where Earl Browder (who would also eventually travel to Spain) shook each by the hand. The men were expected to keep themselves to themselves during the week-long journey aboard the French liner *Normandie*: a voyage whose highlight was the presence on board of dancers from the Folies Bergère. The Party met the cost of the men's passage, using money raised by a front organization, the North American Committee to Aid Spanish Democracy. Few of its donors realized they were helping to finance communist soldiers in the armed struggle against fascism.

Unknown to the American volunteers, also on board the *Normandie* was the Dutch communist filmmaker Joris Ivens. He too was on the way to Spain, his passage paid by Contemporary Historians, a new organization whose stated mission was to 'present the true facts of contemporary history'. Its founders included a number of prominent American writers, including John Dos Passos, Dorothy Parker, Archibald MacLeish and

Dashiell Hammett, as well as Ernest Hemingway. They had commissioned Ivens to make a film that would persuade Americans of the justice of the Republican cause in Spain, reverse the US Government's neutral position on the sale of arms, and raise money for ambulances.

The *Normandie* reached Le Havre on the last day of 1936. If asked, the American volunteers on board were told to tell immigration officials that they had come to France as tourists visiting (albeit rather prematurely) the forthcoming International Exposition, which was due to open in Paris in May. Recognizing the men's true destination, however, the sympathetic French officials waved them through without question. From Paris they boarded the train now dubbed 'the Red Express', its carriages packed with international volunteers for Spain. As they pulled out from the Gare de Lyon they broke out into the *Internationale*, and when one American volunteer sang the Zionist anthem *Hatikvah*, he was joined by hundreds of voices.

Along with numerous Irish, Germans and Belgians, the Americans crossed the Pyrenees without incident, and arrived at what had become the International Brigades' first assembly point in Spain: the medieval fortress of Figueres. The atmosphere was exhilarating, and Horvitz and his idealistic young colleagues

> were soon pretty damned drunk. We were part of an army, a red army. We were going to make a revolution. We were going to make a new world, a much better world; poverty would be abolished, there would be jobs for all, war would be outlawed, fascism destroyed, men and women would be free, free, free; liberty, fraternity, solidarity, long live life, long live the revolution, long live Stalin … Our cause was the most just ever advanced by the human race. Twenty-year-olds, most of us, we believed that as Communists we knew for certainty the solution to every problem the world faced.

They reached Barcelona by train on 6 January 1937. To another

Winifred Bates, *Arrival in Barcelona of first volunteers of the Abraham Lincoln Battalion, January 1937* (IWM)

enthusiastic Catalan welcome they marched up Las Ramblas with the Stars and Stripes, many of them in tears. According to one volunteer, most Spaniards almost universally assumed that *all* Americans were wealthy, so they were deeply impressed that 'these "rich" Americans should have crossed the seas to fight for them;' this explained 'the extra loud cheers' that greeted them. 'At the same time,' he noted, 'our prestige in the International Brigade is great for the same reason.'

They stopped outside the US Consulate to sing *The Star Spangled Banner*. An American clerk sent out to investigate reported that the men told him they were in Spain to 'fight for their principles'. Some claimed to be veterans of the Great War; others were clearly students. As they marched off to a dinner provided by the POUM militia in the Lenin Barracks, one volunteer shouted back, 'We're just the beginning!' André Marty greeted them at Albacete, telling them that they were 'like the Yanks of 1917, come to save Europe from the barbaric Hun.' (An ill-considered remark that angered the German anti-fascists.) By the end of the month, some 300 Americans had crossed the Pyrenees.

Back home, attempts were soon being made to stem the flow of volunteers. According to one American veteran, throughout the war the Hearst press 'characterized the Internationals as the scum of the earth, international bums, gangsters, and murderers,' and by the end of January the US Government had ordered consular officials in France to board incoming liners and stamp American passports 'Not valid for travel to Spain.' According to *The New York Times* on 24 January, the US consul at Le Havre warned sixty-five suspected volunteers arriving on board the SS *Paris* that, according to a 1909 statute, Americans who fought in a foreign war were liable to fines, prison terms and even the possible loss of citizenship. Some volunteers laughed openly at him. Even the closure of the French border with Spain in February did not stop them coming. By late 1938, almost 3,000 Americans had joined the International Brigades, most of them having to cross the mountain border on foot in order to evade the French patrols that started enforcing the Non-Intervention Agreement.

Many of these American volunteers were clearly motivated by world affairs. A majority were either immigrants from Europe or their children, and they were well aware of events in their old homelands. One communist, about to embark for Spain, told his brother: 'Those who feel that I must justify my action, I refer them to the bloody hand of Hitler, no further justification is needed. The dead babies on the streets of Madrid are more articulate than any master of words.' Despite the support for Franco shown by many US newspapers and magazines, popular opinion was moving against the rebels; though most Americans still had no opinion at all on the Civil War. An opinion poll in May 1937 revealed that only one in five supported either side; but of those who did express an opinion, fifty-seven per cent were in favour of the Government, compared with nineteen per cent backing the rebels. (The figures were very similar in Britain: a poll in October 1938 would show fifty-seven per cent supporting the Republic, only nine per cent for the rebels, and a third undecided.) Most Americans with an interest in the Civil War rejected Theo Rogers' claim that Franco was 'fighting for modern civilization against the ruthless barbarism and the bubonic plague of Sovietism.'

'I came to Spain because I felt I had to,' Hyman Katz, a Jewish volunteer from New York, explained in a passionate letter to his mother:

> Look at the world situation … how fascism is grasping
> power in many countries (including the US, where there are
> many Nazi organizations and Nazi agents and spies) – can't
> you see that fascism is our own problem – that it may come
> to us as it came to other countries? And don't you realize
> that we Jews will be the first to suffer if fascism comes?

It seemed clear to Katz that Mussolini and Hitler, 'with their agent
Franco … are trying to set up the same anti-progressive, anti-Semitic
regime in Spain, as they have in Italy and Germany … If we sit by and let
them grow stronger by taking Spain, they will move on to France and will
not stop there; and it won't be long before they get to America.'

And it was not only Jews and communists who recognized the danger.
Canute Frankson, a young Jamaican who had emigrated to the US before
joining the International Brigades, told a friend why he was fighting in 'a
war between whites who for centuries have held us in slavery, and have
heaped every kind of insult and abuse upon us'. As Frankson explained,
he had joined

> a great progressive force, on whose shoulders rests the
> responsibility of saving human civilization from the planned
> destruction of a small group of degenerates gone mad in
> their lust for power. Because if we crush Fascism here, we'll
> save our people in America, and in other parts of the world,
> from the vicious persecution, wholesale imprisonment, and
> slaughter which the Jewish people suffered and are suffering
> under Hitler's Fascist heels.[1]

---

1 Significantly, the rebels' American supporters saw things in similar terms. As Theo Rogers
wrote, the war 'was no longer a struggle of ins and outs. It was Communism against Civilization.
The soldiers of General Franco were fighting the battle of the world against the forces of
Sovietism and Anarchism.'

Whilst these young Americans recognized the need to act, President Roosevelt and his Democrat administration continued to enforce Non-Intervention. Nevertheless, there were some diplomats who feared where US policy might lead. As early as October 1936, in a letter to *The New York Times*, the former Republican Secretary of State Henry Stimson had criticized his country's 'ostrich-like isolationism' in response to German and Italian actions in Ethiopia, the Rhineland and Spain, and the 'erroneous form of neutrality legislation [which] has threatened to bring upon us in the future the very dangers of war which we are seeking to avoid'.

Neutrality 'will not save us from entanglement,' Stimson warned. 'It will even make entanglement more certain. History has already amply shown this last fact.'

IV

Naming themselves after the great President of the American Civil War, the Abraham Lincoln Battalion would form part of the newly-formed XV International Brigade. (Back home, though, the Battalion would be known as the Abraham Lincoln *Brigade*, a deliberate overstatement made by the CPUSA to exaggerate the number of American volunteers in Spain.) They would be fighting alongside the English-speaking volunteers of the 'British' Battalion, together with the Frenchmen of the 6th February Battalion and the Czechs, Austrians, Italians, Bulgarians and Balkan volunteers of the Dimitrov Battalion. It was not long before the Americans were appraised of the nature of the war, and the heavy casualties they could expect: a German veteran informed one fresh-faced volunteer that of the nine hundred men of the Thälmann Battalion who had helped defend Madrid in November, only he and sixteen others remained.

The Lincoln Battalion's base was the little village of Villanueva de la Jara, thirty-five miles from Albacete. William Horvitz described it as like 'a town in a cowboy movie, flat, stucco instead of clapboard, yellowish, dusty.' They were housed in an ancient convent beside a vast church. It was exciting to have a common purpose. 'Our bunch,' one volunteer would write home, 'is a true cross-section of America, auto workers from Detroit, steel men from McKeesport and Pittsburgh, sailors and longshoremen … The real international language here is Yiddish. Jews from Germany, France, England, Poland, Czech, Hungary, Rumania, all the front ranks of the respective movements have come to battle the common enemy of the workers, and of the Jews as a special oppressed minority.'

As well as a number of Canadians, there were also about sixty Cubans and Mexicans with the Lincoln Battalion, as well as some forty of the Irish volunteers who had arrived in Albacete with Frank Ryan. Ryan's talk of 'the common enemy' had not succeeded in quenching their reluctance to serve in a 'British Battalion', and they had voted instead to join the Americans, a number of whom were after all of Irish descent. The British Battalion's commissars told Harry Pollitt that they were 'frankly glad' that most of the Irish were going, whilst the Americans cautiously welcomed the military experience of the IRA men, whilst taking care to hide the discarded prayer books they had been using till then as toilet paper. Ryan, however – who had been away in Madrid when the split happened – was livid when he discovered that his 'Irish Column' was now divided between the Americans and British.

Through January and into February the Lincolns underwent basic training. The most that many of them knew about fighting came from Hollywood movies or novels about the Great War. Hemingway's *A Farewell to Arms* and Erich Maria Remarque's *All Quiet on the Western Front* were among the best known (both had recently been made into films). Their weapons were old Canadian Ross and Austrian Steyr rifles – both with a tendency to jam – and two antiquated Colt machine guns, which for a time did not even have ammunition.

Doug Seacord, a charismatic African-American from Tennessee who was rumoured to have been a gunnery instructor at West Point, took command of the machine-gun company. They named themselves after

Thomas Mooney, the radical San Francisco union leader who was serving a life sentence in Alcatraz for a bombing outrage that had killed ten people (a crime for which he was later acquitted). As one veteran later recalled, 'The guys in that company were tough guys. You couldn't get in if you weren't a hard-core something-or-other.' Seacord invited William Horvitz to join the 'Mooneys'.

Overall command of the Battalion remained a problem. For a while there was no clear officer in charge at Villanueva de la Jara, despite the truckloads of volunteers arriving almost daily. Men milled about, wondering what to do. They played football, while the villagers eyed them with suspicion.

Officially, their commander was James Harris, a Polish-American seaman who had come over in the first batch of volunteers. He was rumoured to have once been a US Marine sergeant, and to have fought in China as an adviser to the People's Army; but he would prove inarticulate and erratic. Eventually, Robert Merriman, a tall, bespectacled thirty-year-old American with the air of a schoolmaster, would replace him. The son of a Californian lumberjack, Merriman had studied economics at Nevada University, where he had served in the Officers' Training Corps before receiving a commission in the US Army Reserve. An economics job at Berkeley had followed. He had been in Moscow with his wife, Marion, writing a thesis on collective farming, when the Spanish Civil War broke out. Believing that the advance of fascism could be checked in Spain, and that another world war could yet be averted, Merriman had decided to join what he thought would be a three or four-month war. He arrived in Valencia by Russian freighter in January. A Party man with military experience, he appeared to be the ideal officer.

Training continued, with the limited resources available. André Marty visited the Battalion to see how they were getting on, and appeared to be impressed. But privately he would call the Lincolns 'arrogant Americans' and 'spoiled cry-babies', and would later threaten to send them all home. The Americans reciprocated: 'The French were the scum of the International Brigades,' one veteran later recalled.

Ill-fed, ill-treated and overlooked, the four hundred or so men of the Lincolns were restless. 'We were becoming nervous,' William Horvitz later wrote, 'tense, anxious to get into the ring. Bring on the enemy.'

V

The men of the British Battalion were also restless for action (and for many, this restlessness found an outlet in drunkenness). New recruits were arriving in Madrigueras almost daily, though some were met with an ominous greeting: 'Welcome to the biggest shambles in Europe.'

The Battalion's commanding officer was an eccentric veteran of the Great War, Wilfred Macartney. Born in Scotland in 1899, Macartney was the son of a successful Scottish-American electrical engineer and his American wife. In 1915, aged only sixteen, he had enlisted in the British Army. Eventually securing a commission in the Royal Scots, he had been badly wounded in the head on the Western Front in September 1918, and was taken prisoner. After the War he found employment in the City, and – having inherited a substantial fortune from his father – led a life of what he himself called 'incurable extravagance': big boxing matches, opening nights in London's West End and cabarets in Paris and Berlin were coupled with a love of fine food, cigars and Savile Row suits, as well as a weakness for cocktails. Tom Wintringham, who had now been appointed commander of the British Battalion's machine-gun company, noted that, even in Spain, if Macartney could not get champagne and good cigars he would rather drink water or tea and not smoke at all. At first sight, Wintringham thought that 'so civilized a being' appeared more suited to the Café Royal or a box seat at the theatre than Albacete.

'I became a Communist,' Macartney would write in 1937, 'because the century became Communist.' Having visited Germany and seen the terrible post-war conditions there, as well as the 'scurrilous conduct of the mine-owners in England and the realization of what a filthy racket the war had been,' he had come to realize 'that the only chance for the huge majority of mankind, including myself, is a Communistic revolution leading to the replacement of a system of universal exploitation, degradation and horror by a Communistic economy in which human beings shall enjoy the full fruits of an universal abundance.' By his own admission, 'apart from his sincere belief in Communism he was a wild and rather reckless young man of the possessing class.'

It was this mix of recklessness, excess (he had squandered all his inheritance) and idealism that had led Macartney to spying. According to the writer Compton Mackenzie, who had been one of his commanding officers during the Great War, Macartney was both an inept spy and a megalomaniac. Within weeks of taking up espionage on behalf of the Soviet Union in 1926 this well-dressed, well-spoken communist was arrested, tried, convicted and sentenced to ten years' imprisonment (including two with hard labour).

Released on licence after eight and a half years, Macartney had been taken in by Compton Mackenzie at his Hebridean home on the island of Barra. There he wrote *Walls Have Mouths*, a first-hand indictment of the British penal system. Published by Victor Gollancz's Left Book Club, it was listed by *The Observer* as one of the best books of 1936, deserving 'all the admiration it has won'. (While not stating what he actually thought of the book, George Orwell called its author one of 'the professed enemies of society'.) Captain Macartney was thus something of a celebrity; and with George Nathan he was the only veteran officer in the whole Battalion. His adjutant was a five-foot-tall Irishman who had served in the Great War, as well as with the IRA and the French Foreign Legion (or so he claimed).

Discipline would prove a problem. The majority of men under Macartney's command hailed from Britain's industrial heartlands of Lancashire, Lanarkshire and South Wales, where poverty, unemployment and radicalism were endemic. A few were veterans of the Great War; some had experience in the armed services; many had none at all. As Wintringham would write, often the men would discuss an order before they obeyed it (or chose not to obey it), and called their officers 'comrade' rather than 'sir'. 'Most of our carefree volunteers,' he wrote, 'saw no point in doing things that displeased them, and some were very insistent on doing what they pleased. That was our problem.'

The recruits also included a few artists and writers, such as Jason Gurney, a young South African sculptor who had been living a bohemian life in London, and Christopher Sprigg, a journalist and writer since described as 'perhaps British communism's sharpest intellectual of his time'. Also at Madrigueras was Esmond Romilly's brother, Giles, who had quit his studies at Oxford University to join up; his friend Tony Hyndman had come with him. An ex-Guardsman, Hyndman had until recently been Stephen Spender's secretary and lover. (Gurney noted that there congregated around Romilly and Hyndman a 'small coterie of middle-class intellectuals … the majority homosexuals'.) Other small national groups with the British Battalion included Cypriots, Maltese, Egyptians and Indians.

And they continued to come, in spite of the attempts by the French and British Governments to prevent them. The former closed its border with Spain, while the latter threatened to enforce the 1870 Foreign Enlistment Act, which (so it claimed) made attempts to enlist in the International Brigades illegal. Undercover policemen spied on Party meetings, while MI5 intercepted the correspondence of known and suspected communists. In London, the Foreign Secretary told the German *chargé d'affaires* that his Government was determined to prevent the 'flow of volunteers to Spain,' in an effort to stop the conflict from spreading to the rest of Europe. To supporters of the Spanish Republic, however, it seemed clear that the British Government's real motive was to aid Franco.

Because of the continued enforcement of Non-Intervention or neutrality policies by the Western democracies, the British volunteers, like the Lincolns, had inadequate equipment with which to train. Wintringham described their few rifles as 'appalling' – rusty, with cracked woodwork – and while their Colt machine-guns worked fine when using factory-loaded ammunition belts, they jammed repeatedly if the belts were loaded by hand: it took Wintringham five minutes to shoot off twenty-five rounds, far slower than shooting a rifle. Their other machine-guns were equally deficient: French Chauchats, 'queer blunderbuss-looking things, very light, with very old and faulty ammunition and weak springs in the tin magazines,' which tended to seize up if they got dusty.

Finally, Wintringham asked Kitty Bowler to help him out with the Colts. She was back in Barcelona, working as a freelance journalist supplying stories to newspapers in Britain and America, as well as broadcasting to the US on behalf of Catalonia's United Socialist Party, the PSUC. Wintringham asked her to go to Valencia and consult two machinegun experts for him there. They advised Bowler that the Colts' ammunition-belts had to be waxed to make them function properly. Armed with this information, Bowler was given a pass to enter Albacete by a senior German communist. Going to the he headquarters of the International Brigades was reckless, as Bowler knew the town was off-limits to non-Party members. But for weeks Wintringham had been encouraging her to come and write a piece about the British Battalion for the American press. 'There is much good human propaganda in this unit,' he had told her, 'and an American or two.' More importantly, it would give them a rare opportunity to be together.

So on 20 January Bowler hitched a lift on a lorry going to Albacete. In Madrigueras she met Macartney, who was so susceptible to her charms that he immediately enrolled her as a temporary Colt machinegun instructor, issuing her with a hand-written note to this effect. But her new position was short-lived. According to her own account – and even before she had met Wintringham – 'At midnight there was a great banging at the door of the cubbyhole where I was trying to sleep. There was Mac tousled and distraught. I was under arrest!'

Given only enough time to dress, Bowler was taken under armed guard back to Albacete, where a 'lean and hard faced' German questioned her. Then she was ordered into an adjoining room, where a sleepy and irritable old man with a walrus moustache and a coat pulled over his pyjamas sat behind a roll top desk. It was André Marty. Though he reminded her 'of a petty French bureaucrat,' he wielded real power.

Spies were the Communist Party's obsession, and it was an obsession

Marty warmly embraced. Famous among fellow-communists for his part in the Black Sea mutiny, he nevertheless lacked experience for the job he had been given in Spain. As the German volunteer Gustav Regler observed after meeting the Frenchman in Albacete, 'it is not easy to turn a mutinous NCO into the commander of an army and Marty covered his forgivable inadequacy with an unforgivable, passionate spy-hunt.' Putting all his energies 'at the service of his mistrust,' Marty 'did not shrink from conducting day-long, soul-destroying interrogations, or even from sacrificing the tranquility of his nights and peace of mind by promptly liquidating doubtful cases, rather than harm the Republic by what he called "petty-bourgeois indecision".' As Franz Borkenau observed, 'the International Brigade has a reputation of being quick in shooting people,' and one volunteer later described Marty as 'a sinister and ludicrous figure … quite literally mad at this time.'

Bowler was shocked when, after an hour of questioning, Marty read out the charges against her: she had travelled from Albacete to Madrigueras without a pass; she had penetrated a military establishment; she had shown an interest in machineguns; and she had previously visited both Italy and Germany. Marty's conclusion was clear: Kitty Bowler was a spy; and spies were to be shot.

Bowler underwent a further three days of interrogation, frequently woken in the night to be questioned by a relay of investigators. Tom Wintringham waited anxiously. As he explained to her in a letter, the 'length and seriousness of the enquiry seems to be due to the circulation of a description of a woman spy, the description resembling yourself.' He added that she had impressed Marty as 'very very strong, very clever, very intelligent'. Although Wintringham admitted that Marty counted this 'as a suspicious point against you – women journalists should be weak, stupid – I got a jump of pride from the words.'

As Macartney was not prepared to intervene on Bowler's behalf, it was probably Wintringham who convinced Marty that the American was not really a spy. Eventually she was released, but orders would soon be issued for her expulsion from Spain.

Wintringham took Bowler to Madrid for a night. 'Just those few hours with you were enough to wash all bitterness out of me,' she wrote to him afterwards. 'You made me strong again … You took a somewhat undirected little lost girl and made a person of her. I love you, love you, all of you, your long tall body, your sweet steadying voice, your brains and good sense mixed with good emotion. *Salut y republica*!'

'You know a good deal about giving a man a good time, and then some!' he replied. 'The total effect on morale of my 24 hours leave was A1 Magnificent, I'm on top of the world!'

Chapter 8

Death in the Afternoon

|

The events surrounding Kitty Bowler's arrest raised further doubts in the minds of some of Tom Wintringham's comrades. Wilfred Macartney defended him. 'Don't get any silly ideas into your head that Wintringham is not pulling his weight,' he warned Harry Pollitt, 'he is the best man in Spain at his work, the ideal staff-officer, a fine machine-gunner.'

This was in contrast to many of the other officers Macartney had encountered. 'Most of the commanders are more or less useless,' he reckoned. Macartney did not record his impression of the officers in the Abraham Lincoln Battalion, but did write to them, suggesting they meet and practise with the grenades they were being issued with. These were, he noted, 'extremely powerful, and very tricky'.

'I've commanded this Battalion for nearly a month,' he told Pollitt in mid-January, 'and by dint of kicking, yelling, nagging, swearing, I've made something of it but nearly killed myself.' However, Macartney reported to Marty's aide, Vidal Gayman, that discipline in the British Battalion was still 'backward'.

The Battalion's political commissar in Albacete, a dour Scottish communist named Peter Kerrigan, reiterated to Pollitt the need to send out good men who understood what they were getting into: '*This is a war and many will be killed*. They must understand this clearly, and it should be put quite brutally.' Kerrigan was also worried about Macartney, who had recently muttered to Wintringham that he was thinking of quitting. Macartney had his own drink problem, whilst Frank Ryan had heard that he had been in the Black and Tans, which hardly made him popular among the Irish volunteers. In another letter, Kerrigan added that Macartney was 'far too irritable,' possibly a sign of his anxiety that the Battalion – now up to seven hundred men in strength – would soon be called into action, and that he had had too little time to prepare them. 'Mac is a rather difficult man to handle,' George Aitken, the Battalion's commissar, explained. 'His temper is none too good.'

Despite the regular letters they sent back to London, the British volunteers felt isolated. In January, Kerrigan wrote angrily to Pollitt stating that, despite their frequent reports and urgent requests, they had been 'ignored. Not a word … Not a wire. Nothing! … For all our serious proposals, *concerning many of which we honestly believe our success and men's lives depend*,' they had received 'bugger all notice or response from your end.'

Morale improved a little when the survivors of the Battalion's Number One Company returned from its disastrous action at Lopera. When they assembled in Albacete's bullring, Marty told them they were 'not only the best [company] in the Battalion but the best in the Brigade,' an example to all for their 'courage,' 'endurance,' 'heroism' and 'unity of purpose'. George Nathan, who had shown his obvious abilities, was promoted Major and placed in XV Brigade's staff.

The problem with Macartney came to an unexpected conclusion on 7 February. As part of his parole arrangements, he had to make a brief trip back to England before returning to resume command. On his last night in Albacete, Macartney offered to swap his heavy service revolver for Kerrigan's smaller weapon. Kerrigan agreed, but in showing him how his pistol worked he accidentally shot Macartney in the arm.

Kerrigan was mortified. It was 'a stupid mistake,' he informed Pollitt, 'and it was just chance that the consequences were not a great deal more serious.' Given that Macartney was, as Kerrigan put it, 'a well known figure in Britain being an author etc,' it could have awkward propaganda implications. Macartney was rushed to hospital, but the injury was not severe. All sorts of rumours were soon circulating: that Macartney had deserted, even that he had attempted suicide. According to Frank Ryan, 'The bastard wounded himself in the left arm with his own revolver … and got the London Daily Worker to say he was "wounded by Fascist rifle-fire near Madrid"!!!' Even when it was accepted that Kerrigan had shot him, it was still whispered that he had done it deliberately, in order to remove Macartney from command and replace him with a Communist Party member. He soon went home to England, but the Party would not allow him to return to Spain, perhaps conscious of the criticisms they had received of his leadership.

With Macartney off the scene and George Nathan now with Brigade HQ, Tom Wintringham was the only credible candidate to take over command when the Battalion suddenly received orders to prepare for action. 'This was a tremendous shock,' one British volunteer later recalled. 'Nobody liked Macartney with his 1914 ideas but to find your battalion commander is not there when you are about to go into battle and a kind of instructor is in command! Well, it's a very demoralising thing, particularly in these mysterious circumstances.' The sculptor Jason Gurney, who had no previous experience as a soldier, reckoned that whilst Wintringham was 'invariably pleasant, informal and unpretentious, I don't think he really knew any more about military affairs than I did.' For all Wintringham's love of military history and knowledge of machineguns, leading a battalion of men into battle was a quite different matter.

Peter Kerrigan reported that though Wintringham appeared reluctant to take over from Macartney, he was not daunted by his new responsibility, and 'is very pleased in a way at the idea of commanding the first British Battalion.' As he prepared his men for departure, the newly promoted Captain Wintringham found a moment to write to Kitty Bowler:

> going at last, and temporarily in command of the battalion. All in the game, and I love it: beautiful new uniform and field-glasses and all. Have no time to tell you how much you helped and are helping to make the person now tackling this

job. But I can tell you I love you, and much more than that I don't need to tell you.

Kerrigan, sorry that he was not going with them, watched the British Battalion leaving Albacete. 'The boys looked splendid,' he wrote to Harry Pollitt.

> They are keen and, I think, very efficient. They know what is expected of them and will do their best to carry out the job. They are anti-fascist, they understand it's got to be fought here and they are prepared to take all the risks implied in this fight. They are too close to it all to see that history is being made here and this generation and the one that follows it will be filled with great pride. After all it is no little thing to hold back International Fascism and help save the peace of the world a little longer.

II

Despite his defeats at University City and Boadilla, General Franco remained determined to capture Madrid. On 5 February, after days of heavy rain, the rebels had launched an offensive to cross the Jarama River, to the south-east of the Spanish capital. Their objective was to cut the city's road and rail links with the Government in Valencia. Some 25,000 Moroccan and Spanish troops, supported by German machinegun battalions, artillery, tanks and planes, were thrown into the attack. If the Republican line broke, Madrid would be virtually encircled, and Franco would be a vital step closer to victory. Along with XI, XII and XIV International Brigades, XV Brigade were being rushed from Albacete to help plug the gap; only the Abraham Lincoln Battalion was left behind to complete its training.

Rebel morale was high: on 8 February, in a separate offensive far to the south, the Andalucian city of Malaga – birthplace of Picasso – had been captured virtually without a fight by Italian troops supplied by Mussolini: fleeing civilians were blasted from the air and shelled from the sea. The Jarama offensive also started well for the rebels. At dawn on 11 February Moroccan soldiers silently knifed the sentries of the André Marty Battalion who were guarding a major river crossing. In the fighting that followed the rest of the French Battalion was virtually wiped out, with the wounded murdered where they lay waiting for ambulances.

That same day the five hundred or so volunteers of the British Battalion arrived at Chinchón, a few miles behind the front line. In contrast to the plains of Albacete, this was fine, hilly country; the ridges and plateaux of the landscape were dotted with olive and orange groves, vineyards and pine and cypress trees. After weeks of rain the sun was finally shining, whilst overhead Russian fighter planes successfully engaged the advancing rebels. Wintringham's men were given the chance to fire ten rounds from their recently issued rifles, before moving into action early the next morning. Their orders were to hold the very left flank of the thinly-stretched Republican line.

Thousands of Moors were already approaching another crossing of the Jarama River when Wintringham's inexperienced volunteers were unloaded at dawn from trucks beside a large abandoned farmhouse; with its courtyard and outbuildings, it would serve as both HQ and cookhouse. One bedroom had once been used by a famous *torero*, and Jason Gurney was fascinated to see its walls covered with bull-fight posters, banderillas, swords and other souvenirs of his fighting career. A few white buildings on the outskirts of Madrid were just visible in the distance, with the peaks of the Guadarrama mountains rising up beyond. After the rain and wretchedness of Madrigueras, Gurney thought that the world looked clean and sparkling.

At around ten a.m., and to the sound of distant gunfire, the three rifle companies of the British Battalion moved forward. Though many of the men were uncertain what they were doing, and no one had a map, their objective was the high ground overlooking the Jarama. In command of No. 1 Company was the IRA veteran Kit Conway, taking over at the last minute from Jock Cunningham, who was down with a fever. Frank Ryan, who now had a position with the Brigade staff, appeared to see off his fellow Irishman.

Bill Briskey, a leader of the London Busmen's Rank and File movement, commanded No. 3 Company, whilst Bert Overton from Stockton, a veteran of the Guards, commanded No. 4 Company. Moving up in support were the heavy machine-gunners of No. 2 Company, commanded by Harry Fry, a Scotsman who had once served with the Brigade of Guards. At the last minute they had received eight German Maxims, together with boxes of brand new ammunition, each containing a filled belt of cartridges. Maxims were the efficient, heavy, water-cooled guns that Bernard Knox and John Cornford had used with devastating effect at Boadilla. They could provide murderous supporting fire.

From his observation post behind the lines Wintringham proudly surveyed his advancing battalion, and remarked to Jason Gurney – who had taken on the role of Battalion scout and map-maker – that there had not been 'a better-looking body of troops' in Spain since the Duke of Wellington had led the British forces in the Peninsular War. In Gurney's unspoken opinion, 'the whole thing looked more like a Sunday school outing than an army.'

George Nathan appeared, smartly dressed in his British Army officer's jacket.

'Your battalion's a bit late, Tom,' he observed, matter-of-factly. He then explained that he had passed on instructions to Wintringham's companies to change their route of march a little.

'The battle seems to be mainly up north from us, over there,' Nathan clarified, waving his swagger stick towards some woods to the north and west, where French International Brigaders were already heavily engaged. Then Nathan walked calmly back to his car and returned to Brigade HQ.

Unfortunately, Nathan's new orders caused confusion among the neat ranks of Wintringham's three rifle companies. Instead of stopping on the high ground Wintringham had indicated, they started to bunch up and move on towards – and then beyond – another objective closer to the river: a white house on top of another ridge of high ground. Soon they were coming under heavy fire from the German machine-gunners in front of them. When rebel soldiers overran the Republican positions to their right, the British Battalion suddenly found itself dangerously exposed; and in front of them, making skilful use of the little cover available, a battalion or more of Moors was advancing up the hill.

In the warm midday sun Wintringham's men were falling before they had had the chance to return a shot. Even before the day was over their exposed position had been dubbed 'Suicide Hill'. Despite Wintringham's best efforts before the battle, the Colt light machineguns that had been distributed through the rifle companies soon jammed; and, to the men's bewilderment, their Machinegun Company was silent.

The eight Maxims of Harry Fry's Machinegun Company were Great War issue. In the rush before action, no one had noticed that, though the shiny cases of ammunition they had been issued with contained the right sort of belt, they held the wrong sort of cartridge: they were bullets made for the latest model of Maxim gun, not Wintringham's twenty-year-old relics. Fry and his men had unloaded the wrong cases from the ammunition lorry. Their guns were useless, and Fry withdrew his men from the action. Worse still, the lorry that was supposed to be carrying the right ammunition had disappeared.

Watching through his binoculars, Wintringham was not fully aware of the disaster unfolding before him. He could see Kit Conway taking control of the situation, 'standing up, strolling along his first line of rifles … with an Irish "don't care a damn" in his pace.' When Moors appeared on a knoll some hundreds of yards to Conway's right, he moved his men to meet the threat. Then Conway was hit. Though mortally wounded, in Wintringham's opinion the IRA veteran's 'example of coolness and disregard for danger, helped to hold [his company] together under the crossfire that with every hour grew deadlier, until a mechanized steady hosing of every visible square foot with fire was sweeping Suicide Hill.'

Wintringham did not know that many of his other leading men were also already casualties, or that his No. 4 Company commander, Bert

Overton, had lost his nerve and had abandoned his men on Suicide Hill. There, according to one survivor, the thin grass and weeds on its crest were 'being slowly mown down, as if a gigantic scythe was passing and repassing, by bullets from the machine-rifles of the Moors and machine-guns of the Germans.' Overton was eventually persuaded to return to Suicide Hill; but he would later be seen lying behind the ridge, 'weeping because so many of his men had been killed and wounded'.

Though the British Battalion was holding on, its position was desperate. They had no entrenching tools, so used corpses as shields. At one point Moorish soldiers were only thirty yards away. Men lifting their heads to fire would be shot through the face.

Orders from Brigade HQ were to 'hold on at all costs.' Support was promised, but to the south of Suicide Hill there were no more Republican troops. If the rebels realized this, and swept around the British flank, the defensive line would be broken in an instant, and defeat would be inevitable. By late afternoon over half the men of Wintringham's rifle companies were either dead or wounded, their Machinegun Company was still without ammunition, and the situation looked desperate.

Eventually, what Wintringham described as a 'weak, hastily-trained Spanish battalion' came up to reinforce them. Led by a captain with 'dark, hurt, scared, [and] very surprised eyes,' they came forward firing their Maxims, blazing the guns blindly into the olive groves. As Wintringham began plotting how he might get his hands on the Spaniards' guns and make better use of them, Fred Copeman appeared, dragging one of Fry's Maxims behind him.

Wintringham asked the former Royal Navy sailor if there was any ammunition for the gun.

'Yes, of course there's f—ing b—ing s—ing ammo,' Copeman exploded, 'but we'll have to fill the belts.'

According to one veteran of the battle, Copeman was 'a great bull of a man' who by this time was 'more or less insane, giving completely inconsequential orders to everybody in sight, and offering to bash their faces in if they did not comply.' Injured on Suicide Hill, he had been returning to the action from a dressing station when he discovered the missing ammo lorry, upturned by the side of the road. It was filled with cartridges for their Maxim guns.

Wintringham and Copeman now found any man available to help them bring up the ammunition crates. Then they hand loaded the bullets into the machinegun belts.

As sunset approached, five Maxims were positioned on the ridge behind Suicide Hill. The survivors of the rifle companies were then finally allowed to retire. It appeared to the rebels that the British volunteers were beaten, and a unit of Moors advanced after them in eager pursuit. 'They were in full dress,' Copeman later recalled, as the Africans charged over Suicide Hill and down into the valley beyond, 'in a solid thick line,' in full cry, their 'flowing cloaks lined in red and red berets or turbans.'

Having assumed effective command of the Machinegun Company, Copeman told the men not to fire until the Moors were much closer. When one young Irishman threatened to start shooting, Copeman knocked him out. All the guns would take part, Copeman insisted,

> working from left to right, sweeping the line together, until ordered to stop. I told them they would experience a sight that should give them confidence during the whole of the war in the weapons they were using.
>
> The pressure of excitement was amazing. Every gunner was bawling to be allowed to fire. I was threatening to shoot the first that tried.

Copeman hid his fear that the guns might not work:

> All sorts of suppositions passed through my mind in a few seconds, producing a million and one doubts – and suddenly it couldn't be held any longer! The order to fire, followed by a stream of curses, threats and invective, was deadened by the blast of these concentrated heavy Maxims. The result

was like mowing down wheat. As the bullets struck home, a still, thick black line appeared on the ground.

One of the machine-gunners was Stephen Spender's lover, Tony Hyndman. As he later recalled, the water-cooled Maxims 'bubbled over with heat, drying up. For the final burst we all urinated into a steel helmet. Some liquid was poured into each gun as the light of the day ended. We cheered. We shouted abuse. The other side was silent, strangely silent.' After the battle, Hyndman would tell Spender how he could 'still see the blood and the dead faces; worse still, the expression in the eyes of the dying. I felt no anti-Fascist anger, but only overwhelming pity.'

'One or two may have got away,' Copeman reckoned, 'but I didn't see them. The firing continued until no hand moved in an attack which must have started with three or four hundred men … Our battalion had annihilated one of the finest units in Franco's army.'

The Republican flank had been held, but at terrible cost to both sides. As the British Battalion regrouped, of the four hundred men who had marched on Suicide Hill that morning, only 125 were fit for further combat. After less than twelve hours' fighting, well over half the Battalion was dead or wounded.

In the darkness they heard an injured comrade, out in no-man's-land, crying for help. A patrol could not find him. 'It is horrible to hear a man's voice, six hundred yards away, calling hour on hour, at intervals, dying away slowly, getting fainter,' Wintringham would write months afterwards. 'I have heard his voice too often, since that night.' He wondered what he was doing there. 'Yes,' he reminded himself, 'hatred of war; trying to stamp war out as one would a forest fire, before it spreads.'

Many of his best men were dead; and more soon would be. They included labourers, miners, a famous speedway rider, a parson from Ulster, and the young writer Christopher Sprigg. George Orwell, who was still idling away his time with the POUM on the Aragon front, had wanted to join the International Brigades: given the bloodbath at Jarama, it was fortunate for him that he had not.

After a bitterly cold night, the fighting resumed early the next morning. Fry's Machinegun Company retained its forward position, and as dawn broke they saw a large section of rebel soldiers camped in the open. They opened a deadly fire upon them.

Though Fry's position offered an excellent field of fire, it was dangerously exposed, so Wintringham placed the forty survivors of Bert Overton's rifle company to guard their flank. But no one had told Wintringham that Overton's nerve had been broken on Suicide Hill. To the right, the Franco-Belge, Dimitrov and Thälmann Battalions were all enduring heavy attack, and Overton's position came under machinegun fire, then shelling. By mid-afternoon, and without orders, Overton suddenly withdrew his men some three hundred yards to the safety of a sunken road.

Exactly what happened next has never become clear. According to one survivor, towards dusk Fry's machine-gunners were simply surrounded and overrun. Others would claim that a group of Foreign Legionnaires approached Fry's company, their fists raised and singing the *Internationale*. Assuming they were rebel deserters, Fry and his men had welcomed them, realizing too late that they had been tricked. According to another report, the rebels had disguised themselves in uniforms taken from dead International Brigaders. However it happened, the British Battalion's deadly machineguns and the thirty men of their gun crews were about to be led away into captivity.

Wintringham knew he had to act fast. All through the battle he had been steadying his nerves, waiting for the moment he would go in to action. 'Why die crying?' he had kept repeating, 'Why die crying?' Now, with the enemy only two hundred yards away, he ordered a counter-attack. One of his men thought that by now they were all 'a little mad … The sheer weight of noise was tremendous and, coupled with a feeling of desperation and excitement, produced a kind of madness among us … Wintringham bawled at us to fix bayonets, which was quite absurd.'

As Wintringham stood up to lead the charge he was shot through the leg. Of the forty men who carried out his command, only Overton and five or six others returned.

Wintringham was stretchered away. He would later complain that beneath Overton's 'self-confident surface,' he was a 'fool, a romantic, a bluffer who wanted to be courageous,' but whose 'cowardice' cost lives.[1] Fortunately, the rebels did not press home their advantage, and that night Jock Cunningham appeared. He had heard of the disaster of the first day's action, and with Frank Ryan now took over unofficial command. But what had once been a Battalion was now little more than a Company, supported by a few young Spaniards.

In the heat of the following afternoon, the rebels attacked again. This time tanks supported them. As the official account of the engagement, written a few weeks later, recorded, the young Spaniards suddenly turned and ran, 'and the rout spread to the whole line. The slaughter was terrible. One would see five men running abreast, and four of them suddenly crumple up ... Here and there, little groups rallied to stem the Fascist advance ... Finally, they too, had to give up the unequal fight ... It was a terrible rout. The Fascist offensive, held up for three days, was again on the threshold of success.'

At the bottom of a hill, on the road from Chinchón to Madrid, men stopped to catch breath. Scattered groups of Spanish, British and Irish lay along the roadside, exhausted and demoralised. Frank Ryan and Jock Cunningham cajoled and rallied them – and led them back up the hill.

As Ryan later wrote in his propagandizing account of their counter attack, 'Whatever popular writers may say, neither your Briton nor your Irishman is an exuberant type. Demonstrativeness is not his dominating trait. The crowd behind us was marching silently. The thoughts in their minds could not be inspiring ones.' Then Ryan recalled a trick from his IRA days. Jerking his head back, he cried out, 'Sing up, ye sons o' guns!'

To the 'resounding chant' of the *Internationale*, 'the song rose from the

---

1 Overton would be courtmartialled for cowardice, and sentenced to ten years in prison. Allowed to volunteer for a labour battalion, he was killed in action later in 1937.

ranks.' As they marched, stragglers still in retreat watched in amazement, then turned to join them. 'Beneath the forest of upraised fists,' Ryan declared, 'what a strange band! Unshaven, unkempt; bloodstained, grimy. But full of fight again.' A Spanish Battalion joined them; *'¡Adelante!,'* they cried. 'Forward!' As darkness fell, survivors from the Franco-Belge Battalion also joined the attack.

Ryan suddenly realized 'with savage joy, that it is *we* who are advancing, *they* who are being pushed back. And then in actual disappointment: "The bastards won't wait for our bayonets!"' The equally exhausted rebels, thinking they were facing fresh reinforcements, had turned and run.

'We are in the olive groves. Firing ceases. We are on our feet, feeling for one another in the inky blackness. I stumble against a soft bundle. I bend down. His spiked bayonet scrapes my hand. He is one of ours. His face is cold. He has been dead for hours … So we are back where we were at midday.'

With his men continuing to fight and die, defending a line from which they would not now be shifted, Tom Wintringham penned a short note from his hospital bed: 'Dear Kitty,' he wrote, 'Hit in thigh while trying to organise bayonet charge. Damn these out of date sports. Nice wound. 2 days hard fighting: done well … Love Tom.'

IV

Accounts of the battle at Jarama soon appeared in the British press. According to *The Observer,*

> Anti-Red reports say that perhaps never have the Government forces put up so determined a resistance, and that many of them died where they stood. It is claimed that during recent fighting in this sector, 1,800 Government troops have been buried … The sterner resistance now being put up by the Reds is attributed to reinforcements of the International Column from Madrid. The whole 15th Brigade

is said to have been thrown into the defence of the Valencia road.

But in a scurrilous story headlined 'Britons Lured to their Death in Spain,' *The Daily Mail* alleged that so-called 'volunteers' had been press-ganged into the British Battalion and that those who did not want to fight 'were lined up and shot; the remainder like cattle were then driven to slaughter ... commanded by an Englishman named Wintringham.'

Notwithstanding such lies, casualties in the XV Brigade had been appalling. Even *The Daily Worker* admitted that British losses of killed, wounded and missing 'must be around 400'. According to Fred Copeman, who praised Wintringham as 'the mainspring of the battalion,' some harsh words about their captain were passing around (including the allegation that his leg wound had been self-inflicted), 'but later experience was to show that Tom had done a good job' in very difficult circumstances. Outnumbered by a properly trained, better-equipped enemy, they had held their ground.

Elkan Vera, *International Brigade volunteers test their weapons before the battle of Jarama, January 1937*
(IWM)

When Robert Merriman and the 450 volunteers of the Abraham Lincoln Battalion – their own training still far from complete – arrived at Jarama as reinforcements on 16 February they were shocked by what they found. Even as they left Albacete, where they had been issued with rifles, helmets and four Maxim guns, William Horvitz observed how each man 'seemed holed in on himself. I was scared … It also seemed I was living a strange, surreal dream.' Disembarking from their trucks, the Americans marched the final miles up to the front. As they passed over the rounded peak of a hill they suddenly heard the *snap-snap* of rifle fire: 'And then,' wrote Horvitz, 'we were at war, for the ambulances themselves dripped blood. Dog-tired soldiers in International Brigade uniforms lay about the shoulders of the road,' and an enemy plane appeared overhead, dropping bombs.

'As we were ordered up a hill to our right,' Horovitz continued, 'two men helping a wounded comrade toward an ambulance asked if we were Yanks. They were Englishmen. They presented us with encouraging words. They had been a full battalion several days before and now were but few.' The British, in turn, thought the Americans in their 'doughboy' uniforms looked 'utterly bizarre', as if they had stepped straight out of the Great War and the era of silent movies.

For their first few days the raw American troops were positioned in the defensive second line. Each afternoon Italian planes flew overhead and dropped bombs. Though no one was injured, aerial bombardment was followed by what Horvitz called the regular 'nightly horror' of being shelled. This resulted in a couple of casualties, including two men who deliberately shot off their toes. But a more serious loss had already occurred. Catastrophically, one of the trucks carrying American volunteers to the front had made a wrong turn, and had ended up in rebel territory. The twenty-one men on board were never seen again.

On the night of 21 February the Lincolns were finally ordered into the front line to reinforce the other three battalions of XV Brigade (now numbering less than 500 men, when only ten days before they had been more than two thousand strong). The next day, William Horvitz saw his first action with the Lincoln's Machinegun Company; to his frustration, his Maxim jammed after shooting a single round. The following afternoon he was ordered to set up his machinegun again, this time in support of an imminent American counter-attack. As he was doing so what felt like a sledgehammer blow struck him on the back of the head. Unconscious for a few minutes, he woke paralysed, certain he was dying. 'It was not as frightening as I had always believed it would be,' he later wrote. 'I remember it distinctly. The best word to describe it is peace. I felt at peace, and very fatigued.'

He received a morphine shot and was put in an ambulance. His initial feeling of peace quickly passed. The pain from the bullet in his spine was soon 'so agonizing I did not stop screaming the length of what seemed an endless ride through hell as above me a dead man leaked blood, piss and shit into my face.' Lapsing back into unconciousness, Horvitz awoke hours later in hospital. Wounded Americans surrounded him. 'The battalion had in clear daylight gone over the top in idiotic World War I fashion and been repulsed, with some twenty dead and sixty wounded.'

The man who had ordered the attack, General János Gálitz ('Gal'), had served and learnt his military tactics in the Great War. An Austro-Hungarian conscript, Gal had been captured by the Russians and had then joined the Red Army, rising through the ranks. Though it should now have been clear that the rebel operation to cut the Valencia road had failed, Gal still hoped for a clear victory. A British volunteer fighting in Franco's ranks at Jarama later described how the Republicans 'put in a frontal assault in broad daylight across a plain dominated by our positions and almost devoid of cover … I wondered what kind of military cretin had ordered such an attack.' And as Herbert L. Matthews, the *New York Times*' openly anti-fascist reporter in Spain observed, the terrain around Jarama was 'a mass of rather sharp hills – easy to defend and suicidal to attack for every inch of it can be covered by machinegun cross fire.'

But Gal appeared obsessed with frontal attacks, and on 27 February he ordered Merriman and his French, British and Spanish comrades to directly assault a rebel-held hilltop. Using his pet phrase, he told Merriman that the Lincoln Battalion was to take the position 'at all costs'. Tanks, planes and artillery were promised in support.

When dawn came there were no tanks or planes, and only a few artillery pieces. A barrage of rifle and machinegun fire was laid down, but this in itself was not enough; moreover, many of the Americans' Maxims had soon jammed. Two tanks appeared, fired a few shots, then left. The Spanish troops who were meant to support the attack likewise took a brief look at the situation before deciding they would not be joining in.

Captain Merriman also thought his orders were suicidal, and he told XV Brigade's Commanding Officer, Lieutenant-Colonel Vladimir Copic (another Austro-Hungarian from the Red Army) that to attack in such circumstances would be disastrous. Copic promptly accused Merriman of cowardice. He sent two men from the British Battalion, the commissar Dave Springhall and Lieutenant George Wattis, with instructions to remove Merriman from his command if he refused to obey orders. Although Springhall and Wattis soon agreed with Merriman's assessment of the situation, they could not rescind Gal's instructions; and unlike the Spanish troops, they were not prepared to simply ignore them. They bravely volunteered to join the American officer in leading the troops, some of whom were refusing to leave their positions, whilst others were threatening to shoot Wattis.

Sixty-five new volunteers who had arrived at the front the previous day from Albacete augmented the Lincolns' numbers. But most of them had received virtually no training of any sort, and some still wore the clothes they had travelled out to Spain in.

'This will be a fuck-up,' veterans of the previous attack told one of them. 'If you want to live, just do as we do.' When they left their trench they advanced just a few yards before diving to the ground and digging in again.

On their flank, Jock Cunningham and George Aitken led a hundred men of the British Battalion into the attack. But like the Spanish soldiers, the remnants of the Franco-Belge Battalion did not emerge from their trenches. The rebel fire was thus concentrated on the Americans. One survivor said that within minutes of going over the top the heaped dead bodies of volunteers from the Bronx Young Communist League protected those who had remained behind. Almost immediately, Captain Merriman was hit in the shoulder, and Springhall was shot in the face. Only Wattis, coolly waving his swagger stick, seemed immune to the bullets as all along the line the attack fell to pieces.

When Merriman's second-in-command fell dead, Wattis became temporary commander of the Battalion. He tried to encourage the Americans on.

'Who the hell are you to give orders to my troops?' a company commander responded. Wattis replied that he was from Brigade HQ. 'Go to hell back there,' he was told.

Afterwards Wattis told a Cuban company commander that he was a coward; he responded by telling the British officer to get out of their trenches.

'I am already doing so,' the British officer replied, 'because I belong with men – not with you.'

As drizzle turned to heavy rain, one American later recalled how 'those who made it back to the trenches were soaked to the skin, covered with mud, and with rifles that were in no condition to fire.' Herbert Matthews reported in *The New York Times* that by the end of the attack, 'of the 400 Americans in the Lincoln Battalion, 108 were left.' Of the casualties, over a hundred were dead. One survivor described the scene afterwards, the ground in front of their trenches littered with corpses, as like 'some sort of stage setting created by a Hollywood mad genius'.

It hardly seemed real, and for many volunteers this sense of disbelief and disconnection with what was happening persisted through the war. 'One likes to imagine that at the end we will all go home again,' one American recorded in his diary later in the year, 'that the game will be over, that all the ones who have been killed will pick themselves up & come home to make their bow, with the rest of the stage corpses. But one knows that this will never happen. [They] are dead forever.'

Survivors of the attack mutinied. In a mass of emotions – disgust, fear, outrage, shock – small groups of Americans started quitting the line. Reaching their cookhouse one shouted angrily, 'On to France!' A squadron of XV Brigade cavalry, mostly Russians, stopped many of them before they got far. Others had gone six or seven miles before they were arrested.

A court martial was hastily arranged. It was reported that Colonel Copic wanted deserters executed, but the Brigade's political commissar, George Aitken, objected, pointing out that it would be 'catastrophic for enlistments'. In the end, a Russian tank officer, having heard that one of the Americans on trial was Russian-born, intervened and broke up the court. Instead, the mutinous, leaderless men of the Abraham Lincoln Battalion were temporarily taken out of the front.

A few days later they held their own meeting. John Simon, a young Jewish medical student from Philadelphia who had joined the Battalion just after the disastrous action, wrote in his diary that some men were crying because they had not known how to use their rifles, whilst a machine-gunner 'broke into tears as he explained how the guns wouldn't work, how they were not properly equipped.' At the same meeting the men elected a new commanding officer from within their own ranks. They chose Martin Hourihan, a former schoolteacher from Alabama who had briefly served as a clerk in the US Army; he was not a member of the Communist Party. They also sent a petition to Copic, requesting their immediate removal from frontline service, two weeks' training under real officers rather than 'self-selected amateurs', and a court martial of those responsible for sending untrained men into action. Copic simply treated it as further evidence of the Americans' insubordination, and ignored their request.

Back home, the US edition of *The Daily Worker* glossed over the tragedy; but many of the Lincolns held Merriman personally responsible for the massacre. In hospital, one of William Horvitz's wounded comrades dubbed their commander 'Fucking Captain Murderman'. They believed that a more confident, more experienced officer would have refused to attack. (Indeed, on his second day in action at Jarama, when promised tank support that had failed to appear, Tom Wintringham had disregarded a direct order from Gal to attack.)

Yet in Wintringham's overly optimistic opinion, despite the failure of their impossible mission, the Americans had achieved something significant:

> They established themselves among their equals as first-rate fighting men. They proved to the Fascists, and to their commanders and fellow-soldiers of our Brigades, that raw inexperienced lads from Brooklyn or Milwaukee could be very dangerous in war. They proved this to themselves and their new recruits training back in Albacete. And in the months that followed, alongside the English and other battalions of our Brigade, the Lincolns showed to the whole of Spain that men could live and remain dangerous week after week and month after month, unrelieved, in the monotony and strain of the trenches.

VI

As Tom Wintringham, William Horvitz, Robert Merriman, Frank Ryan and dozens more wounded men of XV International Brigade lay recovering in hospital, the Spanish Republic's Foreign Minister again linked the war to the threat that fascism posed to the wider world. Addressing a mass meeting in Madrid, he declared: 'To defend Madrid is to defend Paris, London, Prague, the Northern countries and every free and democratic nation in the not distant future.'

The 60,000 Italian troops now reckoned to be in Spain, he said, 'are the best proof that in Western Europe peace is only an ironical and gory fiction.' Though his words were reported in *The New York Times*, there seemed little change in the attitude of the Western democracies; the 'embargo' on international volunteers and arms sales remained in force, whilst being openly flouted by Germany, Italy and Russia.

Even the British edition of *The Daily Worker* appeared to hold a contradictory attitude to the world situation. Whilst encouraging its readers to volunteer to fight in Spain against what it called 'the monstrous horror that is Fascism,' it simultaneously counselled pacifism, and opposed the Government's (albeit half-hearted) policy of rearmament, a policy urged in part by Winston Churchill, who recognised Germany's burgeoning military strength. Part of *The Daily Worker*'s fear was that the British Government was on the side of fascism (a not unreasonable conclusion, given what appeared to be its tacit support for the Spanish rebels). 'That Government,' an article declared in early March, which was 'responsible in large measure for the advance of Fascism in Europe, now seeks to defend its armament policy on the ground that it desires to defend democracy ... Arms in the control of the National Government are arms that will be used to defend imperialism and Colonial exploitation, to maintain capitalism at home and to uphold Fascism the world over.' Rearmament 'is making inevitable an arms race, the end of which, if [the Government] is allowed to remain in power, will be world war.'

Whilst Wintringham expected to recover quickly from his leg wound, it was widely assumed that William Horvitz would die. The prognosis for others was equally unpromising. In the bed next to Horvitz lay an International Brigader who had lost half his face. There was an Englishman 'who'd had a bullet enter his right ear and emerge from his left cheek, yet had not suffered major damage. Mashed faces, shoulders, arms, legs. A Pole who had lost his leg screamed the loudest,' Horvitz recalled. 'They screamed in German, English, French, Serbian, Hungarian. I screamed in New York Gutter, my very own tongue.'

Remarkably, though the bullet in Horvitz's spine would never be removed, he survived. Lying in bed, he fell in love with a Spanish nurse:

She had full dark red lips, her nose was slightly aquiline.

Every time I saw her, my heart somersaulted … I suddenly realized I was alive. It made me happy. It also made me sad. Guilty is probably the right word. So many of my comrades had been killed, and here I was, alive, and damned glad I was.

He found himself wishing that he had had more time to have proved himself at the front, 'to become a hero, to have experienced war to its fullest.' These sentiments amazed him. 'To have proven myself? Be glad you're alive, I kept repeating to myself. All around me were the wounded, men with half faces, with smashed legs, amputees, splintered arms. Be glad you're alive, I said again and again, feeling guilty as hell.'

Within a fortnight of being wounded Wintringham was out of hospital, and with Kitty Bowler he went to Valencia for four weeks' sick leave. There he soon came down with a fever. He was again hospitalized, his overworked doctors assuming the high temperature to be due to the bullet wound in his leg. In fact, Wintringham had contracted typhoid.

A few days later, a nurse was flown out from England: 'poor Tom,' she later recalled, was

> in a very bad way in this terrible hospital … the place was so dirty, full of flies, and shit was all the way up the walls of the loo … He was looked after by this American girl who didn't know anything. He was so wretched, dirty and prickly and horrible that I thought the first thing I'd give him was a tepid sponge bath. A doctor came in furious and made me sign a form that I was responsible for killing him. So I signed the thing. Then I threw poor Kitty out.

Harry Pollitt, over from London on one of his periodic visits to Spain, advised Wintringham to drop Bowler, recommending instead 'with enthusiasm and details the charms of "Spanish dames"'. Later, a very embarrassed-looking British comrade appeared with a Party order, telling Wintringham to leave his mistress. Wintringham would have none of it.

Once he had recovered they decided to disappear for a month or two up the coast, where he would start writing a book about his experiences.

They went to a quiet fishing village on the Costa Blanca, spending six weeks alone together; it was like a honeymoon: 'the sky white clouds shadowed with pink … the clear skies of joy,' as Wintringham recollected in one of his poems. When his wife came to visit, he told her in no uncertain terms that their marriage was over, and that he was leaving her and the children for his American lover.

Back at Jarama, the men of the XV International Brigade were enduring the monotony of trench warfare in late winter. One American volunteer recorded how they would wake in the morning to find mud in their dugouts, blankets soaked, their clothes damp. Food had to be brought up to the front line from their cookhouse, a mile away: 'Most meals were as cold as the morning coffee. The wind whirled and eddied, and mud joined the food on its way to our mouths.' Not till April did the weather – or the supply of warm food – improve.

Jason Gurney, the sculptor from the British Battalion, had managed to get himself transferred to the Lincolns. He later wrote that despite frequent rumours that they were going to be withdrawn for leave and re-organization, nothing ever came of it. They began to feel that they would be 'left to rot on in Jarama for ever … everywhere there was a continuous and unrelenting grumble of discontent.' A principal grievance was the lack of mail, or much news at all from the outside world. This increased the impression that they were 'forgotten men … We were filthy and full of body-lice and began to feel that we were in a trap from which there was no escape.' Some thought that they were being deliberately kept there as punishment for their previous insubordination.

Some men deserted, some just seemed to disappear, whilst others were wounded or killed. Though neither side was strong enough to mount another attack, there was a regular danger from snipers – only two or three hundred yards separated the two lines – and the occasional trench mortar.

Jason Gurney was, like many others, despondent. 'It began to seem that we would sit up there in the dirt and stink of the Jarama trenches until we were gradually whittled away without having achieved anything at all.'

'If there were not the ever-present fear of death,' the American's medical orderly recorded in his diary, 'this life would kill us with *ennui* – there would be nothing idyllic about it.'

There was one visitor, however, who arrived with the spring and who briefly broke the monotony: Ernest Hemingway.

Chapter 9

The Capital of the World

|

It was only once a first draft of *To Have and Have Not* was completed that Hemingway was prepared to leave for Europe. 'I hate to go away,' he told his wife's parents in February 1937, 'but … for a long time me and my conscience both have known I had to go to Spain.' His second wife came from a family of wealthy Southern landowners, and his mother-in-law, Mary Pfeiffer, was a devout Catholic; for this reason she was more sympathetic to Franco than to the Republic. Hemingway (who had actually converted to Catholicism in the 1920s) carefully outlined his position:

> The Reds may be as bad as they say but they are the people of the country versus the absentee landlords, the Moors, the Italians and the Germans. I know the [rebels] are rotten because I know them very well and I would like to have a look at the others to see how it lines up on a basis of humanity. This is the dress rehearsal for the inevitable European war and I would like to write anti-war correspondence that would help to keep us out of it when it comes.

The North American Newspaper Alliance would be paying him well for his reports, which would be syndicated to some sixty US and Canadian newspapers (including *The New York Times*, *The San Francisco Chronicle* and

The Los Angeles Times, as well as the paper with which he had started his writing career twenty years before, *The Kansas City Star*). 'I don't believe in making money out of other people's suffering,' he told his mother-in-law, explaining that he would be donating the money towards ambulances for Spain.

Politics had never loomed especially large in Hemingway's life or writing; some critics even accused him (uncharitably) of 'an indifference to society'. By the mid-1930s it appeared that Hemingway was squandering his extraordinary talent writing articles about fishing and big-game hunting for *Esquire* magazine (experiences which had also inspired his most recent book, *The Green Hills of Africa*, as well as a brilliant short story, 'The Snows of Kilimanjaro'). As Percy Wyndham Lewis suggested in a long essay published in 1934, 'it is difficult to imagine a writer whose mind is more entirely closed to politics than is Hemingway's. I do not suppose he has ever heard of the Five-Year Plan, though … I expect he has heard of Hitler.' Lewis (who admired Hemingway's work) went on to suggest that, although the author was clearly interested in war, he was not interested in 'the things that cause war, or the people who profit by it, or in the ultimate human destinies involved in it.'

In fact, this was not entirely true. As a European correspondent for *The Toronto Star* in the early 1920s Hemingway had covered a number of major political events, and had met (and interviewed) some important national leaders, including Mussolini. But he had eventually sidelined journalism for fiction. Now, as he approached his thirty-eighth birthday, the book Hemingway was completing did show clear signs of a social and political conscience. *To Have and Have Not* contrasted the lives of the wealthy 'haves' holidaying in Key West and Havana with the poverty of the 'have nots' who struggled to make a living – often illicitly – alongside them. These included the novel's hard-boiled hero, Harry Morgan (who, one character noted, 'talks like a radical'), as well as Great War veterans employed on Roosevelt's poorly-paid 'New Deal' projects and brutal, idealistic Cuban revolutionaries who rob Key West's bank to fund their cause. The town at the southern tip of Florida thus served as a microcosm for Depression-era America, a grim picture of a deeply divided, apparently decaying society. And though ultimately a flawed novel, it reiterated what Wyndham Lewis considered the greatness inherent in Hemingway's writing: his voice was 'the voice of the "folk", of the masses, who are the cannon-fodder, the cattle outside the slaughter-house.' Though that voice was itself 'innocent of politics,' Lewis acknowledged this was Hemingway's genius: 'he expresses the soul of the dumb ox; his is the voice *of those to whom things are done.*'

To Have and Have Not was not a dramatic step to the Left, and this latest work of fiction (as well as the contemporaneous short stories) continued to reveal Hemingway's obsession with sex, marriage, violence, cowardice and death, obsessions that he would take with him to Spain. But even before the new novel's publication the author's changing political outlook was being noted by critics, including some in England: in December 1936 George Orwell – himself shortly to leave for Spain – observed in one of his very few published references to the American writer that Hemingway 'is rumoured to be toying with Communism.'

Hemingway set sail for France at the end of February 1937, leaving behind his wife, Pauline, and their two young sons. Accompanying him was his friend, the Brooklyn bullfighter Sidney Franklin. Stopping to secure his press credentials in Paris, Hemingway met Joris Ivens, the Dutch film-maker who was directing the documentary for Contemporary Historians. Recently returned to France after four weeks filming in Spain, Ivens had developed his first rolls of footage. Though he was in a hurry ('Our job was not to make the best of all films,' he later said, 'but to make a good film for exhibition in the United States'), he was pleased with what he had captured. His stated aim was 'to make the camera – and through the camera, the audience – take part in the action.' Like Hemingway, he intended to make the war in Spain seem as real as possible to those who did not witness it first hand.

The two men shared a number of drinks and dinners in Paris. Ivens, who was a covert communist, recognized that Hemingway would be 'an asset to our cause because he wrote such good articles.' In Ivens' opinion,

Hemingway expected Spain 'to be just another war, and that was the way he intended to write about it.' Though the American obviously 'had strong, personal, sentimental relations to Spain,' Ivens felt that 'he saw no particularly deep implications in this war, and was pretty skeptical when I described it as the first test of fascism in Europe, fascism on its first battlefield.' So Ivens tasked himself with making Hemingway 'understand the anti-fascist cause,' and the communist side of the argument.

They caught a night-train to Toulouse, and from there a plane to Spain. 'Flying low down the coast of Alicante,' Hemingway wrote in his first NANA despatch, 'along white beaches, past gray-castled towns or with the sea curling against rocky headlands, there was no sign of war.'

A tiny Spanish chauffeur who resembled, said Hemingway, 'a particularly unattractive, very mature dwarf out of Velasquez put into a suit of blue dungarees' drove them the seven hours inland to Madrid. The Spaniard seethed with patriotism, and as the capital came into view, 'rising like a great white fortress across the plain,' he declared: 'Long live Madrid, the capital of my soul!'

'And of my heart,' Hemingway replied.

||

Hemingway made his base at the Hotel Florida, a large building off the Gran Via in the Plaza del Callao. Many of the international reporters covering the conflict were rooming there, as it was close to the Telefónica building from which they cabled their reports home. The residents included the British correspondents Claud Cockburn and Sefton Delmer, the French writer Antoine de Saint-Exupéry, and the American journalists Herbert Matthews, Josephine Herbst and Virginia Cowles. Robert Capa and Gerda Taro were also regular guests. Only twenty-two years old, Capa had made his name the previous autumn with a photograph apparently showing a Republican militiamen at the moment he was shot dead by a rebel bullet. Capa had followed this coup with a series of pictures of the siege of Madrid and the International Brigades' defence of University

Gerda Taro, *Robert Capa on the Segovia Front,
May/June 1937* (Magnum)

City. *Picture Post* would soon be hailing him 'The Greatest War Photographer in the World'. With a shared love of danger and drama, Capa and Hemingway soon became friends.

Another talented young American writer, Martha Gellhorn, joined the international set at the Florida. An attractive, ambitious twenty-eight year old from St Louis, Missouri, she had first met Hemingway at a Key West bar a few months earlier. Educated at Bryn Mawr (where she had known Kitty Bowler), she had worked for newspapers and magazines in the US and Europe (including Paris *Vogue*) since 1929. Her father was a half-Jewish German-born doctor, and it was whilst visiting Nazi Germany that Gellhorn abandoned pacifism to become a dedicated anti-fascist. She had published two books: one a novel, influenced, in part, by Hemingway; the other a collection of short stories based on her travels through Depression-era America. Both had been well received. Idealistic, politically of the Left (Eleanor Roosevelt was a fan of her work), Gellhorn had told Hemingway of her wish to visit Spain.

So he told her to come. She took a boat to France and, unable to obtain press credentials in Paris, she crossed the Pyrenees illegally on foot. By night, in the cold, she arrived in the blacked-out city of Madrid.

'I knew you'd get here, daughter,' Hemingway remarked when she appeared, 'because I fixed it so you could.' It was a ridiculous claim, and should have warned the young writer of what was to come. But she was impressed by his commitment to the Spanish cause, and against her better instincts she and Hemingway soon became lovers, with adjacent rooms in the Florida Hotel. It was not his first affair, nor hers: an earlier relationship with a married Frenchman had resulted in two abortions (a child, she feared, would prevent her from writing).

Martha Gellhorn and Ernest Hemingway, Spain 1937/8 (JFK Library)

In Madrid, Martha Gellhorn was exhilarated to discover a city at war. Rebel soldiers were still entrenched near the University City, little over a mile away. The sound of gunshots and mortar rounds punctured the night, and almost daily rebel artillery shells fell randomly into the city. By night, it was claimed, Fifth Columnists shot citizens in the streets. Madrid, she wrote, 'was a battlefield, waiting in the dark. There was certainly fear in that feeling, and courage. It made you walk carefully and listen hard and it lifted the heart.'

Hemingway loved it. 'You should have seen Madrid when there were shells falling and sharpshooters on the rooftops,' he later told a Spanish friend. 'The people blossomed anew every morning; it was simply amazing. I'll never forget it; I swear it's the greatest thing I've ever seen in my life.' But, he added, 'I've also seen the filthiest, the most miserable, the most disgusting things here. It was in Madrid that I discovered what a man is really like in his three fundamental parts: his head, his heart, and his balls.'

At first Gellhorn did not know how to respond to this incredible experience. Hemingway advised her to do what she did best: write. So she sent off some articles to *Collier's*, a popular US weekly magazine; they were accounts of day-to-day life in the besieged city, the long queues for food, the hot, twisted steel of an exploding shell killing a little boy, an old woman 'holding the hand of the dead child, looking at him stupidly, not saying anything'. Almost by accident, she discovered that she had become a war correspondent.

Virginia Cowles, a self-assured twenty-six-year-old from New England, also found herself suddenly recast as a war reporter. Yet in Madrid, she was surprised to find that the atmosphere was not one of war at all. 'Bright yellow tram-cars rattled down the avenues,' she later recalled, whilst the shop windows 'displayed Schiaparelli perfume, silver fox furs, jewellery, gloves and ladies' hand-made shoes; movie houses advertised Greta Garbo in "Anna Karenina" and the Marx Brothers in "A Night at the Opera".' Amongst all this, the vivid propaganda posters, the jagged shell-holes in the streets, the camouflaged army trucks and the stone barricades 'seemed as unreal as stage props; the sun was too warm, the people too nonchalant for war. Only the queue lines carried a sense of tragedy.'

One of the most extraordinary places was the Florida itself. Cowles doubted that 'any hotel in the world has ever attracted a more diverse assembly of foreigners.' There were American mercenary pilots serving with the Republican air force; bohemian English ambulance drivers; writers and journalists seemingly from all nations of the world; volunteers on a night's leave from the International Brigades; prostitutes; spies.

Many nights the correspondents gathered in Hemingway's rooms. He kept an array of food in his wardrobe – ham, bacon, eggs, coffee, marmalade – as well as whiskey in the silver flask he took everywhere with him. (Drinking – like writing, fighting, fishing and shooting – was one of the acts that defined Hemingway. 'I have drunk since I was fifteen and few things have given me more pleasure,' he once remarked. 'Modern life … is often a mechanical oppression and liquor is the only mechanical relief.')

'There was a kind of splurging magnificence about Hemingway at the Florida,' Josephine Herbst later recalled, 'a crackling generosity'. When away from the city he would take a gun and shoot hare and partridge; a maid cooked them in his room, and 'the divine odor of cooking' would seep through the hallways. The journalists ate, drank and listened to records, rarely going to bed before the early hours. But despite Hemingway's largesse, most days they were hungry.

Hemingway, of course, was a celebrity, and everyone who met him came away with a story. Claud Cockburn, still covering the war for *The Daily Worker*, would recall how one day the American laid a big map on a table,

> and he explained to an audience of generals, politicians and correspondents that, for some ballistic reason, the shells could not hit the Florida. He could talk in a very military way and make it all sound very convincing. Everyone was convinced and happy. Then a shell whooshed through the roof above Mr Hemingway's head – the first actually to hit the Florida – and the ceiling fell down on the breakfast table. To any lesser [man] than Mr Hemingway the occurrence would have been humiliating. While we were all getting the plaster out of our hair, Mr Hemingway looked slowly round at us, one after the other.
>
> 'How do you like it now, gentlemen?' he said, and by some astonishing trick of manner conveyed the impression that this episode had actually, in an obscure way, confirmed instead of upsetting his theory – that his theory had been right when he expounded it and this only demonstrated that the time had come to have a new one.
>
> Everyone was very happy to have Mr Hemingway there, partly because he was obviously a fine man to have around when there was war and trouble, and partly because to have so famous an author there, writing on behalf of the Republic, made people feel less alone in the world – in a sense, which was no fault of Mr Hemingway, it helped to foster the

illusion that sooner or later the 'world conscience' would be aroused, the 'common people' in Britain and France would force their Governments to end non-intervention, and the war would be won.

It was certainly the case that Hemingway's accounts of the conflict were powerful pieces of pro-Republican reportage and – sometimes – propaganda. An article written in the novelistic, second-person style that he often affected in his newspaper articles reported the immediate aftermath of a Rebel shell bursting in the street close to the Florida Hotel:

'How many dead?' you ask a policeman.

'Only one,' he says. 'It went through the sidewalk and burst below. If it had burst on the stone of the road there might have been fifty.'

A policeman covers the body; they send for some one to repair the gas main, and you go in to breakfast. A charwoman, her eyes red, is scrubbing the blood off the marble floor of the corridor. The dead man wasn't you nor any one you know, and every one is very hungry in the morning after a cold night and a long day the day before …

'Did you see him?' asked some one else at breakfast.

'Sure,' you say.

'That's where we pass a dozen times a day – right on that corner.' But everyone has the feeling that characterizes war. It wasn't me, see? It wasn't me.

Later in the year Hemingway told his mother-in-law that this experience of war had 'completely eliminated all fear of death or anything else.' As he explained, 'It seemed as though the world were in such a bad way and certain things so necessary to do that to think about any personal future was simply very egoistic. After the first two weeks in Madrid I had an impersonal feeling of having no wife, no children, no house, no boat, nothing.'

But he did have a mistress; and, increasingly, a purpose. Joris Ivens introduced him to the Russians who had taken over the Palace Hotel, at the other end of Gran Via from the Florida. In Claud Cockburn's opinion these Russians seemed to be the only people who could do without the illusion that the war could be won, 'and still not become defeatist'. Cockburn and Hemingway both befriended one Russian in particular: Mikhail Koltzov, foreign editor of *Pravda*.

Though some thought Koltzov 'unbearably cynical,' Cockburn felt he had 'a powerful enthusiasm for life – for the humour of life, for all manifestations of vigorous life from a tank battle to Elizabethan literature to a good circus.' He 'positively enjoyed the sense of danger, and sometimes – by his political indiscretions, for instance, or his still more wildly indiscreet love affairs – deliberately created dangers which need not have existed.' Cockburn wrote that 'Spanish politicians often spoke of [Koltzov] to me as the most powerful man in Spain. That sort of phrase is always meaningless. But it was true that he did play a major role in determining the course of Russian policy in Spain.'

Sometimes with Martha Gellhorn or Virginia Cowles, Hemingway visited the volunteers of the International Brigades, either the wounded in hospital, or their comrades still in the front line at Jarama. Many were pleased to have the famous writer in their midst; others were less impressed. Jason Gurney, already disillusioned at the course of the war and convinced it was time for the Republic to admit that defeat was inevitable, later described Hemingway as 'full of hearty and bogus *bonhomie*' when he visited the Abraham Lincoln Battalion. 'He sat himself down behind the bullet-proof shield of a machine-gun and loosed off a whole belt of ammunition in the general direction of the enemy. This provoked a mortar bombardment for which he did not stay.'

Gustav Regler was more impressed. He admired Hemingway's 'calming effect' on the soldiers, but also noted that Hemingway sought something from them, too. 'For him we had the scent of death, like the bullfighters, and because of this he was invigorated by our company.'

Regler introduced Hemingway to the remnants of the French

Ernest Hemingway with the Russian writer Ilya Ehrenburg (left) and the German political commissar and writer Gustav Regler, 1937 (JFK Library)

Battalion that had been virtually destroyed in the early action at Jarama. The German writer watched as Hemingway listened patiently to the stories of the demoralized Frenchmen. 'He stood with his flask ready beside each speaker in turn, snorting to show that he understood. The knives of the Moors seemed to flash again, and the survivors raised their faces to the square-figured man in the shapeless woollen jersey.'

'*C'est défendu, n'est-ce pas?*' they asked.

Hemingway nodded, gripped their shoulders reassuringly, and repeated (with what Regler described as 'an almost childish gravity'), '*C'est défendu.*'

Like Koltzov, Regler would give Hemingway inside stories on many of the military operations and political crises he had witnessed in Spain. 'I let him know our losses and gave him advance information whenever I could, feeling certain that he really understood what it was all about.' This included providing secret material relating to the Communist Party, an organization which Regler felt Hemingway 'respected,' because the American (as much as he came to despise its figureheads such as André Marty and 'La Pasionaria,' Dolores Ibárruri) knew that the Party 'was fighting more actively than any other body'. It increasingly appeared to Hemingway that it was only the communists, with the military aid of the Soviet Union, who were making the fight against Franco possible.

The situation, however, was not seen quite this way by every foreign observer sympathetic to the Republic. In February 1937 George Orwell's old school-friend, the writer Cyril Connolly, visited Spain, and reported on what he had seen in the left-wing weekly paper, *The New Statesman and Nation*. He certainly saw some sense to the communists' policy of supporting 'moderate elements' in the Spanish Government to help establish 'a bourgeois democratic Spain against what they consider the premature revolutionary activities of the Anarchists and the POUM.' And it was clear to Connolly that the communists did not want to frighten off Europe's anti-fascist democracies, and that they wanted to give France and Britain 'authentic evidence of a legitimate and moderate government in power in Spain'. As he explained, the communist and socialist slogan was 'First win the war, then attend to the revolution.'

This, however, contrasted significantly with the policy of the more radical elements in the united front against Franco. The argument of the anarchists and the radical Marxists of the POUM was that the war and the revolution were 'indivisible and we must go on with both of them simultaneously.' They rightly accused the communists of suppressing the revolution. This attitude, as Connolly observed, meant that the POUM 'are severely condemned by the Communist and Socialist press on charges of being Trotskyites, and hence Fascists, of running away in battle and undermining the Government (from which they have been driven out), of consisting of criminals and the rejected members of other parties, and of preparing a counter-revolutionary coup.' The anarchists, meanwhile, were attacked 'as being either visionaries, half-wits, or gunmen.'

To 'prove' their point, the communists pointed to the inactivity of both the anarchist and POUM militias on the Aragon front, where George Orwell was wiling away his time, making night patrols and taking occasional pot shots at the enemy. (When Orwell later read his old friend's article, he was disappointed that Connolly had not dropped by his trench: 'I would have enjoyed giving you tea in a dugout,' he wrote and told him.)

In defence of their supposed 'inactivity', the anarchists explained that no quantities of decent armaments had reached them, and that without modern weapons to support an attack on entrenched positions, the Aragon front would remain dormant. But the communists would not give them Russian arms; perhaps (as Orwell later claimed) because they feared that these radicals would use them in pursuit of the revolution that Stalin did not want; or perhaps simply because those arms (insufficient as they still were) were going to the newly formed, government-sanctioned 'Popular Army' and the International Brigades instead. A message sent to Russia from a Comintern agent in Barcelona complained that the anarchists had 'always enough pretexts and excuses for refusing action … there are not enough forces, not enough weapons, no cartridges, no aircraft and tanks, and so on.' He did not appear to realize that this was true, as Orwell's experience with the POUM was proving.

It was a confusing, precarious situation that generated plenty of infighting and recrimination. 'In fact,' Connolly concluded,

> it would be hard to find an atmosphere more full of envy, intrigue, rumour and muddle than that which exists at the moment in the capitals of Republican Spain; while Malaga falls and Madrid struggles heroically, the further one gets from the front, the dimmer grows the memory of the 19th of July, the louder the mutual accusations and reproaches of the party. They are now even jealous of their one hope, the International Brigades, and it seems useless to clamour for unity of command when there is no one worthy of it.

III

Notwithstanding Connolly's insights into a complex situation, the Republican army and the International Brigades were soon celebrating a major success. On 29 March *The New York Times* ran Hemingway's description of the aftermath of a Republican victory, their first real success since the defence of Madrid.

Having failed to cut the Madrid-Valencia road at Jarama, Franco had changed tactics. His Italian allies, buoyed by their recent triumph in taking Malaga, proposed an attack on Madrid from the north-east, towards Guadalajara, some forty miles from the capital. Three divisions of Italians, supported by Spanish rebel militiamen, advanced early on 8 March. Having broken through the Republican defences, the Italian's lightly armoured columns initially made rapid progress, advancing eighteen miles towards the capital in just two days.

Among the troops rushed to stall the attack were Italian volunteers of the International Brigades' Garibaldi Battalion. The Republican counter-attack, supported by tanks, with numerical superiority in the air and aided by bad weather that made it hard for Mussolini's Italian forces to manoeuvre, was devastating.

According to Hemingway's report, Guadalajara was

> the first battle in this war [to be fought] on a World War scale of organization … It is impossible to overemphasize the importance of this battle, where native Spanish battalions, composed mainly of boys untrained last November, not only fought stubbornly in defense with other and better-trained troops, but attacked in a complicatedly planned and perfectly organized military operation only comparable to the finest in the Great War.

Hemingway explained that he had been studying the ground of the week-long fight for the past four days, 'going over the ground with the commanders who directed it and the officers who fought it, checking the positions and following the tank trails.' He was certain that the battle 'will take its place in military history with the other decisive battles of the world.'

Others shared Hemingway's interpretation. Herbert Matthews wrote at the time (and to his later embarrassment) that Guadalajara was 'one of the twelve or fifteen decisive battles of history'. Tom Wintringham, still recovering from his injury at Jarama, felt that this success had given the Republic an eighteen-month breathing space: whilst they might yet suffer losses and defeats, it seemed clear that the Republican army 'could not be effectively attacked'. This, thought Wintringham, was surely time enough for the rest of Europe to open its eyes to 'the nature of the invasion of Spain,' and act to end it.

In fact, Franco was not especially perturbed by the Italians' defeat, for, confident that neither Britain nor America was going to intervene in Spain, he was no longer pursuing a speedy victory. As he explained to an Italian Chief of Staff: 'In a civil war, systematic occupation of territory, accompanied by the necessary purges, is preferable to a rapid defeat of the enemy armies, which in the end leaves the country still infested with enemies.' A slow war would give Franco the chance to dispose of his political enemies – on both the Left and the Right – one by one.

IV

While General Franco might have been convinced that the democracies would not intervene in Spain, many British and American supporters of the Republic persevered in their efforts to change their governments' opinion. Through much of April 1937, Hemingway helped Joris Ivens and his cameraman on their documentary, now titled *The Spanish Earth*.

The Dutchman was impressed by Hemingway's dedication to the project, and by his quick comprehension and understanding of this new medium. The three men rose early to film the Republican Army's counter-attack against the rebels still holed up near University City. Watching the fighting one day with Virginia Cowles, Hemingway remarked, 'It's the nastiest thing human beings can do to each other, but the most exciting.'

Ivens' film was structured in two parts, juxtaposing the life of the front-line soldiers with that of those who remained at home tilling the dry earth. The latter sequences were shot in Fuentidueña, a small village on the river Tajo some forty kilometres south-east of Madrid along the Valencia road, within earshot of the fighting at Jarama. As well as evicting their priest, the villagers had appropriated the local estate from its owner, who was now fighting for Franco. He had used the land for hunting; according to Ivens, any peasant who dared walk on it was shot. The new owners' collective, however, planned to irrigate it with water from the Tajo. Then they would grow crops to sell in Madrid.

An American reviewer would write in July that this was the primary theme of *The Spanish Earth*: 'the efforts of a peasant people to reclaim for themselves, by irrigation and toil, a land that had been neglected through generations of absentee ownership ... This, says Mr Ivens, is the meaning of the war in Spain. It is, he says, a war for melons, tomatoes, onions – not one for broad principles of ideology.'

John Dos Passos was supposed to be helping Hemingway with the film. The two writers were close friends, with much in common: both had served with the Red Cross in Italy during the Great War, they had first met as young men in Paris, and had visited Spain together long before the Civil War. Dos Passos, though, was well known for his left-wing views; he had visited Russia, and in novels such as *Manhattan Transfer* and *The Big Money* had explored what he saw as the moral emptiness at the heart of twentieth-century America. (Kitty Bowler would recommend *The Big Money* to Tom Wintringham: 'it is so full of the stupid drunkenness we Americans will go in for. You must read it. It will explain so well to you the disgust which first turned me left.') Though his books were well received, they did not sell as well as Hemingway's. 'Sore, broke, and damn sick of everything,' he wrote to Hemingway from New York at the start of January 1937. 'Living in the latter Roman Empire's not much fun.'

Dos, as his friends knew him, had written of his fear that a 'fascist Spain' would mean 'a fascist France and more violent reaction here and in England'. Like Hemingway, he believed the cancer of right-wing extremism had to be stopped before it spread further. He had spent

March raising money to fund *The Spanish Earth* in New York, and had intended to arrive in Madrid in early April. Instead, on arriving in Spain, he had been waylaid in Valencia.

Like Hemingway, Dos Passos had old friends in Spain. He particularly wanted to meet one of them, José Robles, whom he had met during his first visit way back in 1916. Robles came from a well-to-do family, but had left Spain to teach Spanish literature at Johns Hopkins University. He had been home on holiday with his wife and children when the Civil War broke out, and had decided to stay and help the Government. A fluent speaker of Russian, he had found work in the Ministry of War as an interpreter for a senior Red Army general, Ian Antonovich Berzin (known in Spain by the pseudonym Goriev, and one of the men responsible for defending Madrid during Franco's first assault on the city in November). Dos Passos reckoned that given Robles' knowledge and sensibilities, he would be 'the most useful man in Spain for the purposes of our documentary'.

A little while before Dos Passos arrived in Valencia, however, Robles had been arrested. Robles' wife told Dos Passos that she could not find why (or even where) he was being held. Dos Passos used all his contacts to try and find his friend, but after a week in Valencia had only been met by faces that 'took on a strange embarrassment'; and behind the embarrassment he saw fear. All he could learn was that the charges against Robles 'were not serious, and that he was in no danger.'

Going on to Madrid, Dos joined Hemingway and Ivens at the Florida Hotel; but he continued to ask questions. This worried Hemingway. One morning after the Florida had been nearly hit by shellfire, Hemingway invited Josephine Herbst to his room for a brandy, and urged her to talk to Dos Passos. As she later wrote, Hemingway suggested that she 'tell him to lay off making enquiries about Robles. It was going to throw suspicion on all of us and get us into trouble. This was a war. [Pepe] Quintanilla, the head of the Department of Justice, had assured Dos that Robles would get a fair trial. Others in authority had told him the same. He should lay off.'

But Hemingway's request was, Herbst later recalled, 'terribly disturbing'; for she already knew that Robles was dead, shot as a fascist spy:

> I had been in Valencia before coming to Madrid and there had been told, in strictest confidence, and for the reason that Dos Passos was an old friend of mine, that the man was dead. Some of the Spanish were beginning to be worried about Dos Passos's zeal, and fearing that he might turn against their cause if he discovered the truth, hoped to keep him from finding out anything about it while he was in Spain.

Since Herbst had sworn to keep this information secret, she did not feel she could tell Dos Passos. Nevertheless, she felt that Dos should know, 'not because he might bring danger down on us but because the man was dead.' So she asked Hemingway to do the deed. At a lunch shortly afterwards hosted by officers commanding XV International Brigade, Hemingway informed his old friend that Robles had been executed as a spy. This was not perhaps the first Dos had heard of Robles' death, but he was appalled that Hemingway so readily accepted that his Spanish friend had been guilty.

'What's one man's life at a time like this?' was Hemingway's attitude. 'We musn't let our personal feelings run away with us.' For Hemingway, there were greater issues at stake: as he repeated over and over again, though war was terrible, once started, there was only one thing to do: 'It must be won. For defeat brings worse things than any that can ever happen in a war.'

But in Dos Passos' opinion, what was the purpose of winning the war if everything worth fighting for was lost in the pursuit of victory? Though he had been impressed by what the communists were achieving when he visited the Soviet Union in 1928, he had also glimpsed some of the fear: an Englishman he had met there told him he had come to Russia out of enthusiasm for the revolution, but his stay had turned into a nightmare as the government turned on Trotskyists, old revolutionaries and other supposed opponents of the revolution.

Hemingway and Dos were thus each disgusted by the other's attitude. Herbst felt that it was Dos Passos who had the better idea of what was happening in Spain. Hemingway 'seemed to be naively embracing … the current ideologies at the very moment when Dos Passos was urgently questioning them.'

As Dos Passos wrote two years later, it was only in Madrid that he had received

> definite information from the then chief of the Republican counter-espionage service that Robles had been executed by a 'special section' (which I gathered was under control of the Communist Party). He added that in his opinion the execution had been a mistake and that it was too bad.

Spaniards closer to the Communist Party to whom Dos Passos spoke 'took the attitude that Robles had been shot as an example to other officials because he had been overheard indiscreetly discussing military plans in a café.'

In Dos Passos' opinion, 'Russian secret agents felt that Robles knew too much about the relations between the Spanish war ministry and the Kremlin and [that he] was not, from their very special point of view, politically reliable.' The 'intended effect' of his friend's murder had been to make people 'very chary of talking about the "Mexicans" as the Russians were familiarly known'. The 'fascist spy' theory seemed, to him, to be 'the fabrication of romantic American Communist sympathizers': by which, perhaps, he meant Hemingway.

In his most recent novel *The Big Money*, Dos Passos had illustrated the betrayal of radical causes by a Soviet-dominated American Communist Party. Even before he arrived in Spain, he was becoming disillusioned by the far Left with which he had for such a long time been closely associated. Recent events in Russia only added to his – and others' –

unease, and their growing awareness that something was going deeply wrong within the world's first communist state.

To young acolytes such as John Cornford and William Horvitz, communism alone offered redemption to the working class; it was communism and state control of wealth and the economy that would save them from the greed, inequalities and degradation of capitalism. And British and American journalists such as Tom Wintringham and Louis Fischer, who had visited Russia in the years immediately after the Revolution of 1917, had been deeply impressed by what they saw there. But what Marx and Engels had called the 'dictatorship of the proletariat' had been replaced by the dictatorship of just one man: the Bolshevik revolutionary, Joseph Stalin.

In late December 1929, six days after his fiftieth birthday, Stalin had launched a programme to revolutionize Soviet agriculture, speeding up collectivization and forcing better-off peasants (the 'kulaks') from their land, often at gunpoint. Some of those imposing Stalin's diktat did so gleefully; others were not happy at turning weapons on their own people. At the same time, in the first of the Five Year Plans, economic focus was placed on rapid industrialization. By 1932–3 the combined result of these operations – particularly in the grain-growing region of Ukraine – was famine and death, on an enormous scale. Millions died. Yet many Western journalists in the USSR – most notably Kitty Bowler's one-time boyfriend, Walter Duranty of *The New York Times* – went out of the way to deny such a thing. To its Western sympathizers, the Soviet dream – with its promise of solving the puzzle of 'poverty in the midst of plenty' – was simply too big to be allowed to fail. Was not Soviet communism, as the English ideologues Beatrice and Sidney Webb had suggested in 1935, 'a new civilization'?

It was also in 1935 that Stalin instigated a reign of political persecution far worse than anything ever imagined by the Tsars: within three years, more than three million so-called 'enemies of the people' were sent to labour camps, where many were worked to death; more than 700,000 were executed. No one – except Stalin himself – was immune from accusation.

In a series of show trials that began in Moscow in 1936, a series of senior Soviet figures implicated themselves in a variety of improbable plots, conspiracies, 'counter-revolutionary' and terrorist activities. Numerous Bolsheviks who had headed the 1917 revolution were accused of spying for Russia's enemies. Mikhail Tukhachevsky, hero of the Revolution and Marshal of the Red Army, was arrested and executed in 1937 along with many fellow generals. Frequently, army officers summoned back from Spain were arrested: General Kléber, who had led the International Brigades in the defence of Madrid, was sentenced to hard labour, and would die in a gulag. Mikhail Koltzov, too, was recalled. In one of his last conversations with Claud Cockburn, the *Pravda* journalist accurately ran through his own forthcoming trial and execution.

'But,' Cockburn responded, 'the worst you can be accused of is only that your advice was mistaken.'

'Only?' Koltzov replied. 'Only? With all that's been at stake, to give mistaken advice can be criminal.'

Even Nikolai Yezhov, head of the NKVD, the Soviet secret police, disappeared in 1939, victim of the 'great terror' his murderous organization had orchestrated. But the greatest 'enemy of the people' was Stalin's former Bolshevik comrade, the exiled Leon Trotsky. To be accused – or forced into an admission – of Trotskyism was a virtual death sentence.

Many in the West were puzzled by the trials ('a dark mystery,' as Orwell called them), and by the ready confessions of the accused. Opinion ranged from approval of this removal of enemies of the state, to scepticism at their guilt, to sheer confusion. One of the few groups in Spain to condemn the Russian trials openly was the POUM. Their founder, Andrés (Andreu) Nin, had spent the 1920s in Russia, during which time he had worked for Trotsky (and though Trotsky had been critical of Nin's organization, the POUM had invited him to come to Barcelona). Nin thus knew Russia from the inside, and the Communists responded to this dangerous critic and former bedfellow with an almost unbelievable accusation: they claimed that the POUM was secretly aiding

Franco; rumours even reached the POUM's leadership that – on orders from Moscow – the communists in Spain were planning their destruction.

Taking their lead from Moscow, communists worldwide vigorously attacked any opposition to, or criticism of, Stalin and his policies. As an anonymous letter to *The New Statesman and Nation* pointed out in February 1937, 'anyone' – be it in Russia, Britain or Spain – 'who does not accept Stalin's line regarding policy is at once dubbed a Trotskyite, a Nazi agent [or] a Japanese agent.' Absurdly, even the left-leaning *Manchester Guardian*, as this letter-writer pointed out, had been branded by *Pravda* as 'a Fascist-speaking trumpet … open to the Gestapo for the glorification of its hired murderers, wreckers and Trotskyist spies'.

This state of uncertainty, irrationality, fear, accusation and recrimination – what Gustav Regler called 'spy disease, the Russian syphilis' – had now contaminated Spain. Dos Passos's friend had been one of its early victims; as the American wrote bitterly long afterwards, 'With their teamwork and their arms and their slogans the communists had brought with them their terror.'

Chapter 10

Eye-Witness in Barcelona

|

In late April 1937, whilst Ernest Hemingway and Martha Gellhorn were touring the Republican positions in the Guadarrama mountains north of Madrid, there came one of the defining events of the whole war.

Following the defeat of the Italian forces at Guadalajara, Franco had all but abandoned his attempt to take Madrid. Instead, he turned his attention to the north, and the Basque country. The Catholic Basques, who had continued to support the Republic in the hope of securing independence, were an embarrassment for Franco, since they contradicted his (and the Catholic Church's) bold claim that the rebellion was a 'Crusade' against godless 'Reds'. At the end of March, the rebel General Emilio Mola launched an attack of nearly 40,000 troops against them. If submission were not immediate, he warned, he would raze their land to the ground. German planes and pilots of the Condor Legion, under the command of Lieutenant-Colonel Wolfram von Richthofen (cousin of the famous Great War pilot, the 'Red Baron') supported the offensive. By late April, despite stiff defence, the ill-equipped Basque forces were in disorder, retreating to Bilbao, their coastal capital and northern Spain's industrial centre.

The reporter covering the story for *The Times* was a twenty-seven-year-old South African, George Steer. A graduate of Oxford University, Steer had recently been reporting on Italy's invasion of Abyssinia; there he had met the Spanish journalist who soon became his wife. *The Times* was a conservative newspaper, and Steer had originally been reporting the war from Franco's side. But his sympathies lay with the Republic, and Steer had soon been ordered to leave the rebel zone. Instead, he had started covering the other side of the war.

Returning to Bilbao from the front line in the late afternoon of 26 April, Steer had seen bombers massing in the distant sky. But it was only whilst he was at dinner that evening with some fellow journalists that he heard the news over the phone, 'Guernica is in flames.'

If true, it was a major story: Guernica was the spiritual capital of the Basques. It was there, beneath an ancient oak tree, that they had held their parliaments, and it was in Guernica's ancient church that the kings of Spain had traditionally sworn to uphold the liberties of the Basque people.

Immediately, Steer and four journalists from Reuter's, *The Star*, *The Daily Express* and *Ce Soir* called for cars. In convoy they drove through the night the twenty miles to Guernica. Fifteen miles south of the town, the reddening horizon 'seemed to move and carry trembling veins of blood.' As they drew closer, they saw great pink billowing clouds of smoke, reflecting 'some great fire upon them. The skies in their vague, all-embracing way were mirroring Guernica, and pulsed more slowly to the destruction that danced a war dance over the home of seven thousand human beings.'

Finally they saw the town itself: Steer would call it 'undoubtedly the most elaborate attack upon the civilian population staged in Europe since the Great War, and more concentrated than any of their experiences in that holocaust.' Guernica was ablaze. At every window there were 'piercing eyes of fire; where every roof had stood [were] wild trailing locks of fire … and a wild red disorder was taking the place of its rigid geometry.' The five foreign journalists were driven carefully down the main street into town: 'Black or burning beams and tattered telephone wires rolled drunkenly, merrily across it, and the houses on either side streamed fire as vapour rises effortless from Niagara.'

With the narrow streets 'a royal carpet of live coals' the journalists

Guernica in flames, April 1937 (Getty)

could not reach the town centre: 'blocks of wreckage slithered and crashed from the houses, and from their sides that were still erect the polished heat struck at our cheeks and eyes.' At first all they saw were a few dazed militiamen; then, in the dark shadow of the Casa de Juntas, there were 'people sat upon broken chairs, lay on rough tables or mattresses wet with water. Most were women: some hundreds of them were littered around in the open space, and as we passed they groped about, fiddled with dirty pillows, tried to sleep, tried feebly to walk.' For two hours the journalists talked with the survivors.

Conversing 'in tired gestures and words unnaturally short for Spain,' they told Steer what had happened: 'they made the funny noises of bombers poising, fighters machine-gunning, bombs bursting, houses falling, the tubes of fire spurting and spilling over their town. Such was the weary, sore-eyed testimony of the people of Guernica, and it was only later that people who were never at Guernica thought of other stories to tell.'

Trying to calm himself, Steer collected off the ground the metal fragments of incendiary bombs. The stamps impressed upon them told him all he needed to know about the source of this devastation: they had been made in Germany.

Steer's report was published simultaneously in *The Times* and *The New York Times* on 28 April. In dispassionate terms it told how, for over three hours, the town had been bombed by wave after wave of German Junkers and Heinkels, whilst fighter-planes 'plunged low from above the centre of the town to machine-gun those of the civilian population who had taken refuge.' It was Steer's personal opinion that Guernica had been targeted 'in order to terrify the civil population, and through them the militia: and in order to break communications to the rear of a retreating army.' It was also widely interpreted as a test case for new German methods of saturation bombing, 'a rehearsal' (as some called it) for even larger bombardments in the future. Though the little Basque town of Durango had been recently attacked in similar fashion, Steer's story of Guernica gave for the first time the full picture of the horror of aerial attack and saturation bombing of innocent civilians. *The New York Times* followed Steer's report with an editorial condemning the rebels' actions as 'wholesale arson and mass murder'.

The day after the attack the British Consul in Bilbao also visited the town. As he informed Britain's ambassador in Spain:

> to my amazement I found that the township … [was] almost completely destroyed. Nine houses in ten are beyond reconstruction. Many were still burning and fresh fires were breaking out here and there, the result of incendiary bombs which owing to some fault had not exploded on impact the day before and were doing so, at the time of my visit, under falling beams and masonry. The casualties cannot be ascertained and probably never will be. Some estimates put the figure at one thousand, others at over three thousand.[1]

Realizing that they were facing a propaganda disaster, spokesmen at the rebel headquarters in Salamanca immediately denied responsibility. First they claimed that none of their planes had flown that day; then that the Basques had destroyed the town themselves with petrol and dynamite. Many newspapers outside Spain happily reproduced these claims.

Three days after the attack, rebel troops occupied Guernica. When

---

1 The Consul was correct, and an exact figure has never been established; even modern history books range in their estimate of the number killed from some 250 to over 1,600 (though a figure in the lower estimate is now considered more likely).

James Holburn, a *Times* journalist more sympathetic to Franco, then visited the town he claimed there was no evidence of blast damage, and suggested that craters in the ground 'were caused by exploding mines which were unscientifically laid to cut roads.' Steer responded in *The Times*: 'The statement issued from Salamanca that Guernica was destroyed by "Red" incendiaries is false.'

Thereafter, as claim was met by counter-claim, people effectively believed what they chose to believe, and the question of who destroyed Guernica remained bitterly contested for decades. The German press reacted with outrage at Steer's claims that German planes had been responsible. What *The Times* itself described as 'a wave of violent Anglophobia' followed, with the official German news agency attacking the paper for printing 'the most evil kind of atrocity reports'.

Steer received death threats, and started carrying a gun. But as he pointed out, the other journalists who had been with him that night all filed the same story: there was no shadow of a doubt but that German planes had bombed Guernica. When, having visited Guernica in August 1937, Virginia Cowles mentioned the controversy to rebel staff officers, she reported in *The Sunday Times* that one responded, 'of course it was bombed. We bombed it and bombed it and bombed it, and *bueno*, why not?'

'The principle of lying and continuous prolonged lying enunciated by Herr Hitler in *Mein Kampf*,' Steer wrote the following year, was at Guernica 'tried out for the first time in war, like the rest of the German air method of which it was an important part.'

The story dominated the international press; it finally turned many of the undecided and indifferent against the rebels. There was even talk in France of abandoning the Non-Intervention Agreement altogether. In Paris, Steer's report of the bombing was reproduced in the communist newspaper *L'Humanité*. Together with photographs of the devastated town, the report gave Spain's foremost living artist the impetus for a monumental painting that would ensure that no one ever forgot the name of Guernica.

David Seymour, *Pablo Picasso at the unveiling of* Guernica *at the Spanish Pavilion of the International Exhibition, Paris, June 1937* (Magnum)

Earlier in 1937 Pablo Picasso had been commissioned by the Republican Government to paint a large mural for the forthcoming International Exhibition in Paris. By late April, he had still not started work. Then came the destruction of the Basque town. On 1 May, with only a few weeks before the delayed event was due to open, the artist started making sketches. Drawing upon his love of the *corrida*, by the first evening he had come up with most of the key images: the bull (representing what he called 'brutality and darkness'), the dying horse, and the terrified woman with her head and arm thrust upwards.[1] Within days he had added a mother clutching her dead child, bellowing at an empty sky. There were no flames, no planes or ruins, just a vision of war-torn Spain built from Picasso's personal mythology and using his own set of symbols. Over the following weeks he worked feverishly on the immense canvas in his attic studio. It would simply be titled *Guernica*.

Only two days after Picasso started work, violent street fighting erupted

---

1 Like Hemingway, Picasso was an *aficionado*, and in later years there would be persistent rumours that *Death in the Afternoon* had originally been planned in the 1920s as a collaboration between the Spanish artist and the American writer, the former providing illustrations to the latter's text. Hemingway was interested in modern art, and collected works by a number of eminent Spanish artists, including Joan Miró, but could not afford a Picasso.

again in his hometown. The threat had been there for weeks, and now in Barcelona a 'civil war within the civil war' had broken out. It was fought not between rebels and Republicans, however, but between communists, anarchists and the POUM. It would leave more than a thousand dead and wounded. George Orwell was one of the many bewildered participants.

II

For almost four months – from early January until late April 1937 – Orwell had been stationed in or near the front-line trenches of Aragon. Almost immediately upon his arrival he had been promoted to the rank of corporal in a unit that boasted only one other native English speaker, a Welshman named Robert Williams. Some three weeks later, however, a group of around thirty volunteers arrived from London. They had been organized by the Independent Labour Party and were led by the future MP, Bob Edwards. Most were British and Irish working-class men, but there was also an American, Harry Milton, a self-confessed Trotskyist from New York.

Orwell and Williams were sent to join this group. Bob Edwards later recalled the lofty English writer's arrival:

> He wore corduroy riding breeches, khaki puttees and huge boots, I've never seen boots that were so large, clogged in mud. He had a yellow pigskin jerkin, a coffee coloured balaclava hat and he wore the longest scarf I've ever seen … wound round and round his neck right up to his ears, on his shoulder he carried an old-fashioned German rifle, I think it must have been fifty years old; and hanging to his belt were two hand grenades. Running beside him, trying to keep pace, were two youths of the militia, similarly equipped; but what amused me most was that behind Orwell was a shaggy mongrel dog with the word POUM painted on its side.

Orwell thought the ILP men 'an exceptionally good crowd'. The 'best of the bunch' was the twenty-one-year-old Bob Smillie, grandson (and namesake) of the Scottish miners' leader and former Labour MP. But at first some of his new colleagues were suspicious of Orwell, with his middle-class accent, his endless diary and letter-writing, and his habit of frequently disappearing into a book. Although Orwell had given his profession as 'grocer' when he joined the POUM (a reference to the shop he ran in England), it was obvious that he was an outsider.

In February, Orwell's wife arrived in Barcelona. Eileen Blair had been as keen as her husband to come to Spain, and she had eventually secured a job as a secretary for John McNair and Charles Orr in the POUM's offices. Unlike her husband, she had been to University (studying English at Oxford), and had worked for a while in various secretarial jobs. Charles Orr found Eileen 'friendly, gregarious and unpretentious,' and an excellent assistant (though Lois described her as 'nice but very vaguish when she talks,' and complained that she 'is eternally smoking cigarettes'). Charles was particularly impressed by Eileen's devotion to her husband: she soon convinced him that Orwell was 'a good man, a profound man,' and not the 'blundering adventurer' he had at first appeared.

Eileen kept Orwell supplied with tea, biscuits, tobacco and cigars, and when *The Road to Wigan Pier* was published in March sent him copies, followed by press reviews. As Orwell admitted, a number were 'very hostile', in particular Harry Pollitt's in *The Daily Worker*, which viciously attacked both book and author. Another observed that the book revealed Orwell to be 'a man with basically the right ideas, one who would be with the workers in a revolutionary situation, but whose mind is muddled with middle-class prejudices from which, with the best will in the world, he has been unable to escape.' More amusingly, *The Manchester Guardian* suggested that the book 'would have been better if Mr Orwell had not been so anxious to show that he is a real live He-Man.' Some of his British colleagues in the POUM would be less amused at his suggestion that the working classes smelt.

In March, Orwell's commanding officer, Georges Kopp, gave Eileen permission to visit her husband; she travelled to Aragon with Charles Orr, John McNair and sixty new POUM recruits. Lois Orr, who was 'dying' to see the front, was indignant at not being allowed to go with them: 'sex discrimination, I call it,' she wrote to her brother. '*They* said they didn't have facilities for women, so, if I had been a man, I could have gone. That's outright discrimination, I think, especially since the other woman went.' The explanation for Eileen being permitted to go was, perhaps, Kopp's romantic interest in her. At least two people would later suggest that he and Eileen were having an affair. According to Orwell, he and his wife had an open marriage; though over the subsequent years, this would appear to work more in Orwell's favour than Eileen's.

George Orwell (centre rear) with Eileen Blair (kneeling to his left), Harry Milton (kneeling with rifle to his right) and fellow British and American volunteers of the POUM mililtia, Aragon, March 1937 (UCL)

'I *thoroughly* enjoyed being at the front,' Eileen wrote home, and she appeared happy in the photograph that caught her kneeling beside Orwell, his colleagues and their machinegun. 'The whole visit's unreality,' she continued, 'was accentuated by the fact that there were *no* lights, not a candle or a torch; one got up & went to bed in black dark, & on the last night I emerged in black dark & waded knee deep in mud in & out of strange buildings,' looking for the car that was to take her back to Barcelona. She omitted to mention a detail that she added in a letter to Orwell's literary agent the following month: 'The Fascists threw in a small bombardment and quite a lot of machine-gun fire, which was then comparatively rare on the Huesca front, so it was quite an interesting visit – indeed I never enjoyed anything more.'

But for most of the time, almost nothing happened in Orwell's positions. Lois Orr explained the POUM's rationalization for this inactivity in a long letter to her family. Though Aragon 'is the front where the fascists are weakest, as their materials and men are all concentrated at Madrid and Malaga,' since most of the Republican soldiers there were either anarchist or POUM militiamen, the 'Stalinists' refused to arm them properly: 'There has been no ammunition and no guns on this front because the Stalinists are afraid that, if they give them to the anarchists, they will return to Barcelona when they are through with the fascists and finish making the revolution.' And revolution in Spain was the last thing Stalin and the communists wanted at this point.

All told, Lois was unimpressed with the Russians, and the influence they wielded over the increasingly powerful Spanish Communist Party. 'Russia, in spite of all the publicity she has been getting here and abroad as the proletarian brother of Spain,' she complained to her brother, 'has only carried on the most business-like intercourse with Spain in distress.' Everything the Soviet Union did to aid Spain – from arms to food – was done only in exchange for gold.

For weeks on end, with almost nothing else to do, Orwell and his comrades debated the bewildering political situation in Spain. It appeared sometimes that the communists and the anarchists hated one each other more than they hated the fascists, and that everyone hated the POUM. Orwell thought it 'idiotic that people fighting for their lives should *have* separate parties.' His attitude was, 'Why can't we drop all this political nonsense and get on with the war?'

It appeared to Orwell – as it did to Hemingway – that it was the communists who were the ones actually getting on with the job of fighting the rebels, whilst the anarchists and the POUM were simply 'standing still'; the POUM's constant talk of revolution seemed irrelevant to Orwell when there was a war to win first. When he had joined the militia, Orwell had promised himself that he would kill at least one 'Fascist': 'after all, if each of us killed one they would soon be extinct.' Yet in Aragon, he had hardly had the chance to kill *anybody*. Nothing happened. He was sick of it. He wanted to get to Madrid, to join the real fighting there. Along with some of the other British volunteers he talked openly of quitting the POUM for the International Brigades.

Harry Milton, the American Trotskyist in Orwell's unit, thought him politically naïve; they spent hours discussing politics, with Milton trying to argue Orwell out of leaving. Bob Edwards also warned him about André Marty, a man unlikely to look favourably upon as independently-minded and outspoken a figure as George Orwell. Indeed, Edwards was convinced that if Orwell did join the International Brigades, he would end up being courtmartialled and shot. But, like Milton, he had had no luck convincing Orwell out of his decision.

This strong sense of conviction impressed at least one of Orwell's companions, however: the eighteen-year-old volunteer Stafford Cottman. He admired what he called Orwell's

> direct, forthright 'no messy-mindedness' about things. You were either for something or against it. And if you were for it, you batted hard for it, and if you were against it you didn't have anything to do with it. He didn't have all these 'ifs' and 'buts.' And I think this is why he wasn't really a political animal, in the sense that he wasn't partisan to any particular group. And this probably left him free to analyse things and see them more clearly than the rest of us.

The Aragon front, however, was not entirely inactive. One night in

February the rebels launched an attack along Orwell's lines. They were supported by a few machineguns and artillery pieces. It was the first time Orwell had ever been properly under fire, and he was humiliated to discover how 'horribly frightened' he was. But the rebels made no attempt to assault the POUM positions, and after a couple of hours the action petered out; there had been only one casualty among the defenders. Nevertheless, a day or two later, Republican newspapers and radio reported that 'a tremendous attack with cavalry and tanks ... had been beaten off by the heroic English.' To the embarrassment – and anger – of Orwell and his comrades, there would be plenty of this type of overblown reporting.

On another occasion Orwell joined his unit in their own night attack, a diversionary action in support of an anarchist assault near Huesca. With thirty other volunteers he crept forward through the darkness. They silently cut the rebels' wire defences, then flung hand-grenades as they rushed the hilltop position, bayonets fixed. One of Orwell's grenades found its mark: the roar of the explosion was followed by 'a diabolical outcry of screams and groans ... I don't know whether he was killed, but certainly he was badly hurt. Poor wretch, poor wretch! I felt a vague sorrow as I heard him screaming.'

Then he chased an escaping rebel soldier down a communication trench:

> He was bareheaded and seemed to have nothing on except a blanket which he was clutching round his shoulders. If I had fired I could have blown him to pieces. But for fear of shooting one another we had been ordered to use only bayonets once we were inside the parapet ... Instead, my mind leapt backwards twenty years, to our boxing instructor at school, showing me in vivid pantomime how he had bayoneted a Turk at the Dardanelles. I gripped my rifle by the small of the butt and lunged at the man's back. He was just out or reach. Another lunge: still out of reach. And for

a little distance we proceeded like this, he rushing up the trench and I after him on the ground above, prodding at his shoulder-blades and never quite getting there – a comic memory for me to look back upon, though I suppose it seemed less comic to him.

As dawn broke Orwell returned to his lines. After the fear and excitement he was struck by 'the desolate look of everything, the morasses of mud, the weeping poplar trees, the yellow water in the trench-bottoms; and men's exhausted faces, unshaven, streaked with mud, and blackened to the eyes with smoke.' The three men sharing his dug-out were already asleep, clutching their sodden, muddy rifles.

He smoked the last of the cigars that Eileen had brought him as a present from England.

III

In late April, Orwell and his English-speaking comrades finally got their leave. He had spent almost four months in the line; he later described them as seeming one of the most 'futile' periods in his life (and this from a man who had once spent months washing pots in a Parisian hotel).

Their train back to Barcelona was filled with filthy militiamen singing revolutionary songs, and leather-faced peasants carrying bundles of vegetables, sacks of rabbits and live chickens; even sheep were driven into the compartments as they neared the city. Amongst this chaos, as they talked and drank *anis* and ate chocolate and sardines, Harry Milton asked Orwell if he was still intending to join the International Brigades.

When Orwell told the American that he was, Milton 'blew his top'. He began 'to rant and rave like a maniac,' saying, 'They wont take you, but if they do, they'll knock you off. You'll curse the day you were born. They'll canonize you.'

Milton was certain that Orwell would be killed: either murdered for what Harry Pollitt considered the writer's political unreliability, or in action to create another literary hero for the communist cause. 'I was really vulgar and rude,' Milton later recalled, but Orwell 'was cool as a cucumber, and he just walked away from me. He was a very disciplined individual.'

Dirty, dishevelled, unshaven and exhausted by their months at the front, Orwell and his comrades were stared at as they tramped from the railway station to their quarters in Barcelona. 'He arrived completed ragged,' Eileen wrote to her brother, 'almost bare-foot, a little lousy, dark brown, and looking really very well.' He was overcome by a 'ravenous desire for decent food and wine, cocktails, American cigarettes and so forth,' and 'wallowed in every luxury that I had money to buy.'

Yet almost immediately he had noticed that the exhilarating revolutionary atmosphere he had experienced in Barcelona in December had gone. 'The militia uniform and the blue overalls had almost disappeared,' whilst 'prosperous men, elegant women, and sleek cars were everywhere,' and a black market was thriving. Two things struck him. First, to his surprise and disgust, the civilian population had lost much of its interest in the war: the Government had had to resort to conscription to fill the ranks of the new Popular Army, and soldiers leaving for the front now met with comparatively little enthusiasm. Secondly, the old class divisions between rich and poor were once again asserting themselves, in dress, diet, relative wealth. The *Generalitat* was wresting back control from the anarchist committees, and it was clearly no longer a revolutionary war. Paradoxically, the communists had helped this to happen: Stalin and his supporters in Spain knew that if the Western democracies were ever to support the Popular Front, they had to be convinced that the left was not a radical, revolutionary movement. Besides, as a Catalan government official had told Cyril Connolly earlier in the year, in the end it had never been much of a revolution anyway: 'we have only socialized hotels, cafés, theatres, cinemas, barbers and boot cleaners;' and he had described the present regime simply as 'capitalism without capitalists'.

There were plenty of Catalans, however, who were still pursuing the path of radical reform, and such were the political tensions in Barcelona that plans to celebrate May Day had recently been abandoned. As Orwell put it: 'The danger was quite simple and intelligible. It was the antagonism between those who wished the revolution to go forward and those who wished to check or prevent it – ultimately, between Anarchists and Communists.' As he now realized,

> under the surface-aspect of the town, under the luxury and growing poverty, under the seeming gaiety of the streets, with their flowers-stalls, their many-coloured flags, their propaganda-posters, and thronging crowds, there was an unmistakable and horrible feeling of political rivalry and hatred. People of all shades of opinion were saying forebodingly: 'There's going to be trouble before long.'

This palpable ill-feeling – together with Orwell's growing sense that his political opinions lay more with anarchism than communism – did not prevent him from following through with his plans to join the International Brigades. He sought out a communist contact of Eileen's: Hugh O'Donnell, the unreliable and erratic young man who had come out to Barcelona with Kenneth Sinclair-Loutit and the British Medical Unit. O'Donnell, as Orwell noted, was 'very anxious' to recruit him, and introduced him to Walter Tapsell, a British communist serving with the International Brigades.

Orwell and some of his ILP colleagues told Tapsell of their various concerns about their recent service in Aragon, and discussed the possibility of joining the British Battalion. According to the report Tapsell sent back to Albacete, Orwell was the 'leading personality and most respected man in the contingent':

> This man is a novelist who has written some books on pro-letarian life in England. He has little political understanding and says he is 'not interested in party politics, and came to Spain as an Anti-Fascist to fight Fascism.' As a result of his

experience on the front, however, he has grown to dislike the POUM and is now awaiting his discharge from the POUM militia.

In a letter to her brother, Eileen admitted that 'to join the I.B. with George's history is strange but it is what he thought he was doing in the first place & it's the only way of getting to Madrid.' She also noted that, given their association with the POUM, they were both 'politically suspect'; nonetheless Tapsell had offered her the possibility of a job in Valencia, and even maybe one after that in Albacete. A letter home from Lois Orr confirmed the Orwells' plan: George, she wrote in early May, 'is off to join the International Brigade. Eileen is going to Valencia to get a job to be nearer [to him].'

It was also at this time that Orwell encountered John Dos Passos, a writer whom he had long wanted to meet. On discovering that the secret security forces had executed his Spanish friend and translator José Robles, Dos Passos had left Madrid. Hemingway had been disgusted, later claiming that it was fear of the shelling that had driven Dos from the city. But Dos Passos was equally revolted by the way Hemingway – full of boastful bravado – seemed to be revelling in the conflict. After spending a little time in Fuentidueña observing the irrigation project that would feature in *The Spanish Earth*, he had returned to Valencia; from there he travelled north to Barcelona, where Charles Orr had arranged his visit on behalf of the POUM, booking Dos Passos's hotel and accompanying him around the city.

Like Orwell, he was disturbed by what he saw: the furtive looks, the shuttered stores, and 'people glancing back over their shoulders as they walked. In every street there was a smell of burning from the charred ruins of the churches.'

Following a request from Eileen, Orr arranged for Orwell to be in the hallway in front of Andrés Nin's office when Dos Passos arrived for an interview with the POUM's leader. (Orr wanted to be able to invite Orwell into the meeting, 'But who was I,' he later admitted, 'to drag this husband of my secretary, this militiaman – in his baggy, tan coverall uniform – into a private interview? So we just left Orwell standing in the hallway.')

According to Dos Passos (who did not then know anything about the English author), Orwell was aware of his disillusionment with the war. 'Things I've heard,' Orwell said, 'lead me to believe that you are one of the few who understands what's going on.'

The impression Dos Passos had of Orwell was very different from that of others who met him in Spain. They often described Orwell as politically naïve, but as Dos Passos put it in a memoir written long after their meeting, Orwell's face 'had a sick drawn look':

> He seemed inexpressibly weary. We didn't talk for very long, but I can still remember the sense of assuagement, of relief from strain I felt at last to be talking to an honest man. The officials I'd talked to in the past weeks had been gulls most of them, or self-deceivers, or else had been trying to pull the wool over my eyes. The plain people had been heartbreaking. There's a certain majesty in innocence in the face of death. This man Orwell referred without overemphasis to things we both knew to be true. He passed over them lightly. He knew everything. Perhaps he was still a little afraid of how much he knew.

Dos Passos was reminded of the soldiers he had met during his service as a young ambulance driver in Italy during the Great War:

> The men at the front could allow themselves the ultimate luxury of telling the truth. It was worth the dirt and the lice and the danger and racket of shellfire to escape the lying and the hypocrisy and the degradation of the people in the rear. Men who are about to die regain a certain quiet primal dignity. Orwell spoke with the simple honesty of a man about to die.

Before Orwell could transfer to the International Brigades, he had to replace his worn-out boots; and he also wanted to spend a few days by the seaside with Eileen. But rapidly developing events quickly made that impossible. The simmering tensions in Barcelona finally came to a head on Monday 3 May, a few days after Dos Passos had left the city on his way back to France.

At around midday a friend remarked to Orwell in the lounge of their hotel, 'There's been some kind of trouble at the Telephone Exchange.'

Orwell thought nothing of it – until later that afternoon when walking down Las Ramblas he heard shots, and saw anarchist youths firing at gunmen in a church tower. As the crowds in the streets scattered, an American doctor who had been with Orwell's unit at the front suddenly appeared. He grabbed Orwell excitedly by the arm, and led him to the POUM's headquarters at the Hotel Falcón, explaining how he had seen several lorry-loads of Civil Guards driving up to the Telefónica building.

At the time, no one knew exactly what had happened. It later transpired that the Chief of Police, a communist, had decided to wrest control of the building from the anarchists who had held it since the start of the war. The anarchists, it was said, were not running the Exchange effectively: they were listening in to official government calls, sometimes even interrupting conversations to voice their own political opinions. When the Civil Guard had entered the building, however, they were met by machinegun fire.

Some months before, Lois Orr had told her family in Kentucky, 'I love the way these anarchists don't wait for anything or anybody. But when they think they're needed, they go. It makes you feel safe to know that five minutes after you hear cannon from somewhere, hundreds of men are mobilizing with guns cocked, to find out just exactly what is going on – and ready to stop it at all costs.' As Orwell now saw, Barcelona's streets quickly filled with militiamen. He knew immediately where his loyalty lay: 'when I see an actual flesh-and-blood worker in conflict with his natural enemy, the policeman, I do not have to ask myself which side I am on.'

Still exhausted from his months at the front, Orwell now spent an uncomfortable night with a group of German militiamen guarding one of the POUM's buildings, armed only with a small revolver and some crude homemade bombs. By morning people were building barricades, long lines of men, women and children pulling up cobblestones. Soon they were head-high, with riflemen positioned at the loopholes.

The day started quietly, but eventually the shooting resumed. Soon the roar of rifle and machine-gun fire, as well as hand-grenades, 'was almost comparable to the din of a battle'. Communists, anarchists, Civil Guards and POUM militiamen were all firing on each other, almost indiscriminately.

Eventually, the POUM's leaders told their men only to fire if they were attacked. For three days and nights, Orwell and some of his comrades, armed with rifles and bombs, were stationed on the roof of a cinema opposite the POUM's Executive Building near the Plaça de Catalunya. Las Ramblas was deserted, but gunfire echoed around the stone buildings of the city, 'on and on, like a tropical rainstorm'.

'I was in no danger,' Orwell later wrote. 'I suffered from nothing worse than hunger and boredom, yet it was one of the most unbearable periods of my whole life. I think few experiences could be more sickening, more disillusioning, or, finally, more nerve-racking than those evil days of street warfare.'

Though it appeared that the anarchists had the upper hand, there were rumours that the Government in Valencia was sending six thousand armed policemen to restore order, and Georges Kopp heard news that the POUM was to be outlawed.

On the Friday, as the city's supplies of food started to run out, life started to return to normal. By evening, Assault Guards from Valencia were patrolling the streets. Their array of weapons astonished Orwell: they included modern rifles, automatic pistols, and submachine-guns. These policemen were far better armed and clad than Orwell and the militia at the front had ever been. The May fighting, Orwell realized, 'had given the Valencia Government the long-wanted excuse to assume fuller control of Catalonia.' Weapons were impounded, the workers' militias were broken up and redistributed among the Popular Army and numerous anarchists and *POUMistas* were arrested.

Almost immediately the communist press began spinning events in Barcelona to their advantage. According to Claud Cockburn's report published in *The Daily Worker* on 11 May, 'German and Italian agents' had recently 'poured into Barcelona,' preparing 'a situation of disorder and bloodshed' that was to presage a fascist invasion of Catalonia. 'The instrument for all this lay ready to hand for the Germans and Italians in the shape of the Trotskyist organisation known as the POUM.' On the same day, a Comintern agent in Barcelona informed his superiors in Moscow that the Spanish minister of internal affairs 'had proof that the POUMist–Trotskyists maintain regular contact with the fascist espionage-provocateur organizations located in Madrid … No one has any doubt, either, that the Spanish Trotskyists represent an organized detachment of Franco's fifth column.'

The outrageous claim that the POUM had staged a *putsch* in aid of the rebels was soon widely disseminated (along with a poster that appeared around Barcelona which, as Orwell described it, represented the POUM 'as a figure slipping off a mask marked with the hammer and sickle and revealing a hideous, maniacal face marked with the swastika'). Various documents appeared, apparently showing direct links between the POUM and the rebels. In fact, they had been doctored and forged by the NKVD under the direction of their Russian master in Spain, Alexander Orlov. They had then been passed to the communist-controlled Madrid police, directly implicating the POUM's leader, Andrés Nin, in a genuine Falange terrorist cell that had recently been uncovered.

The NKVD's deceit was widely disseminated. On 16 May, *Our Fight*, the paper produced by men of the British Battalion, published the improbable suggestion that 'the plans for an insurrection in Barcelona were worked out in Fribourg, Germany, where a meeting between

POUM, the Gestapo and the Italian Fascists took place.' Orwell, however, later wrote that the accounts in the communist press were so 'self-contradictory' and filled with such obvious discrepancies 'as to be completely worthless'. He would ridicule Cockburn's claim in *The Daily Worker* that the POUM's armoury in Barcelona had included tanks, and virtually accused the journalist of making up certain facts. But the contradictions, exaggerations and even downright lies did not stop the communist account from being repeated in Spain and internationally; and, more importantly, it did not stop it from being widely believed.

Orwell described the atmosphere in their hotel in the days immediately after the Barcelona fighting as 'horrible'. People were 'infected with spy mania,' he later wrote, 'creeping round whispering that everyone else was a spy of the Communists, or the Trotskyists, or the Anarchists.' As he later recalled, 'You had all the while a hateful feeling that someone hitherto your friend might be denouncing you to the secret police.' He may well have been right. Exhausted physically and mentally by the events of the past few days, he had got to the point where even the banging of a door would make him reach for his pistol.

The chaos in Barcelona led to a crisis in the Government. Largo Caballero, the Spanish Prime Minister, already suspicious of the communists, refused to believe the accusations they were making against the POUM, and rejected their demands that Andrés Nin be arrested. On 17 May he was forced out of office. His replacement was the Finance Minister, Juan Negrín, a more moderate Socialist who believed that the only way the Civil War could be won was either through closer collaboration with the Russians, the repeal of the Non-Intervention Agreement, or secret negotiations for a truce with Franco.

As Orwell predicted, the Government in Valencia now took the opportunity to assume fuller control of semi-independent Catalonia. 'The workers' militias were to be broken up,' Orwell wrote, 'and redistributed among the Popular Army. The Spanish Republican flag was flying all over Barcelona – the first time I had seen it, I think, except over a Fascist trench.' Whilst the communists were allowed to retain the barricades protecting their buildings, the rest were dismantled, and stashes of arms were seized from the anarchists. The POUM's newspaper, *La Batalla*, was censored almost out of existence, while the communist papers continued their virulent attacks on the renegade Marxists. Though no immediate action was taken against the POUM, many supporters saw the danger ahead. Whilst Andrés Nin branded the Spanish Communist Party and its Catalan subsidiary, the PSUC, 'the vanguard and the instrument of bourgeois counter-revolution,' Lois Orr complained in a letter home that 'a lot of fair-weather foreigners' were now leaving the country.

Orwell was surprised when Hugh O'Donnell now approached him again about joining the International Brigades.

'Your papers are saying that I'm a Fascist,' Orwell told him. 'Surely I should be politically suspect, coming from the POUM.'

'Oh, that doesn't matter,' O'Donnell responded. 'After all, you were only acting under orders.'

But recent events had made Orwell realize what Harry Milton and the others had warned: he could not join any communist-controlled unit. 'Sooner or later it might mean being used against the Spanish working class. One could not tell when this kind of thing would break out again, and if I had to use my rifle at all in such an affair I would use it on the side of the working class and not against them.'

Furthermore, Orwell knew that the May events in Barcelona had given him great material for a book without having to go to Madrid. As he explained to his publisher, Victor Gollancz, joining the POUM instead of the International Brigades had – purely by chance – brought him

> into contact with Spaniards rather than Englishmen and especially with genuine revolutionaries. I hope I shall get a chance to write the truth about what I have seen. The stuff appearing in the English papers is largely the most appalling lies – more I can't say, owing to the censorship. If I can get back in August I hope to have a book ready for you about the beginning of next year.

Before that, however, Orwell would return to the front.

V

George Orwell and John Dos Passos were not the only foreigners with grave doubts about what was happening. The distorted reports of the May fighting in Barcelona also led some volunteers in the International Brigades to start questioning their loyalties. Many knew no more than what they could read in communist and the Brigades' own newspapers; and these obviously propagated the official story.

Tom Wintringham, who was still recuperating with Kitty Bowler on the Costa Blanca at the time of the fighting, later told her that he had heard from someone in the British Battalion 'that shipments of supplies have been sent from Barcelona to the Fascists via POUM lines.' Fred Copeman noted the 'serious' effect on morale in the British Battalion of the POUM 'uprising': 'Why, men asked, was it possible that these people could obtain arms and even tanks, so far in the rear, when the front line was starved of ammunition?' But when Walter Tapsell returned to Albacete, he reported that he 'was of the opinion that the Spanish Communist Party were not unconnected with the uprising,' and that the POUM had been 'used as a blind'. All this, Copeman noted, 'was dynamite and Tappy's report was not published.'

Others also doubted the Party line. Jason Gurney, who had recently been wounded by a sniper at Jarama, was in the American Hospital in Murcia when he heard about the recent events in Catalonia. He later wrote that 'the wildest rumours' were being spread, both 'officially and unofficially – the POUM had linked up with Franco supporters in Barcelona to raise a revolt in our rear but had been wiped out by the loyal forces of Party stalwarts defending peace and democracy. At the other extreme, the Party had sprung a plot to annihilate the leaders of all opposition parties in the Popular Front in order to turn the bourgeois Civil War into a Communist revolt.'

As Gurney felt that no source of information could be trusted, it was impossible for him to discover the truth. But the rumours

> served to heighten the feeling that the Communists were in control of the situation and that they would exploit it to suit their own advantage without any sort of consideration for anyone but themselves ... The official Party now produced a mass of palpably absurd propaganda, claiming that the POUM were in alliance with Franco who, for all his faults, certainly would not have allied himself with a small party of dissident Marxists. It is never comfortable for a soldier to feel that there is a struggle for power amongst the politicians behind the line, but in a civil war, fought on the basis of a 'Popular Front' alliance of anyone opposed to the principle of Fascist dictatorships, it was disastrous.

William Horvitz, also recovering in the American Hospital, was equally sceptical. He heard stories that it was anarchists who had first attacked the Telephone Exchange, a building that, as was well known, the anarchists had occupied since the first day of the war. 'Why in the world,' he asked himself, 'would they have staged an attack on a building they themselves held? It was a bold Party lie, and if the Party lied about that, could the rest of what it said also be a lie?'

Before coming to Spain Horvitz had been a committed communist. But he had increasingly come to admire both the anarchists and the POUM, considering them 'the genuine anti-Fascists and champions of the Spanish people'. He now realised that what a Trotskyist friend in New York had told him before he left America was true: the Communist Party was 'the most counter-revolutionary party in Spain'. Horvitz also realised that he had to watch what he said:

> I knew if I asked about the events in Barcelona, challenged the Party view, questioned it, my life would be in danger.

Rumors were already floating all over Murcia about comrades, leaders, having disappeared, shot perhaps. ... Those of us who filled the hospitals of Murcia, the wounded of the International Brigades, the very cream of the international Communist movement, heard about it, whispered to each other about it with pained faces, then shut up about it.

Instead, Horvitz spent the days drinking beer, eating peanuts, talking with friends and going to whorehouses.

He also began a relationship with the Hungarian wife of a political commissar in the International Brigades ('the wounded and the medical staff', he reflected later, 'seemed to be so elated to be alive that sex became an urgency'). But the more newspapers and magazines he read, 'the more I was becoming divorced from my Party, my life's blood.'

Despite his best attempts to conceal this, his new mistress noticed. One morning he was called before the Communist superintendent in charge of the hospital:

I had revealed a tiny crack in the foundation of my belief. Tiny cracks widen, become crevices, and soon the foundation crumbles. The edifice comes tumbling down. There is a purpose to the total discipline of a total party running a total state. I am a good example. The best thing to with people like me is to shoot them.

Horvitz was not shot; but years later he would write that one day the superintendent drove him to a church that had been turned into a prison, guarded by International Brigade soldiers. Inside, he was made to watch as a Belgian communist shot three young Spanish revolutionaries in the head. One of them, a skinny young woman, her clothes ragged and dirty, screamed hysterically, '¡Viva la revolución!' Then a German comrade, 'a Communist who escaped from Hitler and came to Spain to fight fascism,' picked up the bodies and tossed them in a corner.

Horvitz's faith in the communist 'adventure' collapsed. For nights afterwards he could not sleep. He cried into his pillow so that his neighbours in the hospital ward would not hear him. He had done nothing to save the three Spaniards, and knew that if he had been handed the gun, he would have killed them himself.

Chapter 11

The Killers

|

Within a few days of his brief meeting with George Orwell in May 1937, John Dos Passos had crossed the border into France. Leaving Spain, he later wrote, was like 'waking up out of a nightmare,' except 'it wasn't the kind of nightmare you can ever wake up from. The nightmare went along with us, back to Paris, back to the States. It's a nightmare you have to learn to live with all day and every day.'

Whilst Dos Passos was waiting to catch the boat train in Paris, Ernest Hemingway appeared. He too had recently left Spain, and would shortly be heading home. He demanded to know what Dos planned to write about the war when he got back to America. Dos was considering an article for the US press about what had happened to José Robles, and about how the Russians and communists were corrupting the Republican government in Spain. Like Orwell, he rejected the argument that anything critical written about the Republic would naturally aid the rebels.

But Hemingway was not having it. 'You do that,' he warned, 'and the New York reviewers will kill you. They will demolish you forever.' He even raised his fists, as if he were going to hit his old friend, before he turned and walked away.

Once home, Dos Passos agonized over what he should do. 'You didn't want to help the enemy,' he admitted, by adding 'to the immense propaganda against the Spanish republic fomented by so many different interests. At the same time you wanted to tell the truth.' He decided that all he could do was describe what he had seen, and through 'surface events' hint at 'the great forces working underneath'.

Thus in an article titled 'Farewell to Europe,' he observed: 'An American in 1937 comes back from Europe with a feeling of happiness, the relief of coming up out into the sunlight from a stifling cellar.' In contrast to Americans, the people of Western Europe were 'facing this summer a series of tragic dilemmas': the greatest dilemma was the inevitable, but unenviable, choice between two competing political forces: communism and fascism. As he explained in a letter written that autumn from his home on Cape Cod to his old friend, the playwright John Howard Lawson:

> I have come to believe that the Communist Party is fundamentally opposed to our democracy as I see it and that Marxism … if held as a dogma, is a reactionary force and an impediment to progress. Fascism is nothing but Marxism inside out and is of course a worse impediment – but the old argument about giving aid and comfort to the enemy is rubbish: free thought can't possibly give aid and comfort to fascism … I now think that foreign liberals and radicals were very wrong not to protest against the Russian terror all down the line. There's just a chance that continual criticism from their friends might have influenced the Bolsheviks and made them realize the extreme danger to their cause of the terror machine, which has now, in my opinion, eaten up everything good in the revolution.

Dos Passos was far more hopeful about the situation in the US. 'Sure, we've got our class war,' he wrote in 'Farewell to Europe', 'we've got out giant bureaucratic machines for antihuman power, but I can't help feeling that we are still moving on a slightly divergent track from the European world.' In his opinion, 'not all the fascist-headed newspaper owners in the country, not the Chambers of Commerce, not the armies of hired gunthugs of the great industries' could change the facts of American political history,

and the fact that democracy has been able, under Jefferson, Jackson, and Lincoln, and perhaps a fourth time (it's too soon to know yet) under Franklin Roosevelt, to curb powerful ruling groups. America has got to be in a better position to work out the problem: individual liberty vs bureaucratic industrial organization than any other part of the world. If we don't it means the end of everything we have ever wanted since the first hard winters at Plymouth.

||

On 12 May 1937, the day before Hemingway was to sail for the States, he read aloud from the manuscript of *To Have and Have Not* at Sylvia Beach's Paris bookshop. The audience included James Joyce, who left quietly after the American had finished reading, and thus missed Stephen Spender, who had also recently returned from Spain. The Englishman read from his poems on the Civil War. The most famous of these would be 'Ultima Ratio Regum' (the 'ultimate' or 'final argument of kings'), which began:

The guns spell money's ultimate reason
In letters of lead on the spring hillside.
But the boy lying dead under the olive trees
Was too young and too silly
To have been notable to their important eye.
He was a better target for a kiss.

Spender had met Hemingway for the first time when they were in Spain. He greatly admired his fellow writer, though he thought that in the flesh Hemingway 'seemed at first to be acting the part of a Hemingway hero'. Spender wondered 'how this man, whose art concealed under its apparent huskiness a deliberation and delicacy like Turgenev, could show so little of his inner sensibility in his outward behaviour.' Though at one point, as they talked about literature, the carapace slipped and Spender 'caught a glimpse of the aesthetic Hemingway,' the disguise was quickly replaced.

Hemingway, in turn, told Spender (who had ignored Harry Pollitt's suggestion that he join the International Brigades) that he was 'too squeamish': a coward. Spender would later allege that during lunch with Hemingway and Gellhorn after their joint reading at Sylvia Beach's bookshop, Hemingway told him Gellhorn had also been 'squeamish'. To get her over her fear, Hemmingway claimed that every day before breakfast he took her to the Madrid morgue to see the corpses.

Back in New York, the press reporters were again waiting to meet Hemingway off the boat. They were eager to hear his opinion on the Spanish war, and as *The New York Times* reported:

> Mr Hemingway said it was his conviction that the Insurgents were doomed to defeat, because he considered Madrid an impregnable city favored with natural defense possibilities which General Franco could never overcome. He pictured the Loyalists as growing stronger every day in forces and morale, and the insurgents growing weaker.
>
> 'The war has changed greatly,' he explained. 'It is no longer a war of militia, but a serious war of trained troops, and the forces of the defenders of Madrid increase their strength every week, and time is definitely on their side. Franco has been hammering away at Madrid since last November, and he lost his chance to take the city that first month.'

Reunited with his family on the tiny island of Bimini, some fifty miles off the cost of Florida, Hemingway spent a few days deep-sea fishing and revising the final draft of *To Have and Have Not.* Then he flew back to New York.

On 4 June, with Martha Gellhorn and Joris Ivens, he showed two preview scenes from *The Spanish Earth* to 3,500 delegates and members of the public attending the opening of the Second American Writers' Conference at Carnegie Hall. The whole theme of the convention was political, with a range of writers lecturing on war, the fate of democracy and the threat of fascism. Hemingway followed Ivens' film clips with a heartfelt speech – the first such public speech he had ever made – in which he told the assembled writers that 'fascism is a lie told by bullies … And when it is past it will have no history except the bloody history of murder that is well known and that a few of us have seen with our own eyes in the last few months.' Gellhorn also spoke at the conference. Her theme was 'Writers fighting in Spain,' and she mentioned, among others, W.H. Auden, Ralph Bates, Claud Cockburn, Gustav Regler and Stephen Spender: 'All of us are concerned in the war in Spain,' she stated, 'all of us have a heavy obligation toward that war.'

John Dos Passos did not attend the conference. A friend, the writer Dawn Powell, told him jokingly that Hemingway's address had been a good one 'if that's what you like and his sum total was that war was pretty nice and a lot better than sitting around in a hot hall and writers ought to all go to war and get killed and if they didn't they were a big sissy.' She added that the sequences from *The Spanish Earth* were excellent, 'particularly a soldier going home on leave'.

Another writer remarked that though Hemingway had seemed a little awkward, he spoke well, and 'it was the speech of the meeting. The audience had come for Ernest; he was there for them. He lapped up the warm acceptance.' Up till now most left-wing Americans had criticized Hemingway for avoiding major political and economic issues in his work. His speech at the conference seemed like evidence of a conversion. Hemingway, it appeared, had finally joined the People's Front.

This was certainly the opinion of the distinguished literary critic Edmund Wilson, who had been following Hemingway's career with close interest since his earliest publications. According to Wilson, the League of American Writers who had run the New York conference was 'an organization rigged by the supporters of the Stalinist regime in Russia and full of precisely the type of literary revolutionists' that Hemingway had until recently been 'ridiculing'. Hemingway had been hit 'pretty late,' Wilson suggested, by the 'hurricane' that had 'seized' many other American writers and intellectuals since the Wall Street Crash – a Marxist–Leninist hurricane in which 'the key to all the mysteries of human history seemed suddenly to have been placed in their hands, when the infallible guide to thought and behavior seemed to have been given them in a few easy formulas.'

The Spanish Civil War, Wilson would argue in 1939, had given Hemingway 'something bigger than big-game hunting and bullfighting' to write about, 'and the fact that the class war had broken out in a country to which he was romantically attached, seems to have combined to make him align himself with the Communists.' In Wilson's opinion, 'the Stalinists had taken him in tow,' and Hemingway would soon be 'feverishly denouncing as Fascists other writers who criticized the Kremlin.' It was an extreme judgment, but it had its point.

||

At the time of Hemingway's New York speech, George Orwell was still in Spain. Given the events in Barcelona and the growing influence of Russia and the Communist Party, Orwell was certain that the Civil War would end with either a Soviet or a Nazi style of dictatorship: either way, and by whatever name, essentially some form of what he considered fascism. The only other conclusion he could foresee was a stalemate, with Spain divided into separate zones of control.

It thus seemed clear to Orwell that the general political trend in Spain was towards extremism of one form or another; on-going events within the Republic did not lessen this impression. Shortly after his return to the trenches near Huesca, news reached Orwell that Bob Smillie had just been arrested whilst trying to cross the frontier into France. The young Scotsman, who had been returning home to lecture on the war, had been thrown into prison in Valencia, on account, Orwell presumed, of his connection to the POUM.

'Whichever way you took it,' he figured, the future for Spain 'was a depressing outlook.' But it did not follow that the Republic was not worth fighting for. 'Whatever faults [a] post-war Government might have, Franco's régime would certainly be worse ... The Popular Front might be a swindle, but Franco was an anachronism. Only millionaires or romantics could want him to win.'

On his return to the Aragon front Orwell was promoted to acting second-lieutenant, in charge of around thirty Spanish and English-speaking troops. Though plans were now underway for a full-scale assault on Huesca supported by the International Brigades, things were still quiet. The weather was warm by night and hot in the day; in the deserted orchards of no-man's-land the cherry blossom was whitening, and Orwell passed the time by crawling out into a ditch concealed by long grass, where he could snipe at a gap in the rebel parapet. Though not a great shot, he was determined to kill someone sooner or later.

He had other routines, too. First thing each morning he would casually light a cigarette and stand in the trench smoking. 'Eric, you know,' a friend warned, 'one of these days you're going to get shot.'

But Orwell did not have a high opinion of Spanish marksmanship. He had been shot at a number of times during the May fighting in Barcelona, but he had never felt at risk. 'They couldn't hit a bull in a passage,' he responded.

At dawn on 20 May 1937, only ten days after his return to the line, Orwell came to relieve Harry Milton from guard duty. 'It was a beautiful, beautiful sunrise,' Milton later recalled, and Orwell climbed onto the step of the sandbag barricade, and stuck his head over the parapet.

Almost immediately there was what Milton described as 'the crisp sound of a high velocity shot.' Orwell was knocked onto his back. He had been hit clean through the neck by a rebel sniper some 175 yards away.

The young American took Orwell's head in his arms, and felt a puddle of blood on his hands. His immediate assumption was that

Orwell 'was a goner'. Still conscious, his mouth filling with blood, Orwell too was certain he was dying. His immediate thought was of Eileen; then he was filled with 'violent resentment at having to leave this world,' and at the meaninglessness of his death. 'To be bumped off, not even in battle, but in this stale corner of the trenches, thanks to a moment's carelessness!'

Milton stopped the bleeding, and Orwell was carried half a mile to the nearest medical post. There his wound was dressed, and he was sent by a series of ambulances to an over-crowded hospital in Lérida.

Within two days, Eileen and Georges Kopp were by his side. Incredibly, as Kopp recorded, considering the bullet had passed right through Orwell's larynx and out the other side, his general state 'was some sort of excellent'. His right arm ached from shoulder to the tip of the middle finger, caused by the bullet clipping a nerve in his neck, and his voice was 'hoarse and feeble', but his breathing was 'absolutely regular' and (as Kopp was pleased to note) his sense of humour remained 'untouched'.

Orwell later wrote matter-of-factly that 'being hit by a bullet is very interesting,' and described how the sensation was like 'being *at the centre* of an explosion … I felt a tremendous shock – no pain, only a violent shock, such as you get from an electrical terminal; with it a sense of utter weakness, a feeling of being stricken and shrivelled up to nothing.'

It was soon clear that, by what Orwell's doctor called 'some sort of unexplainable luck,' nothing essential had been damaged, though the bullet, he was told, had missed his artery 'by about a millimetre.' He could not speak much above a whisper, and there was a chance his voice would never properly recover; but otherwise there was nothing to fear. By the end of May he was back in Barcelona, recovering in a suburban sanatorium run by the POUM.

The writer's Spanish adventure was, however, by no means over.

Throughout Barcelona there still lingered what Orwell described as an air of 'suspicion, fear, uncertainty, and veiled hatred'. The newspapers were censored, food was scarce, and tobacco almost non-existent. The jails were crammed with prisoners from the May fighting, and by ones and twos anarchists and *POUMistas* were disappearing into jail, often without charge. Everyone feared another outbreak of street fighting: 'It was as though some huge evil intelligence were brooding over the town,' Orwell later wrote, and 'it was queer how everyone expressed it in almost the same words: "The atmosphere of this place – it's horrible. Like being in a lunatic asylum."'

Each day Orwell left the sanatorium to visit his wife at her hotel. His voice was improving very slowly under hospital treatment, and as Eileen wrote to her brother, 'He is *violently* depressed, which I think encouraging.' They had decided that the best thing to do was return to England as soon as possible. Though he had been certified medically unfit for further military service, Orwell still had to be seen by a medical board back in Aragon before he could receive his discharge papers. The round-trip took five exhausting days.

He arrived back at in Barcelona on the evening of Sunday 20 June, and found Eileen in the hotel lounge. She nonchalantly put her arm around his neck, and with a smile hissed in his ear:

'*Get out!*'

Totally perplexed, Orwell simply kept responding, 'What?'

Eventually she coaxed him from the hotel and into a café. There she explained what had happened. Four days earlier, the POUM's headquarters in Barcelona had been closed down and converted into a prison, the POUM was declared illegal, and Andrés Nin and the rest of the POUM Executive Committee had been arrested and sent to Madrid. The London edition of *The Daily Worker* reported the whole 'story' under the headline 'Spanish Trotskysists plot with Franco,' declaring that 'there became known, over the weekend, details of one of the most ghastly pieces of espionage ever known in wartime, and the ugliest revelation of Trotskyist treachery to date.' It certainly appeared to Eileen that anyone connected with the organization was being pursued. In the middle of the night six plain-clothes policemen had raided her hotel room, seizing her hsuband's diary, his press cuttings and their letters, as well as a piece of seemingly incriminating evidence: a copy of Adolf Hitler's autobiography, *Mein Kampf*. Fortunately, Eileen had hidden their passports in the bed, which the Spanish policemen had been too chivalrous to search whilst she was lying in it.

Eileen reckoned that already around four hundred people (including Georges Kopp and Charles and Lois Orr) had been arrested. The only reason she was still at liberty, she thought, was as a bait to catch her husband. This was possibly true, as (unknown to Eileen) those responsible for apprehending Nin had apparently included her 'Communist friend', Hugh O'Donnell.

Declaring his innocence, Orwell wanted to return to the hotel. Patiently Eileen reiterated the situation. 'It did not matter what I had done or not done,' he gradually realized. 'This was not a round-up of criminals; it was merely a reign of terror. I was not guilty of any definite act, but I was guilty of "Trotskyism". The fact that I had served in the POUM militia was quite enough to get me into prison.'

Orwell had much to fear. Already many of his colleagues who had not been arrested were on the run, including Harry Milton, who was heading for the Spanish border in a desperate attempt to escape. 'Every foreigner not a Stalinist is suspect and scores and scores have been arrested,' he wrote to a Trotskyist friend in America, warning him of what was happening. 'The streets bustle with armed assault guards and a Hitlerite terror prevails.'

Horrifyingly, Milton had just heard that their young friend Bob Smillie, arrested the previous month whilst trying to leave Spain, was dead. He had died in prison, of appendicitis, it was claimed; but no one had been allowed to see his body. Milton and Orwell's immediate assumption was that he had been murdered. (Orwell would later write that many of his friends in Spain 'were shot, and others spent a long time in prison or simply disappeared.')[1]

It was not the Spanish Government that had ordered this purge of the POUM, but the NKVD under its Russian director in Spain, Alexander Orlov. Largo Caballero, the former Prime Minister, could not believe communist claims that Nin had been 'rescued' by German fascists, and that he was now either with Franco or in Berlin. Despite demands that he be released from prison, nothing more was heard from Nin, and rumours soon circulated that he had been murdered.

So Orwell destroyed his POUM militia card and spent the next few days sleeping rough by night and posing as a bourgeois tourist by day.[2] Spanish bureaucracy required that Orwell's passport be stamped by three separate organizations before he could leave the country; this would obviously be risky, as Orwell reckoned there would be a list circulating of foreign 'Trotskyist' suspects, though he was also sure there would be 'a lot of muddle and *mañana*. Fortunately this was Spain and not Germany. The Spanish secret police had some of the spirit of the Gestapo, but not much of its competence.'

In a brave act, Orwell and Eileen visited Georges Kopp in prison. The first person they saw was Harry Milton, who had been arrested at the border a few days before. Orwell felt 'dreadful' ignoring a man with whom for months he had shared a dug out, and who had helped carry him out of the line when he had been shot. But both realized the danger they were in. 'I may also die of "appendicitis",' Milton had already warned a friend. So they passed each other like perfect strangers.

The prison was filthy and horribly overcrowded, mostly with

---

1 That Smillie was executed was never proven, and an ILP representative who had visited Smillie in gaol told the dead man's father, 'in spite of every curious and mysterious circumstance, I am completely convinced that Bob was not ill-treated nor was he done to death.' Though some of Smillie's comrades in the ILP/POUM always believed he had been shot, Orwell later accepted that the official account was possible; but he still blamed the authorities for not having taken better care of a man who had come voluntarily to Spain to aid their cause.

2 This led him to visit Antoni Gaudí's unfinished 'cathedral', the *Sagrada Família*. He judged it 'one of the most hideous buildings in the world,' and felt that the anarchists had 'showed bad taste in not blowing it up when they had the chance.'

'pickpockets, tramps, thieves, fascists and homosexuals,' Kopp complained. Nevertheless, he seemed in excellent spirits.

'Well, I suppose we shall all be shot,' he remarked cheerfully.

Orwell considered this likely. Like many others in the POUM, it was his opinion that 'everything pointed to a huge frame-up trial followed by a massacre of leading "Trotskyists".'

Though he tried his best, it seemed there was nothing Orwell could do to help his friend. Even the fact that Kopp was now a major in the People's Army, and had been carrying important papers from the Minister of War in Valencia to the colonel commanding engineering operations in Aragon, could not effect his release.

John McNair had been warned that the British consular staff in Spain was 'definitely pro-Franco,' but they still helped him and the Orwells to get their passports in order. The small group then caught a train and crossed the frontier into France without incident. Orwell's first act once over the border was to rush to a tobacco kiosk and fill his pockets with cigarettes and cigars.

George and Eileen had decided they needed a holiday, but the three days spent by the Mediterranean were oddly disappointing. 'It was a strangely restless time,' he later recalled:

> In this quiet fishing town, remote from bombs, machineguns, food-queues, propaganda, and intrigue, we ought to have felt profoundly relieved and thankful. We felt nothing of the kind. The things we had seen in Spain did not recede and fall into proportion now that we were away from them; instead they rushed back upon us and were far more vivid than before. We thought, talked, dreamed incessantly of Spain.

IV

The Orwells decided to head home. Passing back through Paris on the way home Orwell was happy to avoid the International Exhibition of

Arts and Crafts in Modern Life, now in the belated process of opening. He thus missed Albert Speer's historic 215-foot neoclassical Nazi tower, with its eagle and swastika, facing off against the giant chromium-plated statues of the Soviet Pavilion, their garments flowing behind them, brandishing in raised arms a hammer and sickle. He also missed seeing what would become a twentieth-century icon and the definitive painted image of the Spanish Civil War. 'Picasso has done a terrifying fresco in the Spanish Pavilion, a huge black and white thing called "Guernica",' the novelist E.M. Forster reported. 'Picasso is grotesquely angry, and those who are angry still hope.'

'We had an interesting but thoroughly bloody time in Spain,' Orwell told a friend once he and Eileen were back in England. 'We started off by being heroic defenders of democracy and ended by slipping over the border with the police panting on our heels.' He was lucky not to have joined the International Brigades, he admitted in another letter, as '[I] should no doubt by this time have had a bullet in the back for being "politically unreliable", or at least have been in jail.'

Only three weeks after their escape from Barcelona, notes prepared for a Tribunal for Espionage and High Treason stated that it was 'clear' from Orwell and Eileen's intercepted correspondence that they were 'confirmed Trotskyists'. Though this accusation was repeated in *The Daily Worker* it was, of course, absurd; it meant simply that Orwell was not a Stalinist. Indeed, early in 1939 Orwell would write that though Trotsky 'denounces the Russian dictatorship ... he is probably as much responsible for it as any man now living, and there is no certainty that as a dictator he would be preferable to Stalin.'

The future for Georges Kopp, Harry Milton, Lois and Charles Orr and the other imprisoned *POUMistas* was clearly ominous. Their interrogators included a number of Russians, who Lois was convinced were from the Soviet secret police. Given the recent show trials in Moscow, she was overcome by 'a terrifying feeling of utter helplessness,' certain that her end had come. In due course, they were accused of belonging to a secret network of foreign agents working for Trotsky and Franco.

Other prisoners included Belgian, Dutch and English members of the International Brigades. 'The one thing common to us all,' Lois later wrote, 'that had led us by different life paths to this awful impasse, was our devotion to liberty and hatred of the horrible bastard tyranny that the Russian Revolution had bred. We did not believe that any end could justify such means as the Russians were using in Spain.' Orwell agreed. It was now his professed belief that the Communist Party's 'whole line of thought is based on doing evil that good may come.'

Whilst Kopp continued to languish in prison for months to come, the intercession of the US Consul secured the release of Milton and the Orrs. Almost immediately the Orrs boarded a ship in Barcelona and sailed for France, marking the end of what Lois called this 'sinister nightmare.' 'I did not stay on deck to wave goodbye or take a last look at the city ringed by green hills,' she later recalled. 'I went downstairs to the restaurant to eat – French butter, brioche, and strawberry jam. In face of death, affirm life. At a wake, eat.'

Despite what had happened, Orwell was not bitter. 'I have seen wonderful things,' he told Cyril Connolly, '& at last really believe in Socialism, which I never did before.' The Civil War had been a pivotal episode in his life, and Orwell had returned home a different man. Over the next decade he would write three of the defining books of the twentieth century, all of them deeply rooted in what he had experienced in Spain.

V

Though scarcely recovered from the bullet through his throat, even before he reached England Orwell had started writing about his Spanish experiences. His first efforts at getting them published, however, had been unsuccessful. Kingsley Martin, editor of *The New Statesman*, refused to print an article giving Orwell's perspective on the May events in Barcelona and the suppression of the POUM. And Victor Gollancz, who had published *The Road to Wigan Pier*, refused to take Orwell's proposed book. The reason he gave was the same as Kingsley Martin's: he would never publish anything he believed 'could harm the fight against fascism' (even if it was the truth).

'Gollancz is of course part of the Communist-racket,' Orwell told to his friend, the writer John Rayner Heppenstall at the end of July, 'and as soon as he heard I had been associated with the POUM and the Anarchists and had seen the inside of the May riots in Barcelona, he said he did not think he would be able to publish my book, though not a word of it was written yet.' He added that he was

> rather glad to have been hit by a bullet because I think it will happen to us all in the near future and I am glad to know that it doesn't hurt to speak of. What I saw in Spain did not make me cynical but it does make me think that the future is pretty grim. It is evident that people can be deceived by the anti-Fascist stuff exactly as they were deceived by the gallant little Belgium stuff [in 1914], and when war comes they will walk straight into it. I don't, however, agree with the pacifist attitude ... I still think one must fight for Socialism and against Fascism, I mean physically fight with weapons ...

By then though, Orwell had found a publisher. As he wrote to his literary agent, Leonard Moore, on 8 July a 'rather obscure' publisher, Secker and Warburg, 'seem very anxious to get hold of it ... and they hinted that they were willing to make a good offer.' It would prove to be an extraordinary account.

That same day Orwell wrote to his agent, Ernest Hemingway, Martha Gellhorn and Joris Ivens visited the White House to give the President Roosevelt an advance screening of *The Spanish Earth*. It was a remarkable coup, achieved by Gellhorn through her literary friendship with Roosevelt's wife. For the filmmakers, it was their best chance to change US Government policy, and open the way for the Republic to buy American weapons and aeroplanes – which had been exactly their purpose in the making the documentary. For, despite continuing Soviet assistance, such aid was desperately needed. Bilbao had fallen to the rebels only a few weeks before, and it was Italian and German support that had made Franco's victory over the Basques possible. Given such success, Hitler and Mussolini were more than willing to continue their defiance of the Non-Intervention Agreement: some 75,000 Italian troops would eventually see action in Spain, whilst Italian submarines would soon start sinking pro-Republican ships in the Mediterranean (including many British vessels). Little by little, the Republic was losing territory to Franco's better armed, better equipped forces.

Hemingway had been working hard on the script for *The Spanish Earth* and he was angry when Ivens told him to cut back his already parsimonious prose. Orson Welles had agreed to read the commentary; but his voice proved somehow wrong, too rich and rounded for Hemingway's curt narrative.[1] Eventually it was decided that Hemingway himself should provide the film's voiceover. He would assert there that the war could have been over within six weeks if it had not been for the Italians and Germans, whilst graphic footage showed the effect that fascist bombs were having on the women and children of Spain. It seemed obvious that Non-Intervention and American neutrality were keeping the war going.

Hemingway was amused that Gellhorn ate before going to the White House: 'We thought she was crazy at the time,' he told his mother-in-law, 'but she said the food was always uneatable and everybody ate before they went there for dinner.' Gellhorn was right: 'the food was the worst I've ever eaten … We had a rainwater soup followed by a rubber squab, a nice wilted salad,' and a cake some 'enthusiastic but unskilled admirer' had sent the Roosevelts. 'They both were very moved by the *Spanish Earth* picture,' he added, 'but both said we should put more propaganda in it.'

After watching the documentary, the President told Ivens 'that he had

1 By coincidence, William Horvitz later worked for Orson Welles. Welles would tell him that 'only circumstances had prevented him from going to Spain to fight. If the idea [of going] had come to him,' Horvitz wrote, unimpressed, 'I was certain it had come and gone very quickly … Over the years I don't know how many men have told me that they had also wanted to fight in Spain, but one thing or another had interfered. How romantic. How worthy of them.'

liked the film very much, but he could not commit himself in any way.' When Roosevelt had left, his wife spoke more enthusiastically.

'We in the White House think that the Spanish people are not going to lose,' Mrs Roosevelt told them.

If only the arms embargo were lifted, Hemingway and Ivens reiterated, 'Franco wouldn't have a chance.' And when she asked if they thought the Government would win, they told her that they strongly believed it; but it all depended on lifting the embargo.

The presence of Italian and German forces in Spain, together with the bombing of Madrid and Guernica, had helped turn US opinion against Franco: *Time*, *Newsweek* and *Fortune* had all begun to express their sympathy for the Republic. But it seemed no one could convince Roosevelt to change his position. Publicly, the President continued to back US neutrality. Privately, however, as his wife recorded, 'though Franklin knew quite well he wanted the democratic government to be successful,' it was 'political realities' that tied his hands. These 'realities' included Roman Catholic opinion in the US, which remained largely pro-Franco, but on which part of the Democrat vote relied. And whilst Claude Bowers, the US Ambassador to Spain, consistently urged support for the Republic, the State Department was divided. Whilst some feared that a fascist Spain might extend its influence to Latin America, others – in particular Secretary of State Cordell Hull – feared the communist threat more. And there were economic interests to consider. These included US business investments in Spain; but more significant were US oil interests in Mexico, Bolivia, Venezuela and Peru. Hull and others felt that communism, not fascism, posed the greater menace in these countries, which were as economically and socially backward as Spain, and seemingly ripe for their own revolutions.

VI

Two months after his disappearance, Andrés Nin's body was discovered outside Madrid. As *The New York Times* reported in its coverage of the

POUM leader's mysterious fate, the Spanish government found itself between two forces: 'the Communists and their Rightist allies' on one side, and the former Premier Francisco Largo Caballero on the other. Caballero, as the paper observed, was 'the dominant figure' in the varied groups that now believed the communists were 'sabotaging the social revolution that is taking place side by side with the war against General Franco's Rebels.'

Kitty Bowler was another recent victim of the communist witch-hunt: in July she was expelled from Spain as a suspected 'Trotskyite spy'. Tom Wintringham stood by the decision. 'My dear,' he wrote to her, 'the party, our party, yours and mine, is sometimes hard on individuals. But look at the job of work it does as a whole and there's nothing like it on earth or ever has been.'

Back in the States, the fate of Andrés Nin and the vilification and liquidation of his organization by the communists had caught the public's attention. 'You'd be amazed the fuss people make over here about [the] POUM,' she wrote back to Wintringham from New York. At a party one evening she had been attacked on the subject; but, she explained, once she had related some stories of her encounters with the POUM, then 'they grasped it. They weren't aware that every party in Spain was glad to see the last of them.'

Bowler found being home after the excitement of Spain dispiriting. 'This different world, continent, of which you know nothing,' she told Wintringham, 'makes me afraid sometimes it was just a dream … There is so much life in Spain and so much less here. I sit in luxury in a grand cool apartment and think of a funny tiny room with no window that was home.' In another letter she told him how she had been to a party: it was

> agony – all they did was talk of drunken exploits, golf and wall paper. That same old life I fled from years ago. So healthy and handsome and empty these people … Someday it will crash around their heads and they will be on the other side of the barricades and not know why.

She knew it was impossible to return to Spain, and asked Wintringham to tell his 'boys' that for 'a mere glance at them – one hour's eager conversation' she would 'exchange all the baths and comforts of this so-called civilization.'

Since their ordeal on the Jarama, both the British and Lincoln Battalions had been reinforced by new arrivals from home. In fact, so many had arrived from the US and Canada that two additional battalions would be formed: the new American battalion took its name from George Washington, while the Canadians called themselves the Mackenzie-Papineau Battalion (the Mac-Paps for short) after two patriots who exactly a century before had (like Washington) led rebellions against British colonial rule. Like the rest of the volunteers in the International Brigades, they were overwhelmingly working-class; many were immigrants from central Europe, and the vast majority were Communist Party members.

The number of Americans now serving in the International Column impressed Wintringham: 'You met Americans everywhere,' he later observed, 'in the artillery and machine-gun companies, in the driver's cabs of supply trucks, in the postal service.' (Indeed, such was their influence that one Canadian volunteer would complain that 'a clique of American Jews' ran XV Brigade.) Though recovered from the leg wound he had suffered at Jarama, Wintringham was fit only for light duties, and had taken over from Robert Merriman as commander of an officer training school. Of the sixty trainees, fifty were American or Canadian, most with scarcely any previous military experience. He was given six weeks to turn them into NCOs and junior officers. He used his knowledge of history to inspire them, believing that it was possible – as Oliver Cromwell had done – to create a 'New Model Army' out of these raw but politically committed volunteers.

He found that any reference to American history 'had an almost magical effect in getting not mere attention but an eager brain-threshing endeavour to understand.' Talking of Valley Forge and Yorktown, he reminded the would-be officers of how Washington had transformed a half-trained revolutionary force of militiamen into an army that had defeated British regulars. And in an attempt to get 'behind the propaganda slogans' to a realistic discussion of the background to the Spanish war, Wintringham compared it with the American Civil War. Franco's men were the rebels of the Confederate States, led by gentlemen slave owners and trained generals. His men were the Yankees, forging themselves, slowly, into an army more effective than their opponents', proving themselves to be the 'better material for war'. He was deeply moved by the young men he was training:

> What I found out there of the America of the future, the young men who embody the traditions of a people proud of its revolutionary birth and its democracy, was a discovery for me. Those lads, war-salted, who get back to the States are going to move America along even faster than that country has recently been travelling.

Plans were now being implemented for a major new Republican offensive that summer. The largest force yet seen in the war was assembling for a bold assault on Brunete, twenty miles west of Madrid; it included all five of the International Brigades. Under the command of General José Miaja, the hero of the defence of Madrid six months earlier, the aim was to smash through the rebels' lines around the village of Brunete and sweep south-eastwards to cut off their forces in the Casa de Campo and end the siege of the capital.

Since neither Wintringham nor Merriman was sufficiently recovered to return to active duty, command of the British Battalion had passed into the hands of Fred Copeman, the ex-sailor who had dragged up the machineguns on the first day of fighting at Jarama, whilst Oliver Law, an African-American from Chicago, now led the Lincolns. And a Yugoslav-American named Mirko Markovicz commanded the untried troops of the Washingtons. These three English-speaking Battalions formed a Regiment under the command of Major Jock Cunningham, one of the few remaining survivors of the group that had fought alongside John Cornford

Winifred Bates, *British volunteers of the XV International Brigade prior to the Battle of Brunete, July 1937* (IWM)

in University City before Christmas. He too had been wounded at Jarama, and whilst in Madrid recovering from wounds had met Hemingway. Cunningham told his story, Hemingway recorded for the US press, 'clearly, completely convincingly, and with a strong Glasgow accent. He had deep, piercing eyes, sheltered like an eagle's; and, hearing him talk, you could tell the sort of soldier he was.' Cunningham's adjutant was the Alabama schoolteacher Martin Hourihan, whilst George Nathan was XV Brigade's Director of Operations.

Though an Italian submarine had recently sunk a ship bringing more volunteers to Spain (including a number of British and Americans, many of whom drowned), morale in XV Brigade was high. While there were still shortages, some good equipment had been arrayed for the attack, including modern machineguns, tanks, artillery pieces and aeroplanes, most of it supplied by the Russians. And the luxurious former palace of El Escorial had been converted into the International Brigades' field hospital: Kenneth Sinclair-Loutit and Archie Cochrane of the British Medical Unit were stationed there, and Sinclair-Loutit was struck by the organisation and 'total logistic support that comes with being a part of a real Army'. Cochrane was delighted by the arrival of his old Cambridge friend, Julian Bell, the nephew of Virginia

Woolf. Bell had told their family friend, E.M. Forster, 'At this moment, to be anti-war means to submit to fascism, to be anti-fascist means to be prepared for war.' In deference to the wishes of his mother, the artist Vanessa Bell, he had agreed not to join the International Brigades. Instead he had compromised, and had volunteered as an ambulance driver.

'Though Julian had great worldly experience,' Sinclair-Loutit later wrote, 'he had retained a capacity for wonder, an innocence, a candour, and a ceaseless zest for activity. All this made him magically attractive. Though he detested the heartless destruction of war, it did not make him afraid. He was consistently courageous.'

And Frank Ryan, having returned home to Ireland, was now back in Spain. On 4 July he joined the Lincolns at their Independence Day celebrations. 'The one consolation in all this slaughter,' he wrote home to his family, 'is that it is in a great cause. Some men must die lest all men live slaves.' The festivities were cut short when the Americans received their orders to move to the front.

On the night of 5 July tens of thousands of Republican soldiers began to advance.

Chapter 12

The Dangerous Summer

I

As the likes of Stephen Spender, Ralph Bates, Gustav Regler, André Malraux and Pablo Neruda gathered in Madrid for the Second International Congress of Writers in Defence of Culture, the men of XV International Brigade were marching back into war. They went into action on the morning of 6 July 1937. The objective for Jock Cunningham's British and American Regiment was a ridge of high ground beyond the village of Villanueva de la Cañada, which would command the land and vital road beyond. It was high summer, with temperatures over 100°F during the long, hot daytime. The flat plain of Castile was dry and exposed, and there was little cover for the advancing troops.

The heavily outnumbered rebels in Villanueva put up stiff resistance. When Republican troops failed to capture the village, General Miaja needlessly turned this minor obstacle into a major target. Stubbornly, he ordered that it be taken 'at all costs'. The Lincoln and the British Battalions were deflected from their more essential task, and joined the attack. 'We lighted the streets with the red light of bursting grenades' wrote one survivor afterwards, 'as we drove the Fascists before us to the centre of the town.' In one notorious incident, a section of the British Battalion – as William Horvitz bluntly put it – 'did something loco'. On their flank, a group of Moors who were attempting to escape 'shielded themselves with villagers and the English stopped shooting, [because they] didn't want to kill the villagers. They took a lot of losses until they began shooting back.' The Moors and many of the villagers fell dead when the British did finally open fire.

By nightfall, Villanueva de la Cañada had fallen, the village reduced to rubble. Over the following days the Brigade advanced on its original objective, soon named Mosquito Ridge on account of the endless buzz of bullets. Though initially taken by surprise, the rebels were quickly able to strengthen their defences, and with aerial superiority – including the outstanding new German fighter-plane, the Messerschmitt 109 – they counter-attacked.

An Irish volunteer serving alongside Frank Ryan just behind the advancing men of XV Brigade later recalled how, on the road from Villanueva to Brunete, 'we came across rows and rows of bodies, many with their names pinned on slips of paper. Many of them were British lads.' Later, whilst catching a lift to the rear in an ambulance, he heard an Irish and a British soldier arguing. 'It became horribly clear to me ... that just a few miles up the road men were going through a veritable inferno so bad that some had even committed suicide.'

Fred Copeman, the British Battalion's commanding officer, almost lost his mind when his adjutant had his head blown off; his brains landed in Copeman's lap. Once again, the British were furious at the orders they

Gerda Taro, *Claud Cockburn and Fred Copeman, Brunete, July 1937* (Magnum)

received, and Copeman's commissar would later be arrested after telling General Gal that he was 'not fit to command a troop of Brownies, let alone a People's Army.'

Casualties among the North Americans were equally heavy, so much so that the Lincoln and Washington Battalions had to be merged into one unit. The dead included the Lincoln's commanding officer, Oliver Law. According to William Horvitz (who did not fight in the battle, but who was still in Spain recovering from his wound at Jarama) two friends told him afterwards that they had 'killed Law in a mad fury'. They thought Law 'was hopelessly stupid and incompetent and was sending them to their deaths.' It was Horvitz's belief that Law had been promoted beyond his abilities simply because he was black, in other words that the CPUSA wanted to make him an African-American hero, a totemic figure commanding a Battalion named after the man who had ended slavery. Horvitz's contention that Law had been murdered could never be proved; the Battalion's official account stated that Law died a hero, leading his men.

After three weeks of heavy fighting, the Republic had retaken only a few square miles of ground. Brunete, which had been captured early in the offensive, was quickly lost; according to General Walter, this was 'the result of a panic sown by the "fifth column" that the fascists had gotten around our forces.' By 28 July, of the three hundred or so men of the under-manned British Battalion that had started the campaign, only forty-two remained: the rest were either dead, wounded, captured, or simply too physically exhausted to continue – or they had deserted. Those killed included George Nathan. Kenneth Sinclair-Loutit wrote that Nathan had been strolling down a badly-defended position, swagger-stick in hand, ignoring the fire directed at him, and 'showing the crumbling Spanish infantry that holding on was easy'. He was felled not by a bullet, however, but by bombs dropped by a German or Italian plane. He was buried at night, on the banks of the Guadarrama.

Jason Gurney felt that with Nathan dead, there was no one left with sufficient military capability to lead the Battalion. In the immediate aftermath of the fighting, their own political commissar told the survivors that the attack had failed 'because the military command was useless,' and that weak Spanish troops had let them down. Yet remarkably, on 31 July, Tom Wintringham (ever optimistic, or simply blind to the reality on the ground) could write to his mother, 'I think we're beginning to win this war: beginning to force the Fascists to do what we want, however clumsy we are still.' He added more jokingly, 'In the autumn we'll clean up this war and next spring I'll go to China to settle things there.'

Robert Capa, *Gerda Taro and a Republican soldier, Cordova front, 1936* (Magnum)

The Medical Units had also had their losses. Randolph Sollenberger, the American doctor who had come out to Spain with the British Medical Unit, was killed along with two aides and twelve patients when the Condor Legion bombed the Brigades' evacuation and first-aid centre. And Julian Bell suffered a mortal wound when the road he had been helping to repair was suddenly shelled.

Another casualty whose name would appear in the international press was Robert Capa's partner, Gerda Taro. Claud Cockburn, who had befriended the young German photographer, had been deeply impressed by the bravery she showed at Brunete: at one point, whilst they were being strafed by German planes and it seemed they had little chance of surviving, she had continued taking pictures. 'When you think of all the fine people we both know who have been killed even in this one offensive,' she had told Cockburn, 'you get an absurd feeling that somehow it's unfair still to be alive.' One of her last photos taken at Brunete captured the young British reporter with his arm around Fred Copeman's shoulder.

The day before Taro planned to return to Paris, she went with a young American journalist, Ted Allan, to take some final shots of the battle. Having spent the afternoon being bombed, shelled and shot at on the outskirts of Brunete, they walked back to Villanueva de la Cañada. There they had just hitched a lift on the running-boards of a car carrying wounded to hospital when a Republican tank accidentally collided with them. Taro and Allan were both injured, and were taken to the field hospital at El Escorial.

'The tank had slashed open her belly,' the American nurse who tended her reported, 'all her intestines had spilled out.' After an operation, Taro was expected to survive. But at six in the morning she simply closed her eyes and died.

Capa read the news in a French paper the following day. He was devastated, retreating to his studio and refusing food or drink. The French Communist Party organised her funeral, with flowers, music, banners and thousands of mourners. In death, for an instant, Taro was as famous as the man whose proposal of marriage she had declined earlier in the year. *Life* described her as 'probably the first woman photographer ever killed in action.' She was buried in Père-Lachaise, on what would have been her twenty-sixth birthday.

Robert Capa would never marry, but in later life he would often tell people that Gerda Taro had been his wife.

After the debacle of Brunete, the International Column's future looked bleak. Though the communists attempted to present the campaign as a victory, casualties had been heavy, objectives lost, and morale was near collapse. This was made clear in an extraordinary 'Confidential note on the situation of the International Brigades at the end of July 1937,' written almost certainly by Vidal Gayman, the French communist who – under the watchful eye of André Marty – was responsible for running the Column's base at Albacete.

Addressing his Comintern superiors, Gayman wrote bitterly that it was 'the prevailing opinion among high officers in the Spanish army … that the International Brigades are nothing but a foreign legion, an army of mercenaries fighting for money, who therefore have only one right: the right to obey. Do not say I exaggerate. The fact is known, it is patently clear.'

Gayman also believed that the Internationals had been left in the line for long lengths of time, sometimes – like the Lincoln Battalion – for as much as a hundred and fifty days. And in what was actually a common complaint amongst almost *all* Republican units, he believed that the best weapons had been withheld from them. 'The volunteers in the International Brigades are under the impression that they are systematically entrusted with the most difficult sector in every battle,' and they saw this as 'a concerted effort to annihilate and sacrifice the international contingents.' An analysis of the most recent battles, he claimed,

> would demonstrate that the International Brigades have always found themselves faced with the centres of enemy resistance. This cannot be ascribed to chance. I am absolutely convinced, as are the volunteers, that the International Brigades are automatically assigned to attack the most heavily fortified centres of resistance.

Gayman then cited the case of Captain Roehr, a thirty-two-year-old volunteer with a wife and child, who 'fought heroically' at Brunete with XIII Brigade, but 'committed suicide in battle because he could no longer accept the responsibility of demanding renewed effort from exhausted men … I am afraid this brigade will be permanently unable to fight. This brigade is not destroyed, it has been murdered.'

He went on to add that the Commanding Officer of XII Brigade had submitted his resignation, and that increasing numbers of the remaining four hundred Italian comrades were saying that they 'have accomplished their task, and that the time has come to demobilize them.' The morale of XIV was 'in a worrisome state' and it 'cannot be considered a brigade, because its troop strength is smaller than that of two normal battalions.' XV, finally, had 'withstood enormous losses … The English battalion has fallen victim to a wave of collective desertions, which has begun to affect the American battalion. The officers are not excluded from this process of demoralization.'

Others shared Gayman's impression. A report written immediately after Brunete by two senior British volunteers complained that the British Battalion had been 'constantly placed into the heaviest and most dangerous positions with the result that it almost suffered annihilation.'

'Know why we're called the Abraham Lincoln battalion?' William Horvitz heard a fellow American joke in Albacete. 'Because we, too, were assassinated.'

Horvitz claimed that twelve Americans who had quit the front line and gone back to Albacete demanding to be repatriated, having served their time, were taken back to Brunete, tried, and not seen again. He reckoned that at least twenty Americans were executed for desertion, while at least one British volunteer had his card marked for refusing to join a firing squad that was to execute an American. At Albacete, Horvitz found the eyes of those friends who returned from Brunete 'lit up from inside their skulls, very bright, wild, savage, stripped of any civilized patina. Men at war.' They made him 'run around with them, drink a lot, go to bordellos … Savage as they were, they were elated to be alive.'

The volunteers' sense of demoralization was reaching those back home, and the number of foreigners coming out to Spain began to slow. By July 1937, new recruits arriving from Britain had dwindled to around forty a month, and some British commissars suggested turning the remnants of their battalion into a company, and merging it with the Lincolns. Five of the leading figures in the British Battalion – including Jock Cunningham, Fred Copeman and Walter Tapsell – were called back to England to explain the situation. Though both Copeman and Tapsell had effectively suffered nervous breakdowns in the aftermath of Brunete, they were allowed to return to Spain; Cunningham, to his bitter disappointment, was not.

Without 'decisive and rapid action,' Gayman concluded his report on the whole situation, 'the International Brigades will no longer be capable of performing the military tasks with which they might be entrusted by their commanders.' Not surprisingly, another report sent to Moscow shortly after Gayman's stated that 'the commander of the Albacete base was in such a state of depression that we were forced to dismiss him immediately.' Yet other despatches also accepted that there was a 'pessimistic mood' among both the command staff and men of the International Column. Moscow was warned that there was a 'lack of confidence in victory', a mood that had been 'especially strengthened since the operation at Brunete'.

Many of the personnel in the International Brigades' medical units were equally demoralized. Even before Julian Bell's death, Kenneth Sinclair-Loutit had been considering returning home. He, like many others, was deeply depressed by his experiences, and physically exhausted. On one occasion, he had found 'an absolutely splendid Belgian male nurse going around a ward administering lethal injections to patients he considered moribund.' Sinclair-Loutit did not think the man had

> shortened anyone's life by more than a few hours, but this
> was something we never did in any circumstances ... I took
> the nurse outside under the trees, and he broke down totally,

a sobbing hulk, a thirty year old muscular adult male, well educated, with a record of entire commitment to his work. What in fact had happened was that for too long he had been giving far beyond his physical and psychological capacity.

Sinclair-Loutit realised then that he too 'was becoming mortally tired'; it was only the intimate relationship that had developed with one of the British nurses that kept him going.

Shortly afterwards Sinclair-Loutit was given permission to return home. Though the agony of the dying men he had tended was burnt into his conscious, he remained 'convinced that our side in the Spanish Civil war was as right as the other was wrong,' and he continued to hold the 'profound belief' that, 'irrespective of our nationality' the International Brigades 'were fighting for the future of our own homelands.'

For other volunteers, it was not so easy to call it a day and go home. The political commissars with the British Battalion knew that their men had come out as volunteers, many of them expecting a short war; equally, they knew they could not simply be allowed to quit whenever they chose. Added to this, some were becoming disillusioned with the activities of their fellow communists in Spain, and those who spoke their minds too freely could find themselves in danger of punishment. Given these dilemmas, it was not surprising that a number of volunteers chose to desert. According to Peter Spencer, who was still in Spain working as a liaison officer for the British Medical Unit, a number sought his help to get home; he managed to smuggle some out on board British ships bringing food and medical supplies.

Others, such as Stephen Spender's lover Tony Hyndman, were fortunate to have the help of influential friends. On visiting Albacete in 1937 Spender had been appalled at what he found. 'The sensitive, the weak, the romantic, the enthusiastic, the truthful,' he had informed Virginia Woolf, 'live in Hell there and cannot get away.' By late summer, the International Brigades had lost their independence. They were brought under the auspices of the Spanish Republican Army, and increasing numbers of men in their battalions would be Spaniards, not foreigners.

By the time it was clear that the Brunete offensive had failed, George Orwell and his wife were back in what he himself called their 'bloody awful' cottage in Wallington: even in summer it was old, cold and damp; the roof was made of corrugated metal, there was no electricity or hot water, and the kitchen often flooded in winter. Orwell, though, thrived on such deprivations, and he was hard at work on his account of his time in Spain, which he hoped to complete within a few months. And he was also reading and reviewing books published by earlier observers of the war. The first he wrote was a double review of *The Spanish Cockpit* by Franz Borkenau, and *Volunteer in Spain* by John Cornford's comrade in the International Brigades, John Sommerfield. It appeared in *Time and Tide* in July 1937, only shortly after Orwell's return to England.

Since his first trip to Spain when Borkenau had travelled through Catalonia and Aragon with John Cornford, the Austrian journalist had returned to Spain in early 1937; on that visit he had ended up in prison in Valencia. Orwell reckoned that *The Spanish Cockpit* was 'the best book yet written on the subject,' adding that its author 'has performed a feat which is very difficult at the moment for anyone who knows what is going on in Spain; he has written a book about the Spanish war without losing his temper.'

Orwell was pleased to note that, as Borkenau revealed, even as early as January 1937 the communists

> were using every possible method, fair and foul, to stamp out what was left of the revolution. The most important fact that has emerged from the whole business is that the Communist Party is now (presumably for the sake of Russian foreign policy) an anti-revolutionary force. So far from pushing the Spanish Government towards the Left, the Communist influence has pulled it violently towards the Right.

Orwell then quoted Borkenau's suggestion that these 'political facts' were being concealed from the Spanish people, and that this communist-led 'deception' was being maintained 'by means of censorship and terrorism'. Orwell confirmed this, writing that when he had left Spain the previous month, 'the atmosphere in Barcelona, what with the ceaseless arrests, the censored newspapers and the prowling hordes of armed police, was like a nightmare.'

He was far less impressed by *Volunteer in Spain*. Written in hard-boiled, Hemingway-esque prose, it was dedicated to John Cornford. 'Seeing that the International Brigade is in some sense fighting for all of us,' wrote Orwell, 'a thin line of suffering and often ill-armed human beings standing between barbarism and at least comparative decency – it may seem ungracious to say that this book is a piece of sentimental tripe; but so it is.'

It was probably just as well for Esmond Romilly that Orwell was not sent a copy of *Boadilla* to review, especially as (according to Philip Toynbee), Romilly 'believed that the Spanish communists were right and that their grim policy was a necessary one.' Orwell did, however, read W.H. Auden's long poem, simply titled *Spain*, which was published in May 1937. Before leaving for Spain in January, Auden had told a friend that he believed how, 'in a critical period such as ours ... the poet must have direct knowledge of the major political events,' and he had had the intention of either joining the International Brigades, driving an ambulance or working in a censor's office. But on reaching Barcelona Auden had soon discovered that Spanish politics were 'particularly unpleasant ... I found as I walked through the city that all the churches were closed and there was not a priest to be seen. To my astonishment, this discovery left me profoundly shocked and disturbed.'

In Barcelona Auden encountered Orwell's 'friend', Hugh O'Donnell, who refused to issue him with a pass to visit communist units on the Aragon front on the grounds that the poet was making contact with anarchists there. He therefore continued on to Valencia with the intention of eventually reaching Madrid, but within five or six weeks he had left Spain. This pleased his friends and fans, one of whom had agonized that 'as man power he is only one

W.H. Auden, Christopher Isherwood and Stephen Spender in a studio portrait by Howard Coster, London, 1937 (NPG)

unit, but as voice for the cause he is thousands and it would be a fearful loss if he were killed.' Subsequently Auden would talk little about his actual experiences in Spain. He would later state that he had been 'shocked and disillusioned' by his visit, but since he remained opposed to Franco, he did not wish to speak out against the Republic. 'It is always a moral problem when to speak,' he acknowledged. 'To speak at the wrong time can do great harm.' Yet the sentiments expressed in 'Spain' (the proceeds of which would go to Medical Aid for Spain) were far more positive than his later remarks would have suggested.

For Auden's poem lyrically described the sacrifices being made by men such as Cornford who had decided to leave their own country and fight in the Civil War. For those volunteers, their 'tomorrow' and all the activities of youth and everyday life – 'the discovery of romantic love,' the 'beautiful roar of the chorus ... the exchanging of tips on the breeding of terriers' – had been postponed, in many cases forever. For the volunteers, today was only for 'the struggle'.

Though Orwell would describe the poem as 'one of the few decent things that have been written about the Spanish war,' he took umbrage at one particular verse:

To-day the deliberate increase in the chances of death,
The conscious acceptance of guilt in the necessary murder:
To-day the expending of powers
On the flat ephemeral pamphlet and the boring meeting.

Auden was a key figure in British literary circles, and with his friend Stephen Spender its chief young poet. But Orwell felt that Auden – like the rest of what he called the poet's 'soft-boiled and emancipated' class and generation – had no idea of what the terror of war and the politics of despotism were really like. Orwell would call Auden and Spender 'parlour Bolsheviks': young men playing at radical politics.[1]

That phrase 'necessary murder,' Orwell believed, 'could only be written by a person to whom murder is at most a *word*. Personally I would not speak so lightly of murder.' Referring to his time as an imperial policeman in Burma, he observed:

> It so happens that I have seen the bodies of murdered men – I don't mean killed in battle, I mean murdered. Therefore I have some conception of what murder means – the terror, the hatred, the howling relatives, the post-mortems, the blood, the smells. To me, murder is something to be avoided. So it is to any ordinary person. The Hitlers and Stalins find murder necessary, but they don't advertise their callousness, and they don't speak of it as murder: it is 'liquidation,' 'elimination,' or some other soothing phrase. Mr Auden's brand of amoralism is only possible if you are somewhere else when the trigger is pulled. So much of left-wing thought

---

1 This was a view with which Jason Gurney concurred. During his days as a sculptor in Chelsea before he joined the International Brigades, he had moved in the same artistic circles as Auden and Spender. He later wrote that such 'intellectual Communists' were 'amongst the strangest phenomena of the period and existed on no other basis than pure fashion … They discussed "The Revolution" as though they were intimately involved in a conspiracy in which they would burst out with sword and gun onto the streets of London at any minute. It was all very romantic and totally unreal.'

is a kind of playing with fire by people who don't even know that fire is hot.

Perhaps because of Orwell's criticism (or perhaps because of Auden's own reconsideration) later editions of the poem would excise that chilling phrase 'necessary murder'.

In Orwell's opinion, the Republic's chances of now beating Franco were doubtful. 'To win a war,' he told a correspondent in August, either you had to have 'preponderence of arms, which the Government has not got and is not likely to have, or you have got to arouse enthusiasm among the people. But no one can get up much enthusiasm for a Government which puts you in jail if you open your mouth.' The communists, he was convinced, were just as bad as the fascists, and had almost certainly finished off the Republic's chances of winning the war.

That same summer Orwell was asked to join W.H. Auden, Stephen Spender and numerous other prominent British writers to 'take sides' on the Spanish war. Many had agreed, though Evelyn Waugh was one of the very few to express support for the rebels rather than the Republic. 'Will you please stop sending me this bloody rubbish,' Orwell responded curtly to the invitation. 'This is the second or third time I have had it. I am not one of your fashionable pansies like Auden and Spender.' Having fought for six months in Spain, and having seen fascism 'being riveted on the Spanish workers under the pretext of resisting Fascism,' alongside 'a reign of terror' that was filling the prisons, he asserted: 'I am not going to write blah about defending democracy or gallant little anybody.'

Ernest Hemingway was not so obstreperous when American writers were also asked to 'take sides'. 'Just like any honest man,' he stated, 'I am against Franco and fascism in Spain.'

V

Whether or not he was truly and fully aware of the repression that was taking place within the Republic, Ernest Hemingway knew he had to go back to Spain. As he wrote to his mother-in-law, he was sick of 'running against a solid wall of nobody wanting to hear anything true about this war,' and would 'be glad, in a way, to be back at it with no necessity for talking about it.' In fact, unlike Orwell who found on returning home that he could do nothing *but* talk about Spain, Hemingway claimed 'I haven't talked about it much.' Talking did no good; he had to be there.

But, as in the previous winter, he had a project to complete before he could go back. After their encounter with Roosevelt at the White House in early July, Gellhorn, Ivens and Hemingway had flown to Los Angeles where they were to show *The Spanish Earth* again. They quickly raised $20,000 in donations for ambulances. F. Scott Fitzgerald saw Hemingway there, and felt that his old friend 'was in a state of nervous intensity, that there was something almost religious about it.' He telegraphed him to say the film 'was beyond praise'.

When finally released to the general public in August 1937, *The Spanish Earth* was well received. *The New York Times* called it 'the most rational appeal the screen thus far has presented for the cause of Spanish democracy. Mr Ivens's camera argues gently and persuasively, with the irrefutable argument of pictorially recorded fact, that the Spanish people are fighting, not for broad principles of Muscovite Marxism, but for the right to the productivity of a land denied them through years of absentee landlordship.' It then described Hemingway's narrative as 'superb. It is terse, powerful, and at times informative; but it is vengeful, bitter and unreasoning.'

The critic Otis Ferguson wrote in the *New Republic* that much of the film's

> carrying power in understatement should be credited to Ernest Hemingway's commentary ... it isn't vintage Hemingway; but with his knowledge and quiet statement of the odds against survival, that feeling for the people of Spain which comes from his heart, the combination of experience and intuition directing your attention quietly to the mortal

truth you might well have missed in the frame, there could hardly be a better choice.

The rest of the credit went to Ivens 'and his unquenchable feeling for the life of people, at war or at work … what he has brought back is [as] convincing as the real thing.' These positive opinions contrasted with the *Motion Picture Herald*, which found the film 'too stark, bitter and brutal to please the general audience. Its partisanship and propagandistic non-objectivity tend to vitiate whatever message it may carry.' Astonishingly, when the film was released in Britain the film censor took the policy of Non-Intervention to an idiotic level, insisting on the removal of all references to Italian and German participation in the war.

Soon Hemingway was too far away to care about reviews. He took ship from New York on 14 August, shortly after a fight with fellow writer Max Eastman in their publisher's Fifth Avenue office. Eastman had suggested in an essay titled 'Bull in the Afternoon' that Hemingway's outsized personality hid a deeper insecurity. 'It is a commonplace,' he wrote, 'that Hemingway lacks the serene confidence that he *is* a full-sized man.'

'I did not call Ernest a big bully,' Eastman later clarified to a reporter after this set-to. 'I called him a lunatic.'

The incident caught Kitty Bowler's attention. 'Spain is saner than this town,' she wrote to Wintringham. 'The big news of the week is that Hemingway socked Eastman, not for politics but for making references to his virility.' She was still depressed by her fellow Americans. As she added in another letter a few weeks later,

> Most people here seem to have grasped that the [Spanish] government is in the right but their own reaction is to keep out of it, a general attempt to try and blind themselves to the world situation rather than understand it, [an] escapist, fear complex. After the Spaniards' craving for knowledge, this desire for ignorance, so as not to disturb their equanimity, is frightful.

Following a stop-off in Paris, by early September Hemingway was back in Madrid and the Hotel Florida. Martha Gellhorn joined him again. Their rooms became a haven for American volunteers from the International Brigade taking leave in the capital, with the writer providing them with hot baths, food, drink, and sometimes even girls. His regular haunt was a bar named Chicote's, which he had frequented before the war. It would be the scene for two of his most powerful – and most disturbing – short stories. Based on actual experiences, 'The Butterfly and the Tank' and 'The Denunciation' brilliantly captured the brutality of the conflict (though Stephen Spender would describe the latter as 'the most morally repugnant story ever written').

As these stories made subtly clear, things were not going well for the Republic. By that autumn of 1937 two-thirds of the country was now in rebel hands, at a cost, it was being suggested in the press, of nearly a million dead.[1] With the support of the new Prime Minister, Juan Negrín, communists in the Republican Government were continuing in their attempts to consolidate power and present a united front against the rebels; but their policies often had the side-effect of alienating the Republic's supporters (as they already had in Barcelona). A clumsy and sometimes brutal effort to assert central political control over Aragon, for example, had almost led to in-fighting between anarchist and communist units.

It was to Aragon that Hemingway set off with Gellhorn and the *New York Times* reporter Herbert Matthews, where the reinforced and re-equipped International Brigades were supporting a communist-led attempt to achieve what the anarchists and POUM militiamen had said was impossible: capture Huesca and Saragossa. But as they had soon discovered, the rebels had built a series of veritable fortresses with the aid of German engineers. The ambition – held since the very start of the war – of retaking the two cities proved impossible.

---

1 This was in fact a considerable overestimate: the real figure for total deaths, including combatants and civilians, is uncertain, and estimates for the number killed during the course of the whole war range between around 350,000 and 600,000.

As Hemingway reported for the US press, whilst in Aragon he met veterans of the Abraham Lincoln Battalion (now, since the two units' amalgamation, officially titled the Lincoln–Washington Battalion). 'Since I had seen them last Spring,' he wrote, 'they have become soldiers. The romantic have pulled out; the reluctant ones have gone home along with the badly wounded … Those who are left are tough, with blackened matter-of-fact faces; and, after seven months, they know their trade.' He relayed the news of how, in a campaign to take Saragossa, the Americans had first captured the town of Quinto, before attacking and taking Belchite, assaults that had involved considerable house-to-house fighting.

Robert Merriman, back in action as the recently promoted chief-of-staff of XV Brigade, particularly impressed him. This 'former University of California professor,' Hemingway explained, 'was the leader in the final assault. Unshaven, his face smoke-blackened, his men tell how he bombed his way forward; wounded six times slightly by hand-grenade splinters in his hands and face, but refusing to have his wounds dressed until the cathedral was taken.' In an article she wrote for *Collier's*, Gellhorn described Merriman drawing in the dirt a plan of the offensive, 'going over every point carefully as if we were his freshman class in economics back in California.'

'The boys did well,' Merriman told them.

The two writers encountered some American soldiers lounging by a river. It was 'a strange thing,' Gellhorn wrote, 'walking through that olive grove … seeing the faces from Mississippi and Ohio and New York and California and hearing the voices that you'd heard at a baseball game, in the subway, on any campus.'

American casualties had been comparatively light: 23 killed and 60 wounded out of a total of 500 who had taken part in the two operations. But others in the International Brigades had not been so lucky. The Hungarian General Pavol Lukács, whom Hemingway had befriended on his previous trip to Spain, had been killed right at the start of the campaign, when a shell-burst struck the car in which he was travelling with Gustav Regler.

Lukács and his driver died almost instantly. Despite a lump of steel driving a large hole in the small of his back that uncovered the kidneys and exposed the spinal cord, Regler survived. Hemingway visited him at the International Brigades' hospital in Benicasim, on the Mediterranean coast. On the same ward he also met Wintringham. The Englishman had returned to active service in August, only to be severely injured in the campaign that had killed Lukács. On the second day of fighting he had been shot by a sniper: 'A bullet through the shoulder, cracking a bone or so,' he explained in a letter to Kitty Bowler, who was now trying to write a book about her time in Spain. 'Lost a lot of blood. I love you. Being away from you hurts more than silly bullets.' As he would later ruefully observe, for all the months he spent in Spain, he saw action for a total of only four days.

Conscious that his involvement in the Spanish war was now over, Wintringham still hoped to go to China and join the war there – and to take Kitty with him. 'I must have months of real rest,' he wrote, 'or rather real change, a peaceful life for four or six months, before I'll want to go warring again or even war-reporting. Let's go live with Macartney and Compton Mackenzie in their Shetland Isle, and write … I don't mind quite a lot of work so long as it is peaceful & fruitful.'

'I've had a good talk with Gustav Regler,' he added in another letter, 'all about propaganda and heroism and what not.' Regler had been in Moscow before coming out to Spain, and had witnessed the fear and the oppression there. Both men were growing disillusioned with the war and (in their hearts) with the Communist Party. Before the end of the year, both would have left Spain. Wintringham returned home to recover from his wound in England, where he was eventually reunited with Kitty Bowler. His Spanish memoir would be published as *The English Captain* in 1939, but neither he nor Kitty would complete the novels they hoped to write about their experiences.

Gustav Regler went to France to recover from his wound, and wrote *The Great Crusade*. Hemingway would provide a preface for the English translation of the novel. 'I think I can truly say,' he would write there, 'for all those I knew as well as one man can know another, that the period of fighting when we thought that the Republic could win the Spanish Civil War was the happiest period of our lives.' Though Hemingway added that he cried on hearing of Lukács' death, he claimed: 'We were truly happy then for when people died it seemed as though their death was justified and unimportant. For they died for something they believed in.'

In December 1937 the Republic attacked again, this time at Teruel, a small town in Aragon, north-west of Valencia. The fighting, like the weather, was bitter, and thousands of combatants and civilians died; some even froze to death in the sub-zero conditions of an uncommonly harsh winter. When the town finally fell to the Republican forces on 7 January 1938 it was seen as a significant setback for Franco. As *The New York Times* reported, until recently 'world opinion was convinced of the inevitability of an Insurgent triumph.' Now, however, though 'the odds are still on Franco,' Teruel 'proved that the government forces … are far from beaten, and the end of the warfare, barring any large-scale outside intervention in behalf of either side, is not in immediate sight.' Franco poured resources into recapturing the town.

As at Brunete, casualties included press observers. A shell struck a car carrying four British and American journalists covering the war on the rebel side of the lines. Only one survived: 'Kim' Philby, a young graduate of Trinity College, Cambridge, who had moved in the same communist circles as John Cornford, but was now posing as a fascist sympathizer.

Ernest Hemingway, who was reporting on the action alongside Sefton Delmer, Herbert Matthews and Robert Capa, was as at risk as any of the correspondents. In one despatch he wrote of being under fire from heavy machineguns and trench mortars, and of showing a soldier how to knock open the bolt of his jammed rifle. And in a letter to his ex-wife, Hadley, he boasted of how he had 'made the whole attack with the infantry,' entering Teruel 'behind one company of dynamiters and three of infantry,' before writing the 'most godwonderful house-to-house fighting story'. As he later recalled, 'When the civilians came out of their houses they asked me what they should do and I told them to stay in the houses and not go into the street that night under any circumstances and explained to them what good people we Reds were and it was very funny. They all thought I was a Russian and when I told them I was a North American they didn't believe a word of it.'

The Germans continued to experiment with new military hardware, and it was at Teruel that the Stuka dive-bomber first saw action. In comparison, the Republican units commanded by the young communist General Enrique Líster were often poorly equipped; and the harder they fought, the more their limited resources were depleted. In mid January, following the massive rebel counter-attack, the International Brigades were called into aid the Republican defence of the town. The twenty-three-year-old budding poet Laurie Lee, who had been evacuated from Spain at the start of the Civil War, had recently returned to volunteer with the British Battalion. After a long and difficult journey on foot over the Pyrenees he had been shocked by the disorganization and amateurism he discovered in this makeshift army: the hours of boredom spent before anything happened, the lack of arms, training or apparent purpose, the cold, and his frequent arrests on suspicion of spying. At Albacete he met a wounded American volunteer whose colleagues had been massacred by Moors at Belchite when their machine-gun failed.

'We were set up, goddam it,' the American told him. 'Lambs for the slaughter. No pasaran! They pasaranned all over us.'

Yet Lee was also struck by the men's high spirits, at least until the rebels retook Teruel in February. 'The gift of Teruel at Christmas had become for the Republicans no more than a poisoned toy,' he later wrote. 'It was meant to be the victory that would change the war; it was indeed the seal of defeat.'

It was at Teruel, in the last stages of fighting there, that Lee shot a rebel soldier. Afterwards, as the young Englishman lay 'in a state of sick paralysis,' he contemplated what he had done. 'I had killed a man, and remembered his shocked, angry eyes. There was nothing I could say to him now … Was this then what I'd come for, and all my journey had meant – to smudge out the life of an unknown young man in a blur of panic which in no way could affect victory or defeat?'

Within weeks of this moment of self-discovery, Laurie Lee was back in London. And with Teruel retaken, the rebels looked another step closer to victory.

VI

Writing newspaper articles was child's play to Ernest Hemingway, and he had no intention of wasting his best material on the press. Ultimately, what he was doing in Spain was gathering experiences for another book; for Hemingway was a writer who depended (indeed, had always depended) on autobiography as material for fiction.

To Have and Have Not had been published in October 1937. Though an immediate bestseller, it was not well received by the critics; despite the passages of brilliance that electrify all of Hemingway's writing, it would prove to be his poorest novel. Accompanying its long review with a photograph of the author standing amongst a group of smiling Spanish soldiers, *The Washington Post* reported that the book was 'good red Hemingway ... and it sounds for a considerable distance as if Mr Hemingway's experiences in Spain [have] made him into a proletarian writer.' Sinclair Lewis was more cutting. 'Please quit saving Spain,' he advised his old friend, 'and start saving Ernest Hemingway.'

'Hemingway is a very large athletic man possessed of enormous physical vitality,' Cyril Connolly observed in his review of the novel for *The New Statesman and Nation*. In Connolly's opinion, the 'great factor' determining both Hemingway's life and literary style was his physique: 'Boxing, bull-fighting, big-game shooting, tarpon-fishing, soldiering are as necessary to him as a walk in the park to you or me.' Though he feared Hemingway the man was in danger of outshining Hemingway the writer, Connolly disagreed with the fashionable claim 'that Hemingway is finished ... Hemingway has been in Spain for some time now and he is obviously the person who can write the great book about the Spanish war.'

Through the last months of 1937, holed up in Madrid's Hotel Florida with his typewriter and his mistress, Hemingway was indeed writing; but it was not a new novel. It was a play.

Chapter 13

The Fifth Column

I

'Will Mr Hemingway try his hand at a play?' Conrad Aitken had asked in *The New York Herald Tribune* in 1926 whilst reviewing *The Sun Also Rises*. 'He clearly has the ability to make his story move, and move with intensity, through this medium.' Given Hemingway's extraordinary skill at writing fast-paced, realistic dialogue, a play made perfect sense. And without the need to compose much else other than the stage directions, it would take him much less time to write than a full-blown novel.

As he sat at his typewriter in the Hotel Florida, Hemingway did not need to look far for the perfect location for what would prove his only attempt at theatre. The writer who had already based most of his work on his own experience set the greater part of *The Fifth Column* in the Hotel Florida itself. And its lead characters were two American writers: Philip Rawlings and his lover, Dorothy Bridges, were based on Hemingway and Martha Gellhorn. His picture of Dorothy, 'a tall handsome blonde,' was not flattering: in one scene Rawlings calls her 'lazy and spoiled, and rather stupid, and enormously on the make. Still she's very beautiful, very friendly, and very charming and rather innocent – and quite brave.' Other characters included one of Hemingway's 'whores de combat', a beautiful Moorish prostitute in love with Rawlings, and Max, a German soldier from the International Brigades, a 'comrade,' as Rawlings describes him, with an 'amazing' broken face, his front teeth gone, and black gums from where Nazi torturers had burnt them with a red-hot iron.

Rawlings, it soon transpires, is actually working for Spanish counter-espionage. 'I'm a sort of second-rate cop,' he explains, 'pretending to be a third-rate journalist.' His covert mission is to track down fifth columnists in Madrid, who are then brought before the sinister Colonel, an interrogator with the secret police.

Whereas Orwell told his readers that life in wartime Spain was a nightmare, Hemingway's play – like his short stories – actually showed them. Men are killed by mistake; young and naïve American volunteers are threatened with execution; Rawlings and the Colonel question and intimidate prisoners, they talk openly of torture.

'I have seen a politician walk across that floor on his knees and put his arms around my legs and kiss my feet,' the Colonel tells Rawlings in a scene set in police headquarters. 'I watched him slobber on my boots when all he had to do was such a simple thing as die. I have seen many die, and I have never seen a politician die well.'

'I don't like to see them die,' Rawlings responds. 'It's O.K. I guess, if you like to see it. But I don't like it.' Then he asks the Colonel who dies well.

'Fascists, real fascists,' the Colonel replies, 'the young ones; very well. Sometimes with much style. They are mistaken, but they have much style.' And priests also die well: 'Terrific. You know; just simple priests. I don't mean Bishops.'

'Sometimes there must have been mistakes, eh? When you had to work in a hurry perhaps.'

'Oh yes. Certainly. Mistakes. Oh, yes. Mistakes. Yes. Yes. Very regrettable mistakes. A very few.'

'And how did the mistakes die?'

The Colonel answers proudly: 'All very well.'

In between the main action, Hemingway explored his relationship with Martha Gellhorn through that of Rawlings and Dorothy Bridges. When the Moorish prostitute tells him not to make a 'mistake' with 'that big blonde,' he replies: 'I'm afraid that's the whole trouble. I want to make an absolutely colossal mistake.'

'I'd like to marry you,' Rawlings tells Dorothy in bed, 'and go away, and get out of all this.' But he knows he does not mean it. 'Never believe what I say in the night,' he tells her later. 'I lie like hell at night.' Rawlings is bitter, he drinks and starts fights; Dorothy wants to settle down in St Tropez or Paris to have children and write books.

When Max, the German anti-fascist, sees Dorothy wearing a silver fox fur cape, he is suspicious of Rawlings relationship with this empty-headed bourgeoise. Rawlings replies that he is 'bloody well fed up' with the war, wishes he was 'on the Riviera waking up in the morning with no bloody war, and a café crème with proper milk in it … and brioche with fresh strawberry jam.'

'You do it so *every* one will have a good breakfast like that,' Max responds. 'You do it so *no one* will ever be hungry. You do it so men will not have to fear ill health or old age; so they can live and work in dignity and not as slaves.'

The climax of the play comes in a heroic night-time operation, when Rawlings and Max kill numerous rebels and capture a key Fifth Columnist politician.

'You'll get everything,' Rawlings tells the Colonel in the interrogation room, 'the lists, the locations, everything. This thing has been running it.' The following day the Madrid newspapers report the arrests of three hundred Fifth Columnists who have been involved in shootings, assassinations and sabotage around the city.

In an ugly final scene, Rawlings tells Dorothy he is leaving her, describing as he does so all the things that Hemingway had enjoyed doing with his wife, Pauline: watching horse races, drinking in Paris, skiing, shooting lions in Africa, fishing in Cuba. 'I've been to all those places,' Rawlings tells her, 'and I've left them all behind.'

Using words Hemingway knew could be (perhaps *had* been) applied to himself, Dorothy calls him a '*conceited* drunkard. You ridiculous, puffed-up, posing braggart.' He abandons her in tears.

As Hemingway later explained, whilst he was writing *The Fifth Column* the Hotel Florida 'was struck by more than thirty high explosive shells'. (Herbert Matthews reported how one night the rebels fired at least 1,500 shells into Madrid during 'a terrific night bombardment,' the 'incessant flashes' brightening the sky 'like sheets of lightning'. He noted, too that Hemingway, 'in his room at Madrid's most famous hotel – hit thrice tonight – counted 600 shells by 9.45 and exactly 1,152 up to 10.30.') 'So if it is not a good play,' Hemingway suggested, 'perhaps that is what is the matter with it. If it is a good play, perhaps those thirty some shells helped write it.' Some of the most detailed stage descriptions were of the sounds the shells made, being fired, coming in, exploding, shattering windows.

Having completed the play, just after Christmas 1937 he returned to Paris, where he met his wife. Against his wishes, Pauline Hemingway had travelled from Key West with the hope of finding him in Spain, and saving their marriage. The reunion was not happy: at one point, she threatened to jump from the balcony of their hotel. In the New Year they returned to Florida, though Hemingway would soon be telling his ex-wife, Hadley, that he was 'very homesick for Spain.'

His initial attempts to put *The Fifth Column* on stage proved unsuccessful. One producer died after signing a contract, another failed to raise the considerable money required for a New York run. Eventually – regretting that he had not written the play as a novel – Hemingway decided to publish it alongside forty-nine of his short stories, from the first he had written in Paris in the early 1920s, to the most recent written in Madrid.

Like *To Have and Have Not*, the published script was not well received by the critics. Though Hemingway had already guaranteed his lasting fame as a writer, it seemed that perhaps his greatest achievements lay behind him. The influential critic and university professor Lionel Trilling thought that there was 'something vulgar in making Spain serve as a kind of mental hospital for disorganized foreigners who, out of a kind of self-contempt, turn to the "ideal of the Spanish people".' Nor did he think 'that Hemingway's statement of an anti-fascist position is of great political importance … It is hard to believe that the declaration of anti-fascism is nowadays any more a mark of sufficient grace in a writer than a declaration against disease would be in a physician.'

'The heroic Anglo-American secret police agent is the same old Hemingway protagonist of *The Sun Also Rises* and *A Farewell to Arms*,' Edmund Wilson complained, 'though now more besotted and maudlin; but we never doubt that he will do his duty. Indeed, the more besotted and maudlin this familiar old character gets, the more completely he behaves like the hero of a book of adventure for boys.'

Wilson felt that neither the hero's 'breaking-off' with Dorothy Bridges, 'nor the butchery by the Communists of the Fascists – which would have worried him at an early stage [in his career], when he used to write about wars very differently – seems to give rise to the slightest moral uneasiness.' For Hemingway, Wilson went on, 'the Comintern agents in Spain have *carte blanche* to go as far as they like, because they are up against a lot of dirty bastards. [He] ignores the fact that the GPU [the Soviet secret police] in Spain has been executing its opponents of the left as well as Fascist spies.' In Wilson's final analysis, though Hemingway's new short stories were once again excellent, the play was 'silly', with 'trashy moral attitudes'. He would later nickname the play's hero Hemingway's 'Hotel Florida Stalinist'.

'I know that all of you who took no part in the defence of the Spanish Republic must discredit those who did,' Hemingway responded sarcastically in a letter to Wilson (possibly unsent). 'The suppression of the POUM,' he continued,

> the poor old Poum, was a godsend to all cowards as a pretext for taking no part in the fight against Fascism in Spain, and I hope to live long enough to see John Dos Passos … and yourself rightly acclaimed as the true heroes of the Spanish War and Lister, El Campesino, Modesto, Durán and all our dead put properly in their places as stooges of Stalin.

Nothing revolted Hemingway more than a stay-at-home critic writing about something he had never experienced, even if that critic was, perhaps, correct.

II

Whilst Hemingway had been in Madrid putting the finishing touches to *The Fifth Column*, George Orwell was completing his non-fiction account of his Spanish experiences, detailing his service with the POUM and his escape from the secret police. He knew his stance against totalitarianism would make it a controversial publication; when, during the writing process, a Soviet magazine asked him to contribute an article on Spain, Orwell responded that he had served with the POUM. 'Our magazine, indeed, has nothing to do with POUM-members,' the editor replied. 'This organization, as the long experience of the Spanish people's struggle against insurgents and fascist interventionists has shown, is part of Franco's "fifth column" which is acting in the rear of the heroic army of Republican Spain.'

Reactions such this only added to Orwell's sense that he was an enemy of the communists. Kenneth Sinclair-Loutit met Orwell a few times after their return to England, and as he observed:

> the fact that we had both been in Spain at the same time should have served as a bond but, in our particular case, it was regrettably and un-necessarily divisive. He had fought under the flag of the POUM, as indeed had John Cornford when he first went out. I myself did not feel that we had been on different sides, but Orwell's experiences when the POUM, the independent left, was being broken up at the behest of the Soviet Communist Party, had made him suspicious of those like myself who had been in the International Brigade.

By early 1938 the manuscript of Orwell's Spanish book was with the publisher. 'I think the title will be "Homage to Catalonia",' he told a friend in February, 'because we couldn't think of a better one. I'm not starting another for a few weeks.' He was thinking of writing a novel; but as he told Cyril Connolly, 'This bloody mess-up in Europe has got me so that I can't really write anything ... It seems to me we might as well all pack our bags for the concentration camp.'[1]

Like Hemingway, Orwell was convinced that unless something was done soon to check the spread of fascism in Europe, another world war was inevitable; and it also seemed that the obvious place to take that action was Spain. Unlike Hemingway, he believed that in the event of a world war, fascism in some form or another would be the ultimate winner, even in Britain. 'We like to think of England as a democratic country,' he told a friend, 'but our rule in India, for instance, is just as bad as German Fascism, though outwardly it may be less irritating. I do not see how one can oppose Fascism except by working for the overthrow of capitalism, starting, of course, in one's own country.'

Homage to Catalonia was published at the end of April 1938. It began with Orwell's encounter with a young Italian volunteer in the POUM barracks in Barcelona, and ended with his escape from Spain six months later. His final paragraph, describing the last leg of his journey home, was a reverie about a British way of life that had once seemed unquenchable, yet was surely on the brink of annihilation:

> it was still the England I had known in my childhood: the railway-cuttings smothered in wild flowers, the deep meadows where the great shining horses browse and meditate, the slow-moving streams bordered by willows, the green bosoms of the elms, the larkspurs in the cottage gardens; and then the huge, peaceful wilderness of outer London, the barges on the miry river, the familiar streets, the

---

1 He had already thought of a title for his next novel, but had not yet written a line of *Coming up for Air*. As he told another friend, 'what with Hitler, Stalin & the rest of them' it seemed that 'the day of novel-writing was over.'

posters telling of cricket matches and Royal weddings, the men in bowler hats, the pigeons in Trafalgar Square, the red buses, the blue policemen – all sleeping the deep, deep sleep of England, from which I sometimes fear that we shall never wake till we are jerked out of it by the roar of bombs.

Though *The Observer*'s reviewer praised Orwell's book and described the author as 'the giant of … any other writers on the Spanish war,' *Homage to Catalonia* was a failure. Many reviewers ignored it, whilst others sympathetic to the Communist Party attacked it. 'The trouble is that as soon as anything like the Spanish civil war happens,' Orwell complained to a friend, 'hundreds of journalists immediately produce rubbishy books which they put together with scissors and paste, and later when the serious books come along people are sick of the subject.' A decade later, the first print run of 1,500 copies had still not sold out.

His warning, it appeared, had gone unheeded. Unless something changed soon, Orwell feared that Fascism would be victorious everywhere. The suggestion that he would be completing his next book inside a concentration camp became a recurrent dark joke in the writer's correspondence through 1938 and 1939. What he had experienced in Spain, and what he had read of current events in Russia and Germany, did not fill him with hope. Whilst he reckoned on 'another thirty years or so' in which to live and write, 'the idea that I've got to abandon them,' he complained, 'and either be bumped off or depart to some filthy concentration camp just infuriates me.' Though Orwell had gone to Spain a fighter, and had returned still with the conviction that fascism would have to be fought with arms, he found himself increasingly embracing a pacifist outlook. Many in Britain agreed with him that pacifism – the mass refusal by people everywhere to be drawn into any fighting at all – was the only answer to the dangers lying ahead.

The threat of airborne bombs clearly aided the anti-war argument. In a speech in London in July 1938, the MP Marcus Samuel described how a 'wave of horror' had 'swept over Great Britain at the recurrent news

MADRID
THE "MILITARY" PRACTICE OF THE REBELS

4 - 21
35

IF YOU TOLERATE THIS
YOUR CHILDREN WILL BE NEXT
MINISTERIO   DE   PROPAGANDA

that civilians have lost their lives in the bombing of "open" Spanish towns. Not for a long time will the outcry that followed the attack upon Guernica be forgotten.' The great fear, of course, was that if this could happen in Spain, what might happen to British towns and cities in the event of a war with Germany? Orwell was well aware of this threat, something he made clear in two book reviews he wrote in 1938. Of Brigadier-General F.P. Crozier's *The Men I Killed*, he observed in *The New Statesman and Nation* that the author, having spent the years 1899 to 1921 'in almost ceaseless slaughter of his fellow-creatures,' was now a pacifist. One of his arguments against war 'is the fact all known methods of defence against the aeroplane are more or less useless and that the German bombers could probably reduce England to chaos and starvation in a few weeks'. This, Orwell acknowledged, was probably true, even if stating it amounted 'to scaremongering'.

Of George Steer's recently published book, *The Tree of Gernika*, he gave a fuller examination in the pages of *Time and Tide*. Subtitled *A Field Study of Modern War*, the *Times* reporter had written his book in Paris in the months immediately after the bombing of the Basque town. As Steer observed, his account of the attack had resulted in a violent dislike of the rebels 'among the majority of English people'; it had also awakened in them the realization that if this could be done to Guernica by only some forty planes, what could the Luftwaffe do to Hull, or Portsmouth? Although Orwell thought Steer seemed at times an unreliable witness, he spoke 'with undoubted authority' on the destruction of Guernica:

He was in the immediate neighbourhood at the time of the aeroplane-raids, and his account leaves no doubt that the little town was *not* 'burnt by Red militiamen' but systematically destroyed from the air, out of sheer, wanton brutality. Guernica was not even of much importance as a military objective. And the most horrible thought of all is that this blotting-out of an open town was simply the correct and logical use of a modern weapon. For it is precisely to slaughter and terrify the civilian population – not to destroy entrenchments, which are very difficult to hit from the air – that bombing aeroplanes exist … the horror we feel of these things has led to this conclusion: if someone drops a bomb on your mother, go and drop two bombs on his mother. The only apparent alternatives are to smash dwelling houses to powder, blow out human entrails and burn holes in children with lumps of thermite, or to be enslaved by people who are more ready to do these things than you are yourself; as yet no one has suggested a practicable way out.

It was pacifism and – in particular – appeasement that appeared to offer a way out of this terrible dilemma: a way out that had driven British policy since the start of the Spanish Civil War. By rectifying the injustices implemented on Germany by the Treaty of Versailles after the Great War in 1919 and bending to Hitler's territorial demands, many members of the British establishment hoped that the Nazis could be satisfied, and another war thereby averted.

And if Claud Cockburn was to be believed, this dangerous policy was being dictated by a group of wealthy and self-interested Anglo-Americans based at a beautiful country house on the banks of the Thames, some twenty-five miles west of London. They were, as Cockburn dubbed them, 'the Cliveden Set'.

At the heart of Cockburn's alleged 'set' were two wealthy Anglophile Americans, Waldorf, Lord Astor and his wife, Nancy. Educated at Eton and Oxford, Waldorf was the eldest son of the phenomenally rich American businessman, William Waldorf Astor, who had settled in England in 1889. In 1905 young Waldorf had met Nancy, a divorcee from Virginia; when they married the following year they had received Cliveden House as a wedding present. Within easy reach of London, it became the focus of regular weekend gatherings of influential guests from the worlds of politics, journalism and academia.

The Astors were a well-connected family. In 1910 Waldorf was elected Conservative Member of Parliament for Plymouth; when he succeeded his father as viscount in 1919 he was obliged to resign his seat; whereupon his wife was elected in his place, becoming the first woman MP in Britain. The family also had significant interests in the British press. They owned *The Times* (which had recently been described by Cockburn's cousin, the novelist Evelyn Waugh, as 'the most important newspaper in the world') and they co-owned *The Observer*.

Rich and outspoken, it was almost inevitable that the Astors would come to Cockburn's attention. As early as the summer of 1936 he published a series of articles in *The Week* revealing the 'extraordinary position of concentrated political power' they and their Tory companions held. These friends included *The Times*' editor Geoffrey Dawson and his deputy Robert Barrington-Ward; the aristocratic diplomats Lord Lothian and Viscount Halifax; Sir Nevile Henderson, the British Ambassador to Berlin; and the austere, autocratic, umbrella-toting Neville Chamberlain, who in May 1937 replaced Stanley Baldwin as Prime Minister. Cockburn described them as 'one of the most important supports of German influence' in Britain. Or, as a CPGB pamphlet based on Cockburn's accusations ominously put it:

Week-end parties at Cliveden House have made and broken

British Cabinet Ministers. Decisions taken there have brought Europe to the verge of war. Friends of Hitler and enemies of the people are welcome there … The Cliveden Set: their power reaches through British banking, transport, journalism – through Britain's Parliament, across the seas to International Fascism. But their power can be broken …

Even while he was in Spain, Cockburn and his assistants in London continued to publish his weekly dose of political scandal and rumour. *The Week*'s success had brought him under the increasingly close watch of his enemies. He was well aware that the German Ambassador in London 'had me followed about London by enormous blondes'; and MI5 was also on his trail. As Sir Vernon Kell, head of the British secret service, observed in a note to a diplomat at the American Embassy, 'Cockburn is a man whose intelligence and wide variety of contacts make him a formidable factor on the side of Communism.' Though Kell complained that *The Week* was often full of gross inaccuracies, he admitted that on occasions Cockburn 'is quite well informed and by intelligent anticipation gets quite close to the truth.'

Whether close to the truth or not, the articles Cockburn published in *The Week* in November and December 1937 established one of the most internationally successful and enduring conspiracy theories of the century. It had already been revealed in the press that Lord Halifax, who had been invited by Hermann Goering to attend a hunting exhibition in Berlin, was going to meet Hitler at his private headquarters, the Berghof. But Cockburn revealed in *The Week* what he called the 'sensational' news that Halifax would be presenting Hitler with a 'deal', whereby Germany would be given a 'free hand' in central Europe in return for leaving Britain in undisturbed possession of its Empire. According to Cockburn, this proposal had been knocked 'into usable diplomatic shape' during a Cliveden weekend in late October by 'that little knot of expatriate Americans and "super-nationally" minded Englishmen' who for years had 'exercised so powerful an influence on the course of "British" policy.'

According to Cockburn, the Cliveden Set was acting as its own private Foreign Office, advancing a policy favourable to the Nazis. In return for offering Hitler a 'free hand' in Austria and Eastern Europe, the Clivedenites, Cockburn argued, were securing their own wealth and position. In so doing, they were betraying the workers of Britain as well as European democracies such as Spain. This was made clear in the CPGB's penny pamphlet, *Sidelights on the Cliveden Set: Hitler's Friends in Britain*, published in March 1938:

> The hands of Chamberlain and his Cliveden Set are red with the blood of tens of thousands of the Spanish people … Communists say the time has come to hound these people out of public life. The time has come to end the domination of Britain by a gang of millionaires and their despicable agents. It is time the people took things into their own hands, and set up a People's Government to carry out the policy desired by the people and in the interests of the people – a policy of alliance of the peaceful countries against fascist aggression, a policy of social progress at home.

The first act of such a 'people's policy' would be 'assistance for Spain – arms, food, medical supplies,' and the 'withdrawal of Hitler and Mussolini's armies and airplanes'. Other actions would include the formation of a 'Peace Bloc' with France and the USSR, and 'co-operation with the USA'.

Cockburn's accusations hit home. A Labour MP dubbed Nancy 'the honourable member for Berlin', and the Astors were soon receiving hate mail. 'You blasted American whore of a chorus-girl,' declared one writer. 'Go back to your own country!' But the 'Cliveden Set' was not simply a phenomenon of the British press: they were being written about internationally, too. According to Cockburn, the phrase quickly appeared 'in almost every leading newspaper of the Western world … No anti-Fascist rally in Madison Square Garden or Trafalgar Square was complete without a denunciation of the Cliveden Set.' During a visit to America, Anthony Eden would tell Stanley Baldwin, 'Nancy and her Cliveden set has done much damage, and 90 per cent of the US is firmly persuaded that you and I are the only Tories who are not fascists in disguise.'

Ferdinand Kuhn, *The New York Times*' foreign correspondent in London, explained the broader context of the 'Set' to American readers in April 1938:

> British aristocracy by its very nature is more hostile to communism than to fascism … Menace to their wealth, their social position, as they see it, is the creed of communism, and, in their minds, whatever endangers themselves endangers England.
>
> So it is not difficult to see why so many British aristocrats today sympathize with Hitler. They may not approve particularly of his persecution of Catholics or Jews, but they do regard him as a St George who killed the dragon of communism in Germany and prevented Russia from spreading her creed to Western Europe.

Hitler did indeed regard himself as Western Europe's buffer against Soviet Communism, and Kuhn was right in saying there were many in Britain who felt the same way. The MP Harold Nicolson would be shocked when, stopping at his club in May 1938, he encountered 'three young Peers who state that they would prefer to see Hitler in London than a Socialist administration'.

The 'Cliveden Set' was thus not a complete fabrication. Indeed, as early as June 1937 Robert Vansittart, Undersecretary at the Foreign Office, had complained about 'ambulant amateurs' involving themselves in foreign affairs. 'We really must put a stop to this eternal butting in of amateurs,' he had advised the Prime Minister. 'These activities – which are practically confined to Germany – render impossible the task of diplomacy,' for these 'superficial people are always gulled into the lines of least resistance … and we then have the ungrateful but necessary task of pointing out the snags and appearing obstructive. It is quite unfair and should cease.' Nevertheless, the 'Set' was an exaggeration. Cockburn had created it with a political purpose: to raise awareness of the dangers of appeasement, and to help win support for Republican Spain. He was quite happy to employ unscrupulous measures to achieve this. For Cockburn did not judge 'facts' to be the most important feature of journalism, and if it suited Cockburn's purpose his reporting could be far from accurate or truthful.

For by the time of the Spanish Civil War Cockburn had come to the conclusion that 'the real hum-bug of the press begins only when newspapers pretend to be neutral, impartial fact-purveyors, "servants", so help me, "of the public".' What he later considered 'one of the most factual, inspiring and yet sober pieces of war reporting' he ever wrote was an entirely fabricated article he invented in Paris with the Czech Communist Otto Katz, describing a supposed 'anti-Franco revolt' in Spanish Morocco. It succeeded, briefly, in convincing the French Government 'that Franco might lose, and that it was therefore worth supporting the Republicans, and permitting the transport across the border of some field guns that were vitally needed.' As Cockburn recognized, Otto Katz 'regarded journalism simply as a means to an end, a weapon'. It was a lesson Cockburn was happy to embrace.

Having scoured the British press during his research for *Homage to Catalonia*, George Orwell was well aware of Cockburn's tricks. At one point in his book he dissected Cockburn's *Daily Worker* accounts of the May events in Barcelona, concluding: 'It is impossible to read through the reports in the Communist Press without realizing that they are consciously aimed at a public ignorant of the facts and have no other purpose than to work up prejudice.' He phrased it more strongly in private. 'The reason why so few people grasp what has happened in Spain,' he told a friend, 'is because of the Communist command of the press … the accounts of the Barcelona riots in May … beat everything I have ever seen for lying.'

Orwell's horror grew when he read misrepresentative press accounts of the POUM 'spy' trials, which were held in Valencia in October 1938. Though all of the organization's leaders who were tried were exonerated of any connection to the rebels, Orwell noted that even *The Observer* was guilty of erroneous reporting. 'I admit this kind of thing frightens me,' he told an Irish colleague who had served alongside him in Spain:

> It means that the most elementary respect for truthfulness is breaking down, not merely in the Communist and Fascist press, but in the bourgeois liberal press which still pays lip-service to the old traditions of journalism. It gives one the feeling that our civilization is going down into a sort of mist of lies where it will be impossible ever to find out the truth about anything.

Already, the foundations were being laid for Orwell's greatest work of fiction.

IV

When Nancy Astor visited the US in the summer of 1937, she was shocked by the degree of anti-German sentiment in her home country, and appalled that some people were stoking it deliberately. Publicly she voiced her suspicion that Jews might be responsible. Her remarks caused a furore, and in a letter to *The Manchester Guardian* on her return she attempted to defend herself: 'There are in America (as there are here) certain forces which are doing their utmost to keep Britain and Germany at loggerheads, perhaps even to get them involved in a war. The result of such a conflict would imperil civilization whoever was victorious.' This, of course, was also Orwell's opinion. And, in essence, it was the rationale behind the British Government's appeasement policy.

Millions had died in the Great War, and billions had been spent to fund it; few wished to see such folly again. In July 1938, Chamberlain stated that he was compelled 'to strain every nerve to avoid a repetition of the

Great War in Europe'. Though they had been humiliated by the terms of the Treaty of Versailles, it was widely assumed that the Germans felt the same way, too. Most probably did; even Hitler repeatedly professed himself a man of peace with no desire to start another conflict. Yet everything behind the Nazi regime, from the moment it came to power, suggested otherwise. 'With few exceptions,' the US Consul General in Germany had informed the State Department as early as June 1933, 'the men who are running this Government are of a mentality that you and I cannot understand. Some of them are psychopathic cases and would ordinarily be receiving treatment somewhere.' When the British journalist Sir Philip Gibbs toured Europe the following year, he reported in *The New York Times* that though everyone he met in Berlin (including Britons and Americans) told him that Germany's intentions were peaceful, in France 'every man, woman and child believes to the very bones that Germany is preparing and arming for a new war.' Refugees fleeing the country told the same story.

Even *The Times* saw the darkness at the heart of Hitler's party. As an editorial reflected after the 'Night of the Long Knives' in July 1934, when dozens of Hitler's own supporters had been executed:

> the present rulers of Germany have thrown aside all the principles of law and justice which distinguish a modern Western State from an Oriental despotism or a medieval tyranny, breaking down all the safeguards which civilized nations have painfully established for the protection of human life and individual liberty.

The Nazis' anti-Semitism was equally apparent. Their oppression of Germany's large Jewish population had begun within months of gaining power. 'What is Hitler going to do with the Jews?' pondered the American journalist, Vincent Sheean, after visiting the country. There were 600,000 of them in 'Greater Germany', but it 'is clearly impossible for even the German National Socialist party, in all the pride of its absolute dominion, to murder so many people.' Yet he knew about the concentration camps, with their machinegun towers and barbed wire fences, slowly filling with Jews, Catholics, socialists, communists, priests, homosexuals, Gypsies: all manner of enemies or innocent victims of the Third Reich. 'When total insensibility is reached,' he mused, 'the lives of half a million Jews will make no more difference to the Nazis than the lives of six flies.'

Rightly or wrongly, to Cockburn and others on the left, such terror had to be fought by any means necessary, and to attempt to appease such a monstrous regime was reckless, immoral and irresponsible. And Spain was the front line in the international fight against fascism. As Sheean wrote at the time, in the face of continuing Nazi triumphs through the final years of the 1930s 'it was necessary to think of Spain very frequently: otherwise the general level of cowardice, treachery, bad faith and cruelty throughout Europe was too oppressive to be borne. Spain alone had resisted and was still resisting the limitless claims of Fascist imperialism; Spain alone raised its clenched fist against the bombs.'

Of course, what alarmed liberals such as Orwell and Dos Passos was that the communist terror in Russia at the other extreme of the political divide was equally ominous, that it was making itself felt in Spain, and that it could not be ignored. When they chose to make that known, they were viciously attacked. Thus as Hemingway wrote to Dos Passos in March 1938 after his old friend had written a series of articles on his experiences in wartime Spain, 'A war is still being fought in Spain between the people whose side you used to be on and the fascists. If with your hatred of communists you feel justified in attacking, for money, the people who are still fighting that war I think you should at least try to get your facts right.' Angry that Dos Passos was basing his accusations on only a few weeks spent in Spain, Hemingway returned to what had happened to the POUM, and the disappearance of Andrés Nin. 'Then there is Nin,' he told Dos Passos:

> Do you know where Nin is now? You ought to find that out
> before you write about his death. But what the hell. There

were some good Russians in Spain but you didn't meet them and they aren't there now … for you to try constantly to make out that the war the government is fighting against the fascist Italian, German, Moorish invasion is a communist business imposed on the will of the people is sort of viciously pitiful.

'So long, Dos,' he concluded. 'Hope you're always happy.'

Whilst Hemingway's rambling attack on Dos Passos was confined to a personal letter, Orwell was subjected to attacks in the press. *The Daily Worker*, he complained to a friend in 1937, 'has been following me personally with the most filthy libels, calling me pro-Fascist etc.' It was only after he asked Victor Gollancz to intercede that the harassment ended. But he would always be aware that he had powerful communist critics, who – he feared – might stop at nothing to silence him, as they had silenced Nin.

V

There were some on the fringes of political power who perceived the danger inherent in the appeasement and neutrality policies of the Western democracies. Winston Churchill, who was still in the political wilderness of the Tory backbenches, kept out of the Cabinet by Chamberlain, told the House of Commons in April 1937, 'We seem to be moving, drifting, steadily, against our will, against the will of every race and every people and every class, toward some hideous catastrophe. Everybody wishes to stop it, but they do not know how.' William E. Dodd, lately US Ambassador to Berlin, echoed his words when he returned home in January 1938. In a speech at New York's Waldorf-Astoria Hotel he made clear his disgust for Hitler and the Nazis. 'Mankind is in grave danger,' he warned his fellow countrymen, 'but democratic governments seem not to know to what to do.' Whilst the German Ambassador went to the State Department in Washington to complain about Dodd's speech, the retired diplomat Theodore Marburg wrote to *The New York Times* praising it. 'The last hour has come for action by the United States,' he warned. 'It can still save the world … Surely the noisy isolationists, the peace-at-any-price group, do not represent the will of the vast majority of the American people.'

Ironically, through 1938 it was becoming increasingly apparent to the political leaders of the Spanish Republic that the only thing likely to save them from Franco was the outbreak of another full-blown world war. The chances of this happening appeared to become more likely after March 1938, when German troops marched unopposed into Austria. Many Austrians rapturously received the *Anschluss*; it was followed by the immediate introduction of Nazi policies, and soon thousands of Jews had been arrested. Though the Versailles Treaty had expressly forbidden the union of Germany and Austria, the Western democracies again responded meekly.

As German men and matériel continued to help Franco wage war in Spain, it was soon clear that the next objective in Hitler's expansionist programme was Czechoslovakia. In an extraordinary book, *Secret Armies*, the American communist John Spivak devoted a chapter to 'England's Cliveden Set' and the part it was supposedly playing in the spread of fascism, and charted the full implications of the Nazis' increasingly belligerent ambitions in eastern Europe:

> From Austria Hitler got more men for his army, large deposits of magnesite, timber forests and enormous water-power resources for electricity. From Czechoslovakia, if he could get it, Hitler would have the Skoda armaments works, one of the biggest in the world, factories in the Sudeten area, be next door to Hungarian wheat and Rumanian oil, dominate the Balkans, destroy potential Russian air and troop bases in Central Europe, and place Nazi troops within a few miles of the Soviet border and the Ukranian wheat fields he has eyed so long.

That Britain, France and the US had allowed Hitler to keep this steady course unmolested appeared as remarkable as their failure to intervene in Spain. In Spivak's opinion, appeasement 'indirectly menaces the peace and security of the United States ... and will inevitably lead Great Britain on the road to fascism.' He had only one explanation for this astonishing course:

> England has a reputation for shrewd diplomacy. In the past she has used nations and peoples, played one against the other, betrayed, sacrificed, double-crossed in the march of her empire. Since the Cliveden week-end, however, with its resultant intrigues, England has, to all appearances, finally double-crossed herself.
>
> Those who guide her destiny and the destinies of her millions of subjects have apparently come to the conclusion that democracy, as England has known it, cannot survive and that it is a choice between fascism and communism. Under communism, the ruling class to which the Cliveden week-end guests belong, stand to lose their wealth and power. It is the fatuous hope of the economic royalists that under fascism they will sit on top of the roost, and so the Cliveden week-enders move towards fascism.
>
> Hitler's fifth column finds strange allies.

Chapter 14

The Undefeated

|

O n 15 March 1938, only three days after the *Anschluss*, George Orwell was rushed to hospital, bleeding heavily from a haemorrhage in his lung. ('The bleeding seemed prepared to go on for ever,' Eileen told one of her husband's friends.) He was sent to a sanatorium in Kent to recover, and at first was afraid it was tuberculosis; it was eventually diagnosed as a chronic viral disease of the bronchial tubes. He would remain at the sanatorium until September; to his frustration he was unable to start work on his new novel, but he did write a pacifist pamphlet outlining how war was not the answer to the problem of fascism.

The following week, Ernest Hemingway boarded ship from New York, bound for Europe on his third visit to wartime Spain; once again, Martha Gellhorn appeared beside him. Gustav Regler, recovering in France from his injuries, was overjoyed when he heard the news that Hemingway had once again pinned his colours to the loyalist cause. For the Republic was in crisis: on 9 March, in glorious spring weather, the rebels had launched a major mechanized offensive in Aragon. One of their first targets was Belchite. Nearby, the British, Americans and Canadians of XV International Brigade – their numbers now bulked out by large numbers of Spanish conscripts – were resting after their participation in the bitter winter fighting at Teruel.

They were immediately sent forward to stiffen the defence; but already that defence was crumbling. With heavy casualties, they were soon being overrun. As Major Merriman realized, the situation was hopeless. 'Driven before the Insurgents' mechanized steam roller,' Herbert Matthews reported in *The New York Times*, 'scattered by its shattering power or caught behind in the machinery were the remnants of the Loyalists' Fifteenth Brigade.' What the Republicans were experiencing was the forerunner of *Blitzkrieg*: the co-ordinated use of fast-moving mechanized units supported from the air. The way of war was changing, even before the Spanish had mastered the tactics of 1914-18.

And the rebels were giving no quarter to the foreign soldiers of the International Brigades. They blamed them and the Communist Party for prolonging the war that was devastating Spain. When Franco's rapidly advancing forces penetrated into Catalonia – the first foothold they had made in the region since the war began – Herbert Matthews declared that the Republican Army was fighting 'with its back to the wall' (whilst also noting that the response in Barcelona to this crisis was almost 'indifferent').

By 26 March 1938, according to a report in *The Times*, a thousand square miles of Republican territory had been lost, and the war had 'entered its last lap. Nothing now can save the cause of the Government in Spain,' *The Times* correspondent suggested, 'unless foreign intervention comes to their rescue on terms approximately equal to the help Italy and Germany are giving to General Franco.' And any help on such a level 'would have to be "administered" to prevent its being wasted by incompetence.'

A new recruit who joined the remnants of the Lincoln-Washington Battalion during this crisis was Alvah Bessie, a thirty-three-year-old communist from New York. Having graduated from Columbia University in 1924, Bessie had gone on to work variously as an actor, writer and farmer, even living for a while in Paris. His fortunes had changed in 1935 when he won a Guggenheim prize for his first novel, *Dwell in the Wilderness*. Having heard Hemingway's passionate speech at the American Writers' Conference at Carnegie Hall in June 1937, Bessie had left his wife and two young sons in New York to join the International Brigades. As he

Alvah Bessie, Spain, 1938

recorded in the privacy of his notebook, his motivation for coming to Spain had been twofold: 'to achieve self-integration,' and 'to fight fascism.' Of these, he admitted, the first 'far outweighed the second.' As he explained to himself, he wanted to 'submerge' himself in a large body of men, 'seeking neither distinction nor preferment,' thereby achieving 'self-discipline,' 'patience and resignation' and 'unselfishness,' and finally 'to build again a life that would be geared to other men and the world events that circumscribe their lives.' It was undoubtedly a noble ambition, and one in which he was firmly supported by his wife.

With a group of around forty Americans, Germans, Romanians, Italians, Czechs and Serbians, Bessie had crossed the Pyrenees from France at the beginning of February. He recorded with a writer's painterly touch the experience of watching for the first time as dawn rose over Spain: 'magnificent rugged country. Cork trees with trunks stripped, gray-green of olives ripening, lemons ripe ... Rivers winding silver in distance ... Cold, hungry, exhausted.' After a brief period of training in Albacete, along with 125 American and Spanish replacements he joined the 350 or so survivors of the Lincoln-Washington Battalion near Belchite on 18 March.

Like most foreign writers in Spain, Bessie planned to write a book if he survived. 'Things look hard, here,' he recorded in the notebook he kept assiduously: 'the men are worn and discouraged, individualistic. It appears the brigade took a terrific licking at Belchite ... lost lots of men and equipment.' Those killed in the retreat had included the Battalion's captain. They holed up in reserve in an olive grove near Batea, high in the hills above Tarragona. Bessie was both impressed and shocked by the men he had joined:

Militant; hard as rock; fighters; tough guys. In poor shape – dirty, unshaved, ragged, lost all equipment, including rifles, in actual rout of XV Brigade. Soup kitchen blown up. Few men have decent clothes, shoes or even blankets; few have mess kits – we use tin cans and fingers ... Men lie around all day, chewing the fat about the last and previous actions; the men who have been lost in this and previous fights. Talk, too, about union battles back in the States. They have, by dint of long months in the lines, been reduced to a truly animal level – growl at each other, are surly, selfish, though capable at moments of comradeship and generosity ... The strain, however, is obvious and they are not to be taunted or kidded much, about anything. Sabotage apparently accounted for the loss of Teruel and Belchite, after they had been in our hands so long. One major (Spanish) and 2 Lts. and 1 Sgt. were shot yesterday for cowardice.

Another court martial followed, and the Americans' political commissar sentenced some of his fellow countrymen to death for desertion. He was eventually overruled by the Brigade's commander: General Copic feared that news of the executions would leak out to Hemingway and Matthews.

In fact, damaging reports had already reached the international press. Though dozens of deserters were caught and returned, their hands bound, to the Battalion, John Honeycombe, a Communist Party volunteer from Los Angeles who had fought at Teruel, succeeded in crossing the border into France. There he told a *New York Times* reporter that 'Americans have been stood against a wall and shot for the slightest insubordination.' According to his wild overestimate, some 8,500 Americans had already been killed, captured or wounded in Spain; only around 500, he reckoned, now remained.[1]

---

1 The US contingent in the International Brigades never numbered more than around 3,000 men (and a handful of women); another 1,600 or so came from Canada.

'The Communist International is the only thing that keeps this war going,' he told *The Times*. 'The Spaniards are tired of war, they hate the foreigners and are not backward in letting us know it.' In Honeycombe's opinion, the International Brigades were 'through,' the two crack Spanish Brigades were 'played out,' and there was 'nothing left to stop the Rebels; it should be over soon.'

Despite Honeycombe's bleak prognosis, Republican forces reformed and succeeded in stalling the rebel advance. For a week the Lincoln-Washington Battalion remained in reserve positions, waiting to be rearmed. A twenty-two-year-old veteran from Brooklyn, Milton Wolff, was promoted as their new captain. On 24 March, as Bessie recorded in his diary, Robert Merriman told them 'we may go up any time now and sacrifice of all lives may be asked in coming battles to recover terrain lost in the Aragón, and push on.' Rumours circulated: that the French frontier had been unofficially reopened, and that arms were pouring through for the Republic; that Roosevelt had declared 'in favor of revision of neutrality legislation, under pressure of popular feeling about Spain and China'.

Finally they received new Russian light and heavy machine-guns, as well as rifles. A week later, Alvah Bessie came under fire for the first time. Unknown to the men of XV Brigade, as they were being sent into forward positions they were already virtually surrounded by a rapid new rebel advance. Formed mostly of Italian mechanized units, the attack force was aiming to reach the Mediterranean, and divide what remained of the Spanish Republic in two.

The British Battalion was the first to stumble unwittingly into the rebel offensive. When the soldiers at the front of their column, who were advancing on foot, encountered tanks, it was a few moments before they realized that they were enemy vehicles. Walter Tapsell – the man with whom Orwell had discussed the possibility of transferring to the International Brigades the previous year – was one of the first to be killed; he was last seen firing his pistol at an Italian tank commander. The 140 men captured included Frank Ryan. Those lucky enough to be at the rear of the column made a fighting retreat.

The Canadians of the Mac-Paps were more fortunate: they were able to make an orderly retreat through wooded valleys and over hilltops. 'It was like playing cowboys and Indians,' one survivor reflected long afterwards, 'except there were too many Indians.'

Communication between the various units had collapsed. Unaware of what was happening to the rest of their Brigade, the Lincoln-Washington Battalion advanced obliviously into disaster. 'Ordered to stand fast' near Gandesa, Captain Wolff recollected three decades later, 'we found the whole fucking fascist army!' They held out till almost nightfall, when Major Merriman appeared in a bullet-riddled staff car. He told the Americans and their Spanish companions to withdraw to the river crossing at Mora de Ebro (Móra d'Ebre), ten miles to the east. A whole company out on one flank never received the order, and was not seen again. In the darkness, Bessie and his remaining comrades were soon retreating in disorder.

The Battalion split into two large groups. The smaller one, of which Bessie was a part, stumbled in the darkness upon a camp of sleeping rebels. Of around seventy men, he was one of a handful not killed or captured; exhausted, he reached the rendezvous at Mora de Ebro on 1 April.

Later the next day, Republican engineers destroyed the iron bridge across the Ebro. As Bessie recorded in his notebook, safely over the river there mingled 'hundreds of men from all IB units'. There was 'complete disorganization, men wandering around looking for their units. No command, demoralization.'

When Bessie and three others stumbled upon some Mac-Paps, one of the Canadians asked, 'Where's the Lincolns?'

'We're the Lincolns,' one of the four replied. So far as they knew, they were the only Americans to have survived the rout.

II

It appeared that the end of the Republic was quickly approaching. In

Barcelona, Hemingway and Gellhorn once again teamed up with Robert Capa, Herbert Matthews and Sefton Delmer. They were all eager to reach the front line (wherever exactly that might be).

The morning of Sunday 3 April, Hemingway wrote, 'was bright and warm and the pink of almond blossoms colored the grey hills and brightened the dusty green rows of olive trees.' A mile and a half from the coastal town of Reus enemy planes flew overhead, and they watched the bombs fall and the town disappear 'in a brickdust-colored cloud of smoke'. Continuing onwards into the mountains, they became entangled in columns of refugees, pulling their possessions on carts, with goats and sheep tethered to the tailboards. Hemingway was struck by the sight of a woman carrying her newborn baby on top of a mule 'piled high with bedding ... The mother's head swung steadily up and down with the motion of the beast she rode and the baby's new wet-black hair was drifted grey with dust.' Then they began to see soldiers straggling along. Some carried rifles; many others had abandoned their precious weapons.

At first there were only a few of them, 'then finally there was a steady stream with whole units intact. Then there were troops in trucks, troops marching, trucks with guns, with tanks, with anti-tank and anti-aircraft guns, and always the line of people walking.' Then they started meeting troops they knew: 'soldiers from New York and Chicago who told how the enemy had broken through and taken Gandesa, that Americans were fighting and holding the bridge at Mora across the Ebro River and that they were covering this retreat and holding the bridgehead across the river.'

It was impossible to push past the tide of people, so the journalists returned to Barcelona. But the next day Hemingway and Matthews returned in search of survivors from the Lincoln-Washington Battalion (of whom, he reported on 4 April, 'no word had been heard since Gandesa was captured two days ago').

Eventually they found eight Americans among a group of about three hundred soldiers from XV International Brigade; Alvah Bessie was one of them. He had spent the previous day in a truck searching for stragglers, driving all the way down to the shore of the Mediterranean, then back up to the mountains. Three of the Americans Bessie managed to find had stripped off their uniforms to swim the wide waters of the Ebro: six others with them had drowned in the swiftly flowing river.

By the following day, about seventy Spanish and Americans of the Lincoln-Washington Battalion had been rounded up. 'Apparent now that almost 70% of the L-W is missing,' Bessie noted:

> either dead, captured or still wandering in the hills, trying to get across the Ebro. Mail was brought up last night and of hundreds of names read, only about 15 claimed letters. Situation extremely difficult, demoralization great. Many men talk openly of fucking off across the French border, if possible … We may yet be cut off from all escape, north or south. Plans uncertain but possible that we may defend Mora la Nueva.

In only three weeks of fighting almost three hundred Americans had died. Despite rumours over the next few months that he had been taken prisoner, one of those who would never be seen again was Robert Merriman. It would later transpire that he had been killed (along with a large group of his men) leading an ill-judged attempt to cross the enemy lines in daylight. Well over a hundred of the American dead had been shot after being captured; a further 87 had been taken prisoner. Their Government would take little interest in the men's plight, however, for neither the British nor American embassies were well-disposed to help their citizens captured in Spain. 'When Americans enlist to fight under a foreign flag,' the US consul in Seville explained, 'they cannot expect our government to worry about what happens to them thereafter.'

The situation among the British was little better; of the 497 on the Battalion roll who had gone into action little more than a week before, by 8 April there were 350 still unaccounted for, including some of their leading comrades. A letter to Harry Pollitt announced the bad news:

'as you can guess the strain has been terrific and our boys are not in very good shape.' One of their surviving officers 'wanted to pull out immediately for Barcelona' whilst another 'was for refusing to go into the line again ... Should we run the danger of allowing the remnants of the British to be annihilated?'

Despite the disaster, some loyalists were still confident of victory. As Bessie noted in his diary, Hemingway and Matthews both told him that 'plans are being made to get around this apparently impossible situation.' But he was sceptical. Even Matthews' own newspaper was announcing that the rebels looked ready to move on Barcelona, now less than sixty miles from the front lines.

'Unless France comes in here,' Bessie mused, 'Spain is sunk.' But there was, it seemed, a glimmer of hope. 'Hemingway says Roosevelt offered 200 planes to France if France would send them in here,' he wrote, adding plaintively, 'where are they?'

III

Hemingway's remark was not wishful thinking. Although publicly Roosevelt continued to support the US arms embargo on *all* belligerent powers – whatever the morality of their cause – he was in fact acting behind the scenes in a clandestine attempt to provide military planes for the Republic. In March 1938 – only a month before the new rebel offensive – the President had met the Spanish ambassador in Washington, and 'promised to give directives not to hinder the export of any weapons to France and not to enquire about the further destinations of the cargo.' Roosevelt also told the Mexican ambassador that US weapons could soon be shipped to Republican Spain via Mexico.

Though at the time nothing came of these promises, in June the US ambassador in Paris, William Bullitt, was amazed to be confronted by his Spanish counterpart, asserting that Roosevelt had 'personally approved' the sale of US planes to the Republic, and that the President was 'arranging for the evasion of the Neutrality Act ... knowing fully that their destination would be Spain.' Bullitt was even more surprised when Eleanor Roosevelt's alcoholic brother, Gracie Hall Roosevelt, visited him shortly afterwards. Hall (as he was known) told Bullitt that he had 'managed to gather for the Spanish government approximately 150 new and second-hand planes of various makes.' As Bullitt wrote sceptically to the President, Hall had 'said that he had discussed this transaction with you and that it had your entire approval. He stated that you and he ... had discussed all the details and that you had agreed to wink at the evasion of the Neutrality Act involved, because of your interest in maintaining the resistance of the Spanish government against Franco.'

Without implicating the President in this illegal plan, Bullitt also contacted the State Department requesting more information. With clear opposition there, the plan collapsed. Further attempts by Hall to export planes to Spain (with, he claimed again, 'the approval and support of the President') also failed. The depth of Roosevelt's commitment to this covert policy remains unclear. In various speeches, the President warned about the dangerous threat posed to peace by certain unnamed – though obvious – powers: a famous speech at Chicago in October 1937 had warned that the foundations of civilization were under threat; that 'innocent peoples, innocent nations, are being cruelly sacrificed to a greed for power and supremacy'; that 'law, order and justice' were being 'wiped away'; that the community of nations was under metaphorical threat from 'an epidemic of physical disease' and needed to join 'in a quarantine' to prevent its spreading. Yet as the Soviet ambassador in Washington complained in April 1938, Roosevelt's many anti-fascist pronouncements were in such 'striking contrast to [his] actions that it has become nauseating.'

Roosevelt could have done more to support the Republic openly. In April 1938 a resolution to end the arms embargo was introduced in the House of Representatives; it was supported by a petition signed by 206 members of the bar, declaring that the embargo 'constitutes an unprecedented repudiation of well-settled principles of international law as well as a reversal of traditional American foreign policy.' In May, a similar resolution was introduced by Senator Gerald P. Nye, which also called for the lifting of the arms embargo. Nye had stated – rightly – that US policy had simply abetted 'aid for one side as against another, and neither neutrality nor non-intervention is accomplished.' When it seemed likely that the resolution would be passed, Roosevelt went out of his way to defer a decision indefinitely.

Once again, it was public opinion that was at stake. As Roosevelt told his Secretary of the Interior, Harold Ickes, in May, Democratic congressmen believed that 'to raise the embargo would mean the loss of every Catholic vote next fall.' Furthermore, it was feared that a change in US policy would undermine the French and British policy of Non-Intervention. Nye's wish to end what he called 'the policy of coming to heel like a well trained dog every time England whistles' had failed.

Yet Roosevelt only recently had received a letter from his ambassador in Dublin, criticizing Chamberlain's appeasement policy, and the weakness and vacillation of the British government following the *Anschluss*. 'Over here there is the same element that exists in London,' Roosevelt had replied. 'They would really like me to be a Neville Chamberlain – and if I would promise that, the market would go up and they would work positively and actively for the resumption of prosperity. But if that were done, we would only be breeding far more serious trouble four or eight years from now.'

Roosevelt was well aware of the dangers in the international situation; in January 1938 he had approached Chamberlain with the suggestion that the US might host an international conference in Washington addressing world peace. Chamberlain had rejected the offer, a move that contributed to Anthony Eden's decision to resign as Foreign Secretary, frustrated by the Prime Minister's continuing attempts to please and appease Mussolini and Hitler. Eden was replaced by Lord Halifax: the Cliveden Set's stooge, if Claud Cockburn was to be believed.

With Barcelona apparently in his sights, again Franco appeared to hesitate. In March, with Mussolini's enthusiastic support, he had ordered a series of heavy air raids on Barcelona in an attempt to pummel the population into submission. Aside from food shortages and the influx of refugees from elsewhere in Spain, this was the city's first direct experience of the war with Franco since the rebellion had begun almost two years before. Hundreds of air raid shelters were hastily constructed as Italian planes flew overhead, but over three thousand people were killed and injured. International condemnation, however, was swift and strong enough to put a stop to the attacks.

So, perhaps fearful of finally triggering French intervention in the war, Franco decided to avoid launching what would likely prove a costly ground attack on Catalonia. Instead, he ordered his army southwards, towards Valencia. The rebels were confident of a speedy victory against an enemy they now considered on the run. But Léon Blum's French government had reopened the its border with Spain, allowing Russian military equipment into the country. Furthermore, Republican forces had regrouped. Falling back upon prepared defences, they successfully stalled the rebel attack.

Hemingway watched it happen. He was forced to admit that the news from the northern area of the rebel offensive in Aragon had not been good. On 10 April 1938, in the shadow of the Pyrenees, he wrote, 'where the positions could be held by the determined graduates of any good girls' finishing school,' Republican territory had been taken 'as more or less a matter of course'. But on the banks of the Ebro, in a landscape 'almost too romantic-looking to make war in,' 'attack after attack by two Italian divisions … supported by world-war-scale barrages of six-inch, three-inch and the new lighter quicker-firing guns had not succeeded in piercing the Government lines at any point.'

Nevertheless, on 15 April 1938 rebel forces finally succeeded in reaching the Mediterranean. The Republic was cut in two, and Catalonia was isolated from Valencia and Madrid. It was Good Friday, and to the Catholic rebels, it seemed a good omen.

'It's a bloody mess down there, the game's up I'm afraid,' George Orwell wrote to Cyril Connolly from his sanatorium bed. 'I wish I were there. The ghastly thing is that if the war is lost it will simply lead to an intensification of the policy that caused the Spanish Government to be let down, & before we know where we are we shall be in the middle of another war to save democracy.'

But in Hemingway's opinion the Republic was not defeated yet. 'Anyone who thinks the war is over in Spain,' he wrote at the end of April, was either 'a fool or a coward.' Despite the losses of territory, the Republic was still putting up a strong resistance, and he reckoned there was at least another year of fighting to be had.

By late May it was indeed clear that the immediate threat to the Republic had been averted, and Hemingway returned to New York. Once again, he told reporters waiting for him at the dockside that he reckoned the Republic's chances of beating Franco were still good (this despite the four American deserters from the International Brigades who had stowed away on board the liner).

Returning to his wife and family in Key West, Hemingway refused to give up on Spain. In a series of overtly political articles written for the new monthly American magazine *Ken*, he passionately reiterated the need to fight Hitler and Mussolini before their forces overran Europe. In a number of militant essays he declared that the way to avoid the forthcoming world war was 'to end it where it has begun, in Spain, by smashing world fascism's weakest link, the beatable Italian military machine.' This the Spanish could do themselves if only they had the weapons and planes that would come by ending the arms embargo. He also denounced the alleged 'fascists' in the US State Department who had done 'their level, crooked, Roman, British-aping, disgusting efficient best' to end the Spanish Civil War by 'denying the Spanish government the right to buy arms to defend itself against the German and Italian aggression.' And he denounced Chamberlain and the French ministers for betraying the people of Britain, France and Spain. He called on Roosevelt to become a great president by opposing Chamberlain and supporting the Spanish Republic while there was still time.

The Republic's continuing survival made more plausible the negotiated peace that the Prime Minister, Juan Negrín, was optimistically hoping for. In an attempt to assuage international opinion, one of his proposals was that both sides send home foreign participants.

Though they had played an important role in the early months of the war, it did not appear that the withdrawal of the remnants of the International Brigades would be a great military loss for the Republic. The Brigades' base at Albacete had already been abandoned and re-established on a much-reduced scale near Barcelona, whilst many soldiers in the Brigades were no longer international volunteers at all, but drafted Spaniards led by Spanish officers. (This policy, though, had not been a great success, for the different nationalities had not integrated well.) Finally, what remained of the Lincoln-Washington Battalion was, at least in Alvah Bessie's opinion, 'a pretty crummy bunch … with few exceptions, men who are unfit, either physically or, more frequently, psychologically, for the front.' When replacements arrived to refill their ranks, they were young Spaniards, sixteen, seventeen, eighteen years old. 'Many are so young, they cry when reprimanded.' Bessie thought it 'doubtful if they have any conception of what they are going into – more doubtful if they could be held in the event of hot action and attendant panic … It is shit that such babies should have to know this sort of thing – as it is shit that *anyone* should have to know it.'[1]

Things were little better among the remaining British volunteers, as one of the Battalion's commissars had told Harry Pollitt back in April ('our boys are not in very good shape,' he had warned).

Once again, the men had been ill-prepared: 'A great number of the

---

1 However, Negrín would later tell Herbert Matthews 'that he considered his decision to withdraw the volunteers [of the International Brigades] to have been the worst mistake he made as Prime Minister … The Internationals were few, but they were precious.' Matthews would also disagree with the claim that the withdrawal had been made on Stalin's orders, stating that the decision had been solely Negrín's.

lads had never seen action before and had never had training. Just bang in the line immediately they arrived in Spain.' The British commissar accepted that the Brigades' 'military weaknesses' were 'pretty obvious. The enemy is not only superior in armament but also in his knowledge of military tactics and supply of trained officers. Time after time our troops have been cut off or tricked because of the inexperience of our commanders.' But he also placed considerable blame on the man he called 'our old froggie friend': the Brigades' French commandant, André Marty.

'I just take no notice of mad Andre,' the commissar admitted to Pollitt, adding, 'I would not be surprised if his number was up soon as everybody is cursing the old idiot.' By late May, the same commissar was writing that even Marty admitted that 'there is no longer an International Brigade, there are only foreign soldiers mixed with Spanish brigades … Froggie continues to say the most terrible things about the 15th, including the allegation that it has been "ruined" by the Americans etc. He confiscated the personal parcels sent for the Canadians on the grounds that such preferential treatment accentuated national differences and was helping Fascism!'

Once the rumour reached the volunteers that they were to be withdrawn in order to pave the way for a negotiated peace with Franco, it dominated conversation. Most of the Americans, as Bessie wrote, wanted 'badly to go home and talk of nothing else. They discuss the possibility of our withdrawal from every angle and in terms of unmistakable wish fulfillment.'

On 4 July 1938 – after three months out of the fighting – the Lincoln-Washington Battalion held a fiesta. Although they were still being trained in river crossing and mountain assault tactics, Bessie did not believe the Brigades would be sent back into action now. The men 'could not fight with the old-time zest,' he noted, 'realizing that they might be killed on the very eve of returning home.'

V

Bessie was wrong. The withdrawal of the International Brigades remained only a rumour, and on the night of 24 July, in a massive counter-attack, thousands of Republican soldiers recrossed the Ebro. XV International Brigade was part of the massive assault force. Their objective was Gandesa, to retake the territory lost in April, restore the land link between Barcelona and Valencia, and boost the Republic's stature in the eyes of international observers. It was an ambitious and initially well-executed plan (the following month, Mussolini would even be predicting Franco's defeat). But ultimately it was an ill-conceived political gambit. Despite amassing tens of thousands of soldiers, the Republic could ill afford to commit its increasingly limited military resources on another frontal attack against an enemy superior in aircraft, tanks and artillery.

Many of the young Spanish recruits in the Lincoln-Washington Battalion refused to go into action. Company commanders, Bessie noted, 'feel like real butchers, leading these undeveloped, frightened kids into fire – threatening them, forcing them. Many stood up better than expected, many did not.' Once again the Republican attack – begun with great optimism – stalled. The rebels counterattacked, and another grim battle of attrition was fought through long days of intense summer heat.

By mid August XV Brigade was fighting in the Sierra de Pandols south of Gandesa. This high ground, desolate and covered with broken, sliding rock, burned over by incendiary bombs and fought over and lost and retaken, was, Bessie wrote, a 'hellhole'. On the ominously named Hill 666 there was almost no cover from artillery or planes.

'The worst day, so far, of this life,' Bessie wrote on 19 August. After he had helped to capture a key node of rebel-held high ground on the hill, 'hell broke loose':

> For 7½ hours we were shelled, the shells covering practically every inch of our parapets and the *barranco* behind our hill. The strain, unbearable, the shells, thousands, falling in

groups of 3, 4 at second intervals ... Whitney, translator for the company, 1½ years here, scared as a rabbit, nearly hysterical with fear for weeks now, severely wounded two feet from me ... the sight of Whitney, his buttocks nearly torn off, holding them, his face dead yellow, covered with rock dust, screaming. Was lying down, hit on head by rock ... fog of dust and ears ringing for hours. After that, hour after hour of the same, hour in and out, the body utterly exhausted and indifferent to conscious fear, but strained to the snapping point ... sweat and internal pain, waiting, waiting for the shells and mortars, falling to right and left, above and below, to finish us off ...

Through the bombardment Bessie tried thinking of his sons back home in New York, but found it 'all but impossible' to hold their image in his mind. Whilst he could talk rationally with his comrades, everything inside him was saying 'Run for your life and scream out loud.' The pauses were worse than the shelling; waiting for it to resume was 'hell – dry lips, rising gorge, sweat and shaking limbs ... you lie and insanely cover your face with your leather jacket – as though it offered any protection ... hours in and hour out, waiting for them to finish you, like a rat in a trap, chained to the post by the commander's order to stay here.' Yet Bessie survived.

A few days later the British Battalion replaced the Americans, taking their turn to experience a barrage that one survivor described as 'one continuous roll of thunder'. 'Everywhere was the smell of urine, excreta, dead men and dead mules,' recalled another. 'It was hell on earth. If that was hell, Dante didn't have to invent it, that was it.'

The bombardment only stopped to leave the way clear for rebel attacks. In spite of heavy Republican casualties – upwards of fifty per cent in the Lincoln-Washington Battalion alone – these were all repulsed. 'After all these hours it is almost impossible to walk,' Bessie wrote in his notebook, 'you lift your feet like a cat in paper boots, you feel weak and light as a feather, the hands shake uncontrollably, the guts quiver ... still it is possible to function, to talk rationally, even to joke. But how much of this is it possible to stand? For myself, I am afraid of breaking.'

Eventually Spanish forces relieved the English-speaking units on Hill 666. Harry Pollitt visited the British in their reserve positions, and some volunteers were ordered home. Though most returned to the fighting, one Irish volunteer, who had drunkenly fired his machine gun at his own advancing men, was taken away and shot.

Bessie was among the lucky ones: he was offered a job writing for the Brigade newspaper, *Volunteer for Liberty*. He was understandably delighted. 'I truly feel that I have learned as much from front line experience as I will,' he noted, and 'that, as a soldier, I am a negligible quantity, showing no possibilities of leadership. I might – now – and quite possibly – be of some use as a writer.'

On 22 September, Bessie heard the news that Negrín had told the League of Nations in Geneva 'that Spain had decided to repatriate all IB's. Fine speech that caused a sensation in the Assembly and should cause the same abroad … Thus there comes to an end the International Brigades.'

But it was not quite the end. That same day, with the confirmation that all their foreign volunteers were to be sent home, XV International Brigade was called into action for the last time.

Of the 377 men of the British Battalion who went into this last action, two days later over two hundred were still missing. Peter Kerrigan, who was supposed to be writing an account of the men's forthcoming repatriation for *The Daily Worker*, was distraught at what had just happened. As he told Harry Pollitt,

> I was at the beginning of the British Battalion, I saw what our No. 1 Company came through and I will never forget when I was told what our casualties were in those first 3 days at Jarama. But nothing can compare with the end of our Battalion … What I cannot get out of my mind at the moment, is that James Pollock of my branch, the bravest

of the brave, is gone. Jack Nulty of the machine gunners is gone. Young Tommy McGuire whom Bob Cooney said could be a Company Commander, is dead. Liam McGregor, of whom the official citation says: 'He died as he lived, a model anti-fascist fighter.' Clifford Lacey, dead. And then all the lads, we cannot say are dead, but about whom there is so little hope … I cannot write an article in my present state of mind.

The last American to die was James Lardner, a twenty-four-year-old reporter for *The New York Herald Tribune*, and the son of the writer Ring Lardner, who had been an early influence on Hemingway. He had travelled from Paris to Barcelona with Hemingway, and like others before him had been caught up in the excitement of the city. When he asked advice about joining the International Brigade, Hemingway had told him 'that it was a very fine thing if I wanted to fight fascism, but that it was a personal matter that could only be decided by me.' Bessie's request that Lardner work as his assistant on *Volunteer for Liberty* had been turned down, and the young man was killed when his night patrol stumbled upon a rebel position.

Once again, international events overshadowed the final tragedy of the International Brigades, for the world's eyes were turned elsewhere. September 1938 was the height of the Munich crisis, when the fate of Czechoslovakia – and with it world peace – seemed to hang in the balance. Czechoslovakia's diverse population included three million German speakers, and these 'Sudeten Germans' were Hitler's pretext for annexing the entire country. Even if all the German people were not ready for what lay ahead, Hitler himself felt prepared – mentally, strategically, militarily – to fight another pan-European war that might last years. He suspected that the French and British governments – despite their warnings that they were prepared to go to war over the issue – were not; and that without their support, the Russians would not either. Claud Cockburn, who was in Prague to report on the crisis, saw this as 'the moment when there still seemed to be an outside chance that either the League of Nations, or at least Britain, France and the Soviet Union, would stand together on behalf of Czechoslovakia against Germany.' He saw that the Russians, like the Czechs, were ready and willing to fight, if they had the support of the Western democracies. But appeasement was still the watchword of Conservative politicians in Britain; during two desperate visits to Germany, Prime Minister Chamberlain bowed to a mix of flattery and threats from the Nazi leader, and seemed ready to surrender a large part of Czechoslovakia to Hitler.

In New York, an old friend of Alvah Bessie wrote a letter agonizing over the situation. 'Oh Alvie, these have been anxious days,' he wrote on 26 September. 'I'm still afraid of the Tories. Those sons-of-bitches will sell out yet if they can. Not until the Cliveden set is ousted, can we have certainty about England.' On a more optimistic note, Bessie's friend told him that he had attended a 'Save Czechoslovakia' rally that the CPUSA had organized at Madison Square Garden the previous night; there had been 22,000 people inside, another 10,000 outside. According to *The New York Times*, the crowd had 'cheered three hours of militant attacks on the Chamberlain-Hitler proposals.' The speakers included the celebrated journalist Dorothy Thompson, author of *I Saw Hitler*. She had told the audience 'it was useless for Chamberlain to talk to Hitler, since "the sane cannot communicate with the insane", and that the British parliament should address itself to the German people and the German army, telling them "to overthrow their mad leader".'

The last person to speak had been the venerable German writer, Thomas Mann. 'I always loved peace and detested war,' Mann explained in his brief address. 'I detest it even today. But I feel that it would be a shame and an infamy if Europe and the world would accept without resistance this misdeed against a gentle little country which wishes to save civilization and freedom and which would be dismembered and delivered to slavery.' Mann then told them that he believed it was too late for Chamberlain – or any other politician – to try and engineer a European concord:

It is the task of the German people. It would fulfill its destiny by freeing itself of a regime that is leading Germany and the whole continent into the Abyss. Hitler must fall. This and nothing else will preserve the peace.

According to *The New York Times*, 'the Garden was a bedlam of sound as the crowd cheered and clapped for the somber, obviously nervous, tall German who forsook his fatherland when Hitler came to power.'[1]

That same day the paper also reproduced a message Roosevelt had just sent to Hitler and President Edvard Beneš of Czechoslovakia, warning them of the danger of a war in which millions of lives would be lost 'under circumstances of unspeakable horror,' and exhorting them 'to use peaceful means to settle their problems'. As the paper rightly conjectured, Roosevelt was using whatever influence he had 'to avert a European war that he obviously feared would eventually involve the United States.'

'Events in Europe seem [to be] rushing to a catastrophic conclusion,' Bessie jotted in his notebook a few days later. 'Meantime, the men sit here and go batty – fearful that they will never get out of Europe before a general war breaks out.'

In a historic meeting on 29–30 September, Chamberlain flew to Munich for a final conference with Mussolini, Hitler and the French Prime Minister. Whilst Chamberlain privately admitted that Hitler was 'without question the most detestable and bigoted man with whom it had been his lot to do business,' it was agreed that Czechoslovakia would surrender the Sudetenland, in return for a promise from Hitler that this was the end of his territorial ambitions. Though German expansionism had once again been permitted – if on a more limited scale than Hitler had hoped – world war, it seemed, had been narrowly averted. According to one cynical observer, when Chamberlain's plane landed back in England, the huge crowd that greeted him 'seemed ready to roll on the

---

1 A number of high-ranking German Army officers were, in fact, already plotting Hitler's downfall, fearful that he was about to lead them into a war they could not win. Their overtures to the British government would, however, be ignored. Some of them would later be involved in the failed bomb plot of 1944 that attempted to assassinate the Führer.

ground like worshippers at the Juggernaut festival to let Chamberlain ride in glory over them.' Speaking later from 10 Downing Street, Chamberlain declared: 'I believe it is peace for our time.' Coincidentally, it was the same day that *Guernica* arrived in London. Picasso's great tableau and its accompanying drawings were to be displayed for a month in the Burlington Gallery: a stark warning of what would come to London if war with Germany ever became a reality.[1]

Many were disgusted by what they considered Chamberlain's craven peace-mongering. As Claud Cockburn memorably put it in *The Week*, Chamberlain had 'turned all four cheeks' to Hitler. The Labour Party, which had increasingly moved towards support of the Spanish Republic and the ending of Non-Intervention, opposed the treaty, as did a rump of Conservatives headed by Winston Churchill.[2] Even Chamberlain's Foreign Minister, Lord Halifax, was depressed at the deal done with a man he now regarded as 'a criminal lunatic'. As one Foreign Office official observed, it seemed that Britain would do 'anything ... however contemptible to avoid war'. President Roosevelt was soon denouncing the agreement as 'peace by fear'. He would now abandon his idea of the negotiated disarmament of the major powers, and looked at rearmament instead. Stalin, too, was alarmed by what had happened, and even feared that the British were planning a deal with Hitler.

Many international veterans of the Spanish war also saw Munich as a 'sellout'. But in George Orwell's opinion, 'it would be absurd to regard Chamberlain as really a peace-maker.' He told a former militia colleague from the POUM in November 1938, 'Certainly Chamberlain and Co. are

---

1 The exhibition was not a great success, as only around 3,000 visitors came. However, a second showing of *Guernica* at the Whitechapel Art Gallery in the East End of London attracted some 15,000; price of admission was a pair of boots, which were then sent out to Spanish soldiers. The painting would then be sent on to the USA, touring from New York to Los Angeles, San Francisco and Chicago, before returning to New York for the opening of a major Picasso retrospective at the Museum of Modern Art. But the painting had a greater influence on artists than politicians.

2 The Labour Party leader, Clement Attlee, even went to Spain in December 1938; he visited the British Battalion of the International Brigades, who renamed their No. 1 Company in his honour.

preparing for war, and any other government that is likely to get in will also prepare for war.' He reckoned that there was 'perhaps two years' breathing space in which it *may* be possible to provoke a real popular anti-war movement in England, in France and above all in the Fascist countries. If we can do that, to the point of making it clear that no government will go to war because its people won't follow, I think Hitler is done for.'

For Orwell, 'almost anything is better than European war, which will lead not only to the slaughter of tens of millions but to an extension of Fascism.'

VI

By the time of the Munich crisis in the autumn of 1938 Ernest Hemingway was back in Europe. He had spent the summer in Key West, New York and Wyoming, writing short stories set in Spain, his anti-fascist articles for *Ken*, and editing his first edition of collected stories. He included the text of his still unproduced play; the book would be published later in the year as *The Fifth Column and the First Forty-Nine Stories*.

Though the collection was provisionally dedicated to Martha Gellhorn 'with love' – the first public declaration of his new relationship – Hemingway had spent the summer trying to ignore the fact that his marriage was disintegrating. Finally, in early September he returned to Europe, and a reunion with Gellhorn in Paris.

His eye was still on Spain. In late October in Paris he wrote to tell a couple of friends (in the strictest confidence, possibly because it was not actually true) that he been offered 'a staff captain's commission with the French to go with what they were going to move into Spain'. He had turned it down, he explained, partly because of another contract to write journalism for the North American News Agency, and partly because he had told his wife he would not join in the fighting. 'Things here are so foul, now,' he added, 'that if you think about them you go nuts.'

Things certainly did not look good in Spain. Though the fighting continued on the Ebro, the twelve thousand remaining volunteers of the International Brigades had been withdrawn from further action. In locations around Catalonia, those men with a home to return to waited impatiently; volunteers from Germany, Austria and Italy, who could never return whilst their countries were under fascist control, waited anxiously to hear what would become of them. Rumours circulated. Alvah Bessie wrote in his notebook that efforts were 'apparently being made to find sanctuary for them in the "democracies" – France, Britain, Mexico, USSR.' But he added that 'even the so-called "democracies" are looking askance at a sudden influx of war-trained "revolutionaries".'

Robert Capa, *Volunteers from the Abraham Lincoln Battalion, led by Milt Wolff (centre), prepare to leave Spain, October 1938* (Magnum)

Back again for what would prove to be his last wartime visit to Spain, Hemingway went to see the American volunteers off.

'I'm glad to see you got out of this alive,' he told Bessie.

'I am too,' Bessie replied.

'Because,' Hemingway explained, 'I always felt responsible for your being here.'

Bessie was surprised to hear this, but as Hemingway added, bombastically, 'You heard the speech I made at the Writers' Congress ... I know that speech was responsible for a lot of guys coming over.'

On 29 October Barcelona hosted a leaving parade in the International Brigades' honour. Suffering from rheumatism and scabies, Bessie did not attend. Those who did included the Republic's President, Manuel Azaña, its Prime Minister, Juan Negrín, and the Communist Party's popular mouthpiece, La Pasionaria. Robert Capa was there, capturing the faces of the soldiers and the huge crowds. There were flags and military bands, tanks and artillery rolled past, whilst the crowds threw flowers and planes dived almost to street level, dropping leaflets.

'You can go with pride,' La Pasionaria told the departing volunteers in a rousing speech. 'You are history. You are legend. You are the heroic example of the solidarity and the universality of democracy ... We will not forget you; and, when the olive tree of peace puts forth its leaves, entwined with the laurels of the Spanish Republic's victory, come back! Come back to us and here you will find a homeland.'

As Bessie recorded in his notebook, his comrades told him that 'the demonstration and parade were worth everything they've been through. Tremendous enthusiasm of the people – women weeping, holding up children to be kissed, girls breaking into the parade to kiss the men ... Sorry to have missed it.' A British veteran described it as 'no simple march through the streets, but a glorious demonstration of the enthusiasm and affection of the people of Catalonia for the Internationals.'

Though many volunteers had clearly had enough of the war, others felt that they were leaving Spain before their job was complete. Franco's forces looked to be on the brink of victory, and the threat of fascism continued to loom over Europe, its menace made yet clearer less than a fortnight after the International Brigades' leaving ceremony. On 7 November a young Polish Jew, protesting against rampant anti-Semitism in Germany, shot dead a German diplomat in Paris. As *The Times* reported, the Nazi response resulted in 'scenes of systematic plunder and destruction which have seldom had their equal in a civilized country since the Middle Ages. In every part of the Reich synagogues were set on fire or dynamited, Jewish shops smashed and ransacked, and individual Jews arrested or hounded by bands of young Nazis through the streets.' *Kristallnacht*, or The Night of Broken Glass as it would become known, was one of the most horrifying signals to date of life under Nazi rule. As *The Times*' editorial observed, 'No foreign propagandist bent upon blackening Germany before the world could outdo the tale of burnings and beatings, of blackguardly assaults upon defenceless and innocent people, which disgraced that country yesterday.'

The English-speaking volunteers were among the last to leave Spain. Bessie and 148 other Americans finally caught a train for France on 2 December; bands played, and their train was decked with banners, flags and laurel leaves. Back in New York, Bessie recorded, 'there was a terrific welcoming committee of thousands who stood in the bitter cold from 6am (when the ship docked) till noon, when we came off.' A ceremony was held at Madison Square Park. Milton Wolff, last commander of the

Robert Capa, *volunteers from the International Brigades at their farewell parade, Montblanch, near Barcelona, 25 October 1938* (Magnum)

Lincoln-Washington Battalion, placed a wreath at the Eternal Light in the Park, to the memory of those 750 or so Americans of the International Brigades who would never return home. It bore the inscription, 'In memory of those who died for democracy.'

The British who returned home together were also enthusiastically received at Victoria Station, and they marched down Whitehall to lay a wreath at the Cenotaph for their 543 dead comrades. Others who came back alone or in small groups had a less cordial welcome, in some cases from policemen or MI5. Arriving at Folkestone, one volunteer and his friend had their passports examined. The official simply said: 'Two more bloody reds back.'

Many veterans of the International Brigades never had the chance to go home. Some were given Spanish citizenship and rejoined the Republican Army to continue the fight against Franco. Others crossed the border into France, where they were herded into vast concentration camps alongside thousands of Spanish refugees, all trapped in what Gustav Regler called 'an abyss between two worlds'. Cold and hungry, they awaited a very uncertain future.

Chapter 15

For Whom the Bell Tolls

|

The end of the Spanish war came quickly. Two days before Christmas 1938, Franco launched his assault on Catalonia. Once again Barcelona came under waves of aerial attack from Italian bombers based in the Balearic Islands. Though a few aeroplanes were still arriving from Russia, the Republican air force was increasingly overwhelmed, and the city had virtually no anti-aircraft weapons. After three weeks of intensive fighting, short of weapons and reinforcements, hungry and with low morale, the Republican army in Catalonia was on the verge of collapse.

'What a mess in Spain!' George Orwell wrote on 20 January 1939. An anonymous admirer had generously paid for the writer and his wife to travel to French Morocco, where it was hoped the warm North African air would help his lungs recover. Having started work on a novel, he was still keeping a keen eye on international events. 'A friend who recently came out tells me that Barcelona is smashed out of recognition, all the children are hungry … I keep hearing in roundabout ways of Spaniards I knew, always that they are killed. It does seem so meaningless.' Orwell was deeply pessimistic about the future. 'The idea of war is just a nightmare to me,' he wrote in another letter, 'and I refuse to believe that it can do the slightest good or even that it makes much difference who wins.'

'I can see that war's coming,' mused the narrator of Orwell's new work in progress. 'There are millions of others like me,' this English everyman continued. 'Ordinary chaps that I meet everywhere, chaps I run into in pubs, bus drivers, and travelling salesmen for hardware firms, have got a feeling that the world's gone wrong. They can feel things cracked and collapsing under their feet.' Infused with the spectre of approaching war, *Coming Up for Air* would be published later that year, a sort of prequel to the masterpiece that would follow it exactly a decade later.

There were still some die-hard Spanish Republicans who believed that Franco could yet be defeated. On 22 January, Herbert Matthews reported in *The New York Times* that the Spanish government had called on Barcelona 'to emulate Madrid,' and defend itself as the capital had been so valiantly defended two years before. And as the doomed young American volunteer James Lardner had told his mother the previous year, he did not think the rebels would *ever* conquer Catalonia. 'There are too many people here who are fighting for things they believe in, and too few on the other side.' Herbert Matthews expected the coming battle to be hard-fought. 'In spite of everything,' he wrote, 'it is a calm and brave city.'

Robert Capa, *Civilians watching an air battle over Barcelona, January 1939*

Desperately, the Spanish Government and its supporters maintained their call to the Western democracies to end the arms embargo before it was too late. Gradually, political opinion had been shifting in that direction. In January, the former Republican US Secretary of State Henry Stimson once again spoke out in support of Spain's right to buy arms. 'If this Loyalist Government is overthrown,' he wrote in a letter to *The New York Times*, 'it is evident now that its defeat will be solely due to the fact that it has been deprived of its right to buy from us and from other friendly nations the munitions necessary for its defense.' Even President Roosevelt was now privately admitting that the embargo had been 'a grave mistake' and that 'he would never do such a thing again'.

It was General Franco who found his support burgeoning, his armoury bulging. After Munich, Hitler had felt increasingly confident to do as he pleased. It seemed clear to the Nazi leader that the British and French Governments, in pursuit of appeasement, would always back down from a fight. Spain continued to be a testing ground for Hitler's men and matériel, whilst in return Franco provided mineral resources for the ravenous Nazi war machine.

A British journalist who had returned to Spain to report on the battle for Catalonia was Esmond Romilly's former brother-in-arms in the International Brigades, the deserter Keith Scott Watson. Having gone home to write *Single to Spain*, an account of his early experiences in the war, he was now working as a foreign correspondent for *The Daily Herald*. (Romilly's journalistic career, by contrast, had stalled. He had found more profitable work as a copywriter in an advertising firm, and was now on the verge of emigrating with Decca to America.)

On 24 January Scott Watson was sitting in a café drinking the mud-coloured water that passed for coffee in Barcelona when a clerk from the Ministry of Defence told him the Government was about to quit the city.

'We've done everything we can to hold the fronts, but it's hopeless,' the clerk explained. Two armies were now falling upon the city: the Republic's, and Franco's.

Then they heard singing, and watched as a long column of blue-overalled women marched past. They carried a banner with the words *'Barcelona another Madrid! Fortify!'* Pale from long shifts in munitions factories, and shouldering picks and shovels, the women, Scott Watson wrote, 'had a tragic grimness as they marched and sang their Anarchist anthem in the bright sun.'

The government clerk gave the women a bitter look. 'Just two years too late,' he said. 'If the workers had spent less time cutting one another's throats the Iron Belt round Barcelona might have been reality.'

Scott Watson asked how long the city would hold out.

'Unless a miracle happens the Rebels will be here in forty-eight hours …'

In the dark streets later that night Scott Watson watched a long stream of overloaded cars and lorries making its way along the main roads out of the city. In the distance he could hear 'the sullen echo of gunfire [moving] in waves along the dark streets'. The next day, with the city's shops all shuttered up, he saw a ragged line of shallow trenches had been at the edge of the city. From Anarchist Headquarters came the order, 'To the Barricades.' But other than a few overturned trams, there was little response. Individual anarchists, he wrote, 'settled themselves in church towers and vantage points with stubby sub-machine-guns and waited the coming of the Fascists – and death.'

Scott Watson decided it was time to leave. Heading back to his hotel to pack, he watched from the roof as Italian planes bombed the docks. Fires raged in warehouses along the waterfront, and long columns of smoke poured upwards. The hotel manager joined him.

'It's Spain's turn today,' he told Scott Watson. 'Tomorrow England and France will feel the result.'

Scenes on the overcrowded roads north out of Barcelona were chaotic. Before crossing the border into France, Scott Watson watched a final Republican atrocity: the Bishop of Teruel, a rebel colonel and thirteen others were ordered against a cemetery wall and shot.

There was to be no grand defence of Barcelona. The rebels entered the city largely unopposed, and by the end of January posters of Franco were everywhere: Catalan independence was immediately revoked, and even its language would be banned. The Republic's slogans were effaced, along with its supporters: thousands were executed within days, whilst 10,000 refugees had soon crossed the border into France, together with a whole division of the Republican army. Tens of thousands more were *en route* to follow them. *The New York Times* described it as 'one of the greatest mass migrations in history'.

Robert Capa, *Spanish Republicans arriving at an internment camp, France, early 1939* (Magnum)

'The dead sleep cold in Spain tonight,' Hemingway wrote in an elegy to the American victims of the war, published in *New Masses* on Valentine's Day, 'and they will sleep cold all this winter as the earth sleeps with them.' The rains of spring would bring the Spanish earth back to life, but the dead 'do not need to rise. They are a part of the earth now and the earth can never be conquered. For the earth endureth forever. It will outlive all systems of tyranny.' He had found the article 'very hard' to write, he told a friend. 'There is not much to say about the dead except that they are dead. I would like to be able to write understandingly about both deserters and heroes, cowards and brave men, traitors and men who are not capable of being traitors. We learned a lot about all such people.'

From their short-lived capital at Figueres, Negrín and his communist supporters vowed to fight on. But although Madrid, Valencia and over a quarter of Spain was still in Republican hands, many of the Prime Minister's military advisors counselled against continuing the war. On 27 February, in an attempt to force a rapid end to the conflict, the British and French governments simultaneously recognized Franco as the legitimate head of Spain. The US government soon followed suit. In Madrid, an anti-communist coup led by Republican army officers led to fierce in-fighting reminiscent of Barcelona in May 1937. The officers hoped to negotiate a peace with Franco; but the rebel leader was interested only in unconditional surrender.

The last rebel advance at the end of March also went largely unop-posed. Madrid fell quickly; on 1 April, Franco declared himself victori-ous. The war was finally over – though Franco's reprisals were not. Thou-sands more would be imprisoned and executed over the coming years.

II

Only four months after the war in Spain ended, Hitler again tried to face down Britain and France, this time over Danzig and 'German' territory in Poland. Though Chamberlain had given his guarantee to protect Polish sovereignty, Hemingway expected the British Prime Minister to back down once again. 'But you can never tell,' he mused. 'Hitler knows there is everything to gain by war scares and nothing to gain by war. But if you keep lighting matches to show how many powder barrels you have open something may ignite.'

On 1 September German forces marched into Poland. This time Chamberlain did not back down. The British and French governments told Hitler to withdraw his troops, or face war. Their request was ignored. 'You can imagine,' Chamberlain stated in a radio broadcast announcing the declaration of war on 3 September, 'what a bitter blow it is to me that all my long struggle to win peace has failed … Now may God bless you all,' he concluded, 'and may He defend the right. For it is evil things we shall be fighting against: brute force, bad faith, injustice, oppression and persecution; and against them, I am certain that the right will prevail.'

'WAR DECLARED ON HITLER,' shouted the front page of *The Daily Worker* the next day. 'CHURCHILL ENTERS NEW CABINET / NAZIS IGNORE WARNING, CHOOSE PATH OF WORLD SLAUGHTER.' World War Two had begun.

Remarkably, given Hitler's paranoid fear of communism, the Soviet Union was not one of the belligerents ranged against him. Only a few days before the invasion of Poland, the world had been stunned when Germany and Russia – seemingly ideologically implacable foes – had signed a non-aggression pact. Tired of waiting for the British and French to join him in standing up to Hitler, Stalin had made his own peace with the Nazi dictator. They would divide up Eastern Europe between them.

General Franco and Hitler, Hendaye, France, 23 October 1940

The Italians would also not be joining the war: their contribution to the fighting in Spain – and the casualties they had suffered there – had seriously undermined Mussolini's resources. He would not commit his forces to help Hitler until a German victory seemed certain. And General Franco would resist Hitler's earnest approaches to join the war. Despite the indispensable assistance the Germans had given to his cause, Spain would stay out of the Second World War, as it had stayed out of the First. In 1940 the Nazis would forcibly return home many of the Spanish refugees who had been trapped in France at the start of the war; some, such as Lluís Companys, the former President of Catalonia, would be executed. Some foreign refugees, including many veterans of the International Brigades, would be transported to German concentration camps.

III

'Of various speculations of how history might have been different if the Republic had won in Spain,' Claud Cockburn would come to write, 'the only certainty is that if the Civil War had ended otherwise, the subsequent history of Europe would have been incalculably different too.' Millions of people in Europe and America, he suggested, 'saw in that war a climactic event of which the outcome was going to affect, and affect very soon, the lives of people a long way from the Iberian peninsula and previously more or less indifferent to its affairs.'

The question of just why the Republic lost the Spanish Civil War would divide participants and historians for decades. As Cockburn noted in his first volume of autobiography in 1956, no one over thirty-five would 'agree with any generalization anyone makes' about the Spanish Civil War. 'I personally disagree with about half the generalizations I made about it at the time.' But there was some degree of consensus among the foreign supporters of the Republic who had been in Spain.

Ernest Hemingway was not afraid of making his opinion clear. 'The British were the real villains,' he wrote early in 1939. 'All the way through from the very start.' He had come away from the Spanish Civil War filled with contempt not only for Chamberlain, but for the country as a whole. 'What a degenerate people the English are,' he told Maxwell Perkins:

> Their politics have been suicidal ever since the last war. They gave us the worst bitching anybody did in Spain where we fought both Hitler and Mussolini for them for nothing and could have kept them tied up there indefinitely (exactly as the Peninsular war beat Napoleon) if they had only given any aid at all – any at all.

And it was not just the British Government. 'The British volunteers in the International Brigade were the absolute scum of the Brigades,' he continued:

> After the Jarama fight they deserted by whole companies; they were cowards, malingerers, liars and phonies and fairies. They were absolutely panic-ed by the tanks and their officers, when they were brave, were so stupid that their stupidity was absolutely murderous.
>
> Sure plenty of exceptions and some fine ones. But in general the British volunteers were the scum of the Brigades.

Almost equally to blame in Hemingway's occluded opinion were the Catalans. 'They never fought in the whole war,' he complained. 'Maybe they are simply too nice people,' he suggested, before quoting a racist Spanish rhyme that concluded, 'Thank God I am a negro / And not a Catalan.'

By the time of this letter, Hemingway had almost completed his long-anticipated novel of the war. As he had told Maxwell Perkins in another letter, he had been having 'bad dreams every night' about the Republican retreat that had overwhelmed Alvah Bessie and his comrades:

> Really awful ones in the greatest detail. It is strange because I never had any *ever* in Spain about anything that happened. Only the always recurring one about getting out of the trucks and having to attack without knowing where the objectives were ... Last night I was caught in this retreat again in the goddamest detail. I really must have a hell of an imagination. That's why should *always* make stories up – *not* try to remember what happened.

Escaping family and fans to write in a hotel room in Havana, he had started work on a short story; but with increasing excitement he kept on writing, as the short story turned into a novel. After trying out some thirty different titles, and following a long session with *The Oxford Book of English Prose*, he chose a line from a sermon by the seventeenth-century English poet, John Donne. He would call the book *For Whom the Bell Tolls.*[1] 'I think it has the magic that a title has to have,' he told Perkins. And, as Hemingway's Spanish friend José Luis Castillo-Puche would astutely observe: the bell 'does not toll for the defeated Reds or the victorious Whites. The death knell rings out for each and all, for the protagonist and for the most humble "volunteer" in all the brigades, for every soldier who died in the trenches on either side, for every man whose life was snuffed out anywhere in Spain.'

For Whom the Bell Tolls was published in October 1940. It told only one small story from one small sector of the war, but encompassed all Hemingway's insights into Spain, his love of its people and of bullfighting, as well as his opinions on the Republic's defeat. Most obvious was the enemy's superior weaponry – from guns and tanks to aeroplanes – all provided, of course, by the Germans and Italians. It was the last of these – the Fiats and Heinkels moving through the air 'like mechanized doom' – that the partisans and soldiers and civilians of the Republic and the International Brigades had feared most, and which had proved the vehicles of their ultimate defeat.

The novel's hero was an American, Robert Jordan. Loosely based on Hemingway himself, as well as the one-time commander of the Abraham Lincoln Battalion, Robert Merriman, Jordan is – like Merriman – a university academic, and – like Hemingway – a writer, and an *aficionado* devoted to Spain. Though (like Hemingway) he is not a communist, Jordan has accepted communist control of the Republican war effort. He is sent to lead a group of Republican partisans in the Guadarrama mountains on a seemingly doomed mission to destroy a vital bridge in advance of a major offensive. There, Jordan falls in love with a young

---

1 'No man is an *Iland*, intire of its selfe; every man is a peece of the *Continent*, a part of the maine … any mans death diminishes me, because I am involved in *Mankinde*. And therefore never send to know for whom the *bell* tolls. It tolls for thee.'

Spanish girl whose parents have been murdered by the Falange, and who has herself been raped. The most brilliant section in the book described in chilling detail the murder by Republicans of the leading citizens of a small town in southern Spain at the start of the war, while in another powerful incident a group of partisans are bombed to pieces by fascist planes. Less successful were the sex scenes: 'Did the earth move for you?' asks the heroine at one point, coining an enduring cliché.

Nonetheless, *For Whom the Bell Tolls* was quite clearly Hemingway's best long work since *A Farewell to Arms*, and was an immediate bestseller. Written 'with an understanding that rips the heart with compassion for those who live, who do the best they can, just so they may go on living,' Dorothy Parker considered it 'beyond all comparison' his finest work. 'I think that what you do about this book of Ernest Hemingway's is point to it and say, "Here is a book." As you would stand below Everest and say, "Here is a mountain."' Hollywood quickly bought the rights, for what was at the time the largest sum ever paid for a novel.[1]

For Whom the Bell Tolls did not please everyone, in particular American veterans of the war such as Alvah Bessie. *Men in Battle*, Bessie's novel of the war, had already been published, and was an honest account of his experiences with the Lincoln-Washington Battalion. Hemingway had described its author as 'a fine guy and brave soldier and excellent writer and he certainly wrote a damned good book. Very few books read as true as that book did.' But Bessie did not speak so favourably of Hemingway's novel. In the long review he wrote for the left-wing journal *New Masses* he observed that whilst in Spain Hemingway had 'won the respect and admiration of almost every International Brigade man who met him;' but although *For Whom the Bell Tolls* was 'unequivocally on the side of the Spanish people,' and although 'the action is fast and furious, fused with a suspense that is magnificently handled in every incident ... here again is the author's almost pathological preoccupation with blood and mutilation and sex and death.' 'It seems certain,' he continued,

1 Released in 1943, the film stared Gary Cooper as Robert Jordan, and Ingrid Bergman as his young Spanish lover. The politics were largely excised from the script.

that Hemingway did not intend to write a *Cosmopolitan* love story against a background of the Spanish Civil War; yet this is what he has done. It is certain that he did not intend to slander the Spanish people or the Soviet Union; yet his method of telling the story has resulted in both. With minor exceptions, the Spanish people portrayed here are cruel, vindictive, brutalized, irresponsible. Throughout the long narrative there is evidence of much confusion: Hemingway praises the individual heroism of individual Communists, impugns and slanders their leadership, their motives, and their attitudes. He admires the [International] Brigades, and assails their leadership …

In Bessie's opinion, Hemingway had joined 'the company of his enemies, and the people's enemies – clever enemies who will fawn upon him and use him, his great talents and his passion for the people's cause, to traduce and betray those talents and those people.' It seemed that Hemingway had done exactly what he had warned John Dos Passos against (who himself, Bessie noted, 'ultimately became an avowed enemy of the republican government of Spain').

Decades later Bessie would write of Hemingway that 'that the man who could be loyal, generous, warm and modest to those he considered friends could also be (and much too often was) cruel, petty, a braggart, a bully, an anti-Semite and a permanent adolescent,' as well as a liar, 'compelled out of his own sense of insecurity' to create a legend for himself as 'a man of courage, a lover "who bedded every woman he ever wanted," a marksman, an authority on military science, a fighter and a two-fisted drinker.' And as 'a political thinker Hemingway was a child, which explains why his picture of the Spanish Civil War was attacked by the men he so much admired: the American veterans of that war.'

Certainly once the Spanish war had ended Hemingway changed his tune on the men who had fought it. *During* the conflict he had always stated his belief that the Republic would win, feeling it was wrong to undermine the fighters whilst they were still fighting. Afterwards, he spoke ill of the British volunteers, and little better of the Americans. In writing to Maxwell Perkins in November 1939 regarding Bessie's *Men in Battle*, he stated (not wholly inaccurately) that 'what was wrong with [Bessie's] outfit was too much ideology and not enough military training, discipline or materiel.' The Abraham Lincoln Battalion 'has been taught to believe they saved the Valencia-Madrid highway' at the Battle of Jarama, 'but they were pitiful there and uselessly massacred by their incompetent officers ... Bessie never saw the war until it was hopelessly lost.'

Those incompetent officers included André Marty, traduced in *For Whom the Bell Tolls*: 'That old one kills more than the bubonic plague,' a Spanish soldier remarks of the International Brigades' commandant. 'But he doesn't kill fascists like we do ... He kills rare things. Trotskyites ... Any type of rare beast.' La Pasionaria and the Russian officers, journalists and secret policemen holed up in a comfortable Madrid hotel fared little better in Hemingway's emotionally-charged novel.

This change of political tune struck many critics. Edmund Wilson found it remarkable that Hemingway's hero should end up so resembling the hero of John Dos Passos' 1939 novel, *The Adventures of a Young Man*, in which an idealistic young graduate joins the International Brigades, but dies in Spain disillusioned and betrayed by a brutal Communist Party machine that is steadily destroying the very ideals it preaches. Wilson even suggested that Hemingway had 'largely sloughed off his Stalinism'. (Hemingway justly responded, 'I had no Stalinist period.') *Time*, meanwhile, was relieved to see that the author had recovered from what it called his 'Red rash'.

Hemingway rounded off a remarkable year that November, in Cheyenne, Wyoming. Having divorced his second wife, he married Martha Gellhorn; their official wedding photographer was Robert Capa, the pictures published in *Life*. The couple spent their honeymoon in China, covering the Sino-Japanese war. (Other spectators of the Spanish war made a similar journey, including W. H. Auden and Joris Ivens.) On their return Hemingway and Gellhorn established a new home in Cuba:

the move marked a new stage in Hemingway's extraordinary life, though the marriage itself did not last.

IV

The role played by the communists became one of the most controversial explanations as to why the Republic had lost the war. Leon Trotsky, unsurprisingly, was convinced that Stalin's machinations had helped Franco to victory. As early as 1938 in his pamphlet 'Lessons of Spain' he had attacked 'the arrests and murders of revolutionists, the crushing of the mass movement, the disarming of the workers, the arming of the bourgeois police' and 'the artificial restriction of the development of the war industry' in Spain itself. Each, he declared, had been 'a cruel blow to the front, direct military treason, dictated by the class interests of the bourgeoisie ... By turning Bolshevism on its head, Stalin succeeded completely in fulfilling the role of the grave-digger of the revolution.'

Whilst admitting that he preferred communists when they were soldiers rather than proselytizers, Hemingway wanted to underplay the Party's involvement in the war, and blinded himself to the worst actions of the communists in Spain. In an article for *Ken* titled 'Treachery in Aragon', he had even fallen for the communist propaganda blaming the supposedly Gestapo-infiltrated anarchists and POUM for the Republican defeats in Aragon in 1937. Hemingway had nothing but derision for the organization with whom George Orwell had fought. In *For Whom the Bell Tolls*, a Russian journalist speaks of them as 'a heresy of crackpots and wild men ... The POUM. It is like the name. Not serious. They should have called it the MUMPS or the MEASLES. But no. The Measles is much more dangerous ... Poor POUM. They never did kill anybody. Not at the front nor anywhere else. A few in Barcelona, yes.'

Orwell's account of the May 1937 fighting in Barcelona in *Homage to Catalonia* was above all an attempt to disprove the kind of supposition Hemingway had made, that the POUM were fascist collaborators. On his return to England, before he fell ill, Orwell had done all he could to promote the POUM's side of the story. As he told a friend, it was only the fact that the Spanish Government 'had the sense to disregard the clamour of the Communist press' that had prevented 'a wholesale massacre' of anti-Stalinist anti-fascists in the summer of 1937. 'In Spain,' John Dos Passos wrote in a letter to a friend in 1938,

> I am sure that the introduction of GPU [secret police] methods by the communists did as much harm as their tank men, pilots and experienced military men did good. The trouble with an all powerful secret police in the hands of fanatics, or of anybody, is that once it gets started there's no stopping it until it has corrupted the whole body politic ... As far as this country goes, I feel more and more that the Communists are introducing the fascist mentality that has made Europe a nightmare ...

William Horvitz, the communist veteran of the Abraham Lincoln Brigade injured at the battle of Jarama, was of a similar opinion. He returned to New York a hero, fêted by friends in the CPUSA. The Party found him a job, and paid all the necessary medical expenses to help him recover from his war wound. And he continued to give the impression that he was still a 'believer'; but as he later wrote, 'I had in my heart and mind become a POUMist and didn't know what route I was on.' He was bitter that he had learnt nothing about Spain as a country whilst there; wherever he had gone, he would write many decades later, 'I lived under the eye of commissars and Party strongarms ... I might very well have been living in what later became an Eastern European Communist dictatorship.' And whenever he thought of Stalin, 'I get the image of Goya's dark painting of a giant eating a small human being.' The Soviet pact with Hitler in August 1939 ended his clandestine disagreement with the Party, and he paraded up and down the heavily unionized garment district of Manhattan 'denouncing Communism in the iciest terms'. Thereafter, former comrades would vilify him.

But even Harry Pollitt had thought the Soviet pact with Germany was a step too far. Instead of toeing the Communist Party line, he declared that it was time to 'smash the fascist bastards once and for all'. In response, his hard-nosed, hard-line second-in-command, Rajani Palme Dutt, replaced him as the CPGB's General Secretary (until the Germans invaded Russia in 1941, when the Nazis once again became enemies of the Soviet Union). And Claud Cockburn, seemingly one of the staunchest communists, would eventually quietly abandon the Party, retiring to the more tranquil life of a novelist in Ireland.

Tom Wintringham was another increasingly disillusioned veteran. 'Spain woke me up,' he would write in 1941. 'Politically I rediscovered democracy.' He had seen the power and potential of the Popular Front, and had been 'disgusted by [the] sectarian intrigues and the hampering suspicions' of communists such as André Marty, and 'the cynicism of Russian foreign policy'. 'Two bullets and typhoid gave me time to think,' he wrote. 'I came out of Spain believing, as I still believe, in a more humane humanism, in a more radical democracy, and in a revolution of some sort as necessary to give the ordinary people a chance to beat Fascism. Marxism makes sense to me, but the "Party Line" doesn't.' By then, Wintringham had already left the Communist Party; or rather, he had been expelled from it. When in the summer of 1938 Kitty Bowler had left New York to live with (and eventually marry) Wintringham, he had been instructed to choose between his lover and the Party. He chose Kitty. Nonetheless, both of them remained committed to the cause. As Bowler wrote that same summer, 'My greatest hope (Tom's also) both now and as it has been during the last month and more – is that through hard work I can eventually abundantly prove my absolute devotion to the only organization which offers hope for the future.'

Wintringham did not believe that the Communist Party had undermined the war effort in Spain. As he wrote in his 1940 book *Armies of Freemen*, the reason the Republic had lost was 'because Hitler and Mussolini had then – and have now – friends in Britain, powerful enough to prevent us getting arms and food. We lost, too, because the friends of

Fascism here were not fought and rooted out by those who professed to be against them.'

As it was for Wintringham and Hemingway, so for Orwell it was the British who carried most responsibility for the defeat of the Spanish Republic. As he would write in his 1942 essay, 'Looking Back on the Spanish War':

> In 1936 it was clear to everyone that if Britain would only help the Spanish Government, even to the extent of a few million pounds' worth of arms, Franco would collapse and German strategy would be severely dislocated. By that time one did not need to be clairvoyant to foresee that war between Britain and Germany was coming; one could even foretell within a year or two when it would come. Yet in the most mean, cowardly, hypocritical way the British ruling class did all they could to hand Spain over to Franco and the Nazis. Why? Because they were pro-Fascist, was the obvious answer ... It is still very uncertain what plan they acted on in backing Franco, and they may have had no clear plan at all. Whether the British ruling class are wicked or merely stupid is one of the most difficult questions of our time, and at certain moments a very important question.

Orwell found Russia's motives harder to interpret; 'their actions,' he wrote in the same essay,

> are most easily explained if one assumes that they were acting on several contradictory motives. I believe that in the future we shall come to feel that Stalin's foreign policy, instead of being so diabolically clever as it is claimed to be, has been merely opportunistic and stupid. But at any rate, the Spanish civil war demonstrated that the Nazis knew what they were doing and their opponents did not.

Of course, it was not really the British who were *most* responsible for the defeat of the Republic, nor the Americans, even though with hindsight it is possible to say that they could probably have prevented it. Without German and Italian aid, Franco and the rebels would probably have been defeated within weeks. Whether or not Spain might still have gone on to tear itself to pieces is another matter.

V

In the last weeks of peace in Europe, George Orwell again abandoned pacifism (indeed, he would soon be stating that 'pacifism is objectively pro-Fascist'). And he was disgusted by what he saw as the defeatist attitude of the Left in Britain, especially after the fall of France in 1940. 'All this was in marked contrast to the attitude of the common people,' he suggested in one of the regular 'London Letters' he wrote for the American magazine *Partisan Review*,

> who either had not woken up to the fact that England was in danger, or were determined to resist to the last ditch. But certain leftwing writers and lecturers who had fought in Spain, notably Tom Wintringham, did a lot to stem the tide of defeatism.

Orwell was frustrated that his health prevented him from joining the Army. He did, however, join the Home Guard, a defence organization which he likened, for a while, to the Spanish militias, and which owed a lot to the experience of men such as Wintringham, who ran an unofficial training school at Osterley Park in London. 'The whole of the training in Street Fighting given to the British Army and Home Guard since 1940,' Wintringham claimed in 1944, 'is based entirely on my work and that of my assistants who served with me in Spain.'

Many international veterans of the Civil War went on to serve in the armed forces of the Second World War (though others would be rejected:

Gustav Regler was astonished when he was thrown into prison after volunteering to join the French Army: only the intervention of friends such as Hemingway enabled him to escape to America before France fell to the Nazis). Having emigrated to American, John Cornford's colleague Bernard Knox rose to the rank of Captain in the US Army, and he would be awarded the *Croix de guerre à l'ordre de l'armée* after he was parachuted behind Allied lines to arm and organize French Resistance forces (an organization that included many anti-fascist survivors of the Spanish conflict). Esmond Romilly, who had also been living in the US when the war broke out, almost immediately joined the Royal Canadian Air Force. In November 1941, en route for a bombing raid on Hamburg, his plane disappeared over the North Sea. He was only twenty-three. George Steer, the man who reported on the destruction of Guernica, rose to the rank of Lieutenant-Colonel with the Special Operations Executive; he was killed in a car accident in Bengal on Christmas Day, 1944.

Hemingway and Orwell would also experience the war first-hand, though not in the armed forces. Orwell served with the Home Guard until 1943, and his London flat was bombed. Having spent three years of the war working for the BBC, he took a job as a correspondent for *The Observer*. Hemingway, meanwhile, would (like his new wife) again find employment as a correspondent, covering stories that included the D-Day landings. Towards the end of the war the two men finally met, in Paris.

According to Hemingway's account, Orwell sought him out at the Ritz (which, given the way Orwell had sought out John Dos Passos in Spain, may well have been true), and told him of his fear that communists were planning to assassinate him. Orwell, Hemingway later recalled, was looking 'very gaunt' and 'in bad shape,' 'fairly nervous and worried'. He asked for the loan of a gun that he could keep concealed on his person, and Hemingway lent him a small-calibre automatic.

By then Orwell had finished writing *Animal Farm*, his great satire of communism and the Russian Revolution (or, as he called it, 'a sort of fairy story ... a fable with a political meaning'). He had admitted to his agent that the book 'is murder from the Communist point of view,' and knew that the Soviets were prepared to go a long way to kill their opponents: in 1940, Trotsky had been assassinated in Mexico by a Spanish Republican, allegedly travelling on a passport stolen from a Canadian member of the International Brigades.

As the preface Orwell wrote for the Ukrainian edition of *Animal Farm* would make clear, Spain was its greatest inspiration, and the idea itself had come to him not long after his return from Barcelona, when he was still keeping the village shop in Wallington. 'On my return from Spain I thought of exposing the Soviet myth in a story that could be easily understood by almost anyone,' he explained. Then, one day he saw a young boy whipping a huge carthorse: 'It struck me that if only such animals became aware of their strength we should have no power over them, and that men exploit animals in much the same way as the rich exploit the proletariat.' The farm's pigs represented the communist hierarchy – in particular Marx, Trotsky, Stalin and their minions – and the novella charted how the animals' successful revolution was gradually undermined, exploited and cynically destroyed by the pigs. The book was turned down by a number of publishers, who did not wish to offend the Russians (now, of course, allies of the Western democracies). It eventually appeared on 17 August 1945, only eleven days after the bombing war that Orwell had so feared and that had escalated from Guernica to London, Hamburg, Berlin, Dresden and Tokyo, had reached its horrific, atomic climax at Hiroshima.

Animal Farm was excellently received, and is still widely considered one of the best satirical novels since Jonathan Swift's eighteenth-century masterpiece, *Gulliver's Travels*. A US edition appeared in 1946, where it would be the second best-selling book of the year; endless reprintings and dozens of translations followed. Critics on the Right would use the book to attack the Left, misunderstanding – or ignoring – the fact that Orwell was still a socialist. As an interviewer from *Vogue* explained, the book's author was 'fairly much a leftist' and 'a defender of freedom, even though most of the time he violently disagrees with the people beside whom he is fighting.'

Orwell's wife Eileen had died during an operation for cancer a few months before the publication of *Animal Farm*, and in 1946 he and their adopted son, Richard, moved to the remote Scottish island of Jura. Fearful (like Hemingway) that his enemies might still be out to kill him, he kept guns to hand; and though Orwell's sister arrived to assist him, one young visitor found the atmosphere in the large, windswept farmhouse tense and depressing. There, in incredible isolation and increasingly sick, Orwell wrote his last book. Completed in 1948, *1984* was published the following year. The review in *The New York Times* called it 'a work of pure horror … it is probable that no other work of this generation has made us desire freedom more earnestly or loathe tyranny with such fullness.' Unlike Hemingway, who in *For Whom the Bell Tolls* told the story of the Spanish Civil War through one isolated (fictional) incident, Orwell encompassed all that he had experienced of terror, deceit and totalitarianism in Spain (as well as during the Second World War) to create a frightening vision of the near future in which Britain is swallowed up by the United States into the 'super-state' of Oceania under the allegedly benevolent dictatorship of Big Brother, and truth and history are endlessly twisted and rewritten in a world that is permanently at war.

The letters of congratulation included one from John Dos Passos, whose own literary career had stalled since the two men's encounter in Barcelona a decade earlier. '*1984* is a wonderful job,' he told Orwell. 'I read it with cold shivers … Had nightmares all the next week about two-way television. I certainly have to hand it to you.' He suggested that Orwell get in touch if he ever came to America.

Sadly, this would never happen, and Orwell would not live long enough to see the remarkable success of *1984*. His health had never been good, but his time in the cold and mud of the Aragon trenches – together with the bullet wound through his neck – had only served to make things worse. He died of tuberculosis in a London hospital on 21 January 1950, aged only forty-six.

Orwell had never returned to Spain. Unlike Picasso, who also never returned (and who refused to allow *Guernica* to be exhibited in his home country as long as Franco was still in power), Hemingway did go back. As José Luis Castillo-Puche would recall:

> More than once when Ernesto entered a room, there were Spaniards who still glared at him accusingly, as if he were an opportunist without a conscience, a blithe survivor of the hecatomb. These fierce glances hurt Ernesto, and he fled from them ... It was best not to remind [him] of the Spanish War. If he wanted to talk about it, he would say so; if he wanted to be by himself and silently brood about the past, we let him.

Hemingway would not write another book about Spain. His subsequent literary works were meagre: the novella, *The Old Man and the Sea*, and the posthumously published brief memoir of his youth in Paris, *A Moveable Feast*, were his greatest final achievements. Nonetheless, in 1954 he would receive the Nobel Prize for Literature, an award that might have been Orwell's, too, had he lived.

By 1959 Hemingway was already looking much older than his sixty years. In pain from various accidents and injuries, he was increasingly petulant and distracted. Suicide was an idea that had long preoccupied his mind and recurred through his work: in *To Have and to Have Not* he described Colt and Smith & Wesson revolvers as

> those well-constructed implements that end insomnia, terminate remorse, cure cancer, avoid bankruptcy, and blast an exit from intolerable positions by the pressure of a finger; those admirable American instruments so easily carried, so sure of effect, so well designed to end the American dream when it becomes a nightmare, their only drawback the mess they leave for relatives to clean up.

In 1928 Hemingway's father had used a revolver to end his life, a biographical fact that Hemingway (calling it a 'cowardly' act) gave to Robert Jordan in *For Whom the Bell Tolls*. Early on the morning of 2 July 1961 at his new home in Ketchum, Idaho, Hemingway used one of his favourite shotguns to blast his head off. His fourth wife, Mary, found the body.

It is a cruel irony that dictators often live long. With European fascism finally defeated in 1945, many liberals called on the Western democracies to finish the job and remove Franco too. But, as Orwell observed in a phrase that would define the next four decades, a 'Cold War' had begun. Communism was the new enemy, and suddenly Franco was an ally of the West. He was allowed to continue ruling Spain as a military dictatorship until his death aged 82 in 1975. It was not until 1996 that a long-standing promise was finally realized, and the surviving veterans of the International Brigades were given Spanish citizenship.

Dramatis Personae

Wystan Hugh Auden: with his friend Stephen Spender (q.v.), Auden one of the leading young English poets of the 1930s and 40s. Born in 1907 he was educated at Oxford University, and was a vocal supporter of the Left. He visited Spain in 1937.

Alvah Bessie: born in New York in 1904 and educated at Columbia University, Bessie worked as an actor and a journalist before publishing his first novel in 1935. He arrived in Spain in the spring of 1938 as a volunteer for the Abraham Lincoln Battalion.

(Gerald) Lorimer Birch: A Cambridge University graduate and committed communist. In his mid-20s he volunteered with in the Tom Mann Centuria in Barcelona, before transferring to the International Brigades; he served alongside Esmond Romilly in the Thälmann Battalion.

Eileen Blair: Born Eileen O'Shaughnessy in 1905 and educated at Oxford University, she married Eric Blair (George Orwell, q.v.) in 1936; she travelled to Spain early in 1937 to work as secretary for the POUM.

Franz Borkenau: Born in Vienna in 1900, Borkenau was a writer, sociologist and committed Marxist who made to trips to Spain in September 1936 and January 1937. His book *The Spanish Cockpit* (1937) was considered by George Orwell as 'the best book yet written' on the Spanish Civil War.

Kitty Bowler: Born in Massachusetts in 1908 and educated at Bryn Mawr College, Bowler was a wealthy left-wing American journalist who was visiting Russia when the Spanish Civil War broke out. Travelling to Barcelona she met and fell in love with Tom Wintringham (q.v.).

Felicia Browne: born in Surrey in 1904, Browne studied at the Slade School of Art in London before living for some years in Berlin. She joined the Communist Party in 1933. Having travelled extensively in Europe, she was visiting Barcelona for the Workers' Olympiad in July 1936, and soon volunteered with the Republican militia.

Robert Capa: Born Endre (André) Friedmann in Budapest, Hungary, in 1913. Having settled in Paris, he invented the American photojournalist Robert Capa with his girlfriend Gerda Taro (q.v.). They travelled to Spain shortly after its outbreak to cover the Civil War for French newspapers.

Claud Cockburn: born in China in 1904 to a British consular official and educated at Oxford University. He worked as a journalist with *The Times* in Germany and the USA before committing himself to communism and founding *The Week* in 1933. He was in Barcelona for the London edition of *The Daily Worker* (writing under the *nom de plume* Frank Pitcairn) when the Spanish Civil War broke out, and volunteered briefly with the Spanish Fifth Regiment.

John Cornford: born in Cambridge in 1915 and educated at Stowe School, Cornford was a great-grandson of Charles Darwin. A leading figure in the student communist movement at Cambridge University, he travelled to Spain in August 1936, where he volunteered with the POUM militia. He went on to serve with the Commune de Paris Battalion of the International Brigade, and the First Company of the English-Speaking Battalion.

Jon Dos Passos: Born in Chicago in 1896 and educated at Harvard, Dos Passos served as an ambulance driver in Italy during the Great War. He made his name as a writer with books such as the anti-war novel *Three Soldiers* (1921) and *Manhattan Transfer* (1925), becoming an important voice of the left in the USA. A frequent visitor to Spain, he was close friends with Ernest Hemingway (q.v.).

Martha Gellhorn: Born in St Louis, Missouri, in 1908 to parents of German-Jewish descent, Gellhorn was educated at Bryn Mawr College. Travelling extensively in Europe, she became a writer and journalist; she came to Spain in 1937 at the encouragement of Ernest Hemingway.

Jason Gurney: South African sculptor and volunteer with the English-Speaking and Abraham Lincoln Battalions of the International Brigades.

Ernest Hemingway: Born in Chicago in 1899, Hemingway was one of the leading American writers of his day. His first novel, *The Sun Also Rises* (aka *Fiesta*, 1926) was set in Spain. He went to Spain in the spring of 1937 to report on the war for the North American Newspaper Alliance.

William Horvitz: Born in New Jersey in 1915 to working-class Jewish immigrants from Byelorussia (now Belarus), Horvitz was a Communist from a young age. Volunteering to join the International Brigades in late 1936, he was in the first group to leave the US for Spain. Serving with the Abraham Lincoln Battalion, he later anglicized his name to William Herrick.

Joris Ivens: A Dutch communist documentary film-maker who made *The Spanish Earth* (1937) for the group of pro-Republican literary American backers, The Contemporary Historians, which included Ernest Hemingway.

Bernard Knox: As a Classics student at Cambridge University, Knox befriended John Cornford, and was recruited by him to go to Spain in the autumn of 1936, joining the Commune de Paris Battalion of XI International Brigade.

Wilfred Macartney: Born in Scotland in 1899 to wealthy Irish-American parents, Macartney served with the British Army in the Great War. A communist sympathiser, he was imprisoned for spying for Russia in 1927. Published an account of his experiences, *Walls Have Mouths*, in 1936, before volunteering with the English-Speaking Battalion of the International Brigades.

André Marty: French Communist commander of the International Brigades.

Herbert Matthews: A pro-Republican journalist for *The New York Times*, he covered the war in Abyssinia before going on the Spain, experiences explored in his book, *Two Wars and More to Come* (1938).

George Nathan: A working-class Jew from the East End of London, Nathan served with the elite Brigade of Guards in the Great War. After a long period of poverty, he volunteered with the International Brigades, rising to become major in the staff of XV Brigade.

Juan Negrín: Spanish Socialist politician and Prime Minister from May 1937.

Charles and Lois Orr: A young left-wing American couple from Kentucky, the Orrs were on an extended honeymoon in Europe when the Spanish Civil War broke out. Travelling to Barcelona, they found employment with the POUM.

George Orwell was the *nom de plume* of the English author Eric Blair. Born in India in 1903 he was educated at Eton College. Having served in Burma with the Imperial Indian Police, he became a writer. He volunteered with the POUM militia in Barcelona in late December 1936.

Harry Pollitt: English trade union leader and head of the Communist Party of Great Britain.

Gustav Regler: Born in Germany in 1898, Regler was seriously shell-shocked in the Great War. Joining the Communist Party, he spent time in the Soviet Union and published a number of novels before becoming political commissar of XII International.

Esmond Romilly: The son of a British Army Colonel, and a nephew of Winston Churchill, Romilly was born in London in 1918. With his elder brother Giles he launched the anti-public school magazine, *Out of Bounds*. Aged only 18, in October 1936 he cycled to the south of France to volunteer with the International Brigades, serving with German and Austrian anti-Fascists in the Thälmann Battalion.

Frank Ryan: Born in County Limerick in 1902 and educated at Trinity College Dublin, Ryan joined the Irish Republican Army in 1922. Becoming a senior IRA figure and journalist, he led a group of Irish volunteers to Spain in late 1936, and served with the International Brigades.

Keith Scott Watson: A young English journalist who had travelled in Germany and USSR. At the start of the Spanish Civil War he had joined an anarchist column in Barcelona, before transferring to the International Brigades. He served briefly with the Thälmann Battalion before deserting.

Keith Sinclair-Loutit: Educated at Cambridge University, as a young medical student in August 1936 Sinclair-Loutit led the first contingent of the British Medical Unit to go out to Spain.

John Sommerfield: As a student at Cambridge University he was involved in the communist movement with John Cornford, and was recruited by him to go to Spain in the autumn of 1936, joining the Commune de Paris Battalion of XI International Brigade.

Stephen Spender: born in London in 1909 and educated at Oxford University, with his friend W.H. Auden (q.v.), Spender was one of the leading young English poets of the 1930s and 40s. Briefly a member of the Communist Party, he travelled to Spain in 1937. He would later be knighted for his services to literature.

George Steer: Born in South Africa in 1909 and educated at Oxford University, he covered the war in Abyssinia for *The Times* before going on to Spain.

Gerda Taro: born in Stuttgart, Germany, in 1911, Gerda (or Gerta) Pohorylle was the daughter of a Polish Jew. Settling in Paris, with her Jewish boyfriend André Friedmann she invented the American photojournalist Robert Capa.

Changing her own name, she and Capa travelled to Spain shortly after its outbreak to cover the Civil War for French newspapers.

Tom Wintringham: born in Grimsby in 1898, Wintringham served as a despatch rider in the Great War. Going on to Oxford University, he visited Russia shortly after the revolution, and became a leading English communist writer and journalist for *The Daily Worker*. He was sent to Barcelona in August 1936 as a representative of the CPGB, where he met Kitty Bowler [q.v.]. He went on to join the British Battalion of the International Brigades.

INDEX